CW01215100

MODERNISING LENIN'S RUSSIA
Economic Reconstruction, Foreign Trade and the Railways

In this book Anthony Heywood reassesses Bolshevik attitudes towards economic modernisation and foreign economic relations during the early Soviet period. Drawing on hitherto unused Russian and Western archives, he argues that railway modernisation was vital to a strategy of rapid economic modernisation, and that vast quantities of railway equipment were ordered abroad to hasten this process. Following the histories of the principal contracts, this book provides the first detailed case study of the Soviet government's imports policy under War Communism and the NEP, and shows how foreign trade was used to tackle domestic economic challenges. It presents readers with a new perspective on Soviet economic development, and reveals the scale of Bolshevik business dealings with the capitalist West immediately after the Revolution.

ANTHONY HEYWOOD is a Lecturer in the Department of European Studies at the University of Bradford.

MODERNISING LENIN'S RUSSIA

Cambridge Russian, Soviet and Post-Soviet Studies: 105
Editorial Board
Stephen White (*General editor*)   Roy Allison   Mary Buckley
Julian Cooper   Paul Dukes   Saul Estrin
Catherine Merridale   Hilary Pilkington

Cambridge Russian, Soviet and Post-Soviet Studies, under the auspices of Cambridge University Press and the British Association for Slavonic and East European Studies (BASEES), promotes the publication of works presenting substantial and original research on the economics, politics, sociology and modern history of Russia, the Soviet Union and Eastern Europe.

A list of titles in this series can be found at the end of the book.

MODERNISING LENIN'S RUSSIA

Economic Reconstruction, Foreign Trade and the Railways

ANTHONY HEYWOOD

CAMBRIDGE UNIVERSITY PRESS

PUBLISHED BY THE PRESS SYNDICATE OF THE UNIVERSITY OF CAMBRIDGE
The Pitt Building, Trumpington Street, Cambridge CB2 1RP, United Kingdom

CAMBRIDGE UNIVERSITY PRESS
The Edinburgh Building, Cambridge CB2 2RU, UK   http://www.cup.cam.ac.uk
40 West 20th Street, New York, NY 10011–4211, USA   http://www.cup.org
10 Stamford Road, Oakleigh, Melbourne 3166, Australia

© Anthony Heywood 1999

This book is in copyright. Subject to statutory exception and to the provisions of relevant collective licensing agreements, no reproduction of any part may take place without the written permission of Cambridge University Press.

First published 1999

Printed in the United Kingdom at the University Press, Cambridge

Typeset in Palatino 10/12$\frac{1}{2}$ pt [CE]

A catalogue record for this book is available from the British Library

Library of Congress cataloging in publication data
Heywood Anthony.
Modernising Lenin's Russia: economic reconstruction, foreign trade and the railways, 1917–1924 / Anthony Heywood.
    p.   cm. – (Cambridge Russian, Soviet and post-Soviet studies: 105)
Includes bibliographical references and index.
ISBN 0 521 62178 X (hc.)
1. Railroads – Soviet Union – History.
2. Railroads and state – Soviet Union.
3. Railroads – Soviet Union – Equipment and supplies.
4. Soviet Union – Economic policy.
5. Soviet Union – Economic conditions.
I. Title.   II. Series.
HE3138.H48   1999
385'.0947 – dc21   98–38611   CIP

ISBN 0 521 62178 X hardback

To my parents, John and Pauline Heywood

Contents

List of illustrations   xi
List of tables   xiii
Acknowledgements   xiv
Technical note   xvi
List of abbreviations and acronyms   xvii

Introduction   1

PART I Towards economic reconstruction, 1917–1920 the birth of the railway imports policy

1 Prologue   13
   The pre-1914 context   13
   Wartime imports   23
   The Provisional government's largesse   36

2 The revolutionary railway vision   48
   Economic crisis, railway dreams   49
   The question of foreign resources   63
   Decision: imports for railway-led reconstruction   72

PART II Trade and isolation, 1920–1921 implementing the railway imports policy

3 Krasin's first results   85
   The American dream   85
   Success in Sweden   92
   Administrative affairs   103

4 Approaches to Britain and Germany   110
   The British connection   110
   The road to Berlin   120
   The German questions   126

5 Second thoughts	135
Trotskii, railway reconstruction and imports planning	136
Moscow and the Russian Railway Mission Abroad	145
Locomotive swan song	151

PART III Retreat, 1921–1924

6 The new order	163
Change and continuity under the New Economic Policy	164
Retrenchment	171
Politics of scarcity: a conflict of interests	180
Protectionism resurgent	184
7 Denouement	200
The Avanesov commission	200
Demise and results	205
Epilogue: towards Stalinist industrialisation	220
Conclusion	225
Notes	235
Bibliography	285
Index	311

Illustrations

Between pages 160–161

1 Class Ye 2–10–0 decapod, Canadian Locomotive Company, 1915. Courtesy of Queen's Archives, Kingston University
2 Belgian-built 'Flamme' locomotive in 'cemetery' condition, *circa* February 1920. Courtesy of G. V. Lomonossoff Collection, Leeds Russian Archive; copyright Mrs P. Browning
3 Iu. V. Lomonosov and R. N. Lomonosova. Courtesy of G. V. Lomonossoff Collection, Leeds Russian Archive; copyright Mrs P. Browning
4 On the Tallinn–Stockholm ferry, 23 July 1920. Courtesy of G. V. Lomonossoff Collection, Leeds Russian Archive; copyright Mrs P. Browning
5 The Nohab factory, Trollhättan, *circa* 1922. Courtesy of G. V. Lomonossoff Collection, Leeds Russian Archive; copyright Mrs P. Browning
6 M. Billing and colleagues at Nordiska Handelsbanken, *circa* 1921. Courtesy of G. V. Lomonossoff Collection, Leeds Russian Archive; copyright Mrs P. Browning
7 Iu. V. Lomonosov, G. W. Anderson et al., Trollhättan, August 1921. Courtesy of G. V. Lomonossoff Collection, Leeds Russian Archive; copyright Mrs P. Browning
8 The Russian Railway Mission: Lomonosov and colleagues, *circa* 1921. Courtesy of G. V. Lomonossoff Collection, Leeds Russian Archive; copyright Mrs P. Browning
9 The Railway Mission's second anniversary party, November 1922. Courtesy of G. V. Lomonossoff Collection, Leeds Russian Archive; copyright Mrs P. Browning
10 The Railway Mission at work, *circa* 1922. Courtesy of G. V. Lomonossoff Collection, Leeds Russian Archive; copyright Mrs P. Browning

11 G. W. Anderson and Iu. V. Lomonosov. Courtesy of G. V. Lomonossoff Collection, Leeds Russian Archive; copyright Mrs P. Browning
12 W. Hellberg. Courtesy of G. V. Lomonossoff Collection, Leeds Russian Archive; copyright Mrs P. Browning
13 Otto Hagemann. Courtesy of Historisches Archiv Krupp, Essen
14 V. N. Fren. Courtesy of G. V. Lomonossoff Collection, Leeds Russian Archive; copyright Mrs P. Browning
15 A. I. Emshanov. Courtesy of N. A. Zenzinov
16 The Railway Mission's Berlin premises, *circa* 1921. Courtesy of G. V. Lomonossoff Collection, Leeds Russian Archive; copyright Mrs P. Browning
17 F. F. Perno. Courtesy of G. V. Lomonossoff Collection, Leeds Russian Archive; copyright Mrs P. Browning
18 Academician A. N. Krylov. Courtesy of G. V. Lomonossoff Collection, Leeds Russian Archive; copyright Mrs P. Browning
19 The steamship *Odin* in the Kiel canal, *circa* 1922. Courtesy of G. V. Lomonossoff Collection, Leeds Russian Archive; copyright Mrs P. Browning
20 Nohab locomotives delayed at Trollhättan, 1922. Courtesy of G. V. Lomonossoff Collection, Leeds Russian Archive; copyright Mrs P. Browning
21 E^{SH}-4151 on test in Russia, October 1922. Courtesy of G. V. Lomonossoff Collection, Leeds Russian Archive; copyright Mrs P. Browning
22 A locomotive of the type overhauled in Estonia, 1921–1924. Courtesy of G. V. Lomonossoff Collection, Leeds Russian Archive; copyright Mrs P. Browning
23 Canadian-built tanker wagon, 1921. Courtesy of G. V. Lomonossoff Collection, Leeds Russian Archive; copyright Mrs P. Browning
24 Armstrong boilers awaiting shipment, 1922. Courtesy of G. V. Lomonossoff Collection, Leeds Russian Archive; copyright Mrs P. Browning
25 The Avanesov commission, 30 November 1922. Courtesy of G. V. Lomonossoff Collection, Leeds Russian Archive; copyright Mrs P. Browning
26 Sovnarkom meeting with Lomonosov seated at extreme right, October 1922. Courtesy of David King Collection.
27 E^{SH}-4131 in Soviet service, *circa* 1975. Courtesy of A. V. Kazachkov

Tables

0.1	Foreign trade turnover, Russian Empire 1913 and Soviet Russia 1918–1923	page 4
0.2	Concession applications and agreements, Soviet Russia, 1921/2–1925/6	4
1.1	Profile of Russian foreign trade, 1894–1913	16
1.2	MPS goods shipped from North America, spring 1915–April 1918	46
2.1	Russian and Soviet railway traffic, 1913, 1917–1928	50
2.2	Soviet locomotive stock and 'sickness', November 1917–August 1920	51
2.3	Soviet output of pig iron, 1913–1923/4	54
2.4	Soviet output of Steel, 1913–1923/4	54
2.5	Russian and Soviet locomotive production, 1913–1929/30	55
7.1	Quantity and value of Railway Mission orders, 15 October 1920–15 April 1923	210
7.2	Principal Soviet railway contracts with foreign companies, 1920–1923	211
7.3	Value of total Soviet imports and selected products, 1920–1923/4	213
7.4	Values of Soviet contracts for imports, April 1920–1 January 1922	215
7.5	Value of Railway Mission current and completed contracts at 20 November 1922	216
7.6	Deliveries of selected products to the NKPS, 1 January 1920–1 November 1922	217
7.7	Deliveries of selected products to the NKPS, 1 October 1921–1 October 1922, including imports	218

Acknowledgements

Numerous people assisted my preparation of this book and its ancestor, my doctoral dissertation, and I am extremely grateful to them all. I owe special thanks to Mrs Peggy Browning and the Leeds Russian Archive for granting access to the papers of Professor Iurii Vladimirovich Lomonosov, the distinguished engineer–diplomat around whom so much of this study revolves. I am also indebted to the staff of the many libraries and archives in which I have worked, particularly to Mr Peter Morrish, Mr Malcolm Davis and Mrs Pat Shute (Brotherton Library, Leeds), Messrs Peter Nordby and Lars Svensson (Göteborg Regional Archive), and Dr Vsevolod Tsaplin (Russian State Archive of the Economy). Invaluable support was given by Mr Nigel Sill (Steam Traction Ltd), the Russian Ministry of Transport's Main Directorate for Locomotives (especially Mr Aleksandr Kryvnoi), Dr Valerii Tereshchenko (All-Russian Scientific Research Institute for Railway Transport) and the collective of Intertrack Ltd. I also wish to thank Mr Michael Holdsworth and Ms Lindsay Coles of Cambridge University Press for their guidance and patience.

For financial support I am most grateful to the ESRC, the British Council, the Finnish Ministry of Education, the University of Stockholm's Centre for Baltic Studies, the University of Leeds, and the University of Bradford Research Committee.

An earlier version of my discussion of British–Soviet trade negotiations appeared in *Revolutionary Russia*, Vol. 5, No. 1 (June 1992), pp. 53–91. I am grateful to the editor for permission to use parts of the article here. The photographs are reproduced by kind permission of Mrs Peggy Browning, Mr David King, Friedrich Krupp AG, Dr Nikolai Zenzinov and Mr Andrei Kazachkov.

Among the many others who have proffered assistance, advice, encouragement and/or hospitality I should like particularly to acknowledge Mr Sebastian Anstruther, Mrs Susan Anstruther, Dr Hugh Aplin, Dr Robert Argenbright, Dr Gennadii Bordiugov, Mrs Helene Carlbäck-Isotalo, Ms Eileen Consey, Professor R. W. Davies, Dr Tony Edwards, Professor Cliff Foust, Professor Peter Gatrell, Mr Anders Johansson, Professor Sune Jungar, Professor Semen Khromov, Ms Elena Kudriakova, Professor Alexander Loit, Mr Aleksandr Makurov, Dr Mary McAuley, Mr John Morison, Dr Roger Munting, Dr Aleksandr Nikol'skii, Dr Mike Page, Mr Cliff Parr, Dr Sergei Pavliuchenkov, Mr David Price, Dr Arfon Rees, Professor Valerii Shishkin, Mr and Mrs Bertil Thulin, Mr Evgenii Ul'iantsev, Dr Aleksandr Ushakov, Dr John Westwood, Dr Christine White and Professor Stephen White.

Above all I must thank my parents, John and Pauline Heywood, without whose encouragement this research would not have been started; my dissertation supervisors, Dr David Collins and Mr Richard Davies, and the staff of the Department of Russian Studies, University of Leeds, without whose support my dissertation would not have been completed; and my colleagues at the University of Bradford for their subsequent encouragement. Needless to say, the responsibility for any errors of fact and interpretation is mine alone.

Technical note

Russian words are transliterated with a simplified version of the Library of Congress system except for the accepted English forms Moscow, St Petersburg and Archangel. Also, the letter designation of one locomotive class is transliterated as 'Ye' rather than 'E' (see chapter 1, note 76).

Events within Russia prior to 1/14 February 1918 are dated by the Julian (Old Style) calendar, whilst events outside Russia are recorded with the Gregorian (New Style) calendar, though for clarity many such dates are shown in both styles. All later dates are in the 'New Style'.

Because of incomplete data and exchange-rate fluctuations the value of a given contract is indicated in the currency under negotiation unless comparative figures are shown in the sources. For overall comparisons, table 7.1 shows the value of the Soviet railway contracts in Swedish crowns at 15 April 1923 as recalculated by the Russians themselves, together with relevant London exchange rates for 13 April 1923. For the Soviet period ruble values refer to so-called gold rubles, except for one reference to Soviet domestic rubles.

The reliability of published Soviet foreign trade statistics is discussed separately in chapter 7.

Weights and distances have been converted thus:

    1 pood   16.30 kilograms
    1 verst   1.06 kilometres

References from Russian archives normally show the archive's name in abbreviated form, the number of the collection (*fond*), the number of the inventory (*opis'*), the number of the file (*delo*, or *edinitsa khraneniia*), and the number of the folio (*list*). In certain references from the Archive of Foreign Policy of the Russian Federation the file number is followed by the number of a packet (*papka*) and then the folio number. In all cases the reverse side of a folio is designated by 'ob' after the folio number.

Abbreviations and acronyms

AEF	American Expeditionary Force (in France)
Arcos	All-Russian Cooperative Society Ltd
DÖG	Deutsche Ökonomie GmbH
GOELRO	State Commission for the Electrification of Russia
GOMZA	State Group of Machine-building Factories
Gosplan	State Planning Commission
IPS	Inspectorate of Ways of Communication
KhMU	NKPS Directorate of Economics and Materials
Komgosor	VSNKh Committee for State Civil Construction
Mozherez	Moscow Railway Repair Factory
MPS	Ministry of Ways of Communication (until October 1917)
NEP	New Economic Policy
NKID	People's Commissariat of Foreign Affairs
NKPS	People's Commissariat of Ways of Communication
NKRKI	People's Commissariat of Workers' and Peasants' Inspection
NKTiP	People's Commissariat of Trade and Industry
NKVT	People's Commissariat of Foreign Trade
Nohab	Nydqvist & Holm AB
OTK	Basic Transport Commission
RKP(b)	Russian Communist Party (Bolshevik)
Sazherez	Samara Railway Repair Factory
SNK, Sovnarkom	Council of People's Commissars
STO	Council of Labour and Defence
Ts	People's Commissar of Ways of Communication
Tsentrosoiuz	Central Cooperative Society
TsK	Central Committee of the RKP(b)

TsP	Deputy People's Commissar of Ways of Communication
Volkhovstroi	Volkhov dam construction project
VSNKh	Supreme Council of the National Economy
VTsIK	All-Russian Central Executive Committee

Introduction

The transformation of Russia into a major industrial power was a fundamental goal for Lenin and the Bolsheviks. Economic development and industrialisation promised to end centuries of backwardness relative to the West. Technological change was to lead the way from a weak and inefficient capitalist economy – still largely reliant on small-scale peasant production even after a half-century of tsarist industrialisation – towards a prosperous urban socialist society based on scientific planning and modern large-scale production. The transformation of the Russian economy would serve as the catalyst for social revolution by creating the material basis for socialism.

But how in fact did the revolutionaries address economic modernisation during the early Soviet period? After the tsarist regime's prioritisation of railway development and heavy engineering, did Lenin's well-known enthusiasm for nationwide electrification imply a fundamentally new course? How quickly were postwar economic recovery and modernisation to be accomplished? And what of resources? Tsarism's heavy reliance on foreign capital had been criticised by the Bolsheviks for turning Russia into a colony of the major European powers. So did Lenin and his colleagues really want the capitalist world to play a significant part in Soviet economic development? Did they seriously expect to 'normalise' economic relations with capitalist countries given their own commitment to world revolution, their abrogation of pre-Soviet debts, the Allied anti-Bolshevik blockade and the foreign intervention in the civil war? Alternatively, did they prioritise the broader goal of international revolution as the means to Russian economic progress? Or were domestic resources seen as the key?

Traditionally, a paradigm of dramatic collapse and gradual recovery has shaped analysis of the Soviet economy between the 1917 October Revolution and the mid-1920s.[1] Two distinct economic systems and periods have been identified. The first, known as War Communism, prevailed from early 1918 until March 1921. Highly centralised, it was an attempt by the Soviet state to manage all economic activity. Industry, banking, transport and trade were nationalised, grain was requisitioned from the peasantry through a state monopoly, and as the currency collapsed, a moneyless barter economy developed. For some historians, as indeed for many contemporaries, War Communism was a product of communist ideology and it represented the first step towards socialism and communism; for others, it was an emergency improvisation in response to the civil war, or it was considered to be the result of a combination of these motivations. Its fate, too, has been controversial. Though it helped the Bolsheviks to mobilise resources for their war effort and secure victory in the civil war by early 1920, it failed to halt the collapse of output, and the attempt to develop it as a peacetime system ended amidst deep social and economic crisis in the winter of 1920–1. Whether its eventual abandonment represented a major ideological retreat or a return towards gradualist policies which had been interrupted by the civil war in early 1918 has long been a matter of dispute.[2]

War Communism was replaced by the New Economic Policy (NEP), which lasted until Stalin's forced industrialisation at the end of the 1920s. Controversially introduced as a limited reform to conciliate the peasantry by abolishing food requisitions and permitting private trade, the NEP quickly led to the creation of a money-based mixed economy. Heavy industry, railway transport, banking and foreign trade remained state owned within a system of central state regulation, whilst small-scale industry and agriculture were opened to private enterprise. The NEP could not avert devastating famine in 1921–2, and unemployment and price distortions were serious problems, yet it eventually became synonymous with gradual recovery. With the exception of foreign trade, pre-war levels of activity were regained in all the major economic sectors in the mid-1920s.[3]

Within this framework of collapse and recovery the Bolshevik vision for Russia's social and economic transformation has been associated with a plan for nationwide electrification that was produced in 1920 by the State Commission for the Electrification of Russia (GOELRO). According to Coopersmith, electrification was not the only technocratic proposal for economic reconstruction, but it seized the initiative over technologies of the first industrial revolution by 'promising transformation, not simply reconstruction'; electrical engineers steadily acquired political support to the point where 'in

1920, electrification replaced the railroad as the state technology by which the new government intended to accomplish its political and economic goals and distinguish itself from the old government'.[4] The GOELRO project was championed by Lenin himself as 'the second party plan', the means to overcome Russia's poverty and backwardness, and his support helped to ensure that the Eighth Congress of Soviets approved electrification as policy in December 1920. Communism, Lenin famously proclaimed, was Soviet power and the electrification of the whole country.[5]

But given the weak state of the Soviet economy by 1920, how much progress could really be made with the GOELRO plan? The Soviet historian V. Iu. Steklov praised the project as the 'basis of the country's economic development' and 'the first plan for creating the material and technical foundations of socialism', and claimed that 'its completion ahead of schedule was a triumph of planning in the development of the country's economy'.[6] However, Coopersmith demonstrates that the plan's actual results were modest, not least because its authors neglected its dependence on other sectors of the economy and because it received only a fraction of the necessary resources. In particular, the planners assigned great importance to foreign technology and investment, yet these failed to materialise to any significant extent.[7]

This lacuna reflected the general pattern of utter collapse and sluggish growth that scholars have identified in early Soviet foreign economic relations.[8] This sector suffered so badly during the First World War and civil war that the overall turnover of Soviet imports and exports for 1919 was officially recorded at just 3 million gold rubles, and was colourfully described by B. E. Shtein as mere 'foraging by a besieged fortress'.[9] The revival of foreign economic relations – potentially crucial for modernisation – began after the lifting of the Allied blockade in January 1920, and its basic features have been uncontroversial. A legal framework for Soviet–Western trade was constructed through a series of bilateral intergovernmental trade agreements, and Soviet trade missions were opened in London, Berlin and other European capitals. The annual trade turnover grew to 361 million gold rubles by 1923, foreign borrowing resumed on a limited scale, and foreign investment was attracted to concession projects (see tables 0.1 and 0.2). But the sector was one of the economy's weakest at the end of the NEP, with the annual trade turnover below half of the 1913 level in the 1927/8 financial year.[10]

Soviet historians interpreted this growth as a major success in the face of intense capitalist hatred.[11] Western accounts have tended to

Table 0.1. *Foreign trade turnover, Russian Empire 1913 and Soviet Russia 1918–1923 (million gold rubles, average 1913 prices)*

Year	Export	Import	Turnover	Balance
1913	1,520	1,375	2,895	+145
1918	8	105	113	−97
1919	0	3	3	−3
1920	1.4	29	30	−27
1921	20	211	231	−191
1922	82	270	352	−188
1923	218	143	361	+75

Note: Figures for 1920 as given.
Source: Vneshniaia torgovlia SSSR za 1918–1940gg., p. 14.

Table 0.2. *Concession applications and agreements, Soviet Russia, 1921/2–1925/6*

Year	Applications	Agreements
1921/2	224	18
1922/3	579	44
1923/4	396	55
1924/5	256	103
1925/6	482	110
Total	1,937	342

Note: Figure for the total number of agreements as given.
Source: Adapted from Sutton, *Western Technology*, vol. I, p. 9.

emphasise its relative insignificance compared to Russia's pre-war foreign trade and financial situation.[12] However, a new dimension has been given to this picture by Christine White, who has shown that the Soviet government managed to sell a much larger quantity of gold, platinum and other precious metals during and after the civil war than has been believed. Further, she has demonstrated that substantial trade was conducted during the civil war between the West and non-Bolshevik Russia, which of course may have benefited the Bolsheviks at least to some extent after they captured these areas.[13]

Perhaps the most contentious issue, raising overtly political questions, has been whether and when the Bolsheviks became genuinely interested in the economic value of relations with the capitalist world. Soviet analyses often acknowledged that Bolshevik trade overtures to the Western powers during the civil war were designed mainly to secure a peace treaty. But they also argued that from at least 1918 Lenin consistently 'regarded trade and economic contacts between the socialist state and the capitalist world as the economic basis of peaceful coexistence between states of differing socioeconomic systems', not least in the belief that such ties could greatly assist the Soviet economy's revival and modernisation.[14] Western histories have displayed a range of opinion. For instance, Kennan doubted that there was much real Bolshevik interest at this stage. The NEP, by revealing a readiness to use private capital, did set a precedent for attracting foreign capital, but the results were negligible because although 'Western countries made no difficulties about the Soviet demand for trade', neither the Soviet nor Western governments were prepared to compromise their principles over Russia's prerevolutionary debts (abrogated by the Bolsheviks in 1918) and Western claims against the Bolshevik regime.[15] Carr, however, felt that the Bolsheviks did entertain serious hopes from early 1920 that imports of machinery and capital could greatly help Russia's shattered economy, yet they encouraged capitalist hostility by remaining committed to world revolution. Thus, 'foreign trade played virtually no part at all in the Soviet economy during the period of war communism', and only with the NEP and the Anglo-Soviet Trade Agreement in March 1921 was there a beginning 'in the necessary policy of the "breathing space" for economic reconstruction through peaceful cooperation'.[16] More recent specialist studies have tended to follow a similar line.[17]

The present study places these issues of economic system, modernisation and foreign economic relations in a new light. Its focal point is an extraordinary yet little-known decision taken by the Soviet government on 16 March 1920. A secret resolution of the Council of People's Commissars (Sovnarkom), signed that day by Lenin himself, allocated 300 million gold rubles to fund imports of railway equipment.[18] This sum was enormous in the circumstances, for it equated to perhaps 40 per cent of the Soviet gold reserve, and it may well prove unparalleled during at least the 1920s if not the whole interwar period.[19] Why, then, was so much gold made available for such imports? Why was railway equipment prioritised? What was the outcome of this decision? And what is the broader historical significance of this policy for Soviet economic strategy, the nature of War Communism, modernisation and economic relations with the West?

So far as the release of gold is concerned, one might suggest that if the Bolsheviks really believed international revolution and foreign proletarian assistance to be imminent, they might see little or no reason for maintaining gold reserves. From this perspective it could make sense during the short intervening period to try to spend the remaining gold on imports from capitalist countries and thus derive at least some immediate economic benefit from it. On the other hand, if Lenin's talk of peaceful coexistence with the capitalist world implied, as of early 1920, a potentially long delay for international revolution, Sovnarkom's decision to allocate so much of the available gold raises major questions about Bolshevik economic priorities. What was the rationale of these imports? Why was just one sector favoured? And why were the railways chosen?

As the sole form of rapid year-round transport – the country's 'arteries' – the railways were essential for the Bolsheviks.[20] The building of railways had played a leading role in the tsarist modernisation of Russia since the Crimean War. It had radically improved the transport system *per se*, stimulated industrial production and trade, opened up new regions for colonisation and development, and accelerated Russia's integration into the international economy by providing new opportunities for foreign trade and investment. In a political sense railway transport helped the government exert its authority, bind the regions more closely together and strengthen the empire's defence capacity. So when the Soviet leadership began tackling the economic crisis in late 1919, it naturally viewed the railway crisis as one of its most urgent problems. Crisis resolution, then, would seem to be the obvious explanation for the proposed imports. In fact, the situation was much more complex. This book will argue that the key to the decision was a strategy of rapid economic modernisation: the Bolshevik leadership prioritised railway development, not electrification, as the stimulus for beginning economic modernisation immediately in the spring of 1920, and it saw imports as a potential means to quicken that process.

As for the expenditure of the gold allocated by Sovnarkom, this study traces the subsequent acquisition of locomotives, wagons and other goods for the railways between 1920 and 1924, and argues that these contracts accounted for a major proportion of early Soviet foreign expenditure. It also shows how a special trade organisation known as the Russian Railway Mission Abroad was created in the autumn of 1920 to manage these orders. Further, it questions the traditional understanding of the management of the Soviet foreign trade monopoly by demonstrating how, under the leadership of a distinguished specialist railway engineer and administrator called Professor Iu. V. Lomonosov, the Railway Mission actually operated largely outside the jurisdiction of the monopoly's guardian, the People's Commissariat of Foreign Trade (NKVT).

This study, then, is in effect a biography of the Soviet government's railway imports policy between 1920 and 1924. It aims, firstly, to reassess Bolshevik attitudes towards railway development and modernisation in the early Soviet period and thereby to open a new perspective on the demise of War Communism and the first years of the NEP. Secondly, it seeks to revise our understanding of early Soviet foreign trade by providing the first case-study of imports policy in relation to one specific sector of the economy. Focusing on the origins, negotiation, financing and outcome of principal contracts, this book analyses the growth of Soviet foreign trade primarily as a means to tackle domestic economic challenges. In particular, it shows how a given commissariat – in this case the People's Commissariat of Ways of Communication (NKPS) – viewed the question of foreign economic relations, and how imports priorities and plans were formulated. Further, moving beyond the official statistics of trade turnover and deliveries based on customs data, this study may facilitate a re-evaluation of the pattern and volume of the growth of Soviet foreign trade, and more generally the impact of the NEP, based on the dates and values of contracts. Finally, it may help to clarify how the Soviet regime conducted business with Western firms, a subject about which little is known.

It may seem strange that if this purchasing operation was so large and important, historians have scarcely noticed it. The explanation appears to lie in a combination of operational secrecy, avoidance of scandal, censorship and chance. The policy's existence did soon become known publicly thanks to occasional press reports, the involvement of foreigners, and the publication of several lengthy technical reports in the mid-1920s.[21] And as détente dawned in the Brezhnev era, the construction and delivery of the locomotives even served as the background for a curious though soon forgotten Soviet–Swedish film romance starring Bibi Anderson.[22] But in the 1920s the policy's scope and highly sensitive political and commercial details were mostly kept secret, especially because so much gold was involved. Also, as scandal enveloped the policy in 1922, there may have been a reluctance to confront the issue fully because of Lenin's responsibility as signatory of the original Sovnarkom resolution of March 1920. Crucially, the censorship of later decades even involved distortion of the official statistics so that the principal compendium on interwar trade, published in 1960, greatly understated the actual railway-related expenditure and omitted many items.[23] Apart from Lenin's involvement, an important reason for this was Lomonosov's defection to the West in 1927: for some thirty years he could scarcely be mentioned in the USSR, and though there was some limited scholarly discussion of his mission in the late 1960s, his name remained problematic for historians.[24] Only with Gorbachev's *glasnost'* did a serious biographical article at last appear in 1985.[25] In the meantime, the exiled Lomonosov embarked on another monumental endeavour, producing over 15,500 manuscript pages of memoirs; but ironically, refusing to compromise over length, he could not find a publisher.[26]

Historical analysis of the railway imports policy has thus been cursory and, at worst, factually inaccurate. The sole treatment of significant length is within a 1947 volume commemorating the centenary of the Swedish company Nydqvist & Holm AB (Nohab), which naturally concentrates on the firm's own involvement.[27] In general, the policy has been seen simply as a relatively limited exercise intended to help solve the prevailing railway crisis.[28] As for the outcomes and their significance, Nove is typical in stating merely that 'scarce foreign currency was used to import locomotives and components' in 1921, and that railway engines and other foreign equipment contributed greatly to the economy's recovery.[29] The more specialist literature about Soviet foreign policy, trade and transport has scarcely been more forthcoming and, significantly, has even displayed confusion over the quantity of locomotives ordered.[30]

The present study has been made possible by the discovery of Professor Lomonosov's personal archive in England and the easing of access to official archives in Moscow.[31] Lomonosov's collection contains a wealth of primary material such as his diaries, correspondence, official documents, technical books and photographs. His voluminous unpublished memoirs have also survived, complete with carbons of numerous telegrams, letters, protocols and reports. Among the mass of relevant and mostly hitherto unused material in Russian archives is the collection of the Railway Mission itself, which is still virtually intact and includes correspondence and copy protocols of meetings of the NKPS Collegium, Gosplan committees, and the Bolshevik Party's Politburo, Orgburo and Central Committee. In the former Central Party Archive, Lomonosov's correspondence with Lenin, and a large file pertaining to the Railway Mission are contained in the collection of Lenin's secretariat. Unfortunately, restrictions on access to certain papers of the Politburo, Central Committee, Sovnarkom, NKVT and the gold departments of the People's Commissariat of Finances, as well as the Archive of the Foreign Policy of the Russian Federation, mean that some aspects of the initial policy decision remain unclear. But it did prove possible to obtain extensive data about the policy's implementation, including shipments of gold to the West.

Western primary sources include papers from the foreign ministries of Sweden, Germany and Great Britain, which help to show whether or how the railway contracts influenced the development of general trade and diplomatic relations. Documents from the US National Archives clarify some of the prerevolutionary background to the Soviet orders and the problems faced by Soviet representatives in establishing relations with the United States. Papers in company archives and other collections contain useful details of the various business negotiations. Finally, further information has been gleaned from published compendia of documents, newspapers and journals, official reports, technical works and other publications dating mainly from the 1910s and 1920s, as well as from memoirs and secondary literature.

The following chapters are grouped chronologically in three parts. Part 1 aims to explain the vital policy decision: chapter 1 considers its pre-Soviet context, whilst chapter 2 discusses the collapse of the economy and railway traffic, and responses to this, between October 1917 and December 1919, before presenting the railway imports policy as a central feature of Soviet postwar economic reconstruction strategy. Part 2, comprising chapters 3, 4 and 5, analyses the implementation of the policy between March 1920 and the introduction of the NEP in March 1921, covering the placement of several major contracts in the West and, to a much lesser extent, simultaneous developments within Russia. In part 3, chapter 6 traces events between March 1921 and July 1922, whilst chapter 7 considers this policy's dénouement and its relation to the subsequent onset of Stalinist industrialisation.

PART I

Towards economic reconstruction, 1917–1920
the birth of the railway imports policy

1 Prologue

Much of the explanation for the railway imports policy of 1920–4 must be sought in the Bolshevik leadership's economic strategy and assessment of the international situation in the winter of 1919–20. But the policy also had roots in the epoch prior to the October Revolution. The Bolshevik government was well aware that railway development had been among the most important driving forces of pre-war industrialisation between the 1860s and 1914, not least through the tsarist regime's policy of industrial protectionism. At the same time, the Bolsheviks knew that the foreign sector had always been important for the Russian railways, especially as a source of investment funds in the pre-war era and as a supplier of urgently needed equipment during the First World War. An overview of these issues will help to clarify the extent to which Bolshevik policy was shaped by precedents from the pre-Soviet period.

The pre-1914 context

The state-led industrialisation of Russia from the 1860s onwards was intended to create a modern, self-sufficient industrial economy quickly. It reflected not only the tsarist state's traditional preoccupation with overcoming Russia's economic backwardness relative to the West but also a growing realisation that, to quote Marks, 'the road to power for nation-states in the nineteenth and twentieth centuries lay along the path of technological advance'.[1] The shocking defeat on home territory in the Crimean War of 1853–6 and the humiliating terms of the subsequent Treaty of Paris marginalised the position of Russia in Europe and called into question her status as a great power. National pride was damaged, as was the prestige of the regime itself both at home and abroad. Increasingly, state officials understood that only by modernising the country's economy and military forces could the regime hope to restore its reputation, guarantee its future and resume an active role in European affairs.

Formidable problems were inherent in this process of modernisation. The country's vast size hindered rapid communications and stretched the available resources. Other significant geographical obstacles included harsh climatic conditions, a lack of east–west waterways and poor accessibility of natural resources. The abolition of serfdom was among the most important prerequisites for industrial modernisation, yet this presented a complex social, political and economic challenge in itself. In the economic arena, a chronic shortage of domestic investment capital raised the thorny question of whether foreign capital could be used on a large scale without prejudicing the country's political and economic interests. Furthermore, radical economic and social changes might themselves cause revolution. If economic modernisation was the key to the regime's long-term future, it was potentially also the means of its early destruction.

The tsarist state was thus faced with making unpopular compromises between stabilising its own authority and promoting potentially destabilising industrial modernisation. The Emancipation Act of 1861 abolished serfdom on terms which attempted to satisfy the incompatible interests of landowners and peasants but which broadly failed to satisfy either. The subsequent drive to expand the industrial economy prompted two particularly important and difficult compromises. One was the acceptance of heavy short- and medium-term reliance on foreign capital and imports, a tactic which provoked persistent nationalist ire. The other was the prioritisation of industrial development over the balanced development of the industrial and agrarian sectors, at the cost of continuing rural backwardness, low agricultural productivity and vulnerability to famine. This was especially so during the forced industrialisation drive of the 1890s masterminded by the Minister of Finances, Count S. Iu. Vitte, who was accused of causing famine and selling Russia to foreign capitalists.[2]

Nationalist indignation notwithstanding, the foreign sector became vital for Russia's economic modernisation, with investment capital coming mostly from Western Europe.[3] Germany emerged as the main supplier in the 1870s whilst Bismarck promoted the Dreikaiserbund, but French capital predominated from the 1890s until 1914 as a key component of the Franco-Russian alliance. Much of this investment went into commercial enterprises or government securities and railway loans. Thus, in 1913 total foreign capital investment was some 8,445 million rubles, of which 3,971 million rubles were in state loans,

975 million in state-backed railway loans and 2,602 million in joint-stock companies.[4] In fact, Russia became Europe's largest debtor with a national debt of 8,811 million rubles in 1914, of which the foreign share was some 48 per cent.[5] Moreover, once account was taken of the returns on foreign direct investment and interest payments on loans, a large balance of payments deficit necessitated further government borrowing abroad.[6]

The value of the external trade turnover grew dramatically in absolute terms, especially after 1890. Averaging 554 million credit rubles between 1866 and 1870, it climbed to an average of 1,079 million in 1891–5 and 2,641 million by 1909–13. The average balance of trade was unfavourable in the decade 1866–75, but careful management helped to ensure that surpluses were usually recorded thereafter, their size varying with the harvest and resultant export earnings. The generally positive balance and the accumulation of large gold reserves facilitated currency stability and the eventual move to the gold standard in 1897, and these conditions also helped to attract foreign investment from the 1880s onwards.[7]

Export earnings came mostly from agricultural products, semi-manufactured goods and such raw materials as timber, flax and oil. As for imports, machinery and other manufactured goods accounted for between a quarter and a third of the total value, whereas raw materials and semimanufactured goods such as cotton, metals and coal amounted to approximately one half. (See table 1.1.) Within these broad categories, however, were some significant changes over time due to tariff increases and import substitution, and, as will be seen below, this was particularly important with regard to railway supplies. Among the trade partners Germany became pre-eminent: in 1913 she supplied some 52.6 per cent of total imports by value, especially machinery, chemicals and new technology, and purchased nearly 32 per cent of exports, particularly grain. By comparison, second-placed Britain accounted for only about 13.9 per cent of Russian imports and 18.8 per cent of exports.[8]

Domestic industrial development encompassed heavy engineering and metallurgical plants, chemicals, mining and oil extraction as well as light industries such as textiles and food processing. It led, in particular, to the eclipse of the Urals by the Donets Basin (Donbass) as the empire's centre of heavy industry on the basis of its rich iron ore and coal deposits, whilst the Caucasus became the world's leading oil producer by the turn of the century. But railway development dominated the initial stages of this modernisation process, and it

Table 1.1. *Profile of Russian foreign trade, 1894–1913 (percentages of total exports/imports)*

Year	Foodstuffs		Raw materials and semimanu- factured goods		Animals		Manufactured goods	
	Export	Import	Export	Import	Export	Import	Export	Import
1894	56.9	18.4	37.5	54.4	2.0	0.7	3.6	26.5
1898	52.5	16.6	40.3	48.3	2.4	0.6	4.8	34.5
1903	61.3	20.1	31.9	52.5	2.0	0.8	4.8	26.6
1908	54.4	23.2	37.8	47.6	2.5	0.8	5.3	28.4
1913	55.3	17.3	36.9	48.6	2.2	1.3	5.6	32.8

Source: C. White, *British and American Commercial Relations*, p. 6.

remained among the driving forces of economic expansion in 1914. To cite Westwood: 'Tsarist economic policy placed railway development in the forefront, as both end and means.'[9]

Russia's railway age had begun in the late 1830s. It immediately raised the issue of tension between technological progress and political stability, some government ministers fearing that railways might encourage political unrest by allowing the population much greater freedom of movement. But the Tsar, Nicholas I, had witnessed railway operation in England and sensed that it might have important economic, political and strategic benefits for the empire.[10] He sanctioned the building of a short experimental line between St Petersburg and Tsarskoe Selo, and the successful opening of this venture in 1837 laid most doubts to rest, besides confirming the technical practicability of railway operation in Russian conditions. Opponents persisted, but the fact that only two main lines were built by the mid-1850s was due mainly to a chronic shortage of domestic finance and the government's reluctance to borrow heavily abroad. However, the difficulty of supplying Russia's army during the Crimean War produced the necessary impetus for prioritising railway construction and overcoming this financial barrier, and as early as 2 September 1854 an instruction was issued to begin surveying a Moscow–Khar'kov–Odessa route.[11]

Western perceptions of pre-war tsarist railways have tended towards the exotic, especially the epic construction of the trans-Siberian railway and the choice of a track gauge of 1,524 mm instead of the European standard of 1,435 mm.[12] In fact, after the uncertain start, the basic pattern of railway development was relatively mundane.

The authorities concentrated on creating a national network of so-called common-carrier railways – routes belonging to private or state-owned railway companies which were in turn supervised by the Ministry of Ways of Communication (MPS) and legally obliged as a public service to carry all traffic offered, as opposed to the non-public so-called feeder railways usually built and operated by industrial enterprises. Thanks to government encouragement, including financial incentives for private investors, a construction boom ensued in the 1860s and 1870s. Mainly funded by foreign capital, this effort delivered a core common-carrier network of some 20,000 km which radiated from Moscow to the iron ore deposits of the Urals, the coal, ores and new heavy industry of the Donbass, the grain of the Volga region and Ukraine, and the Baltic and Black Sea ports. As in the economy at large, the 1880s were a decade of consolidation for the railways, though a number of strategically important lines were completed in the extreme west, the Caucasus and Central Asia. In the 1890s the 'Vitte system' of rapid industrialisation produced a second railway boom, which was mostly state-funded, and by 1903 the common-carrier network extended to 58,400 km. After a short lull, further construction took the total to some 70,500 km by 1913, including the completion of the trans-Siberian route and more lines in Central Asia.[13] Correspondingly, the number of railway staff rose from about 32,000 in 1865 to some 815,500 in 1913, and the locomotive stock grew from a mere 401 in 1860 to 20,057 in 1913.[14] Freight traffic virtually doubled during every decade except the 1880s, reaching 76.8 thousand million tonne-km in 1913, and 29.3 thousand million passenger-km were recorded in 1913, equating to 244 million journeys.[15]

Railway construction was expected to drive Russia's economic modernisation in three main ways. Its primary function was to improve transport facilities for economic, political and military purposes. The iron horse promised to overcome or reduce the major geographical problems of vast distances, difficult climate, poor accessibility of natural resources and lack of suitable waterways. New markets might be developed at home and abroad, and whole regions such as Eastern Siberia and parts of Central Asia could be opened for settlement and economic development. Many railways in border regions and elsewhere were planned mainly for military shipments, whilst others were devised to support imperial expansion and colonisation.

Secondly, railway construction required a very significant share of the available resources. Though investment trends were similar to those in other sectors, the amount was generally much larger.[16] Indeed the first railway boom dominated the opening phase of industrialisation: in 1861–73 investment in 53 railway companies represented 65 per cent of total investment in new joint-stock companies, mainly from private sources.[17] When the state subsequently became the main investor, its investment in new railways and track improvements totalled some 3,588 million rubles (at contemporary prices) between 1895 and 1914, the annual figure peaking at 358 million in 1902 and never falling below the 109 million of 1895. As Gatrell remarks, railway investment (excluding transport equipment) represented as much as 25 per cent of total net investment in 1896–1900 and possibly more than 30 per cent if equipment is included.[18]

Thirdly, there was the question of potential 'backward linkages' to Russian industry. The construction and operation of railways generated an enormous direct and indirect need for almost every conceivable metal and textile product, as well as coal, timber, lubricating oils and other chemical products. Government officials realised very quickly that railway development could be used to spur the growth of other industries, expanding existing communities and creating new ones. The question of exploiting this potential arose as early as the 1840s, and after several decades of dependence on foreign suppliers, protectionism became a cornerstone of government policy concerning railway procurement from the late 1860s until 1914.

The foreign sector always occupied a controversial place in tsarist railway development, though its roles varied over time. It was an Austrian engineer, Franz Anton von Gerstner, who promoted the Tsarskoe Selo Railway, and foreign capital would remain essential for the railway sector for the remainder of the tsarist period in the absence of sufficient Russian state or private capital. During the Crimean War, having prioritised the creation of a railway network, the Tsar even used third parties to inform British financiers that their capital would be welcome for postwar railway development.[19] Foreign finance duly became the key to the boom of the 1860s. However, financial scandals were soon such a serious economic and political problem that the government changed course towards state intervention in the late 1860s, and for several decades state borrowing abroad became the primary means of raising the necessary capital for the railways. Later, after 1905, foreign private capital reacquired some importance when the government began to encourage private sector investment again.

The foreign loans were used for two main purposes. One was the construction of railways, especially a small number of top-priority routes during the 1880s and then the boom of the 1890s. The other was the purchase of existing, often impoverished, private railway companies in order to establish state control over railway finances, procurement policy and traffic operations.[20] By 1890 some 29 per cent of the network was state-owned and managed by the MPS, this figure rising to 70 per cent by 1900 thanks to further purchases and government-sponsored construction. Concurrently, the remaining private railways were gradually amalgamated into a small number of large companies and subjected to close control by the MPS, an arrangement which endured until 1918.[21]

Imports, too, were essential for constructing early railways. However, the government began promoting import substitution in the 1840s when it required the American contractors for the proposed Petersburg–Moscow line to use Russian materials and equipment wherever possible and to adapt the Aleksandrov iron foundry in St Petersburg to produce rolling-stock.[22] Two decades later the need for speed meant that the boom of the 1860s was deliberately fuelled by concessions on imports tariffs for iron, rails and other railway equipment, but a conscious policy of using railway development to stimulate domestic industrial growth emerged by the end of that decade, and this remained in place until 1914. The initial measures included the reinstatement and raising of customs tariffs, and a requirement for railway lessees to purchase a proportion of their equipment in Russia.[23]

But this protectionist policy had its problems. Russian engineering companies were nonetheless slow to appear and expand. Although four locomotive-building firms materialised in 1869–70, they refused to increase production significantly until the state raised customs tariffs and provided generous subsidies with a guarantee of sales. To complicate matters further, some private railways stubbornly insisted that imported locomotives were cheaper, and, when forced by the government to back down, they rebelliously announced a surplus of stock and placed their state-imposed engines in store.[24] Not until the 1880s, with the help of high tariffs, did domestic suppliers of railway equipment at last corner the market. Thus, locally produced rails met about 99 per cent of requirements by the 1890s.[25] Similarly, another five factories opened between 1892 and 1900 to cover the increasing demand for locomotives.[26] As a result, the net expansion of 9,427 locomotives on the network in 1893–1904 included only 1,077 imports, or some 12 per cent of the growth. The majority of these foreign engines were German, which reflected Germany's emergence as the principal trading partner; the USA was also prominent, whereas British deliveries were almost non-existent after 1880.[27]

Import substitution helped to ensure that the relationship between the engineering factories and the railways remained tense, especially once recession struck in 1900 and the state had to reduce its orders for railway equipment by as much as 10 per cent.[28] The government's response to the recession was well intentioned but had costly long-term side effects which would persist into the Soviet period. The engineering companies were permitted to regroup into powerful cartels, and a so-called Committee for Railway Orders was created under the MPS to channel state orders for rails and rolling-stock to Russian firms at high prices for the duration of the crisis; rails, for example, were bought from eight factories at the peak-demand prices of 1899.[29] This arrangement certainly protected jobs and plant, but its retention until 1915 at the factories' insistence meant that the exchequer and the private railways were faced with long-term high prices which, moreover, encouraged the factories to underproduce rather than diversify into alternatives.[30] The few remaining private railway companies also complained bitterly of their inability to influence design and technical decisions, and of overcharging, late delivery and poor quality. In 1913 they even petitioned the government for the right to choose their suppliers, to import equipment at will, to build engines and rolling-stock themselves and to own fuel deposits; but their plea was refused.[31]

By the outbreak of the First World War the overall results of tsarist industrialisation were famously and perhaps fatally mixed.[32] On the one hand, there was evidence of substantial progress. A railway system now connected the major cities of the empire, including the trans-Siberian route to Vladivostok. Many modern industries were well established – iron, steel, mining, heavy engineering and light industries such as textiles and food processing – with a tendency towards large well-equipped plants. Unsurprisingly, absolute levels of industrial output had grown substantially. For instance, average annual coal production increased from about 355,500 tonnes in the early 1860s to some 29,995,000 tonnes just before the First World War. The annual output of pig-iron rose from about 295,000 tonnes to approximately 3,848,500 tonnes over the same period. Overall, it has been estimated that Russian industrial output in manufacturing and mining grew on average by as much as 5 per cent per annum between 1888 and 1913.[33]

On the other hand there were also serious shortcomings on the eve of the war. Many areas of engineering and chemical production were still underdeveloped, especially high technology, and the agrarian sector remained weak despite its importance for export earnings. Industrial investment was concentrated in the St Petersburg and Moscow regions, the extreme west and the Donbass, and most railway activity was likewise in European Russia. The average annual increase in total real output per capita between 1860 and 1913 remained low at perhaps only 1 per cent because agricultural output – the largest sector – grew very slowly. Indeed, Russia's high rates of industrial growth partly reflected the fact that her industrialisation began from a much smaller base in the 1860s than was already enjoyed by her major foreign rivals, who themselves achieved much further progress during this period. It has even been argued that Russia lost ground: placed ninth/tenth jointly with Italy in a ranking of industrial progress of world powers in the 1860s, she was tenth behind Italy in 1910. Similarly, whereas Russian national income per capita, measured at 1913 prices, grew from 71 to 119 rubles between 1861 and 1913, the national incomes of the other major powers all grew at faster rates, including a spectacular increase from 450 to 1,033 rubles per head in the United States.[34]

The state of the railways was a particular concern. The key issues, which were to have an important bearing on early Soviet policy and which have excited perhaps the liveliest controversy, were the railway system's financial health, physical condition and adequacy. At the time the railways had few defenders: the government was concerned about excessive costs and debts, the public objected to delays and high prices, and harassed railway officials were happy to highlight obsolescence so as to justify new equipment. Subsequent analyses by Soviet officials and historians, shaped by both Russian Marxism and the railways' wartime crisis and collapse in 1915–20, usually concluded that the system was underdeveloped and offered a poor service, for which profit-led penny-pinching was to blame, and this view has been widely accepted in the West.[35] Russia, it has been argued, had far less track per person and per square kilometre than her international competitors, and ports such as Murmansk, Archangel and Vladivostok were poorly connected to the main network. Also, the accident rate was worsening in the years immediately preceding the First World War. There were frequent shortages of wagons, and the number of locomotives relative to traffic was decreasing. Typical of the neglect, in this view, was the fact that locomotive production by Russian factories declined to just 313 engines in 1912 compared to a possible output of more than 1,200.[36]

However, a contrasting positive assessment of the situation has also been advanced.[37] By again encouraging private investment in railway construction after a break of over thirty years, the state was able to concentrate on measures to improve productivity. Detailed planning of principal freight shipments was introduced, attempts were made to eradicate poor management, and existing lines were upgraded, especially by adding second tracks and by strengthening bridges and laying stronger rails for heavier trains.[38] This policy can be seen as a sensible compromise that helped to relieve bottle-necks, and in any case lines to the secondary ports were generally being built or improved. Furthermore, the comparisons of track mileage against population and area have been misleading through their inclusion of vast tracts of uninhabited wasteland. Also, greater efficiency in the use of equipment may explain the apparent shortfalls of stock and high rates of track utilisation, and greater efficiency may also explain why traffic and income were rising rapidly whilst operating expenses were decreasing. As for locomotives, the introduction of higher-powered types logically enabled the withdrawal of a much larger number of old, weaker engines. Fewer engines would be needed because better productivity was expected from the latest, most powerful designs, notably two classes which, with modifications, were built for four decades under tsarist and Soviet rule. One was the Class E freight locomotive with a 0–10–0 wheel arrangement (that is, with ten coupled 'driving' wheels but no other non-powered supporting wheels at either end), which appeared in 1911; the other was the Class S 2–6–2 passenger engine of 1910.[39]

Immediate difficulties notwithstanding, the MPS expected a bright future for the railways. Some 13,000 km of new routes were under construction, and many more lines were considered essential. Also, the ministry expected traffic to increase rapidly during the second half of the decade, and it was drafting plans for a big expansion of the locomotive stock, including a new phase of modernisation, to cope with this growth and defence needs. Its Commission for Rolling-stock and Traction wanted state orders for some 390 Class Shch 2–8–0 engines (a medium-powered freight design of 1907) and up to 100 Class S passenger engines in 1915, followed by up to 1,000 new 'powerful' engines in 1916 and a further 1,000 each year thereafter until 1920.[40] Here, however, the commission encountered a technical issue which would resurface in 1919–20: whether to continue with the latest 'powerful' freight type (the Class E 0–10–0) or introduce larger and more modern but more expensive engines for even heavier trains. Typically, the commission favoured a new type but could not agree on a design. Some engineers, including Professor Lomonosov, advocated a 0–10–2 arrangement as the extra rear axle would allow a larger firebox and more efficient burning of fuel. But the Chairman, Professor N. L. Shchukin, and others preferred a 2–10–0 as it could have a larger boiler, give a smoother ride, would yield higher speeds and cause less wear to the track.[41]

On the eve of the war, then, the railways remained vitally important for the economy, defence and the tsarist regime's political control. Almost certainly, as the example of the locomotive-builders implies, the 'backward linkages' between railway development and industrial growth were becoming much less straightforward than has often been assumed.[42] But the railway system was one of the country's largest employers, and it was still the only form of fast year-round long-distance transport. It was the key to successful military mobilisation. A large amount of construction work was in progress, and much more capacity was wanted, not least for defence purposes. In short, the railways remained central to government and popular thinking about the future. To judge by the MPS's traffic predictions, they may even have been set for a new 'boom'.

Not only were the railways important to the state, but foreign capital remained vital for railway construction. Private investment, whether domestic or foreign, continued to be seen as politically undesirable but was now reaccepted as indispensable. With regard to procurement policy, the tradition of fairly strict protectionism prevailed. Unfortunately, it still soured relations between the engineering industry and the railways, imports naturally gaining the allure of the unattainable for the latter. Significantly, this chronic tension would endure into the Soviet era.

Wartime imports

Russia's declaration of war against the Central Powers in 1914 evinced a wave of popular patriotic fervour. State officials, generals, politicians and populace expected a short and victorious campaign. But the mood soon changed. Nobody was prepared for the long trench-based struggle which ensued. Problems in the war economy soon assumed crisis proportions. Shortages of armaments loomed as early as the autumn of 1914, yet the government failed to organise an effective response, and a supply crisis developed during the winter of 1914–15. Morale was shaken by the army's retreat from Poland in 1915, and the troops and public became increasingly restive. Ultimately, amidst military stalemate and chronic food shortages, the tsarist regime fell in the revolution of February 1917 and was replaced by the Provisional government.[43]

Like the country as a whole, the railway and foreign trade sectors faced unprecedented challenges. Demand for their services increased rapidly, and both sectors faced a difficult struggle to comply. Desperate times required desperate measures, and one was to abandon protectionism concerning railway supplies. Large state railway orders were placed abroad, mainly with North American companies. By February 1917 the MPS had ordered nearly 1,000 new locomotives, 20,000 wagons and several hundred thousand tonnes of rails, spare parts and other equipment. Thereafter the Provisional government sought a further 2,000 engines and 40,000 wagons as well as rails and workshop equipment. This major change in railway procurement policy would represent an important precedent for Soviet officials in 1920, and the remainder of this chapter provides an introductory overview of the main events pending further research.

The railways were inevitably at the heart of the war effort.[44] The short-term demands of mobilisation apart, they had to cope with rapidly growing traffic and fundamental changes in traffic flows. For instance, a drastic decline in coal imports from Poland and Great Britain inflated demand for coal from the Donbass, which the railways now had to ship throughout the country. Grain, which had previously been exported through north-western and southern ports, was redirected westwards to feed the army. Particularly troublesome was the need to reroute most imports and exports through Vladivostok and Archangel because of the enemy blockade: the Pacific port depended on the barely complete and slow trans-Siberian route, whilst Archangel could be reached only by a low-capacity single-track narrow-gauge (1,067 mm) railway from Vologda, the conversion of which to Russian standard gauge (1,524 mm) was not completed until 1916. A line to Murmansk from the Petersburg region was under construction in 1914 and provisionally opened in 1916.

The railways' actual performance in 1914–16 was respectable yet worrying. As in other belligerent countries traffic initially declined through the cancellation of commercial shipments to facilitate mobilisation. But shipments reached record levels in 1915 and again, after their habitual winter decline, in the summer of 1916.[45] However, congestion and long delays were common on principal routes by 1915, causing shortages of food and fuel and a contrasting abundance of complaints and recriminations. Thus, for example, Archangel and Vladivostok were soon choked with goods awaiting shipment inland.[46] Moreover, these problems were perhaps fatally compounded by the army's sudden retreat from Poland in the summer of 1915. The commandeering of rolling-stock for the evacuation caused severe shortages of wagons in the rear, disrupting vital shipments of coal, raw materials and food. Also, by late 1916 the strain was beginning to tell on the railways' equipment. When labour disruption spread in the winter of 1916–17, the usual winter traffic dip became a precipitous collapse during 1917.

Historians have disputed whether the railways failed the country, as was widely believed at the time, or the country failed the railways. Unsurprisingly, scholars who have characterised the pre-war system as underdeveloped and ill-equipped have emphasised the railways' inadequacies. But others with a more sanguine view of the pre-war situation have defended the system's wartime record with the possible exception of organisation.[47] Whichever argument is correct, the tsarist government itself did perceive a significant expansion of railway capacity as a military and economic necessity for both the war effort and the postwar period. Moreover, it took important steps to this end, including its decision to allow railway imports.

Some decisions simply addressed the short-term emergency. Wagons of 1,000-pood capacity (16.3 tonnes) were permitted to carry 1,200 poods (19.56 tonnes); the maintenance of locomotives, rolling-stock, track and structures was reduced to enable their use for longer periods; and spare parts, tools, metals and other supplies were approved for purchase abroad.[48] However, other measures also had potential long-term benefits. Interestingly, these included some degree of modernisation with at least one eye on the postwar future. As in the final pre-war years, existing infrastructure was upgraded, particularly by adding second tracks, laying heavier rails and increasing the size and length of marshalling yards; and railway workshop capacity was gradually expanded. Also, orders for new engines and rolling-stock were increased, including imports, though not yet to the full extent of the 2,000 additional engines and 70,000 freight wagons requested by the railways and the Special Council for Defence.[49] Great efforts were made to complete lines already under construction in 1914, partly using imported rails, and nearly 10,000 km of new routes were opened.[50] Indeed in an interview in November 1915, the minister, A. F. Trepov declared that Russia needed a new network of railways and that railway construction would be continued. A commission chaired by deputy minister I. N. Borisov produced a far-reaching ten-year construction plan, and in mid-1916 the MPS requested the State Duma's approval for the first phase, a massive five-year programme costed at some 600 million rubles per year.[51]

Imports were by no means an easy option because the war was devastating Russia's foreign trade.[52] The country immediately lost her most important trade partner, Germany. Worse, by December 1914 the German–Turkish blockade of the Baltic and Black Seas was forcing reliance on the secondary ports of Murmansk and Archangel in the north, and Vladivostok and Nikolaevsk in the Far East, which were all poorly served by the domestic transport network. Exports and export earnings collapsed. Extensive efforts were made to import armaments, railway equipment and other supplies, but the cost was high. The Treasury's ability to pay for orders was impeded by the loss of export earnings, wartime restrictions on the international movement of currency holdings, and chronic difficulties in obtaining new foreign credit. Also, deliveries were often badly delayed through production problems, sabotage and a shortage of sea-going tonnage. A trade surplus of 146 million gold rubles in 1913 had become a deficit of 1,873 million in 1916, and the foreign debt jumped to 13,800 million gold rubles over the same period, yet overall Russia had relatively little to show for her expenditure.[53]

Russian ministries began sending purchasing agents abroad from August 1914, concentrating on Britain, France, Japan and especially North America. Later, from 1915, Russian government supply committees were formed as coordinating agencies in these and other countries, with overall coordination delegated to the Russian Government Committee in London. Naturally, military contracts predominated, the main priorities being field guns, howitzers, shells, hand grenades, rifles, cartridges and boots. But MPS purchases, mostly of railway supplies, were also very significant. Of the Russian state orders worth at least US$1,176 million placed in North America between mid-1915 and the Bolshevik Revolution, contracts for the Main Artillery Directorate accounted for some $767 million, whilst MPS contracts formed the second largest share at just over $167 million or some 14 per cent of the total.[54]

The key examples of locomotive and wagon policy suggest that the idea of importing railway supplies arose, as with purely military purchases, very early in the war, that the MPS took the initiative, and that one reason for this was lobbying by American industrialists. By late August 1914 there was talk of a possible MPS emergency order in America for 250 locomotives and 10,000 wagons. Also, continuing the discussion of traction modernisation, the MPS was considering ordering prototypes of new 2–10–2 freight and 4–6–2 passenger types from the United States as successors to the classes E and S.[55] Neither of these ideas progressed much further at this stage, but the idea of imports did become established, thanks partly to Samuel Vauclain, a vice-president of the Baldwin Locomotive Works of Philadelphia, USA:

> When war was declared between Germany, England, France and Russia we were running at about one third capacity and I concluded we might obtain some foreign business if someone who knew how to handle it could get into Russia. We had a representative in Russia in whom we had little confidence. His wild cablegrams indicated little knowledge of our business, so I decided to go to Russia ... We found the Baldwin representative trying to carry on business in his room on the fourth story of a house remote from the city's centre. After contacting with the Vice-Minister of Communication concerning locomotives and assisting his engineers in the construction of equipment for war purposes, we concentrated upon narrow-gauge locomotives for the railroad running north to Archangel. For the Russian artillery department, an order for 100,000 military rifles was cabled to the Remington Arms Company.[56]

By stressing rapid delivery Vauclain won a contract for thirty so-called 'Mallet' locomotives for the vital Archangel line, and within a few months he was back in Russia seeking new contracts, such were his optimism and determination.[57]

But domestic issues were also important in the policy change. One problem was tension over the Committee for Railway Orders, whose latest three-year reprieve was to expire on 1 January 1915. The cartels, facing shortages and greater regulation of production, pressed hard for a five-year extension, lobbying ministers and the chairman of the Council of Ministers. But the MPS now withdrew its support. The minister, S. V. Rukhlov, wanted to undermine the syndicates' power and argued that subsidies were unnecessary since contracts worth over 40 million rubles were being planned. Opposed only by the syndicates and the Ministry of Trade and Industry, the abolition of the committee was approved in late October 1914.[58]

Other problems concerned factory capacity and contract terms. The engineering industry made increased railway-related output conditional upon receiving large long-term contracts on similar terms to military contracts. The demands included higher prices, large deposits, firm guarantees for supplies of materials and fuel, exemption from military conscription for their workers, and the right to miss delivery deadlines because of wartime difficulties.[59] Locomotive orders were also delayed because some factories wished to concentrate on the Class S and out-dated Class Shch so as to avoid any retooling, whereas the MPS wanted maximum deliveries of the Class E so as to increase line capacity by operating heavier trains. However, armaments work apart, probably the main cause of delay with locomotive contracts was failure to agree prices, the government resisting the pressure to match those offered by the military.[60] As for wagons, the MPS specified its requirement for 1915 as 60,000 compared to maximum factory capacity of about 43,000, and so it concluded that some 17,000 would need to be imported.[61] Track materials were more troublesome. There had already been difficulties with supplies in 1913 caused by shortages of cast iron, and the war exacerbated the problem, especially when some of the rails factories switched to making armaments.[62]

The engineering factories persisted with their demands through the winter. In January 1915 the wagon-builders' cartel, Prodvagon, was still seeking three-year contracts and large advances to support expansion of its annual capacity to 60,000 so as to cover virtually all the demand.[63] However, Russian industry as a whole adopted a more conciliatory position over wagons. In December 1914 the Council of the Congress of Representatives of Trade and Industry urged the Council of Ministers to approve subsidies and priority for supplies of materials and parts, and also demanded contracts for 49,000 wagons – its estimate of Russian capacity – for delivery in 1915. But the delegates agreed that any shortfall should be covered by imports because the wagon shortage was already causing an industrial 'crisis'.[64]

In the end all sides were probably reasonably satisfied. The railways received far fewer resources than desired, but they did at least win access to foreign suppliers, whom the private railways at least had long regarded as more efficient, technologically advanced and responsive to customer concerns. The autumn of 1914 saw Vauclain's 'Mallet' contract plus orders for 4,890 tonnes of rails and more than 2,000 sets of points from the United States.[65] Meanwhile, the Shchukin commission swiftly approved a new 2–10–0 heavy freight design for urgent mass production abroad.[66] A special interministerial meeting then allocated 53 million rubles for essential MPS imports in January 1915. Several months later the Council of Ministers authorised orders in North America for 400 locomotives of the newly approved type plus 17,700 American-type high-capacity four-axle wagons (equivalent to 40,000 standard Russian twin-axle 16.3-tonne wagons). Approval to import a further 35,000 standard wagons followed in June.[67]

As for the engineering industry, by mid-February 1915 Prodvagon had firm orders for delivery that year of 36,115 wagons, and conditional orders for another 7,289. In addition, the MPS agreed to higher prices for wagons and to the principle of three-year contracts, probably in exchange for a commitment to boost wagon output to 63,000.[68] Meanwhile the locomotive-builders complained to the Shchukin commission that the urgent foreign order for 400 freight engines would force Russian factories to reduce their 1916 production targets. They forecast considerable surplus capacity because the MPS was actually planning to order only 620 engines in Russia in 1916, whilst the private railways were likely to order only about 150. But, significantly, they acquiesced to the imports provided that the foreign locomotives began entering service within six months of the contract.[69] The syndicate's protocols are silent on the point, but one may speculate that with the government refusing to raise prices for rolling-stock, the factories were hoping to get more lucrative military contracts instead. The engineering industry had already begun suspending private and state railway contracts in late 1914, probably partly for this reason, and this trend was encouraged in 1915 by the shell shortage and the general war mobilisation of industry.[70]

Why, then, did the government permit these imports instead of giving railway production the same priority and pricing as armaments? Increased domestic output was certainly wanted, but a key problem was the severity of the shortages of basic armaments such as shells, rifles and cartridges, and of machine-tooling and raw materials, especially metals. Wagon parts, for instance, needed steel akin to that used for shells, whilst the same machinery could make gun barrels, and though the wagon shortage was among the most critical bottle-necks, the armaments crisis was even more important.[71] Thus, a combination of urgency and shortages was probably enough to justify wagon imports as a stopgap, though the MPS was obviously keen for a modern American design into the bargain. As for locomotives, the selection of a new modern type which could not be built in Russia without retooling – itself problematic – suggests that the government accepted the logic of trying to increase line capacity quickly by introducing bigger engines to pull significantly heavier trains.

In the event, the engineering industry's relationship with the MPS and railways remained fraught throughout the war. Underproduction continued despite objections from the MPS and the Special Council for Shipments, which planned railway traffic. The severe shortages of raw materials persisted, and other problems included the evacuation of key companies from the Baltic provinces such as the Russo-Baltic Wagon Works and the Phoenix Works in 1915. It is thus scarcely surprising that, for example, Prodvagon built some 7,500 wagons fewer than planned in 1915, whilst production of much-needed rails slumped from 650,370 tonnes in 1914 to 265,690 tonnes in 1916.[72] Locomotive output reached 870 in 1915, but dropped to 576 in 1916, the delivery shortfall of 474 in 1916 being deferred to 1917.[73]

The placement of foreign railway orders began in earnest in the spring of 1915. A contract for 20,000 wagon axles in April was followed by agreements for 13,160 wagons, 28,700 wheelsets and 25,000 steel tyres. The 400 2–10–0 freight engines were ordered in July 1915: 50 from the Canadian Locomotive Company of Kingston, Ontario; 100 from the Schenectady works of the American Locomotive Company (Alco); and 250 from the Baldwin Locomotive Works. In July and August orders were placed for 204,900 tonnes of rails and 41,700 tonnes of associated fittings such as rail joiners and bolts. By the end of the year 56 shunting and medium-powered freight locomotives had been ordered for the Murmansk Railway from the H. K. Porter Company.[74] As for technical supervision, a so-called Commission of Ways of Communication in America was established under the chairmanship of a senior MPS technical inspector, Count S. I. Shulenburg. This organisation worked in close cooperation with the Russian Supply Committee in America, and was eventually incorporated into the latter in 1916.[75]

The 2–10–0 locomotives, which were the product of the Shchukin commission's modernisation deliberations, were officially designated as the Class Ye but were known familiarly throughout Russia as the 'decapod' (*dekapod*). They represented a certain technological advance over the 0–10–0 through their extra axle, modern bar-type frame and various other features. Moreover, though larger and heavier than the 0–10–0, their maximum axle-loading was no greater, at 16.2 tonnes. Unfortunately, this weight was heavy by Russian if not American standards, and like the 0–10–0 the decapods had to be concentrated on routes relaid with heavy rails, mainly in Siberia and the Donbass.[76]

After assembly in America each locomotive was dismantled and packed in some thirty-four crates. As with the bulk of the railway purchases, most were then shipped to Vladivostok, where they began arriving in late 1915. Next they were forwarded to the Chinese Eastern Railway workshops in Harbin, Manchuria, where representatives of the builders provided technical assistance in the reassembly process. The first locomotives eventually joined the operating stock after trials in early 1916 – a delay which reflects the general difficulties faced by the supply committees during the war: shortages of tooling, materials and shipping, the closure of the Panama Canal in 1915–16 and, ironically, delays in transporting imports inland from Vladivostok.[77]

The first decapods had a frosty reception on the railways themselves. Many staff were suspicious of the unfamiliar design features and unhappy with the large American castings, for the maintenance of which many depots were not yet equipped. There were many complaints about substandard riveting, and the boiler tubes were apparently prone to develop leaks. Also, there were many derailments of the much-heralded leading axle. Most dramatically of all, the boiler of one unfortunate Baldwin decapod exploded in May 1917. Complex design and poor assembly were blamed – an analysis strongly disputed by Baldwin but which at least made a change from the usual alleged cause of such eruptions, drunkenness.[78]

In other respects, however, the locomotives' performance was encouraging. For instance, they could easily haul long trains weighing over 3,260 tonnes, which represented great potential as goods yards were expanded to accommodate such trains.[79] In time, the decapods generally became well regarded. The tsarist MPS did not hesitate to request many more, albeit with improvements, when possible new imports were discussed in 1916, whilst in 1923 Siberian engineers described the decapod as the best class in their service, and in 1925 many of its features were recommended for new Soviet designs.[80]

The commissioning of the foreign-built wagons also involved controversy. As with the decapods, their full potential could not always be used. The larger wagons had to be restricted to routes relaid with heavy rails, and most sidings were still too short to hold the very long trains for which these wagons, with their modern automatic brakes and couplings, were ideally suited. There were also other problems, some quite peculiar. For example, the Russians insisted on shipping coal in covered rather than open wagons, and because the American vans had two rather than four doors, the loading and unloading of coal was more difficult. But the most serious complaint, especially from 1917 onwards, concerned their Westinghouse automatic brakes, and threatened to discredit the ministry's dream of equipping the network's entire stock with modern brakes: numerous wagons were disabled because, as enterprising or desperate railwaymen quickly discovered, their rubber brake pipes were ideal for making boot soles.[81]

In general, however, the most intractable difficulties with railway imports were not human or technical but financial. In July 1916 Rukhlov's successor at the MPS, Trepov, informed the Tsar that the ministry had still to order some 5,000 of the 17,700 high-capacity wagons authorised in the spring of 1915 and all of the 35,000 standard wagons sanctioned in June 1915. The delay was blamed entirely on a shortage of hard currency.[82]

Initially, the Russian government's primary source of wartime foreign credit was Great Britain, first through agreements with the bank of Baring Brothers and then with the British government.[83] The first credit was for £12 million, granted by Barings in October 1914, and was approved by the British government on condition that Russia supplied gold and bullion worth £8 million to maintain the value of sterling. A credit of £20 million followed in January 1915, and a further £20 million was raised in Britain in April 1915, half of it from a public issue of Treasury bills.

By this time moves were afoot to organise a more substantial supply of aid. A special conference about inter-Allied financial assistance produced an agreement which, among other things, defined Russia's credit requirement as £100 million. France and Britain each supplied £50 million, the British contribution being paid by Barings in two instalments of £25 million in June and July 1915. However, this money lasted only a few months, and a fundamentally new approach was required to cover Russia's needs. A further inter-Allied conference was thus convened in September 1915, producing a financial framework which, by and large, endured until the February Revolution. It was agreed that from October 1915 Britain would provide a monthly credit of £25 million for one year by discounting Russian government Treasury bills. The Russian government was to ship £40 million in gold to London as security. Britain would fund Russia's foreign military contracts except those in France and – to the Russians' resentment – would supervise the placement of new orders.[84]

In June 1916 another conference was held in London to discuss future needs. However, agreement was not reached until October. The

British reluctantly granted a six-month extension of the monthly credit scheme, whilst the Russians equally reluctantly agreed to ship a further £20 million in gold after 1 January 1917, if needed, to prevent British reserves dropping below £85 million.[85] Accordingly, yet another conference was required in early 1917, this time in Petrograd (formerly St Petersburg). Inevitably these talks also proved arduous, and were still continuing when the February Revolution swept the Tsar from power.

It would seem that some of this British money was used to fund MPS orders in North America in 1915–16. However, the ministry did also seek assistance from other foreign sources.[86] One scheme, for which in December 1915 Trepov requested the approval of the Minister of Finances, P. L. Bark, concerned an 18-month loan at 9 per cent interest. It involved the Russian industrialist Putilov and an irrepressible Swedish banker, Olof Aschberg, who earned large fees as an intermediary between the tsarist government and American banks, and who would later offer loans to the Bolsheviks. Another plan envisaged an order for 3,000 wagons in Finland, equivalent to that country's annual production capacity. A third project involved orders for up to 97,000 tonnes of rails. Some of these proposals did lead to contracts, but most probably remained just ideas.[87]

The MPS made a special effort to stimulate British interest in its plight in the spring of 1916. Its aim was to gain complete support for a massive new programme of imports with both funding and shipping tonnage. The justification was again urgency, rapidly rising demand for transport, and worsening industrial underproduction despite 'compulsory' orders.[88] In March the ministry defined its immediate needs as $27,603,000 and £272,000.[89] Then, in early April (New Style), it sent a more detailed description of its requirements, specifying rails, wagons, tools and spare parts costing $25,192,730 (urgently needed) and £5.78 million (for slightly later delivery).[90] A month later the MPS made an additional, much larger request, compiled by Shchukin. This document sought 1,300 new decapods ($52,877,500), 34,915 standard wagons ($62,737,890) and 126,038.54 tonnes of rails ($8,975,560). Further, it specified equipment for the Harbin workshops and new workshops in Vladivostok to speed the assembly of imported locomotives and wagons ($500,000), and more equipment for frontline and other workshops ($11,250,000). Also wanted was equipment valued at £422,400 for the Murmansk Railway, and just over $24 million to pay for earlier orders.[91] In addition, Trepov and Bark approached the British ambassador, Sir George Buchanan, for assistance in securing exemption from British Treasury 'formalities' for rolling-stock and motor car orders because of urgency. With some justification the Russians complained that whereas the British required shipping tonnage to be available before orders could be permitted, the Russian government could not procure cargo space until British approval was certain.[92]

Buchanan recommended every effort to meet Trepov's wishes. The minister seemed 'capable and energetic', and costs had risen by 5 million rubles whilst a decision was being made in Britain.[93] But Whitehall was appalled. The War Office bridled at the 'insinuation' of undue delay. It explained that there had been only two Russian applications for railway material: one in October 1915 for £2 million, which had been approved after two weeks; and one for a large order via a middleman named Skidelski, which had also been agreed – despite an 'exorbitant' deposit of 65 per cent plus a price 30 per cent higher than previously paid direct – on condition that shipping tonnage was guaranteed. In the War Office's opinion, 'the latter transaction induces grave doubts as to the advisability of giving this particular Government Department *carte blanche*'.[94] Similarly, the Ministry of Munitions felt that allowing Russia a free hand would be 'disastrous' for the market in railway equipment given the large British, French and Italian requirements.[95] And the Treasury bluntly refused the money on the grounds that insufficient tonnage was available even for the earlier requests, the Russian government had exhausted all agreed credit, and a moratorium would probably be needed on all orders in the United States 'except in quite exceptional circumstances'.[96] Only the Foreign Office seemed even vaguely sympathetic: an official fretted that having been conveyed in writing, 'this unwelcome decision' might create a bad impression.[97]

When Bark then failed to secure a new British loan quickly, Trepov lost patience and obtained the Tsar's personal permission to place orders without a guarantee of British credit. In the first instance he wanted 6,000 high-capacity wagons and 176,040 tonnes of rails, a figure which he increased to 431,950 tonnes by 1 July 1916.[98] The MPS duly invited tenders for 100 more decapods – a move which Buchanan intended to support unofficially – and ordered rails from at least two American companies.[99] In short, Trepov tried to present London with a *fait accompli*. He informed the British Foreign Office and Treasury that the American companies had demanded an immediate response about the rails, that the MPS had waited until the last possible moment, and that he hoped to obtain British credit and shipping for them in due course. However, the British Treasury refused to pay for Trepov's contracts or obtain tonnage because the orders were contrary to the recent Anglo-Russian agreement.[100]

The result was such a cash shortage that Bark tried to stop the delivery of eighty second-hand 2–10–0 'Flamme' engines ordered from the Belgian State Railways in August 1915, and a contract for twenty-seven new and twenty-six second-hand engines from Japan. Only with the next Anglo-Russian financial accord in October 1916 did the situation improve. The MPS was at last granted access to British money, and purchases of more American decapods were immediately planned. However, despite continuing Foreign Office sympathy, the British Treasury remained wary of the transport ministry's vast appetite for cash and was doubtless horrified at MPS claims in November 1916 that 320 million rubles were needed for new American orders. Significantly, there were even angry suspicions, fuelled by railway construction in the Urals and Central Asia, that the equipment was really wanted for long-term railway development, not the war effort. After only 300 more decapods had been ordered from Baldwin and Alco in late 1916, the exasperated British Treasury announced a moratorium on large Russian railway orders. As a result, there were no further British-funded locomotive orders until contracts in April 1917 for fifty-three more Baldwin narrow-gauge 'Mallets' and another seventy-five decapods. These proved to be the last locomotives ordered with British finance.[101]

It is worth adding that whilst contemporary commentators all described the railway situation as serious or even critical during 1916, not all believed that imports were essential for salvation. L. M. Levi, S. S. Ostapenko and a few other engineers argued that major improvements could be effected through organisational changes, especially better planning.[102] Their criticisms were often pertinent, but these dissenters carried little weight by late 1916 as national shortages of food, fuel and raw materials became acute and were blamed (fairly or otherwise) on the railways. Perhaps, too, the authorities doubted their own ability to improve organisation and management. Bizarrely, no less an authority than the Special Council for Defence declared that the last hopes for improvement rested on new orders for locomotives and wagons from the United States, even though council members must have known that such equipment could not reach Russia for at least a year even if given priority for shipping.[103] Imports of equipment were now, it would seem, regarded virtually as a panacea for all the railways' ills.

The Provisional government's largesse

After the revolution of February 1917, the new Russian government quickly displayed a positive attitude towards railway investment, including postwar modernisation. It continued discussions begun in 1916 about immense long-term domestic programmes whereby the Kolomna works would produce 1,000 Class E or equivalent engines and 15,000 wagons in 1918–22, whilst the Russia Company would supply 1,470 Class E engines, 15,600 wagons and 100,000 tonnes of locomotive and wagon tyres in 1919–25.[104] For the short term it approved an MPS request of 31 March/13 April to place immediate foreign orders for 2,000 more engines and 40,000 wagons for delivery by 1 July 1918, together with workshop equipment for Harbin and Vladivostok, at a probable total cost of up to $200 million in addition to maximum domestic output. So urgent were these orders, the ministry argued, that it might even be necessary to try to buy regauged second-hand locomotives. But the imports would have long-term value too: traffic would continue rising after the war and obsolete stock needed to be replaced.[105]

With domestic shortages and underproduction continuing, one new reason for the government's acquiescence to more imports was a much greater sense of crisis. The latest statistics showed a sudden serious deterioration in railway performance with a leap in quantities of 'sick' rolling-stock. For instance, whereas locomotive unserviceability was similar to the pre-war norm during 1916 and January 1917, averaging 16.7 per cent, it jumped to 18.4 per cent in February and to 20.3 per cent in March.[106] Yet, ironically, these particular statistics may have been more alarmist than alarming. A consultant American engineer later observed that in 1917 the railways began describing as 'sick' any engine that was out of service for more than twelve hours, even if merely for routine maintenance.[107] If, as was usual, MPS reports to the government did not explain such technical nuances, the government simply would not be able to understand the figures properly.

A second reason for the approval of more imports was the sea change in Russo-American relations. Whereas Washington had maintained a certain distance from the tsarist regime, it was very sympathetic towards the Provisional government and granted official recognition almost immediately. Thus, the new ministers could reasonably hope for large American loans if, as happened within a month, the United States joined the war against Germany. Certainly the Provisional government gave high priority to trade relations with the USA. The Minister of Trade and Industry, A. I. Konovalov, and the Foreign Minister, P. N. Miliukov, defined closer economic ties as one of their main objectives, and a special trade mission was organised to negotiate credits and contracts.[108] In short, the USA's entry into the war seemingly tempted ministers to try to spend their way out of trouble with American credit.

The Russians initiated discussions for possible US loans on about 17/30 March. The Minister of Finances, M. I. Tereshchenko, had been informed that Britain and France were each to borrow $500 million from the United States, and he asked the US ambassador, David R. Francis, for the same favour. The Secretary of the US Treasury, William G. McAdoo, responded positively. He requested details of Russia's requirements and suggested that his government could purchase Russian government obligations. Tereshchenko then confirmed Russia's request for $500 million, promised to spend the money entirely in the United States and suggested a 5-per-cent dollar bond for the full sum. An Act of Congress duly authorised this loan on 11/24 April, and McAdoo opened a credit for the first instalment of $100 million on 3/16 May.[109] Significantly, however, the Russians viewed this loan as merely a beginning. A commission was formed on 26 March/8 April under a Deputy Minister of Trade and Industry, B. A. Bakhmet'ev, to consider how much American money should be requested in total, how relations with Britain would be affected, and whether Russia could accept Washington's terms for the initial $500 million.[110]

In the meantime, railway requirements costed at $220 million, including 2,000 locomotives and 40,000 wagons, were specified in the expenditure plan communicated by Francis to Washington on 7/20 April. The remainder of the loan was earmarked for agricultural equipment and Russian industry. No major new military orders were planned yet, probably owing to chronic delays with earlier contracts.[111] American consent was soon forthcoming with a promise to facilitate the railway purchases and deliveries.[112] Next, the MPS representative in the USA, Count Shulenburg, was instructed to hold preliminary negotiations for 500 decapods and 10,000 wagons, pending further instructions. In Petrograd there was initially talk of creating a special railway mission, but a simpler solution was found. When the government's proposed economic mission was formed under Bakhmet'ev in late April, it included an MPS delegation headed by a deputy minister with authority to settle all technical questions relating to the railways.[113]

This man from the ministry was Professor Iu.V. Lomonosov. Born in 1876 to a landowning family of modest means in the Smolensk region, he studied with distinction at the Institute of Ways of Communication in St Petersburg.[114] A larger-than-life character in every respect – he was nicknamed 'Monster' by his family – he joined the railways in defiance of his father. He earned international recognition as well as membership of the prestigious MPS Engineering Council in 1913 at the age of just thirty-six by successfully applying an academic approach to the design and operation of steam locomotives, including the development of locomotive testing on a rigorously scientific basis. No less significant was his pioneering work with diesel traction, which would help the USSR achieve a world lead in this technology in the 1920s. He also distinguished himself as an administrator, becoming a deputy head of the MPS Directorate of Railways in 1912 with responsibility for traction, new railways and health care. During the First World War he not only continued his scientific work, testing different types of locomotive fuel, but also reorganised railway traffic in Moscow and Romania and represented the MPS on the Special Council for Defence.

By 1917 Lomonosov was thus among the most senior of those railwaymen who would later be labelled bourgeois specialists or 'spetsy'. Yet his politics were unconventional for an official of his standing and help to explain his later support for the Soviet government. In 1905–6 he was active in the military–technical organisation of the Social Democratic Party's Central Committee, helping to prepare and distribute bombs under the command of Leonid Krasin, the future commissar of transport and foreign trade. After 1907 Lomonosov's commitment to political activism and the Bolsheviks waned, but he evidently continued to hold radical beliefs. He played a notable part in the February Revolution, helping to prevent the trains carrying General Ivanov's troops from reaching Petrograd, and also helping to print the abdication proclamations.[115] Unfortunately, however, his career was marred by controversy both before and after 1917. The most important problem was tension with colleagues, especially his rivals and immediate superiors.[116] Perhaps, therefore, it was inevitable that he would quarrel with Bakhmet'ev in America. Overall financial responsibility clearly lay with the ambassador, and the professor found this increasingly irksome when serious difficulties arose with the locomotive and wagon orders, especially after the Bolshevik revolution.[117]

But this argument was still in the future when Bakhmet'ev's

mission arrived in Washington in June 1917. Naturally, as the largest single element of new expenditure, the proposed railway orders were high on its agenda, and Lomonosov was immediately involved. Since Shulenburg had already negotiated draft contracts for the first 500 locomotives and 10,000 wagons, including 250 decapods each from Baldwin and Alco, Lomonosov had to settle the technical matters and help organise clearance from the US Treasury, War Department (including the Council of National Defense) and State Department. In the first instance negotiations were conducted with the Advisory Committee of the Council of National Defense, chaired by Daniel F. Willard, and the Council's committees for locomotives and rolling-stock, at this time chaired by none other than Samuel Vauclain. The successful outcome was confirmed by an exchange of letters between Bakhmet'ev and the Treasury and State Department. The Baldwin order was then signed on 22 June/5 July, the Alco contract followed on 26 June/9 July and the wagons were ordered on 28 June/11 July and 12/25 July, shared between the American Car and Foundry Company (6,500) and the Standard Steel Car Company (3,500). The budgeted cost was $46 million, set against the $100 million credit of 3/16 May.[118]

Lomonosov was therefore left with two main concerns. One was to succeed Shulenburg as head of the New York-based MPS mission, which was by now a formidable part of the Russian Supply Committee with several hundred employees and responsibility for placing MPS orders, supervising quality control and organising the shipment of finished products to Russia.[119] The other preoccupation was to order the remaining locomotives and wagons as quickly as possible, at a planned cost of about $90 million and $53 million respectively, as well as workshop equipment and automobiles for some $25 million. In fact Lomonosov had tried to order all 2,000 locomotives and 40,000 wagons immediately, but had been thwarted by the fact that the American authorities were having second thoughts. Indeed, whereas the signing of minor contracts continued into the autumn of 1917, and McAdoo opened further credits against the $500 million loan for various purposes, the main business of ordering locomotives and wagons broached broader questions in Russo-American and inter-Allied relations, and it came to a protracted halt.[120]

In his reports to Petrograd Bakhmet'ev apparently played down the difficulties. On 21 July/3 August he cautioned that delay was likely because of worries on the part of the Treasury and a lack of coordination between the relevant US departments, though he himself wanted to postpone signing the contracts in order to secure better terms.[121] Several weeks later he reported that the US government had confirmed the credit for the remaining proposed 1,500 engines and 30,000 wagons, but again he noted his intention to await better market conditions, though not so long as to miss the planned delivery dates.[122]

There was indeed some poor coordination on the American side, to judge from correspondence in early August between McAdoo and the Secretary for War, Newton D. Baker. The Treasury, too, was certainly raising objections.[123] Also, it was certainly possible that better terms might be reached because government price controls at below-market rates were expected for metal products, and a delay of even a few months would not seriously compromise the delivery schedule. But the postponement was in fact imposed by the Americans because the orders raised issues of general inter-Allied supply cooperation. The US authorities wanted to prioritise a locomotive order for the American Expeditionary Force in France (AEF), and they had serious misgivings about the proposed Russian contracts. Russia's unfolding political drama probably encouraged this unease, but there were also genuine doubts about America's ability to finance and deliver Allied war supplies on the scale being demanded and about whether the Russians really needed more railway equipment.[124]

During the spring and summer of 1917 it emerged that Russian and American diagnoses of the railway crisis differed fundamentally. The US administration did recognise the importance of efficient transport for Russia's war effort: a War Department official observed in March 1917 that for Russia 'war at the present time is quite as much a matter of transportation and production in the workshops as of strategy upon the battlefield'.[125] But whereas most Russians defined a shortage of modern equipment as the main problem, the Americans were more concerned with good organisation and management.[126] This dichotomy was most evident over the trans-Siberian route. The Russians insisted that only much more American rolling-stock could increase traffic from Vladivostok. But the sceptical Americans, supported by the British, wanted to send American engineers to clarify precisely what assistance was needed. Evidently unhappy, the Russians had no choice but to agree.[127]

John F. Stevens, a highly experienced American railway engineer, duly arrived in Vladivostok with several colleagues and assistants on 19 May/1 June 1917. After studying the trans-Siberian line this advisory commission travelled to Petrograd, arriving on 30 May/12 June.

There they met MPS officials and also inspected the lines to Murmansk and Archangel and the routes between Petrograd, the Donbass and the front headquarters, ruffling numerous Russian feathers in the process. Most of the commission then returned home in the late summer and autumn, though Stevens himself would remain in the Far East until 1922 alongside the Russian Railway Service Corps, a much larger American group deployed in 1918 to manage the Chinese Eastern Railway and the main lines of non-Bolshevik Siberia.[128]

Stevens was certainly impressed by what he saw and heard in 1917, but often unfavourably. Though usually complimentary in public, he and his team could be bluntly critical in private. Stevens agreed that much of the stock was obsolete by US standards, and at his most biting he later (in 1921) described Russian trains as 'strings of matchboxes coupled by hairpins and drawn by samovars'.[129] But obsolescence did not mean uselessness, and the key problem was actually that the railways were working at only 60 per cent of available capacity.[130] The commission saw widespread labour trouble as a fundamental reason for this. 'Everywhere', Stevens later wrote, 'discontent, idleness and insubordination dominated', and 'apathy and apparent indifference' were endemic on the railways.[131] This was encouraged in turn by the food shortage, caused in the Americans' view by the reluctance of peasants to sell produce at low government-imposed prices.[132] Poor management was also a major problem: for example, delays on the trans-Siberian railway were caused by coal traffic that was needlessly allowed to congest the main line in the Tomsk area.[133]

An inter-Allied conference in Petrograd in June 1917 highlighted the differences between the analyses. British and American representatives told the Russians bluntly that the railways' existing capabilities had to be reappraised because losses of ships would restrict deliveries to 850 engines and 20,000 wagons in 1917. In any case, the British and Americans maintained, much of Russia's transport and industrial crisis was due to continual price increases, capitulation to workers' demands and a failure to make proper use of existing facilities.[134] Not surprisingly, the Russians resented such criticism, and there were many sharp exchanges with the Stevens mission.[135] Stevens himself, deeply frustrated by what he saw as the obstructive attitude of Petrograd officials, complained bitterly to the British Military Attaché, General Alfred Knox, that the Russian government's attitude was quite clear: 'They want us to put a big bag of money on their doorstep and then to run away'.[136]

The irony was that Stevens felt forced to oblige. On 20 June/3 July he informed the Minister of Ways of Communication, N. V. Nekrasov, that he completely agreed about the need for new equipment, and he reiterated this point the next day in a public statement intended to bolster Russian morale.[137] At stake, he believed, was Russia's continued participation in the war. As he telegraphed to the US Secretary of State, Robert Lansing, and the Council of National Defense on 19 June/2 July:

> This whole nation [is] imbued with the one idea that additional engines and cars are necessary to maintain [the] army and navy, also to provide foods and other needs, and is the salvation of the people of Russia. [It is] expedient for moral effect [that] rapid action be taken to insure [sic] continuous operations now and through next winter, otherwise complete collapse may be expected. This commission strongly recommends furnishing from the United States immediately thirty thousand additional American type freight cars and twenty-five hundred additional [decapod] engines ... We have committed our Government to a fair price and the earliest possible delivery. A prompt confirmation of this programme by our Government is vital to the Allied cause and the aims of this commission.[138]

However, that confirmation was not forthcoming. Stevens's telegram, and especially his statements of 3 and 4 July, put the American administration in a difficult position in three respects, thereby helping to provoke a broader policy debate about the scale and purpose of Russian borrowing. Nearly two months would elapse before the Americans made even an interim decision.

In the first place, Stevens's earlier reports of unused capacity had spurred second thoughts about the proposals. A steel shortage and the desperate locomotive needs of American railways and especially the AEF reinforced these concerns. Partly for this reason, therefore, the Russians were restricted to 500 locomotives and 10,000 wagons in early July. When Stevens's public statements were eventually received a few days later there was indignation that he had pledged so much equipment, the more so because, it was felt, he lacked the authority to do so.[139] Secondly, the proposed quantities were so vast that, coinciding with a Canadian request for 100,000 tonnes of rails for use in France, they raised questions about the coordination of Allied purchases in general. Over the following few weeks pressure from the Treasury and the War Department forced the creation of the so-called Allied Purchasing Commission, which would henceforth coordinate all Allied contracts in the United States. Bilateral agreements to this effect were negotiated with each of the Allies, the Russian one being signed on 11/24 August; and needless to say, there could be no question of signing any large contracts before this matter was settled to the Americans' satisfaction.[140] Thirdly, and equally importantly, there was the matter of Russian borrowing *per se*. Having agreed to lend Russia $500 million, McAdoo now feared a cash-flow problem in meeting his obligation if the remaining locomotives and wagons were contracted immediately.[141] Thus, when Bakhmet'ev applied at precisely this time for credit totalling $733 million for August–December 1917 (including $154 million – the largest single sum – for the remaining locomotive and wagon orders, to be paid in 1918), McAdoo reacted negatively. As he told Lansing on 25 July: 'I have no thought of allowing the further credit except possibly to meet August payments on orders placed on British credit and possibly other urgent sums on contracts placed independently and requiring payments in the month of August.'[142] In short, the US Treasury was seriously alarmed by the emerging scale of Russian needs and especially potential railway expenditure which might prove to be unnecessary.

The locomotive and wagon orders were central to the subsequent discussions and eventual compromise. After several weeks of heart-searching the War Department and Council of National Defense recommended in their favour. Though critical of Stevens's initiative and with the caveat of first priority for the AEF, the chairman of the Council's Advisory Committee, Willard, reported to Secretary Baker on 3 August:

> [The key question is:] given a certain amount of money and a certain capacity to manufacture cars and locomotives, where and how can that money and these cars and locomotives be used so as to contribute most towards the winning of this war? From my own limited point of view, it seems to me that engines and cars to the extent I have recommended – that is to say, 1,500 of one and 30,000 of the other, with a new erecting shop at Vladivostok costing not to exceed $2,000,000, and sufficient credits in connection therewith – would contribute more towards winning the war if sent to Russia than would be the case if the engines and cars were kept in this country and the money used for some other purpose.[143]

The Treasury did try to limit the likely financial damage. In a memorandum of 15 August the Assistant Treasury Secretary, Oscar T. Crosby, complained about Stevens's 'extraordinary outgivings', but reluctantly concluded that the United States could not remain indifferent to his pledges. As a compromise Crosby suggested a statement to Bakhmet'ev:

that if his Government still insists upon this rolling-stock order that [sic] very heavy reductions must result in advances which might otherwise be made for other purposes indicated by them (the Russians). Possibly, placing the matter in this light, a request might be gotten from the Russian Government, if that seems to be the right method, to diminish the orders that have been indicated by Stevens.[144]

However, Crosby's proposal was rejected. The final decision, which was communicated to Bakhmet'ev on 10/23 August, attempted to honour Stevens's pledge whilst avoiding any expenditure for the time being. McAdoo opened a further $100 million credit from the May loan, bringing the sum advanced to $275 million, and promised a further advance to fund the remaining locomotives and wagons, but he wanted the order deferred until lower prices had been introduced, though preferably not later than 1 November.[145]

Once price controls were inaugurated in September 1917 Lomonosov himself raised the matter of the proposed locomotive and wagon orders, with Vauclain's support. Again the American reaction was equivocal, this time partly because of the Russian political crisis. For example, Crosby asked Willard whether provision could be made for the equipment to be regauged if it could not be delivered to Russia, and Willard replied by suggesting that perhaps only 750 locomotives and 15,000 wagons should be ordered at that time. But ultimately the Americans viewed their undertaking of 23 August as binding, and the Russians were able to invite tenders for the contracts.[146]

Formal discussion of the draft contracts commenced in Washington on 25 October/7 November. Lomonosov led the Russian negotiators, whilst the American delegation comprised representatives from Baldwin and Alco for the locomotives and four other companies for the wagons. Lomonosov records that the two sides differed over price by some $20 million and that he cut the American figure by $9.6 million. However, this reduction – about $5,000 less per locomotive than in July – may partly reflect the new price controls. For their part the companies secured amendments to the payment schedules.[147] The next day the two sides reconvened, and according to a rather melodramatic account by Lomonosov, their meeting was interrupted by a newsflash about a Bolshevik coup. Lomonosov was asked to telephone Bakhmet'ev for further information, but the ambassador reportedly told him to deny the news and continue working as normal.[148] Accordingly the relevant protocols were signed forthwith, specifying the agreed changes and committing the parties to conclude appropriate contracts.[149] As Lomonosov reported to Bakhmet'ev, the documents would be signed during the following week and the total cost, including a $7 million contract for spare parts, would be $133 million.[150]

Perhaps, as many Americans seemed to feel, these negotiations should have been broken off in July 1917. Arguably such orders were never essential for the Russian war effort unless for morale. At any rate, owing to the Bolshevik coup, the negotiating process now came to an undignified sudden end when the US Treasury and War Department refused the Russians' application for clearance to sign the final contracts. Despite some intense lobbying – for example, Vauclain urged Willard to support the project as 'one of the most important war measures we now have' – the necessary credit was never opened and the contracts could not be signed. Apparently Vauclain and Lomonosov devised a plan in early December to appeal to President Wilson, but Bakhmet'ev vetoed it.[151]

This casualty of the revolution was subsequently joined by others, despite numerous Bolshevik protests over the next few years. In general, goods purchased with British credit but not yet delivered to Russia were seized by the British authorities and in many instances sold to fund the settlement of claims. As for American-financed orders, the US authorities required Bakhmet'ev's mission to liquidate the uncompleted contracts and use its assets to pay its liabilities.[152] And the MPS contracts obviously figured prominently in this new process. Again some of the biggest headaches were presented by locomotives and wagons. For example, several settlement schemes were suggested for the contracts with Alco and Baldwin of June/July 1917, just as the first products were being outshopped, and again Lomonosov and Bakhmet'ev clashed: the former was determined to save the engines whereas the latter's duty was to liquidate the contracts. Eventually, as far as those locomotives were concerned, it was agreed on 11/24 January 1918 that, firstly, the money already paid on these contracts would be accepted as full payment for the first 100 engines, which would be passed to the Russian mission; secondly, the American government would buy the next 200 engines and lease them, regauged, to American railways; and thirdly, production on the remainder of the order would be suspended, although for a non-returnable deposit of $500,000 the Russians would have the option until December 1918 of resurrecting the contract at a price of $55,730 per engine. Also, a related protocol committed the US War Depart-

Table 1.2. *MPS goods shipped from North America, spring 1915–April 1918*

Item	Tonnes
5,000 coal wagons	268,000
8,100 covered wagons	321,000
Spares, gondola wagons	55,500
Spares, covered wagons	4,600
695 locomotives	198,750
Rails, accessories	385,800
Spare parts, miscellaneous	25,000
Miscellaneous	150,000
TOTAL	1,408,650
(Total value: 87,615,252.93 roubles)	

Source: Otchet o deiatel'nosti Russkogo zagotovitel'nogo komiteta v Amerike i ego likvidatsionnoi komissii, Part II, Vol. 3, pp. 37, 61: US National Archives, Record Group 261, box L37.

ment to buy rails and fittings worth $500,000 from the mission so as to enable the Russians to pay the locomotive deposit.[153] The June/July 1917 wagon contracts were settled in September 1918 by curtailing the order from 10,000 to 4,000.[154]

Of the MPS goods delivered to the Russian mission a large proportion did reach Russia, either before the US government prohibited shipments in early 1918 or when deliveries to the White forces were permitted, mainly during 1919, though some of the equipment went to the Chinese Eastern Railway.[155] (See table 1.2.) Again the decapod locomotives provide a good example. As of January 1920 a total of 1,281 had been ordered by the tsarist and Provisional governments and 1,081 had been built. Of those, 881 had been handed over to the MPS mission and despatched to Russia (including 8 lost at sea in 1915 and nearly 200 sent to the Whites in 1918–19), though 124 eluded the Bolsheviks by remaining on the Chinese Eastern Railway at the end of the civil war; 200 remained in the USA as the property of the US War Department.[156] Similarly, about 3,000 of the 4,000 wagons built under the June/July 1917 contracts had reached Russia by early 1920.[157] Some equipment, however, was sold off, including all 53 'Mallet' engines built by Baldwin in 1917–18. Also sold were most of the 212,790 tonnes of rails and rail fittings stranded in the United States, including approximately 145,000 tonnes to the US Director General of Military Railroads.[158]

Further research is needed for a full picture and assessment of the wartime railway imports policy. In particular, it remains unclear how the MPS estimated its requirements and, given the pertinent criticisms by Levi, Stevens and others, how valid those estimates were. In the meantime, the available evidence suggests a mixed verdict. It seems likely that, given the domestic shortages of armaments, tooling and metals, the 1914–15 foreign railway orders represented a sensible attempt to supplement domestic deliveries quickly to cope with the emergency. Mostly reaching Russia in 1915–16, these imports probably did make a worthwhile contribution to the war effort, especially the locomotives acquired for the Archangel and Murmansk railways, and the first decapods on Donbass coal trains and the trans-Siberian route. Also, the decapods and wagons did provide the benefit of experience with modern American equipment. That said, the wagon shortage was arguably the most important bottle-neck, and if credit was so scarce, it might have made more sense for the MPS to prioritise these orders over the 1915 decapods.

The later plans have an increasing air of unreality and escapism. Ever larger quantities of locomotives and wagons were demanded despite inevitable funding and delivery problems. One senses that Stevens was right in seeing the issue as a fixation with equipment combined with an inability to recognise and confront the problems of organisation, management and labour discipline, and that postwar modernisation was also an important motivation. Not without reason did the Americans quickly become disillusioned. As for the goods actually ordered in 1916–17, few reached Russia before mid-1917 and thus did not significantly aid the war effort. On the other hand, these deliveries, supplemented by the shipments to White forces in 1918–19, obviously did help Russian and Soviet railways during and after the civil war .

The salient points of this prologue, then, are a pre-war tradition of foreign investment and import substitution in railway development and operation; the centrality of railways in contemporary thinking about the economy; chronic tension between the railway engineering industry and its customers; the departure from import substitution in 1914; the railways' wartime interest in issues of postwar modernisation; Lomonosov's experience as head of the MPS mission in America; and the tangible legacy of military, railway and other equipment stored mainly in North America which would soon attract Bolshevik attention.[159] It is thus with the Bolsheviks' worsening railway crisis in 1917–19 and their ideas about postwar recovery and imports that the next chapter is concerned.

2 The revolutionary railway vision

If the condition of the Russian economy was frequently described as 'critical' during 1916 and 'catastrophic' in 1917, it was sometimes characterised as 'supercatastrophic' (*sverkhkatastroficheskii*) during the subsequent civil war. Superlatives were certainly appropriate. By December 1919, when the Bolsheviks were beginning to scent military victory, the output of the industrial sectors had collapsed to perhaps, on average, a quarter of 1913 levels. Agricultural output had also slumped, the transport sector seemed near final breakdown for want of serviceable rolling-stock and river barges, whilst foreign trade was virtually moribund from this internal crisis and an Allied naval blockade.[1]

Yet for many engineers this appalling cloud had a silver lining. The revolution and the embattled atmosphere of War Communism excited utopian visions and social fantasies about dismantling the old order and building a new socialist world.[2] For these engineers, widespread destruction and a technologically minded new government implied the possibility of radical technical and technological innovation. In particular, electrical engineers seized the moment to 'spread the gospel of electrification for societal transformation'.[3] According to Coopersmith, they gradually accumulated political support and developed theoretical rationales and organisational frameworks for nationwide electrification. Above all, their vision chimed with the revolutionary times in promising socioeconomic transformation, not simply reconstruction.[4]

This vision of electrification challenged railway transport's traditional role as the pre-eminent agent of socioeconomic development. But railway engineers had their own vision. They too debated technical issues and wanted political support. Not only should railways drive the rebuilding and modernisation of the country, but society could make a qualitative leap forward through the technological transformation of the railways themselves. And this perspective, a hybrid of tradition and innovation, helped to shape Soviet policy in 1920.

Economic crisis, railway dreams

The food, fuel and transport crises were the Bolsheviks' three worst economic problems by late 1919, and transport was treated as the most serious. As Trotskii told the Seventh Congress of Soviets on 7 December 1919:

> Now everything depends on transport. I will state frankly that we have a number of divisions on the Eastern front which, following the rout of Kolchak, we could now move to the south to put a quick end to Denikin. Where is the problem? The problem is transport. Of course, we will overcome it. The food supply system has a large quantity of food stored in elevators and warehouses. So where is the problem? Transport.[5]

Krasin, the Bolshevik electrical engineer then responsible for the transport system as head of the People's Commissariat of Ways of Communication (NKPS, which replaced the MPS after October 1917), warned that 'we are facing a virtually complete transport stoppage unless heroic measures are taken'. And Lenin himself declared in February 1920 that 'unless we achieve the same sort of miracle with transport during the next two months as we did against Kolchak, we face catastrophe'.[6]

New slogans epitomised this anxiety. The apparent success of 'Everything for the Front!' in the civil war inspired a new and equally urgent cry: 'Everything for Transport!' Similarly, in January 1920 the party's Central Committee published a special appeal, 'To Transport!', summoning all party members to the fray.[7] And the phraseology of these slogans encapsulated the Bolsheviks' intended *modus operandi*. Having apparently won the war by the 'shock' tactic of concentrating their limited resources at a key point of one or another front, they addressed the so-called 'bloodless front' in similar fashion. They hoped to penetrate the 'front of destruction' (*front razrukhi*) by focusing on one key sector of the economy. To quote the title of an article by Lenin which appeared in *Pravda* on 8 February 1920, 'If it's war, let's fight' (*Kol' voina, tak po-voennomu*).[8]

The Bolsheviks' primary concern was railway transport. They understood that, as the railways still represented the country's

Table 2.1. *Russian and Soviet railway traffic, 1913, 1917–1928*

Year	Freight tonne-km (000,000,000)	Freight tonnes (000,000)	Passenger-km (000,000,000)	Passenger journeys (000,000)
1913	65.7	132.4	25.2	184.8
1917	63.0	115.2	—	—
1918	14.2	37.2	—	—
1919	17.5	30.5	—	—
1920	11.4	31.9	—	—
1921	14.0	37.9	—	83.6
1922	18.2	44.6	9.4	91.1
1923	26.2	60.7	12.8	121.8
1924	36.5	70.7	16.7	170.4
1925	52.6	92.4	20.5	227.3
1926	73.5	122.2	22.8	259.9
1927	82.6	139.6	22.4	258.1
1928	93.4	156.2	24.5	291.1

Notes: 1913 data is for the territory of the USSR pre-1939; a figure of 76.8 thousand million tonne-km is noted for the Russian Empire in 1913.
Figures for 1917–21 are for Soviet-held territory.
The tonne-km are given for the tariff distance.
Comparable statistical data for passenger-km (1917–21) and passenger journeys (1917–20) is unavailable.
Source: Davies (ed.), *From Tsarism to the New Economic Policy*, p. 312.

'arteries', a cessation of railway traffic would probably doom the government, which was precisely the threat confronting the Bolsheviks by the winter of 1919–20.[9] And the scale of the problem was enormous. NKPS traffic statistics were naturally rudimentary at this time, but they clearly show a terrible slump. The Russian Empire's freight traffic was 76.8 thousand million tonne-km in 1913, whereas the figures for Soviet territory, containing the hub of the network, were down to 14.2 thousand million in 1918 and 17.5 thousand million in 1919. (See table 2.1.) According to M. M. Shmukker, passenger traffic rose in 1918 to 110 per cent of its 1916 volume due to the sudden demobilisation of troops, but then collapsed to 58 per cent of its 1916 level in 1919 and shrank further in 1920 and 1921.[10] And yet the NKPS could scarcely cope with even this minimal traffic. Essential food and fuel consignments were often delayed for days, and even urgent military shipments and the special trains of senior commissars routinely suffered long stoppages. Intending civilian passengers were simply left to fend for themselves.[11]

Table 2.2. *Soviet locomotive stock and 'sickness', November 1917–August 1920*

Month	1917 Stock	Sick (%)	1918 Stock	Sick (%)	1919 Stock	Sick (%)	1920 Stock	Sick (%)
Jan.			21,078	31.1	8,758	47.7	9,618	58.3
Feb.			15,209	35.0	8,829	49.5	9,863	59.2
Mar.			14,692	35.3	9,150	52.4	9,963	60.6
Apr.			13,322	36.5	8,961	52.8	12,155	60.7
May			11,895	38.1	9,032	52.5	13,464	60.5
June			9,383	39.5	9,404	49.6	18,750	59.0
July			9,506	40.0	9,574	48.5	18,568	58.2
Aug.			9,060	41.0	9,771	51.8	18,086	58.4
Sept.			8,989	41.5	9,609	51.5		
Oct.			8,852	43.1	9,170	52.2		
Nov.	20,887	27.4	8,900	45.5	9,203	53.7		
Dec.	22,402	29.4	8,955	47.8	9,283	55.4		

Source: Klemenchich, *Itogi raboty zheleznykh dorog*, p. 10.

Equally dramatic was the breakdown of the railway system's physical health, already weakened during the World War. Indeed, locomotives rusting in so-called 'cemeteries' came to symbolise the railways. An authoritative report of March 1920 showed that between January 1918 and December 1919 the Soviet locomotive stock shrank from 21,078 to 9,283 and the steamable stock from 14,519 to just 4,319, dropping to only 3,750 in February 1920. In other words, 59.2 per cent of the Soviet locomotive stock was classed as 'sick' in February 1920.[12] (See table 2.2.) Even more ominously, officials expected a level of 75 per cent by the spring, as was already being recorded on two or three lines. If that happened traffic would effectively cease because there would be insufficient engines to cover the railways' own internal needs.[13] In ironic contrast to the famous revolutionary slogan 'Our Locomotive, Fly Forward!' (*Nash parovoz, vpered leti!*), derived from Marx's dictum that revolution is the locomotive of history, Soviet locomotives seemed near their hour of reckoning.

The causes of this metamorphosis were numerous and varied. In general, the railways inevitably suffered from the ubiquitous shortages of fuel, food, skilled personnel, raw materials and spare parts – all exacerbated, of course, by the transport sector's continuing collapse. A comment in a railway journal in 1919 oversimplified the situation and completely ignored peasant resistance to food requisitions, but certainly contained a large grain of truth: 'There's no food because transport is in a bad state, and transport is in a bad state because there's no food.'[14]

A major contributing factor was problems with railway employees and administrative structures. Not only did many technical and managerial personnel refuse to work for the new regime, but rank-and-file workers were often hostile too. Indeed the existence of Lenin's government was threatened in October and November 1917 when the railway trade union, Vikzhel, adopted an extreme syndicalist position. A strike ultimatum from the Vikzhel leadership, dominated by Mensheviks and Socialist Revolutionaries, forced the Bolsheviks into coalition with the Left Socialist Revolutionaries and ensured the appointment of a Vikzhel member as People's Commissar of Ways of Communication. Only by encouraging worker executive committees to take control of railways and form a pro-Bolshevik trade union, Vikzhedor, could the Bolshevik leadership eventually marginalise Vikzhel in early 1918.[15]

However, this resort to workers' control brought its own organisational crises. Worker committees began nationalising railways and sacking managers on their own initiative contrary to NKPS policy. Very quickly the administrative authority of the NKPS was badly undermined, and managerial confusion spread. It would take many months, much argument and the declaration of martial law on the railways in November 1918 to re-establish centralised administrative control.[16]

Railway morale and labour discipline disintegrated. In April 1918, before the escalation of the Allied military intervention, the People's Commissar of Ways of Communication complained:

> Every day we receive reports from the lines about the catastrophic position of the railways which point to the extremely careless attitude of officials towards their duties ... All the groundless demands and shirking of work indicate that railway officials have not become conscious of the fact that they are the builders of the new Russia. One cannot silently ignore the following sad facts of transport's collapse: everybody knows that the lines currently have sufficient rolling-stock and officials, yet many areas of the Russian republic are still suffering food and other shortages; the whole problem is that productivity has collapsed completely, work proceeds sluggishly, the number of sick locomotives and wagons increases by the day, repair work is being done any old how, locomotives spend weeks and months being washed out or having minor repairs, expenses are increasing and are devouring state money.[17]

And these difficulties were compounded by uncertainty at the top of the NKPS. Once Vikzhedor was established, the first People's Commissar, the Vikzhel-sponsored M. T. Elizarov, was unsurprisingly dismissed in February 1918. However, his successor, A. G. Rogov, lasted only a couple of months before being replaced by P. A. Kobozev. He in turn was succeeded by V. I. Nevskii in July 1918, before Krasin took charge in March 1919, the fifth commissar in sixteen months.[18]

Military action brought its own disruption. The civil war was fought along and for railway routes, and many engines, wagons, bridges, buildings and other installations were damaged, destroyed or lost to the Whites. A report to the Red Army's General Staff identified 2,247 bridges as destroyed or damaged between 1 January 1917 and 1 April 1920, as well as 729.2 km of track, 2,246 points, 33 depots, 22 workshops, 257 water-pumping stations, 1,718 other buildings, 3,633 telegraph instruments, 9,439 telephone sets and 77,853.8 km of telegraph wire.[19] That said, the overall impact of war damage on railway traffic was arguably less than was claimed. Severe damage was probably confined mainly to south Russia and certain areas of Western Siberia, many of the destroyed bridges were on secondary routes which were not essential for through traffic, and in any case many temporary replacement bridges were constructed very quickly.

Shortages of spare parts and equipment constituted a particularly dangerous bottle-neck. Whether or not Soviet industry suffered extensive war damage, the output of metal and metal products became minimal and would still be low in the mid-1920s. (See tables 2.3 and 2.4.) Moreover, armaments production had priority for the available metal. For instance, military work occupied 60 per cent of the Briansk locomotive factory's capacity during the second half of 1919, leaving little room for the railways and other deserving causes.[20] At the same time, the virtual death of foreign trade eliminated the only alternative source of supply. Thus, the railways had to forage for supplies to keep trains running, and they often had to cannibalise their existing equipment.

Data from the NKPS Directorate of Economics and Materials painted a bleak picture, even if one allows for an inflated definition of NKPS requirements. For example, the directorate reported that in 1919 the GOMZA state machine-building group, which included the Sormovo, Kolomna and Briansk locomotive factories, produced on average only about 21 per cent of the locomotive parts ordered by the NKPS, including only 10 per cent of the order for new wheels and no

Table 2.3. *Soviet output of pig iron, 1913–1923/4 (tonnes)*

Year	South	Urals	Centre	TOTAL
1913	3,083,960	909,540	193,970	4,187,470
1914	3,035,060	854,120	172,780	4,061,960
1915	2,730,250	819,890	117,360	3,667,500
1916	2,870,430	764,470	158,110	3,793,010
1917	2,145,080	715,570	146,700	3,007,350
1918	205,380	255,910	52,160	513,450
1919	27,710	58,680	26,080	112,470
1920	14,670	81,500	17,930	114,100
1921	28,851	70,090	18,745	117,686
1922	87,368	75,632	25,428	188,428
1922/3	112,062.5	138,093.6	48,671.8	298,827.9
1923/4	369,211.3	242,429.9	38,679.9	650,321.1

Source: calculated from Chernov, *Metallopromyshlennost' SSSR*, p. 51.

Table 2.4. *Soviet output of steel, 1913–1923/4 (tonnes)*

Year	South	Urals	Centre/North	TOTAL
1913	2,715,172.5	902,139.8	684,551.1	4,301,863.4
1914	2,793,820	927,470	658,520	4,379,810
1915	2,472,710	938,880	674,820	4,086,410
1916	2,634,080	943,770	673,516	4,251,366
1917	1,778,330	824,780	461,290	3,064,400
1918	118,990	151,590	130,400	400,980
1919	79,870	78,240	39,120	197,230
1920	43,684	117,197	36,186	197,067
1921	52,160	83,130	57,376	192,666
1922	126,325	132,845	99,593	358,763
1922/3	196,235.7	211,036.1	185,314.7	592,586.5
1923/4	396,269.3	310,091.2	282,234.5	988,595

Source: calculated from Chernov, *Metallopromyshlennost' SSSR*, p. 52.

boiler tubes at all. According to the directorate, Soviet industry produced only about 11 per cent of the tools and 37 per cent of the ferrous metals needed by the NKPS, whilst demand for rails was met, insofar as it was met at all, mainly by lifting existing track for reuse elsewhere.[21]

Locomotive construction suffered especially badly. Again, like the NKPS traffic statistics, the figures given in Table 2.5 are rudimentary – other sources give slightly different totals – but they certainly highlight the contraction of output. Having a potential annual capacity of

Table 2.5. *Russian and Soviet locomotive production, 1913–1929/30*

Year	Kol.	Votk.	Nev.	Brian.	Putil.	Khar.	Sorm.	Lugan.	TOTAL
1913	95	—	83	66	100	114	114	82	654
1914	129	20	81	103	68	110	114	138	763
1915	132	13	116	119	72	207	108	150	917
1916	52	24	34	54	2	207	58	159	590
1917	48	12	43	38	11	106	57	105	420
1918	37	—	22	25	7	64	41	25	221
1919	22	—	16	19	11	—	24	4	96
1920	32	—	2	4	—	28	9	9	84
1921	25	—	1	—	—	9	27	12	74
1922	28	—	2	—	3	17	14	7	71
1923	24	—	3	15	12	35	26	48	163
1924	46	—	4	7	19	28	19	51	174
1925	40	—	—	28	18	28	37	65	216
1926	74	—	—	67	25	56	62	96	380
1927	124	—	—	69	25	97	72	86	473
1928/9	195	—	21	125	50	137	91	194	813
1929/30	187	—	45	122	48	126	90	208	826
TOTALS									
1913–25	710	69	407	478	323	953	648	855	4,443
1913–29/30	1,290	69	473	861	471	1369	963	1,439	6,935

Notes: The factories concerned were: Kolomna; Votkinsk; Nevskii; Briansk; Putilov; Khar'kov; Sormovo; and Lugansk.
These figures probably do not include narrow-gauge engines, at least until 1917; some 400 narrow-gauge engines were built for military use in 1914–17.
1928/9 data covers 1928 and January–September 1929; 1929/30 covers October 1929–September 1930.
The rules indicate zero return.
Source: Rakov, *Lokomotivy otechestvennykh zheleznykh dorog*, pp. 127, 255.

over 1,2000 new locomotives, the seven main factories of Russia and the Ukraine built approximately 917 engines in 1915, but only about 10 per cent of this number for the Soviet railways in 1919. Apart from suffering the familiar supply problems, the Putilov and Nevskii works in Petrograd and the three GOMZA locomotive factories were primarily committed to military work, whilst the Khar'kov and Lugansk plants were under White control for long periods.[22] Less obviously, confusion in Moscow also contributed to the contraction of locomotive production. In late 1918 it was decided to suspend locomotive construction forthwith and concentrate on overhauling existing locomotives.[23] But only a few weeks later a representative of the Department of Metal at the Supreme Council of the National Economy (VSNKh), M. A. Lomov, convened a conference on new locomotive-building policy and produced a series of thoughtful decisions aimed at high efficiency through economies of scale: there would be only four types of engine, having as many common parts as possible, and each factory would build just one type.[24] The Department of Metal's Collegium duly endorsed this policy, but in July 1919 the government again halted rolling-stock construction in favour of repair work.[25]

Despite these measures, the number of locomotive overhauls actually completed at VSNKh factories remained insignificant. Apparently, targets of 1,377 heavy overhauls and 2,939 intermediate repairs, involving no less than 21 factories, were set for 1919, but only about 96 heavy and 83 intermediate locomotive overhauls were finished. The factories themselves felt that they were ill-equipped for this type of work, but probably more important reasons for this dismal showing were the emergency use of their capacity for military work and the general shortages of supplies and reliable skilled labour.[26]

To cope with the transport crisis, especially on the railways, was obviously the main concern of the NKPS during the civil war. But like the electrical engineers, railway officials and engineers also looked ahead to postwar reconstruction. The way forward, in their view, was to prioritise transport, involving the complete reconstruction of the railways. By early 1920 the NKPS was adamant that 'the reconstruction of transport is the surest way to the reconstruction of the country's whole economic life'.[27] Nor did this mean simply a recreation of the railways' pre-war operating patterns and technical level. To judge by articles published during 1918–19, engineers felt that the chaos and destruction offered an unprecedented opportunity for Russia's railways to lead the world through revolutionary technical and technological change.

The foundations for this debate were laid by engineers such as V. I. Grinevetskii, author of the most wide-ranging and influential contemporary analysis of the Russian economy and its prospects for postwar reconstruction.[28] An advocate of national economic planning, Grinevetskii was scathing about many aspects of pre-war development, including the transport system. His assessment of the railways was particularly negative, and though it has since been criticised by Westwood and others, it was widely shared at the time both within

Soviet Russia and elsewhere.[29] Briefly, he maintained that enforced economies had meant insufficient capacity (especially on north–south routes and the trans-Siberian and Archangel lines), and an inadequate stock of locomotives and wagons. Thus, he argued, the railway system had inevitably failed to cope during the war and its condition had deteriorated. These difficulties were now compounded by technical and administrative chaos and a precipitate rise in costs, which was plunging the railways into deficit.

Grinevetskii did advocate the electrification of industry as a key priority to secure supplies of fuel and raw materials.[30] But more traditionally he also envisaged a railway-led recovery with substantial foreign investment. He described the technical and economic restoration of railway transport as 'not only the most urgent but also the most difficult task in the business of rebuilding Russia', and he further emphasised the backward linkage between the network's recovery and the fate of its equipment supplier and leading customer, Russian industry.[31] Significantly, his definition of railway 'reconstruction' was remarkably expansive: firstly, the repair of locomotives, rolling-stock, track and installations, and the provision of new equipment; secondly, the building of an authoritative administrative and technical management apparatus, and the appointment of properly trained managers to the individual lines; and thirdly, mechanisation, staff cuts and technological innovation – dieselisation was one of Grinevetskii's special enthusiasms – to minimise costs and enhance efficiency and productivity. Similarly, he considered that to ensure Russia's future economic position it was essential to construct new lines, including not only conventional trunk and local routes, sidings and industrial feeder railways but also, definitely in the realm of superlatives, a network of 'supermainlines' for high-speed long-distance freight traffic.[32]

Among many others with grandiose plans for the Soviet railways was N. Erofeev, who passionately believed that Russia's desperate predicament presented a unique opportunity for revolutionary progress:

> At first glance it might seem paradoxical to affirm that our transport system's present unprecedentedly difficult situation contains conditions which are especially beneficial for the system's future development. Nevertheless, that is the case. Much which has been a brake on development and which has seemed an insuperable factor is now so broken that there is no reason to take it seriously into account when making innovations or to imitate what already exists. It is possible to introduce radically new designs, at the same time ensuring that the

obsolete past is written off as soon as possible. There is no doubt that we are on the eve of a period of intense development of the railways. After this the arithmetical relationship of the old to the new will be such that the latter will not be rare disharmonious elements being incorporated into the old but, on the contrary, the old will be in the minority. The complete disappearance of the old, with its replacement by new forms instead of tedious modification, will happen with minimal disruption.[33]

Such arguments justified the airing of numerous projects ranging from the worthy to the outlandish. For example, A. N. Shelest pressed for the development of diesel locomotives to replace steam, whilst E. E. Nol'tein wanted all rolling-stock fitted with automatic couplings.[34] Similarly, although the Putilov works in Petrograd was hard-pressed with military production, some of its engineers published outline specifications for a complete new collection of steam locomotives; these engines were to have standard and interchangeable parts, and ranged from the familiar 0–8–0 and 0–10–0 wheel arrangements to new 2–10–2 and 2–12–0 freight designs and the exotic 4–4–2–2–0 'Chernomorets' and 6–4–2–2–0 'Aralets' high-speed passenger types.[35] But for sheer revolutionary optimism few campaigners could match those who lobbied long and hard for Russia's track gauge to be changed from 1,524 mm to the standard European 1,435 mm. Declaring that this was a question of 'now or never', one ardent writer even coined a topical new battle-cry, 'Railways of the World, Unite!'[36]

This enthusiastic internationalism, however, was overshadowed by defence concerns: the military and the Cheka political police objected strongly to any alteration of the track gauge, and that idea progressed no further.[37] Indeed, unsurprisingly, little immediate progress was made on any of these issues. Yet the debates do seem to have influenced government policy in some respects despite the civil war emergency. The regime authorised a certain amount of new investment, and by the autumn of 1919 the NKPS had begun laying detailed plans for peacetime development – a turn of events which would help the railways obtain virtually absolute priority for investment in early 1920.

One instance of attempted wartime investment was the building of new railways: the NKPS 1919–20 construction plan envisaged a considerable amount of work, albeit mostly with rails scavenged from existing lines, and some work was completed.[38] Another example was a project for two vast new factories that would overhaul engines and wagons on a mass-production basis. One plant was earmarked for

Liublino near Moscow and known as Mozherez (*Moskovskii zhelezno-dorozhnyi remontnyi zavod*), whilst the other, Sazherez, was planned for Samara. Ministerial approval for the Mozherez factory had been granted as long ago as January 1913 and confirmed by the State Duma in July 1914, with a planned annual capacity of 435 locomotives and over 6,000 carriages and wagons. The war caused a postponement, but construction did commence after Sovnarkom ratified the scheme in 1918.[39] A report of mid-1919 stated that 100 million (Soviet) rubles had already been spent on the factory, that housing was being built for some 20,000 workers, and that the NKPS was placing great hopes on the project.[40]

An interesting product of the enthusiasm for reconstruction and development was the so-called Commission for the Improvement of Transport. This was apparently similar to a high-level commission chaired by Shchukin from 1910 which had failed to complete its work because of the war. Early in 1919 the newspaper *Ekonomicheskaia zhizn'* (*Economic Life*) reported that the new commission was already pondering the introduction of bigger and more powerful engines, the strengthening of bridges to accommodate them, and the raising of speeds through track and signalling improvements. Perhaps wisely, the newspaper did not clarify the commission's attitude to the destruction of old bridges by the Red and the White armies.[41]

The appointment of Leonid Krasin as head of the NKPS in March 1919 initially cast a sober shadow over such forward-looking reveries. An experienced manager, Krasin immediately attempted to define clear, practical objectives for the commissariat. Cutting straight to the heart of the reconstruction issue – the question of resources – he specified the commissariat's first priority as the partial restoration of the railways to accommodate the most urgent military and economic needs. Full reconstruction, which he seemed to interpret as returning the railways to their pre-war condition, would have to await better times and, significantly, foreign help. As he declared in a speech to Moscow railwaymen in April 1919:

> At the present time the process of healing transport, of making it healthy, is a matter of life or death. For the time being we cannot contemplate restoring transport completely to its pre-war level – such a task is currently beyond not only our power but also that of other governments, because we do not have sufficient metals, other materials and grain to fulfil this task. We will have to restore transport to its former level and correspondingly develop domestic industry by using foreign assistance, which will depend on the forms

in which our relations with other countries take shape. [This will be the case] whether fraternal assistance arrives from the other Soviet Republics which will spring up throughout Europe or, at worst, we have to resort to some sort of assistance from so-called foreign capital, be that in the form of rails, locomotives and wagons, or by the acquisition of various materials and tools, which we need for the expansion of the railway network. We will also have to do this in order to resurrect other sectors of our extractive and manufacturing industry. At present our task is more modest, it is the revival of transport to an extent sufficient to meet our most urgent requirements – our requirements for military shipments and our industry, the real needs of the populace.[42]

In spite of this practical approach, innovation, reconstruction and development did remain as topical as ever, and Krasin himself became supportive. In August 1919 the NKPS founded a special journal, *Zheleznodorozhnaia tekhnika i ekonomika* (*Railway Equipment and Economics*), as a discussion forum, and created a Technical Committee in September 1919 to conduct such research. In its first statement the journal's editorial board apologetically agreed that the war prevented much practical progress from being made immediately. But the editors insisted that the transport system would have to be reconstructed because it was the 'main nerve of all economic activity'. Warming to their theme, they claimed hopefully:

The time will come when the civil war ends and processes of destruction turn completely into processes of creation. Then the building of a new life, and in particular of economic life, will begin on a grand scale and it will be possible to start in earnest on not only the reconstruction but also the further development of our transport ... We must prepare ourselves for this time from both economic and technical perspectives. Our journal will be devoted wholly to this task, on an all-Russian scale.[43]

Krasin himself endorsed this argument at a meeting to inaugurate the Technical Committee. Admittedly, he stated firmly that the Technical Committee had to help transport to satisfy at least the country's minimum requirements, and that full reconstruction could follow only after military and political circumstances had changed. But he agreed that it was vital to conduct theoretical research in the meantime so that practical work could commence as soon as the war ended and the country's foreign relations were put in order. At the same time he related reconstruction more explicitly than ever to foreign assistance:

> The question of repairing rolling-stock and restoring damaged lines, installations and buildings is the priority both in practical work and in the analysis of general issues which the Technical Committee must resolve. In this connection it will be necessary to study the prospects which will open up in the near future when we get an opportunity to order rolling-stock abroad. There are no grounds for dreaming about the complete reconstruction of railway transport without foreign help in some form or another. Sooner or later – in this we must believe – this help will come to us, and it is by no means a pointless exercise for us now to consider what contracts we will have to offer foreigners for rolling-stock and what instructions we will need to give.[44]

Continuing, Krasin said he wanted research to be carried out into various other 'practical objectives', which he saw as means to increase traffic capacity. These included the fitting of modern automatic couplings and brakes to freight wagons, the construction of new lines, the development of new types of fuel, electrification, the standardisation of equipment and parts, and the remodelling of major junctions. And, doubtless upsetting military colleagues, he even agreed that the committee should at least consider the idea of converting the network to the standard European gauge.

Coincidentally, one of the keenest technical innovators, Professor Lomonosov, re-entered the scene at precisely this juncture. After the October Revolution he had stayed in the United States, trying to safeguard the railway contracts. During the first half of 1918 he made a series of increasingly pro-Soviet public statements, and was dismissed from the post of head of the MPS mission in America by ambassador Bakhmet'ev after declaring his full support for the Soviet system in a speech in June 1918. When L. K. Martens formed his Soviet Bureau in New York early in 1919 Lomonosov joined as a journalist and technical specialist. However, asserting that his proper place was on the Russian railways, Lomonosov left the USA in May 1919 on an eventful journey which took him home via Stockholm, Berlin and a risky crossing of the front line near Dvinsk.[45]

Warmly welcomed by Lenin, Lomonosov was appointed chairman of the newly-formed Technical Committee. Needless to say, the professor was soon galvanising the researchers into action. During the autumn of 1919 they calculated, for example, that the railways immediately needed 4,000 new freight locomotives of Class E or Ye or both to replace obsolete and war-damaged stock. These engines were no longer particularly modern in world terms – indeed the bogie-less

E could be criticised for being hard wearing on the track – but as the most modern freight classes in Soviet service they had several advantages: the designs were relatively recent yet tried and tested; they were well known to Soviet railwaymen; and construction of the E would not require complete retooling at Soviet factories. Thus they could usefully serve as a form of interim modernisation, bearing the main burden of freight traffic whilst the track and bridges were strengthened to accommodate a qualitative leap forward with much heavier and more powerful locomotive types.[46]

Following Krasin's commands, the Technical Committee also investigated such issues as the construction of high-capacity wagons, the fitting of automatic brakes and couplings, electrification and dieselisation. The question of new railways and supermainlines particularly stirred the imagination, and soon the committee was engrossed in compiling a list of priority routes. It also debated desirable types of engine for trains of up to 6,000 tonnes on these lines, and decided that in conjunction with the Russian locomotive factories the NKPS should produce outline drawings for 4–8–2, 4–10–2 and 2–12–2 wheel arrangements, whilst a massive 2–10–0 + 0–10–2 articulated engine should be developed for banking work on gradients.[47]

Curiously, perhaps the most passionate and incongruous modernisation debate was over the specifications for a new standard Soviet sleeping carriage. Led by A. S. Raevskii of the Putilov works, one group favoured Scandinavian practice whereby 3 tiers accommodated 42 passengers per 44-tonne coach; but a traditionalist group objected that this arrangement contravened basic standards of comfort, and advocated the twin-tier arrangement of the old tsarist third class, which carried 28 passengers in a 41-tonne coach. And so, as the civil war reached its climax and most long-suffering railway passengers endured horrendous conditions, the Technical Committee's engineers built a test rig at their Moscow premises for a practical experiment. Raevskii slept in it for twelve nights, such was his commitment. By contrast, Lomonosov's one night there produced an uncharacteristically and unhelpfully non-committal verdict: he was comfortable only when sleeping alone.[48]

By December 1919, then, railway engineers and the NKPS were looking beyond the immediate crisis to a future of railway modernisation and expansion which would lead the country's socioeconomic development. But what of the vast material, financial, technical and human resources essential for their proposed programmes? With the honourable exceptions of Grinevetskii, Krasin and perhaps one or two others, the railway engineers were reluctant to address this elementary practical problem, at least in their published articles.[49] Krasin and Grinevetskii both stressed the importance of foreign resources, including imports and investment, and with Soviet industry virtually *hors de combat* for the time being, the crucial question was whether this was realistic.

The question of foreign resources

In their famous *Azbuka kommunizma* (*ABC of Communism*), published in 1919 at the height of the Allied blockade and military intervention, N. I. Bukharin and E. A. Preobrazhenskii anticipated thriving economic relations between proletarian Russia and proletarian Europe. Their economies would be coordinated under an overall plan, which would enable the rapid revival and modernisation of Russia's economy. Russia could exchange raw materials for assistance, especially from Germany, the advanced capitalist country which seemed the most ripe for revolution:

> [Russia's] backwardness, the comparatively undeveloped state of her industry, and so on, would all be overcome if Russia were to form part of an international, or even merely a European soviet republic, and thus to be associated with more advanced lands ... Should the proletariat prove victorious in Germany, we [would] establish a joint organ which would direct the common economic policy of the two soviet republics. It would decide what quantity of products German proletarian industry should send to Soviet Russia; how many skilled workers should migrate from Germany (to the Russian locomotive factories, for instance), and, conversely, what quantity of raw materials should be sent from Russia to Germany.[50]

But as Richard Day has shown, there had long been disagreement between Lenin and Trotskii in particular about when the revolution would spread abroad. Trotskii believed that a Russian revolution could not survive without revolution abroad and that this proliferation would occur quickly, whereas Lenin was sceptical on both counts.[51]

According to Day, Trotskii derived his view from his analysis of imperialism, particularly his expectation that class-conscious imperialist governments would take coordinated action against any socialist revolution. In his *Itogi i perspektivy* (*Results and Prospects*), published in 1906, Trotskii argued that Russia's technical backwardness would doom a Russian revolt to foreign intervention and failure unless revolution spread to other countries:

> Left to its own resources the working class of Russia will inevitably be crushed by the counter-revolution the moment the peasantry turns its back on it. It will have no alternative but to link the fate of its political rule, and hence the fate of the whole Russian revolution, with the fate of socialist revolution in Europe.[52]

Yet, he believed, a Russian socialist revolution would certainly not be defenceless. The Russian proletariat could provoke international revolution by repudiating the tsarist regime's debts, for this would precipitate an economic and political crisis in France 'which can only end with the transference of power into the hands of the proletariat'; and this would ignite revolution in other countries, thereby creating international allies for the Russian working class.[53]

By contrast, Lenin emphasised the differences between individual capitalist states, especially their varied levels of growth. He concluded that some societies would be less ready for revolution than others, that a Russian uprising might not necessarily spread abroad immediately, and that capitalist economies might even stage a limited recovery, though at the cost of increasing reliance on exports, especially of capital. It was also conceivable that during the transition to world socialism a socialist Russia might exist alongside ideologically hostile states, and that since the latter would be desperate for access to Russian markets, Russia could industrialise, as before, by exchanging timber and other natural resources for foreign industrial equipment and allowing limited foreign investment in strictly controlled forms.[54]

Unfortunately for Lenin and Trotskii, their analyses were confounded in their optimism and confirmed in their pessimism. To Bolshevik eyes events like the German monarchy's collapse and the establishment of Soviet power in Hungary and Bavaria heralded European revolution, but the breakthrough did not occur. Nor was it produced by the Soviet abrogation of Russia's foreign debts in January 1918 and the nationalisation of industry, transport and trade in 1917–18. Contrary to expectation, Bolshevik Russia was soon isolated and besieged.

In response, as Richard Debo and others have shown, the Bolsheviks debated whether Soviet Russia could survive in perhaps total isolation and whether relations with foreign capitalism were feasible and desirable. The party's left wing became particularly dubious. For instance, in January 1918 the chairman of the VSNKh, N. Osinskii

(V. V. Obolenskii) feared that strong capitalist powers could deprive Soviet Russia of her economic and political independence, and other left-wingers doubted that agreements could really be secured and maintained. Bukharin denied the possibility of peaceful coexistence with foreign capital, whilst Trotskii remained convinced that the Russian Revolution's salvation lay exclusively in European revolution. But Lenin disagreed: political and economic settlements with capitalist countries would be both essential and feasible, both to defuse the foreign military threat and for possible economic and political benefits.

Central to these arguments was the relationship with Germany. In January 1918, after some three and a half years of war, Lenin recommended acceptance of the Germans' harsh terms for peace, but he was outvoted in the Central Committee, not least through fear of German economic domination. However, the Central Committee's mood changed by late February with the disastrous failure of Trotskii's 'No war, no peace' tactic and the German army's renewed eastward advance, and the Russians duly signed an even more onerous peace treaty at Brest-Litovsk in March 1918.

The Treaty of Brest-Litovsk – the first major agreement between Soviet Russia and a capitalist power – was a milestone for the Bolsheviks in not just foreign policy but also foreign economic relations. By encouraging a major escalation of the civil war through full-scale Allied military intervention, it eliminated any remaining scope for Soviet–Allied trade; and by defusing the military threat from Germany, it enabled the start of Soviet–German trade, not to mention opportunities for revolutionary propaganda within Germany itself.[55] The foundations had been laid for Soviet Russia's distinctively dualistic foreign policy, encompassing both contact with foreign capitalists and the cultivation of revolution abroad.

The prospect of trade with Germany concentrated minds on organisational issues. In the autumn of 1917 the nationalisation of all foreign trade operations was planned for the longer term to enable the proletarian state, in Lenin's words, 'to defend its internal economic independence'. But the strong fear of German economic imperialism in the spring of 1918 helped to generate a Sovnarkom decree of 22 April whereby only state-authorised agents were permitted to trade, responsibility for all related planning and operations being entrusted to the People's Commissariat of Trade and Industry (NKTiP).[56]

Significantly, the chance of trade with Germany was taken very seriously by the NKPS, to judge by the establishment within its

Directorate of Economics and Materials of a special Bureau for Foreign Orders in the summer of 1918. The new bureau, which was soon involved in a commission concerned with implementing the Brest-Litovsk treaty, had three main tasks: firstly, to determine import quotas and the proportion of overall NKPS requirements to be imported; secondly, to establish, in conjunction with other Soviet organisations, an appropriate procedure for planning and making purchases; and thirdly, to have full responsibility for all proposed NKPS foreign orders.[57]

It was through Soviet–German relations, too, that Krasin became involved in Soviet efforts to develop foreign trade. Following imprisonment by the tsarist authorities for revolutionary activity, in 1908 he emigrated to Germany where he joined the Siemens-Schückert Electrical Company of Berlin as a junior engineer. After 1908 he almost completely withdrew from politics. In 1911 he returned to Russia to manage the firm's Moscow office, and in 1914 became managing director of its St Petersburg office. During the war he rallied to the Russian flag, serving, for example, on the electrical section of the Central War-Industries Committee. After the February Revolution he evacuated his wife and children to Scandinavia, and he reacted sceptically to the October Revolution. At first Krasin declined Bolshevik offers of employment, but in early 1918 Trotskii persuaded him to assist the Soviet delegation in the first Brest-Litovsk negotiations, though afterwards Krasin rejoined his family in Sweden. However, in the late spring he was contacted by an old friend, A. A. Ioffe, the new Soviet representative in Germany, who wanted to use Krasin's commercial contacts and influence to develop German–Soviet relations; and although Krasin agreed only on condition that his efforts would be unofficial, he quickly returned to the fold.[58]

Krasin was convinced that international trade would be indispensable. On 25 May 1918 he wrote to his wife that '... it will probably be my job to organise trade and barter relations with foreign countries. This is at present one of the most vital tasks.'[59] Initially he expected Soviet Russia to trade with Germany and Scandinavia, and later perhaps also with the United States. He hoped that the German army's advance into the Ukraine would be stopped if trade relations could be re-established, and believed that in any case 'we shall have to do a business deal with the Germans or they will come and take what they want without paying anything for it, and then there won't be anything left for us to sell to Sweden and Norway and other countries'.[60]

During the summer of 1918 Krasin participated in negotiations about a supplementary agreement to the Treaty of Brest-Litovsk, and also secured a number of commercial contracts, including one for much-needed coal for Petrograd. Then, in mid-August, he left Germany for Moscow to join the VSNKh Presidium. From November 1918 he worked as chief of supplies for the Red Army and also as head of the NKTiP, in which capacity, of course, he took responsibility for the republic's foreign economic relations.[61]

Unfortunately for Krasin, his arrival at the NKTiP coincided with Germany's capitulation to the Allies, which isolated Soviet Russia and apparently nullified most of his recent work. Surprisingly, though, the German surrender did not completely kill Soviet interest in foreign trade. For instance, the NKPS bureau continued to function much as before, at least for several months: in early 1919 it had just finished studying proposals to order rails in the Ukraine and rolling-stock in the USA and was busy examining the needs of railways which had recently been under German occupation.[62] More significantly, a debate ensued in the Soviet press about the relationship between isolation, international economic relations and Russia's long-term economic development.

Ardent proponents of foreign trade were opposed by prophets of isolation. For example, on 1 January 1919 M. Savel'ev argued in *Ekonomicheskaia zhizn'* that isolation would trap Soviet Russia in an economic cul-de-sac.[63] But R. Arskii, a publicist associated with Trotskii, retorted that Russia was a besieged blockaded fortress which had to survive alone and attain economic self-sufficiency.[64] Arskii agreed that imports from America and Europe would be most helpful, but disputed that they were vital: if necessary, Russia could successfully develop her economy unaided, thanks to her abundant natural resources and the repudiation of her old debts. At least for the time being, he concluded, Russia's economic plans had to be based on the premise that this isolation would continue. Blockade notwithstanding, normal life could certainly be restored, albeit in a very primitive way, by concentrating initially on repairing equipment and industry and by using the energy of the masses.

A few weeks later these arguments resurfaced in the specifically railway context of repairing the large quantity of unserviceable engines and wagons. That this work was important and urgent was not disputed. And there was agreement that the VSNKh locomotive-building factories were ill-suited and ill-equipped for repair work. Furthermore, there was broad support for creating a network of massive dedicated repair factories to supplement the existing NKPS workshops, each serving a group of railways and benefiting from all the advantages of mass production. Indeed, the Mozherez and Sazherez projects had already been approved. But how could this scheme be completed quickly? An engineer, M. Lapirov-Skoblo, called for radical government measures to inaugurate the repair factories as soon as possible: instead of the pre-war approach of gradually completing them using Russian industrial output, the government should obtain foreign equipment and supplies so that several factories could be built quickly.[65] But V. Ia. Chubar', a member of the VSNKh presidium and of the management of GOMZA, protested that the only realistic policy was to create military-type enterprises using the significant quantity of evacuated mechanical equipment stored in recently liberated Ukrainian warehouses. In this way the factories could be completed within just eighteen months, the severity of existing conditions notwithstanding.[66]

Krasin, meanwhile, was still doggedly trying to negotiate contracts with foreign companies, seeing Scandinavia, in particular Sweden, as his best chance for a breakthrough. The Swedish government had defied the Allies during the First World War by permitting exports of iron ore to Germany, and during 1918 by allowing Swedish–Soviet trade to develop even as the Allies expanded their anti-Bolshevik military intervention. Indeed, V. V. Vorovskii, the semi-official Soviet representative in Sweden after the Bolshevik revolution, reported to Moscow in 1918 that 'the political and press circles in Sweden sympathetic to Germany were benevolent towards the Soviet government and viewed its peace proposals with great interest'. True, after Germany's capitulation the Swedish government changed tack, expelling Vorovskii in January 1919 and recognising the Allied blockade in practice, but it did not officially accept the Allies' invitation to join the blockade, and certain Swedish businessmen displayed particular interest and persistence concerning Soviet Russia during 1919.[67]

One Swedish idea was a ten-year concession to construct and repair locomotives. In a report to Krasin dated 22 February 1919, a Russian engineer, A. I. Belonozhkin, explained that the Swedes proposed to build locomotives in Europe and ship them as kits to Russia for reassembly under a concession arrangement at the Nicholas Railway's Aleksandrov workshops, the Putilov factory and the Nevskii shipyard in Petrograd, where certain parts would also be produced and repaired. Prices for locomotives and overhauls would be set at 40 per cent above the pre-war rate – a new 0–10–0 would thus cost 84,000 gold rubles rather than 60,000 – and payment would be made with raw materials valued at pre-war prices. Finally, the Swedes would be entitled to import any goods, materials and provisions necessary for the workshops on the same terms without payment of customs duties.[68]

Nothing came of this idea, even though Krasin immediately gave approval in principle provided that the concession would be subject to Soviet law, including the labour code.[69] But in the meantime Krasin did have some success in other Swedish dealings. The most notable instance concerned a Swedish ship, the *Eskilstuna III*, which breached the blockade in May 1919 and delivered axes, saws, scythes and several Swedish businessmen to Petrograd. This Swedish delegation was led by a socialist lawyer, Wilhelm Hellberg, and included an entrepreneur named Gunnar W. Anderson, who hoped to supply industrial products worth 500 million Swedish crowns over a three-year period. After several meetings with Krasin in Moscow, the group successfully returned home with a cargo of flax. But this business soon collapsed. Returning from Petrograd on a second sortie later in the summer, the *Eskilstuna III* was intercepted by the British Navy, its cargo was confiscated and no further sailings were made.[70]

Krasin's appointment to the NKPS in March 1919 (he remained head of the NKTiP) produced a closer link between railway needs and imports policy. In particular, as already mentioned, he stressed his view that foreign goods and capital would be essential for the railways' postwar recovery and development. He also ensured that railway equipment featured in the national imports plan for the second half of 1919, which prioritised manufactured goods.[71] Moreover, the NKPS report for the Seventh Congress of Soviets declared that it was 'essential to organise the delivery of all necessary materials and metals from abroad at the very first opportunity, since Russian factories are in no condition to rouse themselves quickly so as to meet the country's needs in full'.[72]

Clearly Krasin was laying foundations for the future. And in this regard Professor Lomonosov provided important support upon his return to Moscow in 1919. For months the People's Commissar for Foreign Affairs, G. V. Chicherin, and his deputy, M. M. Litvinov, had been calling fruitlessly for the West to resume trade. In particular, they had been trying with Martens, Lomonosov and others to persuade the US government to allow new Soviet contracts and deliver the remnants of the wartime equipment.[73] Now Lomonosov could give the Bolshevik leadership an all too rare first-hand account of foreign conditions. Whilst he was dubious about the prospects for immediate orders in the United States, he was quite optimistic about Europe: during his return journey from the USA he had had talks with businessmen in Sweden and Germany and even, in great secrecy, with officials of the German Foreign Ministry.

Lomonosov's business adventures began after his arrival in Stockholm from New York in early June 1919, when a Bolshevik sympathiser named Stark sought his views about the participation of Swedish industry in the rebuilding of Russia's railways. Cautiously basing his replies on his knowledge of the transport situation in 1917, Lomonosov suggested that Russia would probably need 5,000 modern engines like the decapods or the Class E, and 40,000 wagons, as well as boiler tubes, metal tyres, tool steel and machine tools. Lomonosov believed that eventually the USA could best supply locomotives and rolling-stock thanks to its large and partly idle industrial capacity, and so he suggested that countries like Germany and Sweden could assist with repair work on the railways.[74]

There followed a meeting on 11 June with about a dozen Swedish industrialists and bankers. Taking the chair, a banker, Åkerström, proposed the formation of a private company or concern which would offer extensive credit to Russia in exchange for gold-backed guarantees and accept payment in timber and flax. Lomonosov, for his part, became convinced that Sweden would not be able to deliver locomotives since her maximum monthly output was only twelve, but he believed that there was great potential for acquiring Swedish materials and machine tools – an impression that was confirmed by visits to two machine-tool factories working at only 30 or 40 per cent of capacity.[75]

Lomonosov also met Olof Aschberg, the Swedish banker who had had lucrative contracts with Russia during the First World War.[76] But only when an opportunity arose to discuss business with Germany was Lomonosov's imagination really fired. At the beginning of August a German consortium offered exploratory talks in Berlin and intimated that the German government would allow him into the country and facilitate his onward travel. For Lomonosov a major attraction of this offer was that it enabled him to continue his journey, for he was being denied permission to travel via Finland, yet he was certainly also curious to assess the capabilities of German industry. Seizing his chance, he left Sweden surreptitiously and first met the German businessmen on 14 August in Berlin, talking mainly with a small firm named Briske & Prohl which hoped to act as an intermediary. In turn came further talks and, on 23 August, a meeting with a director of one of the leading firms in the Verband (association) of German locomotive-building companies, the Hannoversche Maschinenbau AG. Lomonosov learnt that the German locomotive factories had enough work for some twelve months but would then be able to supply up to about 1,000 0–10–0 engines per year at approximately 900,000 German marks each, roughly the price of American decapods in 1917.[77]

Lomonosov's first contact with the German Foreign Ministry was arranged apparently at the latter's request. A furtive meeting occurred on 18 August with Walter Bartels, a member of the Foreign Ministry's Political Department, at a club called the Berliner, and a second meeting was held the next day. On 25 August Lomonosov met an official whom he described as the Director of the ministry's Russian Section, and on 26 August he had talks with the Director of the Department for Trade Policy, Karl Edler von Stockhammern.[78]

In general the Foreign Ministry's interest in Lomonosov stemmed from the terms of the Treaty of Versailles. Between November 1918 and May 1919 the ministry had opposed the resumption of Soviet–German trade for fear of antagonising the Allies. But it had been shocked by the harshness of the treaty – the Minister, Ulrich Graf von Brockdorff-Rantzau, had resigned in protest – and had begun to show a slightly more friendly though still cautious attitude towards Soviet Russia. In June 1919 the ministry recognised a Bolshevik, V. L. Kopp, as an official Soviet representative for discussions about prisoners of war, and it had since held informal talks with Kopp about the prospects for trade.[79] Caught between East and West, Germany was searching for a way forward.

According to the report which Lomonosov later submitted to Krasin, the head of the Russian Section believed that Russia and Germany were being driven together by history, that a political and economic agreement with Russia was one of the German government's basic aims, and that the main obstacle was Allied policy.[80] Stockhammern was evidently more restrained, though still positive. He highlighted several obstacles, including British naval supremacy in the Baltic, the lack of a Soviet–German land border and the absence of private merchants in Russia. When asked whether the German government would hold talks of the type which an American representative, William C. Bullitt, had conducted in Moscow earlier that year, Stockhammern replied that such negotiations and official co-operation would be impossible before about February 1920 owing to

Germany's restricted freedom of action. But Stockhammern agreed that the fall of the Soviet government was not in Germany's interests, and he repeated his country's desire to cooperate with Soviet Russia, at least to the extent of meeting other Soviet representatives like Lomonosov. He even gave Lomonosov permission to order railway materials and spare parts immediately on condition of absolute secrecy – an opportunity which Lomonosov exploited to sign a provisional contract with Briske & Prohl for locomotive tyres, boiler tubes and other equipment.[81]

If Lomonosov's report gave Krasin at least some grounds for optimism, further reasons emerged during the autumn. For example, on 9 October 1919 the German Foreign Minister, Hermann Müller, publicly voiced a desire for friendly relations 'with the East'.[82] Moreover, although the Allies were organising an international boycott of the Soviet regime's gold at precisely this time, there were rumours of a serious rift within the Allied camp and of the possibility that Great Britain might restore trade relations. Privately the British Prime Minister, David Lloyd George, was arguing that the threat of Bolshevism could be reduced by opening trade relations with Soviet Russia so as to improve living conditions for the Russian people, and in the early autumn he commented publicly that Russia's grain and raw materials were vital for Europe. When the British government then consented to hold negotiations with Litvinov about the release of prisoners of war, a real change in British policy began to seem possible in Soviet eyes.[83]

With Krasin and his sympathisers encouraged by these hints and rumours, and others merely scenting a trap, the issue of foreign economic relations thus became topical again in Moscow in late 1919 just as the Bolshevik leadership began confronting the Soviet transport crisis and economic development. The resultant debate was short but crucial.

Decision: imports for railway-led reconstruction

By December 1919 the railway crisis was at the top of the Bolshevik agenda as the gravest threat to the regime's survival. But Lenin and his colleagues were sufficiently confident to be looking already at questions of reconstruction and the building of a new socialist society, with Trotskii presenting controversial theses about economic strategy to the Central Committee on 16 December.[84] As for what should be done, railway and electrical engineers were anxious to press their respective visions for socioeconomic development. In ideal circumstances railway development and electrification would generally complement each other, as was envisaged by Grinevetskii. Indeed, Lenin saw both of these approaches as binding devices in nation-building.[85] But resources were so scarce that in reality they competed for priority.

Lenin was the most important advocate of nationwide electrification. By early February 1920 he was preaching that it would drive industrial development and overcome 'that backwardness, that fragmentation, dispersion, the darkness of the countryside which is the chief cause of all the stagnation, backwardness and oppression to this day'.[86] Not least, an electrification programme could seize the popular imagination. Thus, at Lenin's suggestion the All-Russian Central Executive Committee (VTsIK) established the so-called GOELRO commission of scientists and technologists to draft a detailed plan within just two months.[87] The tightness of this deadline emphasised the sense of urgency about resuming the modernisation drive. But did the VTsIK decision represent victory for the electrifiers in their battle for investment priority? Certainly it was an important step towards the creation of the GOELRO plan, which would eventually appear in December 1920, some eight months late. But in the winter of 1919–20 political support had yet to switch from the railways to electrification. If one looks at the debate about resources and possible imports and foreign investment at the beginning of 1920, the railways, not electrification, appear as the first priority for a rapid breakthrough on the 'bloodless front' to relaunch the process of national modernisation and development.

This debate was couched in the terms employed by Savel'ev and Arskii a year earlier, and the two leading protagonists were Krasin and Trotskii. There was common ground in that both were gravely concerned about the railway system and both were keen to start the reconstruction and development of the economy. But they differed over the question of imports and foreign investment. Krasin maintained that rapid economic development was essential for the regime's survival and prosperity, and that foreign resources would therefore be vital; he was convinced, too, that they would become available. By contrast, Trotskii expected continuing diplomatic and economic isolation, and hence a slower rate of economic growth and modernisation based on domestic resources, especially labour conscription.[88]

Historians have regarded these two positions as basically irreconcilable. For instance, Day has contrasted them as integrationist and isolationist, whilst for Dongarov Krasin's stance was European and progressive whereas Trotskii's was Asiatic and primitive, the two sides of a 'Great Dilemma' about economic development.[89] As for the outcome, Day has argued that Trotskii triumphed at the Ninth Party Congress in March 1920 but was later defeated by his opponents; Dongarov has implied that the dilemma was eclipsed by the Polish invasion of Russia in April 1920; and others have in effect accorded the honours to Krasin, noting that he was authorised to hold trade negotiations with the British government.[90] Yet arguably the leadership actually kept its options open by devising a compromise over railway development.

Krasin insisted that foreign economic relations could be revived quickly because the prospect of getting Soviet gold and raw materials would tempt foreigners into direct trade or investment as concessionaires in, for instance, railway construction and timber extraction.[91] As for expenditure priorities and the organisation of trade and payment, Krasin expounded his views in theses presented to Sovnarkom on 27 January 1920 and, in revised form, on 10 February.[92] Apart from proposing to transfer responsibility for foreign economic relations from the NKTiP to a special new commissariat, later known as the People's Commissariat of Foreign Trade (NKVT), the revised document noted that given the limited supply of exportable goods and the absence of credit, imports would initially have to be purchased with gold, foreign currency and bonds. Thus, only certain vital goods could be afforded, with priority (as in the ill-fated 1919 imports plan) given to imports that would rebuild productive capacity. This meant expenditure on, first and foremost, new railway locomotives and locomotive spare parts, along with general railway material and equipment for railway workshops. Also to be ordered were agricultural equipment, spare parts for foreign-built machinery, and medicines and chemicals, but only small quantities of food and consumer goods.

By contrast, Trotskii launched what Day describes as a 'personal campaign to dispel any lingering hopes of aid from abroad'.[93] He believed that substantial aid would not appear even if relations were re-established with the West because the recovery of Europe's own shattered economy was likely to consume most of America's exports. Significantly, Trotskii accepted the importance of at least trying to obtain foreign goods and credit. But he insisted that since no real benefits could be expected, long-term Soviet economic strategy had to be based solely on locally available resources, including, controversially, the militarisation of labour. On 6 January he declared that 'perhaps we will manage to import locomotives and other items from America, but we must not pin our hopes on this. We must talk about what we can do in the country during an epoch of nearly total blockade.'[94] And he returned to this point on 12 January:

> Of course, if it was not for the blockade, if we could immediately place orders with the Germans and British for 2,000 locomotives, machines, craftsmen and technicans and get raw materials and food, then a new factor would enter our economic situation which would greatly improve the position. But for the moment this is not the case ... The key to changing the situation is not the instantaneous and extraordinary delivery of all kinds of gifts from abroad but the social factor. This factor is the organisation of the labour force. This is our key lever.[95]

For Trotskii, therefore, the most appropriate economic strategy was, essentially, an extension of the politico-economic system which had brought victory in the civil war. He wanted strict 'shock' priorities, central economic planning and labour conscription, which would allow the use of manpower, where necessary through coercion, as the economy's main driving force during a gradual modernising process of mechanisation.[96]

Over labour conscription Trotskii was virtually isolated in the party leadership, supported only by Lenin in a crucial vote on 12 January.[97] But the debate about foreign trade was probably more evenly balanced. Although it seems impossible to identify precisely the support within the party leadership and commissariats for each of the rival positions, several individuals did publicise their views. For example, Krasin was supported by the chairman of VSNKh, A. I. Rykov, who derided Trotskii's proposals.[98] A. I. Lezhava, the Bolshevik chairman of the Central Cooperative Society (Tsentrosoiuz) and a firm proponent of foreign trade, agreed with the idea of importing transport materials before all else, whilst Karl Radek, a prominent official of the Communist International with expertise about Germany, called for maximum concessions to Allied demands and every effort to open contacts with Germany.[99] More backing for Krasin may have come from technocrats like those appointed to the GOELRO commission in February 1920, whose plan would advocate heavy reliance on foreign capital.[100] Conversely, Trotskii's stance on foreign trade was defended by Arskii in *Izvestiia* on 16 January, and by an unsigned *Pravda* editorial on 21 January.[101] Similarly, one of

Rykov's subordinates, Lomov, agreed with the idea of trying to import railway equipment but doubted that any help would materialise.[102]

Lenin, to judge by his speech to the VTsIK on 2 February, was closer to Trotskii than to Krasin, though he did not necessarily share the assumption of long-term isolation. To be sure, Lenin welcomed that day's peace treaty with Estonia and hailed the removal of the Allied blockade in mid-January as the demise of the Allied Entente's most powerful weapon, which had been strangling Russia's economy.[103] But these remarks were largely polemical. Revealingly, he stated that the main economic task of 'the next few months' was to resolve the transport and food crises, and that then the modernisation of Russia could at last be started.[104] But, he warned, echoing Trotskii, Russia would have to rely mainly on her own resources: although it might be possible to import a certain amount of machinery, which would assist industrial development, Russia could not expect much foreign help, not least because the capitalist countries' economies were themselves in a sorry condition.[105] In other words, Lenin shared the interest in resuming the modernisation process, but, unlike Krasin, he did not regard foreign resources as fundamental for success.

In this period between mid-December 1919 and early February 1920, then, the opposition to Krasin's plan was couched mainly in terms of impracticability. Significantly, no one appears to have questioned the desirability of locomotive imports, at least in published reports. Even Trotskii clearly felt that locomotive imports would be a good thing if they happened. The idea that Soviet factories should produce the locomotives and other equipment needed for the reconstruction and modernisation of the railways, and that this could stimulate industry through the backward linkages, was apparently not voiced in the press at this juncture. Whether such views were advocated privately at this time remains to be discovered.

Lomonosov, it should be added, was now vitally concerned with the immediate transport crisis, having recently been appointed to head the NKPS Technical Directorate. However, he evidently took little part in the discussions about possible imports. To judge by his speech to the Third Congress of Economic Councils on 23 January 1920, his main concern was the crisis: he merely reminded delegates that locomotive imports would not solve the immediate shortage since none could be delivered before the next autumn even in ideal circumstances. A few days later he left Moscow to inspect railways in the south and contracted typhus there in mid-February, which effectively removed him from the scene until April.[106]

The Krasin–Trotskii debate came to a head during the month after the Allied Supreme Economic Council's decision of 16 January to permit trade with 'the Russian people'. Most obviously, the few Soviet representatives in the West redoubled their efforts to stress Russia's desire for trade. Litvinov told Reuters that Russia wanted new machinery, agricultural equipment and railway materials in exchange for gold, and during the following weeks he called for motor trucks, railway locomotives and factory machinery.[107] Similarly, on 17 January Kopp approached the German Foreign Ministry about resuming Soviet–German relations.[108] At the end of January, Ioffe, now participating in the Soviet–Estonian peace negotiations at Tartu, affirmed Russia's urgent need for machinery and railway equipment, whilst one V. N. Polovtseva was quoted on 1 February by a British newspaper, *The Observer*, as saying that 'it is very important that you should first send cargoes of such things as railway materials for transport and agricultural implements for farming'.[109] In mid-February, Kopp stated that Germany and Soviet Russia would sign an economic agreement, that Russia needed machinery, coal and medicines, and that Russia would ask for German technical workers and engineers. And a fortnight later the senior Soviet representative in Tallinn, I. E. Gukovskii, announced that he had just received a quotation for American locomotives.[110]

More significantly, the Allied announcement provided both Krasin and Trotskii with new ammunition. Krasin could cite the policy change as evidence that Western governments were bowing to pressure for trade, whereas Trotskii could highlight three barriers which the Allies had been careful to retain or erect: firstly, the Supreme Economic Council still refused the de facto political recognition which the Soviet government, having nationalised Russia's foreign trade, needed in order to conduct trade operations itself; secondly, the Allies were determined to continue the international boycott against Soviet-held gold; and thirdly, ignoring the nationalisation of Russia's trade, the Allies had stipulated that trade be conducted exclusively through private Russian cooperative organisations.[111]

Decisions taken during January and early February suggest that the Bolshevik leadership sought a compromise over foreign trade which accommodated Trotskii's scepticism and Krasin's optimism as in effect minimum and maximum variants. On 19 January the Politburo approved Trotskii's theses about labour armies, and on 22 January the Central Committee accepted his December theses as the basis for the party's proposals on economic strategy for the forthcoming Ninth

Party Congress.[112] Meanwhile, treating the Entente's decision to allow trade with Russia as a blatant attempt to restore capitalism through the cooperatives, the Politburo decided on 17–18 January to secure complete Bolshevik control of the cooperative apparatus, especially in areas like the Ukraine and Far East where trade routes might be established. The next day, 19 January, the Politburo instructed Krasin, V. P. Miliutin (a deputy chair of VSNKh), G. E. Zinov′ev and N. N. Krestinskii (Commissar of Finances) to report to Sovnarkom about how trade with the West should be organised.[113] Then, on 27 January, Sovnarkom approved Krasin's theses about foreign trade subject to certain amendments.[114] Furthermore, Sovnarkom used its control over the Moscow-based central cooperative organisation, the Tsentrosoiuz, to appoint Krasin, Litvinov and other prominent communists to a special Tsentrosoiuz delegation, which would have extensive powers to negotiate trade agreements with foreign governments and offer Soviet gold to foreign firms for railway equipment and other goods.[115] Also, the NKPS, VSNKh and other commissariats were asked to compile shopping lists of essential imports.[116]

That the railways were to be the first priority in economic reconstruction and, logically, imports policy was emphasised by a VTsIK resolution of 7 February about transport policy. Here, too, policies advocated by both Trotskii and Krasin were included. The statement began by unambiguously defining the twin objectives of arresting the decline in railway traffic and commencing railway reconstruction as 'the first priority and most important task of Soviet power'. It next specified measures to achieve immediate improvements in traffic by using human and other resources already available within the republic. Following Trotskii, the resolution not only gave the railways priority for food and metal supplies, but also demanded the mobilisation of communists and other workers to the transport sector and the introduction of martial law on the railways. Then, in its final paragraph, it described the purchase abroad of complete locomotives, workshop tooling and spare parts for the NKPS as 'the most urgent task of Soviet foreign trade'.[117] Thus, Krasin too was allowed an opportunity to prove his own theory and obtain imports for the ongoing repair work and railway reconstruction. Although many commissariats wanted imported goods, the needs of his NKPS would take first place.[118]

It is unsurprising that the railways won such precedence for imports given that the sector was prioritised for the breakthrough in economic reconstruction, and it was perhaps also thanks partly to

Krasin's dual roles as head of the NKPS and infant NKVT. Needless to say, the NKPS and Krasin were delighted with the VTsIK's categoric support. The commissariat promptly sent Sovnarkom a formal application for imports of 5,000 new locomotives and 100,000 wagons, together with tools, spare parts and raw materials.[119] Imports of such large quantities of rolling-stock were internationally unprecedented, and the figures underline the extraordinary nature of the proposed policy. In mid-February, Krasin told George Lansbury, the editor of the British labour newspaper the *Daily Herald*, that 'it must be understood by the workers of Europe especially that trade with Russia will set the wheels of industry going at full speed everywhere', and that 'Russia could immediately take 2,000 locomotives from Europe and America and almost any quantity of rolling-stock – besides vast quantities of other goods – for which she can pay in gold and commodities.'[120]

Lenin too expressed enthusiasm for possible railway and other imports, though this was perhaps simply rhetoric for foreign consumption.[121] In an interview with an American correspondent, Lincoln Eyres, published in *The World* on 21 February 1920, he commented that he was uncertain of the Allies' motives for lifting the blockade and that the situation in the United States was difficult to fathom. However, he thought it auspicious that although American bankers were apparently more afraid of Soviet Russia than ever, some entrepreneurs seemed to understand that business with Russia was more sensible than war. American locomotives, cars and other industrial products, Lenin asserted, would be more necessary for Russia than goods from any other country. And he saw 'no reason why a socialist state such as ours cannot have unlimited business relations with capitalist countries. We are not against using capitalist locomotives and agricultural machines, so why should [the capitalists] object to using our socialist wheat, flax and platinum?'[122] In any case, Lenin observed, Europe's economies could not recover without Soviet raw materials, and if Europe remained weak the resultant low level of transatlantic trade would debilitate the American economy, too.

By contrast, Trotskii and some like-minded colleagues again publicly voiced doubts about importing locomotives. Again their objections focused on the likelihood of this trade, not on whether the attempt should be made. For example, Arskii and a minor NKPS official, Ia. Shatunovskii, insisted that there was really no hope of importing new locomotives, though they did condone making an effort to purchase spare parts and raw materials for the NKPS.[123] Trotskii acknowledged in a speech to the Third All-Russian Congress of Trade Unions that new engines were desperately needed, but added that Europe was obviously too exhausted to produce them.[124]

Interestingly, at least one statement of outright opposition to the railway imports policy now appeared in the press. Writing in *Ekonomicheskaia zhizn'* on 21 March, E. Al'perovich, deputy chair of the VSNKh Department of Metal, raised the spectre of possible deindustrialisation and dependence on the capitalist world if these imports materialised. In his opinion the case for total government support for the Soviet locomotive-building factories was 'incontrovertible'. The factories were vital for defence as well as transport, and there was 'no salvation without them'. The only answer was 'maximum support for those of our factories which can be used only to build new locomotives', amounting to a firm production plan with exceptional government attention and assistance.[125]

This case for reviving Soviet industry to reconstruct the railways was strong and emotive, not least in terms of Russian self-reliance amidst hostile capitalist encirclement. And since domestic industry had a history of opposing imports before the war, it is obviously possible that the idea of rolling-stock imports aroused hostility from VSNKh officials, the engineering factories and the metalworkers' trade union. However, no campaign of opposition appeared in the press, and as yet no other evidence of such opposition has been found. Indeed, one might also speculate that many or most industry officials did not oppose the railway imports policy. They may well have regarded it as simply unrealistic, and they probably doubted that the Soviet engineering industry could build more than a few hundred locomotives within a similar sort of timescale even with maximum government support. They may have acknowledged that a rapid breakthrough in re-equipping the railways could be achieved, if at all, only with large-scale imports.

Be that as it may, the leadership kept faith with its compromise. On the one hand, crucially, a large proportion of the gold reserve was assigned for purchasing imports. The NKVT was allocated 100 million gold rubles on 13 February for its 1920 expenditure programme, and on 16 March Sovnarkom formally released an additional 300 million gold rubles specifically for 'locomotives and spare parts for the repair of railway transport', the latter decision giving Krasin the opportunity to begin to realise the railway modernisation dream with the imports policy.[126] On the other hand, the Ninth Party Congress publicly endorsed Trotskii's economic strategy, including his assertion that it would be impossible to import the necessary engines quickly. And the congress further proclaimed the importance of organising the mass production of spare parts, and subsequently complete locomotives, at Soviet factories on the basis of careful planning and the latest production methods and techniques.[127]

In this light Trotskii's appointment as acting head of the NKPS on 23 March has special significance. Part of the explanation for his assignment must be his reputation as an effective troubleshooter and organiser, and his job could be viewed as a postwar civilian version of his role as head of the military commissariat and organiser of the Red Army. Indeed, V. V. Fomin, Commissar of the NKPS Operations Directorate, specifically asked the Central Committee to assign Trotskii, as a firm pair of hands, to the NKPS whilst Krasin travelled abroad with the Tsentrosoiuz delegation, and requested that the NKPS be reorganised to resemble the military commissariat.[128] Yet perhaps the main purpose of the appointment was to create a situation where both Trotskii and Krasin would be trying simultaneously to tackle the railway crisis and railway reconstruction, and where their respective strategies would complement each other as, in effect, minimum and maximum approaches. Plans for reconstruction and modernisation were to be based on domestic resources, though ideally large-scale imports would quicken their implementation. The duration of this dualistic arrangement was probably expected to be brief because Krasin anticipated quick progress and planned to be abroad for only a few weeks or months, whilst Trotskii himself insisted that his NKPS placement should last only until Krasin's return.[129] But the fact remained that both men were set to address the same task in their different ways. Whether the result would be a coherent policy or a pantomine horse remained to be seen.

By March 1920, then, the regime was concentrating on quickly solving the railway crisis and beginning railway reconstruction, and it had allocated a large part of its remaining gold for railway imports. A real sense of impending catastrophe explains why the regime focused on resolving the railway crisis. But why were the railways also given precedence over heavy industry and electrification for reconstruction and development? The details of the lobbying and decision making remain unclear, but one can suggest several reasons. Firstly, the Bolsheviks were confronting the shortage of resources by adopting a sector-by-sector approach to economic development akin to their handling of the civil war, when resources were concentrated on one or another front to repel the greatest threat. Secondly, the railways were already at the centre of attention thanks to the railway crisis, which also underlined their continuing indispensability: without them the economy would disintegrate, defence would be impossible and the regime would probably fall. Thirdly, railways still symbolised political, economic and social progress, as shown by slogans like 'Our Locomotive, Fly Forward!', and they were expected to continue to stimulate industrial development, not least in the NKPS view that the reconstruction of transport was 'the surest way' to national economic reconstruction. Fourthly, the fact that railways were an established technology of immediate importance actually gave them an advantage over new technologies like electrification, which by definition lacked that contemporary importance. Fifthly, just as Krasin had wanted, the NKPS could point to the detailed planning already undertaken by its Technical Committee not just to reconstruct but to transform the railway system. Revolutionary in its dismissal of 'tedious modification', it was also hard headed in wanting several thousand new locomotives like the decapods or Class E as a form of interim modernisation. And finally, there was a real if perhaps naive sense that restoring and renewing the locomotive and wagon stocks would ensure a dramatic breakthrough on the transport front.

Superficially, this approach recalls the 'Vitte system' of the 1890s, when railway development and foreign capital were the driving forces of rapid industrialisation. In fact, there were important differences. With scant resources available, the Bolsheviks sought a quick breakthrough with the reconstruction of just one sector of the economy. Furthermore, they were prepared at least temporarily to abandon the pre-war policy of industrial protectionism and try to import capital equipment to force the pace of railway reconstruction. In other words, the idea of importing up to 5,000 locomotives was essentially a short-term emergency measure akin to, and possibly inspired by, the railway imports policy of 1914–17. Potential speed of delivery was more important than 'backward linkages' to heavy industry, which would be restored in due course.

The obvious problem with this sector-by-sector strategy was that it virtually ignored the complex web of links between the railways and other sectors of the economy, especially heavy industry. Arguably the whole idea was fundamentally unfeasible, but revolutionary enthusiasm and a grand vision for economic reconstruction held sway over such practical realities, and their first substantial product was the railway imports policy, funded to the tune of 300 million gold rubles. Time would tell whether it would be a real leap forward or a misguided and costly blunder.

PART II

Trade and isolation, 1920–1921 implementing the railway imports policy

3 Krasin's first results

The departure of Krasin from Moscow in March 1920 at the head of the Tsentrosoiuz delegation marked the beginning of a year which one might call the heroic period in interwar Soviet–Western trade relations. Krasin, who based himself in Scandinavia for several months and then in London from late May 1920, aimed to implement an imports plan of epic proportions with its unprecedented goal of 5,000 locomotives and 100,000 wagons, not to mention the other railway supplies and requests from other commissariats. Trotskii meanwhile took control of the NKPS with his own distinctive agenda for reconstruction. Trotskii's achievements and problems at the commissariat have been discussed elsewhere and need be examined only briefly in chapter 5; the success of Krasin and his colleagues in agreeing a series of remarkable contracts for the NKPS by March 1921, notably three firm agreements for 1,700 new Class E freight locomotives, forms the main subject of this and the following two chapters.

The American dream

Although Chicherin, Litvinov, Krasin and others had been calling for trade with any and every capitalist country, they evidently preferred the United States.[1] One reason for this was the substantial amount of equipment ordered by previous Russian governments – including 200 decapod locomotives – which remained there. Furthermore, it was widely felt that only the USA had sufficient spare capacity to mass-produce quickly enough the desired vast quantities of equipment. True, the US government was still cold-shouldering the senior Soviet representative there, L. K. Martens, but American businessmen, it was felt, might jump far more readily than West Europeans at trade with Russia.

Such, at least, were the arguments confidently expounded by the transport correspondent of *Ekonomicheskaia zhizn'*, I. D. Mikhailov, in a series of articles targeted at sceptics like Trotskii, Arskii and Shatunovskii in March and April 1920.[2] Mikhailov identified a shortfall of at least 5,000 locomotives and 250,000 wagons, and asserted that Soviet factories would take perhaps 10 and 13 years to replenish the locomotive and wagon stocks respectively. But speed was vital, and imports were thus the only option. These would have to come from America and possibly Britain, not least because all other Western countries needed to concentrate on renewing their own stock. Mikhailov further insisted that the prospects for trade were excellent. Firstly, he claimed, Americans were very anxious to trade: in December 1919 American military representatives had offered the decapod locomotives and Russian-type wagons to the Paris office of the Tsentrosoiuz. Secondly, wartime production statistics suggested that American companies could build most of the necessary locomotives within just four or five months. Finally, many factories were short of orders and could undercut British prices. Thus, Mikhailov concluded, only the worldwide shortage of merchant ships would present a major problem.

In principle the Soviet leadership was making US–Soviet trade conditional upon a peace treaty and the establishment of diplomatic relations. In such terms, for example, did Chicherin couch a demand for peace negotiations on 24 February 1920. Declaring that the Soviet army's victories 'have brought quite near the prospect of re-establishing relations between Soviet Russia and the United States of America', Chicherin asserted that 'American commerce and industry are able to help in the largest measure the great work of the reconstruction of Russian economic life; that the United States can play a gigantic role in the realisation of this problem; and that numerous prominent representatives of the American business world are quite willing to take an active part in this work.' Once peace had been established, he continued, Russia could concentrate on this work and America could provide great assistance. Repeating, therefore, the offer made in December 1919 by the Seventh All-Russian Congress of Soviets to discuss peace with each of the Allied and associated powers, the Soviet government wanted to hold negotiations with Washington as soon as possible.[3]

But in practice there was flexibility over this linkage, at least concerning railway equipment. During the late winter and spring of 1920 the Russians sought American railway supplies through at least three different channels without making their proposals contingent upon a peace treaty. One attempt involved a petition to the US government via Colonel Stevens, the railway expert who was now stationed on the Chinese Eastern Railway at Harbin, and Colonel Benjamin O. Johnson, who was based in Eastern Siberia as commander of the US-staffed Russian Railway Service Corps.[4] A message was transmitted to Johnson on 23 March by an NKPS plenipotentiary in Siberia, Iu.V. Rudyi, in which the Americans were offered a monopoly in supplying railway equipment to Soviet Russia:

> The Moscow government wishes to know whether it may acquire a certain quantity of decapod steam locomotives and other railway equipment from the United States, and the earliest possible date when equipment ordered at the current time can be delivered to ports on the Black Sea or Baltic Sea. Payment for railway items can be made by means of a deposit placed in one of the neutral countries, which could be specified by the United States. The payment will be made in foreign currency, in dollars or in gold ... With regard to the American railway engineers being recalled from Siberia, is it possible for Mr Stevens to leave two or three engineers through whom the Soviet government will be in constant contact with the United States concerning matters of supplying railway equipment etc? A directive has been received from the Moscow government that discussions about the acquisition of railway items and equipment should not be conducted with any state except the United States.[5]

Johnson and Stevens were both quite positive about this telegram, albeit without discussing it in detail or actually endorsing the proposals. Sending the message to Stevens on 24 March, Johnson commented:

> While [the] Soviet has disposed of all military opposition to their Government still internal conditions are frightfully bad and unless economic relief is furnished at once the present Soviet Government will last but a short time. If [the] Soviet Government falls there is nothing but absolute anarchy to take its place. If anything is to be done it should be done at once. Delay would result in aid coming after conditions had gotten away from [the] Soviet Authorities and [the] carrying out of our plans will fall with the fall of [the] Soviet.[6]

Stevens forwarded the message and commentary to the Secretary of State on 26 March, and concluded: 'Personally I believe that they are much better than the last Government and if the economic situation can be remedied there is hope for success to their efforts and undoubtedly they have the support of the majority of the people.'[7] However, these opinions cut no ice in Washington. On 31 March

Bainbridge Colby replied for the Secretary of State: 'This Government has no intention of recognizing the present Moscow Government and it to any negotiations with the Soviet representatives [sic]. This Government has reached no decision as to the resumption of trade relations with Russia. When a decision is reached, you will be notified. The subject however is receiving earnest consideration.'[8] And there this correspondence terminated.

In the meantime Martens continued his campaign within the United States to generate government and business interest in trade. Nothing had come of his attempts to win control of the Bakhmet'ev mission's assets in 1919, which had continued to be shipped to anti-Bolshevik forces or sold.[9] By March 1920 Martens had received instructions from Moscow to concentrate exclusively on acquiring railway equipment, and this occupied his bureau in two ways: the purchase of US war surplus equipment, and the negotiation of new orders; in both cases the priority was locomotives.[10]

Naturally Martens was extremely interested in the decapods owned by the US War Department. After 113 were advertised for sale on 18 March, he submitted a bid on 5 April. Since the decapods had been converted for 1435 mm-gauge track and leased to American railways, Martens offered $44,200 per engine for delivery in as-built condition, dismantled and packed in shipping cases. He wanted a large number of them within sixty days of the contract being signed, and the remainder within six months. As for payment, he volunteered a cheque for $25,000 as evidence of good faith and suggested that his government could either deposit the full purchase price in gold in an Estonian bank for the US Treasury or deliver the gold to an American representive in Estonia.[11] The American War Department apparently responded by beginning negotiations, but the proposed sale was soon blocked on the American side, and Martens was left disappointed, though perhaps not surprised.[12]

Martens also tried to negotiate directly with American engineering companies, and he soon identified the Baldwin Locomotive Works as a cautiously willing supplier. On 19 March Baldwin's Foreign Sales Manager, A. W. Hinger, confirmed that the company could commence delivery of 100 Russian-type decapods per month four months after signing a contract, provided that the technical specifications of the 1917 order were employed. True, Hinger's offer was conditional upon State Department approval, and an irrevocable bank credit in US gold dollars sufficient to cover the contract would need to be opened in the United States in Baldwin's name. Such terms were dictated by the 'unsettled conditions in Europe, uncertainty of financial changes from day to day, and the fact that at the present time your Government has not yet been officially recognised', and therefore they could be modified if the situation improved before a contract was signed. Also, adding that Baldwin would be 'glad to be of every assistance possible compatible with our own interests and the policy of our Government', Hinger agreed that Soviet representatives could inspect the factory during the following week. He even suggested that Vauclain, now the company's president, might be persuaded to visit Russia since he already knew Professor Lomonosov through their wartime cooperation.[13]

At this time Vauclain was busy abroad offering locomotives to various European countries. Indeed he later boasted that the 150 engines which he sold to Poland 'kept the Bolshevists from overrunning [Poland] and so preserved that western bulwark for sane Europe'.[14] Nevertheless, it seems likely on balance that Vauclain was favourably disposed towards Martens's approach. Not only had Vauclain shown no political qualms about supplying engines to Russia in late 1917 and early 1918, but Hinger's letter of 19 March could scarcely have been so accommodating, relatively speaking, without his approval.

Replying on 25 March, Martens made large orders conditional upon a US–Soviet peace treaty, but offered to start placing smaller orders immediately. Welcoming Hinger's interest and suggestions, he reported that his government accepted the company's conditions 'as the basis for a more detailed agreement'. And since 'the rehabilitation of the Russian railroad system to a state of adequate efficiency will require the immediate construction of not less than fifteen thousand [sic] locomotives', he was ready to place 'initial orders' in the United States for 2,000 engines and would be pleased to give Baldwin a large share. Obviously credits for such an enormous order could 'hardly be arranged until the whole matter of Russia's foreign credits has been agreed upon and normal relations have been established between the United States and Russia', but Martens had also been instructed to start signing contracts without delay. Subject to agreement about price, he therefore wanted to order 100 decapods immediately for delivery to a Russian or Estonian port on the company's financial terms.[15]

But the company responded guardedly. Hinger had ascertained in Washington that trade with Russia was still prohibited and that Baldwin would be denied export licences for these engines. He therefore felt that, since the US authorities were discussing this issue with several European governments and were likely to make an official statement within a few weeks, further talks should be postponed until after the promised announcement.[16]

Unfortunately for both parties the American authorities kept their counsel for several months. Not until 7 July 1920, at the height of the Polish–Soviet war, did the State Department remove its restrictions on trade with Soviet Russia, and even this retreat was carefully guarded with caveats. Firstly, the US government would not officially recognise any Russian authority, would not issue passports for travel to Russia, and would not assist any would-be traders, who would have to operate entirely at their own risk. Secondly, export licences would be refused for goods which could be used for military purposes. Individual licences would still be required for motor cars, associated parts, railway locomotives, rolling-stock and other railway materials, and they would be provided only when exporters presented convincing evidence that the products were destined solely for civilian purposes.[17] Furthermore, railway equipment – the Russians' main priority – would be treated as war material for the 'duration of Bolshevik hostilities', on the instructions of the Secretary of State himself.[18]

The State Department's announcement was interpreted by the British establishment, for instance, as an essentially political move and a signal to prepare for future trade.[19] But the Russians treated it as a severe setback, at least as far as railway supplies were concerned, and they saw no option but to concentrate on the third, sometimes quite dubious channel of communication with America which they had been cultivating assiduously since the previous winter: various American and European commercial agents and intermediaries.

As early as 11 February 1920 it was reported that Krasin had asked the Mayor of Riga to order 600 locomotives as well as rails, tools and machinery from the United States, and that up to 5,000 locomotives would be ordered eventually.[20] Meanwhile in Tallinn Gukovskii began talks with the Estonian representatives of several American companies, including the agents of Baldwin and the American Steel Car Company, and W. H. Coombes, who acted for the Pressed Steel Car Company. Gukovskii also attempted to enlist the Estonian government as an intermediary.[21] Little or nothing emerged from the Latvian mayor's efforts, but Gukovskii's work yielded some curious results. His most bizarre achievement was a draft contract to obtain all 5,000 planned locomotives from a group represented by a certain Captain Windrower.

It appears that a final contract was virtually ready by late April when an NKPS official named Anchits arrived to discuss the technical details.[22] But the deal was delayed, perhaps because of tension between Gukovskii and his superiors about whether the final negotiations should be held in Tallinn or Moscow. Doubtless, too, Krasin and other colleagues objected to placing all Russia's eggs in this one basket, especially if the price seemed high or the terms onerous.

Gukovskii was also responsible for a draft contract for the supply of 113 locomotives through Estonia, these undoubtedly being the same War Department decapods for which Martens was bidding. Krasin did specify one significant condition in this case: the gold would have to go to a neutral country such as Sweden or Denmark because he believed that Estonia would invent some pretext to hold both the gold and the locomotives. Otherwise Krasin considered this contract acceptable, and he suggested that as long as the Estonians did not withdraw, Lomonosov could be sent to Tallinn to sign it.[23]

In the event Krasin himself took charge of the negotiations about the final contract and concluded a deal worth nearly US$6 million with the Revalis Company, a trading firm recently founded by the Estonian government with offices in Tallinn and New York. Signed in Copenhagen on 27 April 1920 with the head of Revalis, a Russian-born former operatic impresario named Maks Rabinov, this contract was possibly Krasin's first major purchasing agreement after his arrival in Western Europe.[24] Revalis was to buy the US War Department's 113 decapods, arrange and fund their return to original ex-works condition, and deliver them to Tallinn or another Baltic port. The Tsentrosoiuz would pay for the loading operations at the American port and for onward shipment, and would appoint its own representatives to check the condition of the engines and supervise tests with a full-length train over a distance of at least 53 km. The price was $52,000 per engine at the American port, exclusive of loading and shipment, making a total of $5,876,000 for all 113 engines, and the operation was to be completed within 4 to 6 months.

Unsurprisingly, the Soviet government's precarious international position ensured relatively demanding terms of payment. The sum of $235,040 (4 per cent of the total) was due when the agreement was signed, and 30 days later a major British or Scandinavian bank was to confirm a Tsentrosoiuz deposit of $293,000 as a guarantee for future payments; then, as each engine was loaded on the ship, the Tsentrosoiuz would pay its full price of $52,000, with the deposit of $235,040 being put towards the final 12 engines. But at least the agreement did specify fines for late delivery, up to a maximum of $5,200 per engine, and all monies would be returned to the Tsentrosoiuz if the US government blocked the export of the engines.

Krasin thus unwittingly undermined Martens's rather lower bid for the same engines. But by mid-May Krasin could at least take heart that the implementation of his contract was proceeding smoothly. On 15 May the Eesti Pank (Bank of Estonia) provided the requisite guarantee and on 17 May Revalis acknowledged receipt of the 4 per cent deposit. A few days later Rabinov reported that the US government had authorised the engines' departure for Tallinn subject to an advance payment of $600,000, that a US Navy minesweeper would collect the gold and that 65 engines had already been prepared.[25]

However, although Krasin met this new demand for $600,000, Rabinov failed to complete the final arrangements in Washington. Briefly, Revalis agreed a contract with the New York legal firm of Cuthell, White, Bayles and Appel, which in turn signed a contract with the War Department, thereby sealing the fate of Martens's bid. But when arrangements were made for collecting and shipping the gold on a steamer operated by the US Shipping Board, the State Department's Russian Division discovered the project and voiced its objection to the Shipping Board and the Secretary for War. The latter, though keen to dispose of the locomotives, humoured the State Department by inserting a clause in the contract prohibiting any subsequent transfer of the locomotives to Soviet Russia until such time as authorised by the State Department, and treated the matter as shelved. Through an embarrassing misunderstanding, however, the Shipping Board's steamship *Wheeling Mold* still collected approximately $325,000 in Russian gold consigned to the War Department's Director of Sales, leaving Tallinn on 21 August. Hurried consultations led to the gold being reconsigned, probably to Revalis, in whose care it remained until repaid to Krasin in 1921 after the deal's protracted death throes.[26]

Evidently several US–Soviet railway contracts did come to fruition in 1920–1. For example, one involved the little-known Glover Locomotive Works. But none concerned locomotives and all were minor, with nothing on the scale that was achieved in Western Europe.[27]

Success in Sweden

It was in a European country that Krasin recorded his first enduring breakthrough. Logically, his main hopes lay with Britain and

Germany, and he quickly sought introductions to leading companies through several former business colleagues and acquaintances. Yet it was Sweden, with a small engineering sector, that yielded his first major success.[28]

The omens had been poor. In contrast to the adventurous sponsors of the *Eskilstuna III* during 1919, the Swedish government had generally deferred to Allied policy, albeit without participating officially in the blockade. Indeed, in March 1920 the Swedish Foreign Minister, Baron Erik Palmstierna, personally assured the British ambassador, Colville Adrian de Rune Barclay, of his anxiety to be guided by the British government's attitude towards trade with Soviet Russia. And, like Britain, Palmstierna denied Litvinov an entry visa for trade negotiations, prompting Chicherin to retaliate with a boycott of Swedish merchants in Tallinn.[29]

Yet when the Tsentrosoiuz delegation paused in Sweden for a few days in early April en route to Copenhagen and London, Krasin obtained an unofficial audience with Palmstierna. The latter insisted upon merely an informal exchange of views pending the outcome of Krasin's meetings in London, and he almost certainly told Krasin explicitly that the resumption of Swedish–Soviet trade required the Entente's approval. But Krasin was encouraged, persuaded by this veiled expression of Swedish interest and by his first business discussions – principally with a consortium of thirteen companies – that, as he reported to Lenin, Sweden was 'literally choking for want of an opportunity to sell its wares'.[30]

In one important respect diplomatic circumstances were working in Krasin's favour. The Supreme Economic Council had intended, but failed, to inform the neutral countries officially about the lifting of the blockade, and this sin of omission naturally made Swedish policy-makers and businessmen fearful of Allied scheming to steal a march on potential competitors.[31] In short, like Germany, the Swedes found themselves looking both East and West, struggling to weigh their interests. That said, the Swedish government's expectations concerning trade were evidently modest. In early March, an internal report by a Foreign Ministry official warned that Swedish industry could not hope to compete with the USA in meeting Russia's tremendous need for railway equipment, though it might be able to sell small items such as spare parts or even send skilled labour.[32] On 20 March, at a special conference attended by Foreign Ministry officials, the Minister of Finances and representatives of major companies, Palmstierna preached caution and predicted that the volume of trade with Soviet Russia would probably be very small.[33]

Yet Palmstierna was certainly keen to prepare for the future in close cooperation with local industrial interests. The conference of 20 March was an important beginning, with much thought given to establishing a special central organisation to coordinate Swedish–Soviet trade. Similarly, although Palmstierna and the Swedish Prime Minister, Hjalmar Branting, baulked at meeting Krasin officially, they did see him unofficially and later sent a member of their Customs and Treaties Committee, Emil Hamrin, to Copenhagen to liaise with him on Sweden's behalf, much as the British government despatched a senior official of the Ministry of Food, E. F. Wise, to Scandinavia at this time for preliminary meetings with the Soviet delegation.[34]

The delegation's brief sojourn in Sweden was described in a Swedish Foreign Ministry report of 7 April.[35] Krasin had visited the Ministry twice on 1 April, and the Russians had conferred with many industrial interests, offering gold for transport equipment. No contracts had been signed, but several were expected. Negotiations were to continue in Copenhagen, whither most of the Russians had proceeded, but Krasin and several of his technical experts expected to visit Sweden frequently, and Krasin wanted to station one or two representatives permanently in Stockholm with full powers to conclude contracts. Equally, he hoped to see Swedish representatives similarly installed in Petrograd and Moscow. But at the same time, the report continued, Krasin was not authorised to discuss such difficult political issues as Swedish Red Cross personnel missing or detained in Russia, or Swedish claims against the Soviet government.[36]

A detailed Swedish analysis of the delegation's negotiations was dominated by locomotives.[37] One of Krasin's technical advisers, V. P. Ivitskii, had met a group comprising the Motala workshops, the Falu workshops and the Trollhättan-based Nydqvist & Holm AB (Nohab). Ivitskii, formerly a director of Russia's Sormovo locomotive factory, had instructions to obtain as many locomotives in Sweden as possible, and Nohab had agreed to build Swedish-type engines modified for Russia's broad gauge. Specifically, the Swedes could supply 300 engines over three years – 50 in the first, 100 in the second and the remainder in the third – and would submit a formal offer within a fortnight. Suggesting payment in gold, the Russians intimated that whilst Swedish prices would exceed American levels, they could save the cost of maintaining their own quality control staff in Sweden because the work would be done so much better. Ivitskii trusted in any case that the Swedes would offer reasonable terms, especially as a Soviet contract would provide much-needed employment and would be an important advertisement for Swedish industry. Indeed, Krasin and Ivitskii were hoping that the Swedish government would support the project by allowing Russia priority over orders for the Swedish state railways.

Over the next two weeks several despatches from Hamrin supported the new impression that Sweden could secure a locomotive contract. For instance, on 12 April Hamrin surmised that strong Soviet desire for contact with Scandinavia might well produce orders for several hundred engines in Sweden if their price was competitive, even though most Soviet railway needs would be met by the United States. Hamrin added that he had just informed Erland Uggla, the Director of Svenska Järnvägsverkstad AB of Linköping, that the Russians wanted offers.[38] Two days later Hamrin notified the Foreign Ministry that he was holding daily discussions with Ivitskii and his NKPS colleague, B. D. Voskresenskii, and that the Soviets were willing to give 'maximum orders' to Sweden.[39] On 16 April Hamrin said that Uggla was submitting an offer on behalf of three companies – Motala, Falu and Nohab – and, on 21 April, Hamrin confirmed having forwarded Uggla's formal proposal to sell 300 locomotives.[40] In a separate development Hamrin also reported that Bofors, the famous Swedish armaments firm, had sent its own representative to Copenhagen to discuss producing steam locomotives for Russia in conjunction with the Swedish firm Atlas Diesel AB.[41]

These developments, it might seem, represented solid progress for Krasin, especially given the Branting government's refusal to entertain him officially. In the first place, his colleagues were regularly meeting a relatively important Swedish official, who was even trying personally to facilitate contracts with prominent companies. Secondly, Hamrin's involvement potentially implied the possibility of financial agreements with the Svenska Riksbank (Swedish State Bank) and perhaps with well-established private Swedish banks.[42] Yet Krasin was apparently unimpressed. He scorned Uggla's prices and embarked upon an entirely different – and arguably rather less reliable – course.[43]

Unease about such a possibility crept into Hamrin's reports from about mid-April. In a despatch dated 15 April he related rumours that a Swedish engineer from Trollhättan, probably a Nohab representative, was expected in Copenhagen for talks with the Soviet group; this, Hamrin grumbled, would fuel suspicion that Swedes could not be trusted because Uggla was also representing Nohab.[44] Six days later a bemused Hamrin noted that Krasin had had meetings with a certain Gunnar Anderson, who was said to head a group of Swedish exporters.[45] By 24 April Krasin had told Hamrin that he was negotiating with Anderson about a credit arrangement for 100 million Swedish crowns, but would not reveal further details; he merely commented that the contract would be conditional upon Swedish permission for a resident Soviet trade representative in Stockholm – a job for which Krasin wished to appoint a Bulgarian communist, B. S. Stomoniakov.[46]

This Anderson was the businessman of *Eskilstuna III* fame and scarcely the epitome of respectability in the Swedish business community. Born a merchant's son in 1889 in Nohab's home town, Trollhättan, Anderson had become manager of a wool factory very early in his career and had founded his own trading company oriented towards business with Russia in 1914. But according to a confidential testimonial commissioned by Hamrin from the Swedish General Association of Exporters, the wool company had gone bankrupt, and although Anderson had probably reaped a large wartime profit from his trading business he lost money in the collapse of a separate venture which he had helped to found in 1917. Ominously, Anderson was characterised as very enterprising but 'too energetic', and he was regarded with considerable caution in business circles. In short, the commentary wryly concluded, any figures quoted by Anderson should be discounted by 50 per cent.[47]

It is unclear exactly when Anderson and Krasin renewed their acquaintance, or who made the first move, but Hamrin's perplexed reports confirm that they were deep in discussion by 21 April. Their progress was such that on 26 April – one day before the Revalis agreement was signed – Anderson and Krasin initialled two draft contracts. One was between the Tsentrosoiuz and the so-called Swedish Concern, an exporters' consortium of which Anderson was the principal representative, to provide Soviet Russia with goods worth 100 million Swedish crowns on credit against a gold deposit of 25 million crowns. The second agreement, between the Tsentrosoiuz and Anderson, was for Nohab to build 1,000 large freight locomotives. Krasin's chief condition for signing final contracts was that the Swedish government should permit a permanent Soviet trade representative in Stockholm and guarantee that Soviet property imported into Sweden would not be seized in connection with any Swedish state or private claims against the Soviet government.[48]

No public statement was made about these negotiations, but

rumours were soon flying about a massive Swedish–Soviet contract for perhaps 1,000 locomotives, possibly involving Nohab. Hamrin was bewildered, as were Uggla and others. One aspect particularly hard for them to fathom was the alleged involvement of Nohab. Nothing was known, for instance, to Andreas Ljungman, who, as one of Nohab's seven shareholders, sent a puzzled letter to Hamrin on 29 April. The directors of the other locomotive factories were similarly bemused. Hamrin could only conjecture that this was a case of financial interests negotiating a sale without even having contacted Nohab itself.[49]

The enormous size of the rumoured locomotive project caused particular bemusement. Sweden and Nohab were unlikely candidates for what would probably be, by quantity, the largest single order in the history of European locomotive construction. Although the Swedish engineering industry depended heavily on the Russian market between 1890 and 1917, it had exported very few locomotives there; and whilst Nohab was Sweden's largest locomotive-builder it was small in world terms, having outshopped fewer than 1,200 locomotives for all customers since 1865.[50] Erland Uggla was confident that it would take 10 years to build 1,000 engines in Sweden, and he was certain that only his consortium could make an appropriate Swedish bid.[51] And that raised the question of why, if the Russians wanted locomotives quickly and the rumour proved true, they should order so many from Sweden.

In fact Hamrin's guess was accurate. Anderson told the Russians at the outset that he had a purchase 'option' for Nohab shares which was valid until 15 May.[52] However, the Nohab board minutes make no reference to any such arrangement; the only relevant note, dated 31 May, simply records that Nohab had jointly offered with other factories to build 300 engines, that the deadline had not yet passed, that there would probably be new talks with the Russian government and that the various factories had agreed to continue their cooperation.[53] To judge by Ljungman's confusion, Anderson presumably had a private share-purchase arrangement with one or more of the seven shareholders, not the company itself.

Meanwhile Krasin and Litvinov requested Moscow's permission to proceed. Describing the contracts to Chicherin on 27 April, they stressed how they were insisting on permission to open a trade mission in Sweden. They acknowledged that the contracts could collapse under Entente pressure against Sweden, but as they felt that this was 'hardly likely', they requested Chicherin to prepare gold worth 32 million crowns for the initial payments.[54] A week later, on 4 May, they reported the Swedish government's decision to allow a trade mission, and repeated their request for the gold to be readied.[55] And on 8 May, still without a final response from Moscow, they sought NKPS approval of the Swedish contract.[56] But Moscow's eventual verdict, dated 8 May, was unsettling. Krasin and Litvinov were authorised to sign the Swedish contracts but were also warned that the Politburo regarded the locomotive contract mainly as a device to generate interest among the principal European and American locomotive-builders which could deliver much more quickly. Also, gold expenditure was now being restricted because the political conjuncture was insufficiently favourable for the bulk of the gold reserve to be exported, and so final contracts involving gold payments should not be signed without prior authorisation from the Politburo.[57]

Unsurprisingly, given the terms of his mandate, Krasin vigorously objected to this ruling as an unacceptable infringement upon his freedom of action. But the Politburo rebuffed him with a telegram of 11 May, complete with a reminder to be frugal with the gold reserve, and again with a resolution dated 25 May.[58] Indeed, not until early June was this clash more or less resolved, when Krasin was empowered to conclude railway contracts on his own initiative up to a total value of 300 million gold rubles, the sum allocated by Sovnarkom the previous March.[59]

The Krasin–Litvinov telegram of 4 May actually presented matters in a brighter light than perhaps was justified, for the Swedish assent was still merely informal. But after some brinkmanship that lasted almost until the deadline of 15 May Palmstierna did provide formal written assurances. His letter stated that His Majesty's government had decided, following representations from Swedish industrial interests, to permit a Tsentrosoiuz trade delegation in Sweden on a temporary basis on certain conditions: that a similar Swedish group would be allowed into Russia; that Russian delegates would be Tsentrosoiuz members and would not engage in political propaganda of any sort; and that the delegation would have a maximum of fifteen persons. The Swedish government would not confiscate any gold or other property imported by the Tsentrosoiuz into Sweden, provided that Swedish state property in Russia – the embassy and consulate buildings and their contents – was returned to the Swedish government. But these commitments, Palmstierna warned, applied only to the proposed Tsentrosoiuz delegation, not to the Soviet government as such, and so they would not affect Swedish state and private claims registered against the Soviet authorities.[60]

It is interesting to observe that, though Krasin's delegation had by now eclipsed the Europe-based Russian cooperatives and had been described in internal Swedish memoranda as the 'Soviet delegation', Palmstierna would only accept a Tsentrosoiuz delegation. This distinction was presumably intended to mollify the Allies and leave open the question of Swedish claims. Nevertheless it was sufficient for Krasin. He signed the two contracts with Anderson on 15 May, the lawyer William Hellberg acting as witness, and the next day Krasin confirmed his acquiescence to Palmstierna's terms.[61]

The value of the credit agreement with the Swedish Concern remained unchanged at 100 million Swedish crowns.[62] Orders worth 25 million crowns were to be negotiated by mid-June, and the remainder would be placed within 14 months. These goods could be ordered through the Concern from any Swedish factory of Russia's choice, but the Concern's own factories would be given preference. The terms of payment were severe, reflecting Soviet Russia's poor bargaining position. The Tsentrosoiuz was to provide gold worth 25 million crowns as a guarantee and part-payment, which would be deposited in Swedish banks and of which the bulk – 16 million crowns – would go to Nordiska Handelsbanken, a small Göteborg-based bank. Nordiska was to sell this gold on world markets at the best obtainable prices in conjunction with the Swedish State Bank, and the Tsentrosoiuz could oversee these sales. The rest of the sum owed by the Tsentrosoiuz was to be paid in raw materials and other Russian products. Finally, and crucially, the credit contract would become invalid if the Tsentrosoiuz did not order 100 locomotives from any Swedish firm within three weeks.

The locomotive contract was regarded as a supplement to the credit agreement, and was signed by Anderson, not Nohab.[63] The first clause allowed Anderson just two weeks to secure Nohab's consent to build 1,000 freight engines for the Tsentrosoiuz. Succeeding clauses specified that, for instance, all the factory's capacity should be working on the Russian order within six months. The first 100 engines were to be a modified version of the Swedish Class R 0–10–0, for delivery between August 1920 and October 1921; the specification of the remaining 900 was to be agreed separately – a Russian design was almost certainly envisaged – and these would be supplied at 200 per year. The delivery schedule could be altered if the locomotive type was changed.

The financial aspects of the contract were particularly complex, partly because of the tense international situation but also, it would seem, because Krasin wanted to avoid a fixed price in expectation of falling prices. The initial 100 engines were priced at 275,000 crowns each, this figure to be reduced if production costs proved lower than anticipated. The price of the remaining 900 engines was to be determined later and would allow for the company's actual costs, interest on capital and a 10 per cent increment on Nohab's share capital of 6 million crowns; the increment was to be paid to the company's shareholders. The Tsentrosoiuz was to have its own inspectors at the factory to monitor all technical and financial issues, and Nohab was to give them every facility. Also, the Tsentrosoiuz was to advance 7 million crowns, which were to remain at Nohab's disposal for the duration of the contract and then return to the Tsentrosoiuz with interest. Payments were to be made after the delivery of every tenth engine, in cash or, subject to special agreement, in kind.

The most intriguing and probably crucial feature of this contract was the advance payment of 7 million crowns, especially once Krasin and Anderson had signed a special document on 21 May modifying the terms of the original contract. According to this supplementary agreement a sum of 4 million crowns (as opposed to 7 million) was to be advanced to Anderson as a representative of Nohab, whilst a further 3 million crowns would be credited to him personally in the Nordiska bank by 29 May. The latter sum was to serve as security for a Nordiska loan of 3 million crowns to Anderson so that he could acquire a majority shareholding in Nohab nominally worth 3,252,000 crowns; and all Nohab dividends were to be used for the amortisation of, and payment of interest on, Anderson's loan. Once Anderson had paid off the loan, this money would be placed at Nohab's disposal, and upon completion of the contract Nohab would repay the full 7 million crowns to the Tsentrosoiuz with interest.[64]

In other words, Krasin ensured Nohab's participation by helping Anderson to buy control of the company, whilst Anderson, all being well, stood to reap a handsome personal profit, including the guaranteed 10 per cent increment on his shareholding. Until this time Nohab had remained a family firm, with members of the Nydqvist family possessing 3,220 of the 6,000 shares (nearly 2,000 of the 3,222 share votes); the remainder were held by the famous SKF ball-bearing company (2,748 shares and 1,200 share votes) and 4 minor shareholders (in total 32 shares and no more than 32 share votes). But now overall control passed to Anderson. First elected to the Nohab board on 29 June 1920, he became Managing Director on 2 July. He obtained a majority holding of 3,252 shares by buying out the Nydqvist family and the 4 small shareholders, and by mid-December 1920 he had almost total command, owning 5,947 of the 6,000 shares.[65]

Krasin later wrote: 'Without the conclusion of this Swedish contract, we would probably have been months without any opportunity to make more or less major purchases with our gold, and in this respect one must not underestimate the significance of the Swedish contract in our general battle to break the blockade.'[66] These remarks emphasise the broader political and economic significance of the two contracts, but they also leave much unexplained. Why did Krasin order so many locomotives in Sweden, and why through Anderson? After all, delivery was likely to take years, and the Swedish government's assurances could surely have been obtained with a much smaller and cheaper order through Uggla.

According to Lomonosov, Krasin was sceptical about the other locomotive proposals. Certainly Krasin was dismissive about Uggla's price, and Anderson's quote was very competitive given that the Swedish state railways were paying some 400,000 crowns per new freight locomotive.[67] But that had to be weighed against Hamrin's supportive involvement. Perhaps, then, Krasin had some prior commitment to Anderson, possibly agreed the previous year in Moscow. Or he may have felt that full, punctual completion would be more likely with Tsentrosoiuz control over Nohab, which was practicable with Anderson but very improbable with Uggla. Most likely, Krasin wanted to reach a quick spectacular agreement, partly to tempt other foreign companies but perhaps mainly to dazzle sceptical comrades in Moscow: in this respect Anderson was a far more attractive proposition than Uggla, who would have insisted on ten years for delivering this huge quantity.[68]

A Swedish historian, Åhlander, has suggested that Krasin may have planned to transfer the locomotive order to German companies as soon as possible.[69] This idea is certainly plausible, and the Politburo was realistic in treating the contract primarily as a signal of intent for other countries. But the deal involved the Tsentrosoiuz in a major financial commitment to Nohab's future, and it seems unlikely that Krasin would alienate Nohab and Anderson's Concern, not to mention the Swedish government, by effecting such a cancellation. Probably Krasin expected this order to be discharged in Sweden, but with a considerable proportion of the work subcontracted to German and British factories.[70]

What, then, were the Branting government's motives for in effect authorising the two contracts?[71] One possibility is anger at the Supreme Economic Council's silence about the lifting of the naval blockade. In the British Foreign Office's Northern Department, Owen O'Malley minuted that the Swedes did not ask for the British government's views regarding a contract by which Soviet gold would go to Sweden, but – pointedly – they had asked to be kept informed of 'all decisions' taken by the Council concerning trade with Russia.[72] It is conceivable, too, that the Swedish officials were surprised by the turn of events and, at a time of potential unemployment in engineering, were tempted by the size of the locomotive order. And doubtless they did not expect Anderson to cope with his vast undertakings, Palmstierna allowing him to proceed partly so that his problems could provide useful experience for more reputable traders. Indeed, such a course of action was mooted by Hamrin on 24 April.[73]

It is also possible that Krasin and the Swedish government both hoped to conceal details of the affair from the British and French governments. On 15 June Colville Barclay complained to the British Secretary of State for Foreign Affairs, Lord Curzon, that it was 'very difficult' to get reliable information about Russian contracts. With regard to Anderson and Nohab, he continued:

> These transactions would appear to be in the nature of a large private speculation on [Anderson's] part, rather than an agreement between Krassin [sic] and the firms concerned in the delivery of the locomotives. It is said that it is manifestly impossible for Swedish firms to deliver 1,000 locomotives of Swedish manufacture in five years. The Swedish government have not been asked to take any action, and in my despatch No. 418 of May 19th, I had the honour to enclose a communiqué issued by the Minister for Foreign Affairs stating that firms are acting on their own responsibility.[74]

And this note was written, of course, a full month after the two contracts were signed.

If this chapter's analysis is correct, the Nohab contract may be seen as a huge personal gamble on Krasin's part. The main justification for large-scale locomotive imports had been potentially much quicker delivery than domestic industry could achieve. Yet the Nohab contract's five-year schedule was not only considered impossible by Swedish experts like Uggla, but could probably be matched by Soviet factories given even a modest recovery. Krasin had achieved his breakthrough, but at the cost of creating an ill-justified hostage to fortune.

These two Swedish contracts concluded the first main phase of Krasin's foreign activity. But before he could concentrate on trade with Germany, and especially on forging a trade agreement with Britain, he had to ensure that the necessary gold was transported to Tallinn and assign Tsentrosoiuz representatives to Trollhättan. As far as appointments were concerned, he asked a German acquaintance from Siemens-Schückert's Stockholm office, a certain Herr Stol, to monitor costs at the Nohab factory. He also asked the NKPS to send an engineer-inspector to Trollhättan, and proposed that Professor Lomonosov should visit Sweden – however briefly – after about a month to resolve the technical issues arising from the design of the first 100 locomotives and organise the technical inspections.[75] Ironically, this suggestion was one which Krasin would soon regret.

Administrative affairs

Professor Lomonosov had experienced an unnerving few months. Immediately after his speech to the Third Congress of Economic Councils in January he had begun inspecting newly captured railways in south Russia but had caught typhus and was lucky to survive. During a subsequent southern tour in early May he had caused a spectacular crash at Novorossiisk in which one person was killed and three locomotives and several carriages damaged. Shortly afterwards, when Lenin considered appointing him as People's Commissar of Ways of Communication – a job which Lomonosov coveted, even though he was not a party member – there was little support among NKPS and party mandarins who were disgruntled by the professor's sometimes high-handed ways. Finally, when Lomonosov returned from a fruitless visit to Tallinn (to meet at Lenin's behest the Americans with whom Gukovskii had been negotiating), he had been appalled to learn that he was being posted to distant Turkestan.[76]

Initially, Lomonosov was unsure about Krasin's request for him to visit Sweden. Though fearful of being accused of sabotage at Novorossiisk, and apprehensive about moving to Turkestan, Lomonosov still hoped to be appointed as Trotskii's first deputy and eventually as People's Commissar. However, reasoning that a short stay in Europe might allow tempers to cool, he soon warmed to Krasin's idea.[77] The reality, though, would be very different from the brief technical visit envisaged by Krasin. Lomonosov was given very broad powers and his appointment was to have a profound impact on almost all purchasing activity abroad for the NKPS for nearly three years.

Probably the first departure from Krasin's concept came on 8 June when the Politburo gave Lomonosov the right of People's Commissar to resolve 'all matters pertaining to orders for steam locomotives'.[78] This vague wording – a more precise phrase such as 'all technical matters' would have matched Krasin's suggestion – may have resulted from a failure to understand the limited nature of Krasin's proposal. But equally, and perhaps more likely, it may reflect a tactical decision to try to use Lomonosov in the battle to establish diplomatic relations with the West.

Lomonosov records that there were several days of discussions about his proposed official status.[79] The issue was how best to exploit the breach in the foreign front line. Apparently, Lenin and a deputy commissar for foreign trade, A. L. Sheinman, wanted to break the formal distinction between the Tsentrosoiuz and the Soviet government, and openly have only representatives of the Russian Soviet government abroad; thus, Lomonosov should have a government mandate. Chicherin, however, wanted to preserve the distinction and give Lomonosov a Tsentrosoiuz mandate so that, under Krasin's arrangement with the Swedish government, he could use diplomatic couriers and ciphers, and thereby act as 'a disguised chargé-d'affaires in Stockholm'. Eventually a compromise emerged whereby Chicherin's reasoning was accepted, but Lomonosov would also be a plenipotentiary representative of Sovnarkom.[80] In other words, he would have both a government mandate and Tsentrosoiuz documentation.

The extent of Lomonosov's powers also provoked debate. Mindful of the nature of Krasin's original suggestion, a leading Tsentrosoiuz functionary, L. M. Khinchuk, preferred a mandate which limited Lomonosov's powers to steam locomotives. But Chicherin and later Sheinman envisaged Lomonosov enjoying much broader prerogatives as acting chairman of the Tsentrosoiuz delegation in Sweden. Lomonosov himself, recalling his frustrating subordination to Bakhmet'ev in 1917, was evidently keen to have his tasks defined precisely and to retain some degree of independence from Krasin, so much so that he asked Trotskii for written instructions on 11 June.[81] The eventual decision gave him, like Krasin, a full Tsentrosoiuz mandate with power of attorney authorising him to sign important documents.[82] Meanwhile his Sovnarkom mandate would cover all railway contracts abroad. But crucially, this government mandate, which was signed by Lenin, Trotskii and Chicherin on 17 June, was imprecise and failed to distinguish between technical and commercial issues:

> [Lomonosov] is being sent to Sweden on a temporary basis to sort out all matters connected with orders for locomotives, and furthermore comrade Lomonosov is granted the power of People's Commissar – that is, the right to make final decisions about problems on the spot – with regard to all railway orders abroad, including orders for the overhaul of locomotives.[83]

While these decisions sought to preserve flexibility, they would prove disastrous for relations between Krasin and Lomonosov. Their broad scope would already annoy Krasin, and the latter would soon endeavour to reassert his own authority for all non-technical issues. Equally, the ever ambitious Lomonosov had little desire to be, in his view, merely Krasin's technical adviser, and despite promising not to intervene in commercial and financial issues he was soon doing precisely that – a deviation which, to be fair, was partly Lomonosovian wilfulness but by no means entirely so. Krasin was doubtless sufficiently realistic not to expect that technical issues could be resolved in isolation from other concerns. But he did demand total subordination, which ultimately implied a right to override Lomonosov's decisions. Yet, of course, this was anathema to Lomonosov, who could also point to his mandate as People's Commissar.

The potential for trouble was illustrated almost immediately over a technical issue which vitally affected the whole business of ordering new locomotives. Krasin's contract of 15 May specified the first 100 locomotives as a Swedish type modified for Russian use. But an NKPS conference chaired by Trotskii on 9 June agreed that new foreign locomotive types were absolutely unacceptable, not least because they would be 'non-standard' and hence expensive to maintain. Instead, following the NKPS Technical Committee's thinking of the previous autumn, and reflecting concern about differences between European and American production techniques, it decreed that only the Russian Class E should be bought in Europe and the Class Ye decapod in America.[84] Trotskii therefore instructed Lomonosov to cancel Krasin's contract for Swedish-type engines and ensure that Nohab constructed only the Class E 0–10–0.[85]

In Western Europe 100 engines constituted a large class. But for the Russian railways, accustomed to classes numbered in hundreds and sometimes thousands, such quantities were small and, indeed, 'non-standard'. The decisions during the First World War to purchase, for example, eighty second-hand Belgian locomotives were due to the exceptional circumstances; the difference now was that the NKPS was wanting reconstruction and modernisation. An opportunity to standardise existing and new equipment was seen as an important gain of the revolution and an essential ingredient for efficient management. Yet if the NKPS decision of 9 June thus made domestic technical and political sense – and Lomonosov fully concurred – Krasin was livid, fearful for his whole achievement in Sweden. As he thundered in a telegram to Lomonosov on 1 July:

> The cancellation of the order for 100 locomotives is inadmissible. The order was made after exhaustive investigation of the matter by Ivitskii and Voskresenskii, and was signed by me. The locomotives will be delivered relatively quickly, and will doubtless be better than all others in terms of the quality of their work. The Technical Council's verdict cannot change signed contracts, this is tomfoolery, not work. I regard this simply as the odious manner of Russian bureaucrats to refashion orders which have already been placed on the pretext of getting unprecedented designs.[86]

There were dubious assertions here, especially concerning delivery times and quality. But fortunately for all concerned, Lomonosov successfully renegotiated the contract on 28 July so that all 1,000 engines would be the Russian Class E with, ironically, a corresponding extension of the delivery schedule.[87] The immediate fracas was thus resolved relatively painlessly, but it was an ominous portent of future dramas.

In mid-June Lomonosov's impending departure from Moscow provoked a flurry of NKPS activity. When Krasin had left in March, the NKPS had provided a weighty imports plan comprising twenty-two separate shopping lists compiled by its Directorate of Economics and Materials. Once in Europe Ivitskii and Voskresenskii produced a composite list of first priorities which included 2,000 locomotives, no wagons, and reduced amounts of most other items. They then sent their proposal to Moscow for ratification by the NKPS and the VSNKh Council for Foreign Trade. On 5 June a special commission of the NKPS Directorate of Economics and Materials began revising the NKPS plan, and by 18 June it had formulated new lists, which reemphasised all 5,000 locomotives. These lists were handed to Lomonosov, and the NKPS also submitted them for consideration by the VSNKh.[88]

Thus, armed with mandates, the latest NKPS imports programme and Trotskii's promise to provide 2 million Swedish crowns for initial maintenance expenses, Lomonosov left Moscow for Sweden on 18

June. He was accompanied by two engineers – Professor V. N. Fren and the diesel enthusiast A. N. Shelest – and by Shelest's wife, N. P. Shelest, as the small mission's secretary and interpreter.[89] The group did not progress very far, however. They languished in Tallinn for nearly two weeks because Palmstierna refused them visas until Moscow, firstly, had confirmed agreement to admit a Swedish trade representative to Russia, and secondly, had allowed the departure from Russia of Elsa Brändström, a Swedish Red Cross worker whom the Swedes believed had been detained by the Bolshevik authorities in Omsk. The trouble was that whilst the first demand presented no difficulty – Chicherin obliged on 24 June – no trace could be found of Miss Brändström. As late as mid-July Chicherin was still trying to trace her, only to discover – to his considerable irritation – that she had left Russia on about 5 July with official permission from his own commissariat.[90]

It was during the enforced stay in Estonia that, whether exceeding the terms of his mandates or not, Lomonosov participated in his first locomotive negotiations since his new appointment. This involved the resumption of his work in Tallinn a month earlier alongside Gukovskii and the NKPS engineer, Anchits. As before, potentially the most important business concerned American decapods. Exploratory talks with two trading groups produced prices of $63,000 and $68,000 per locomotive, and a contract was drafted for the Estonian Trading Company and American Foreign Trade Corporation to supply 150 engines within three months. But these prices were much higher than the factory prices of 1917 or those agreed in the Revalis contract, and given the US government's continuing opposition Lomonosov and Gukovskii did not proceed to a final contract.[91]

Lomonosov also negotiated with Estonian companies about overhauling Soviet locomotives in Estonia. To judge by a report from the Swedish consulate, the concept probably originated during the Soviet–Estonian peace talks at Tartu in January 1920, and negotiations were definitely under way by May, when Lomonosov himself participated during his brief trip to Tallinn. Now, with the help of Estonian government ministers, it was provisionally agreed that the Estonians would repair 500 Class O freight engines and keep 170 of them – or their agreed value in oil – as payment.[92] Further talks were held that autumn by the new chief trade representative, G. A. Solomon, and it was Solomon who signed a final contract on 5 October 1920 for the repair of 230 (rather than 500) locomotives.[93]

Lomonosov and his group – known within the NKPS as the 'Mission of Collegium Member Lomonosov' (*Missiia TsCh Lomonosova*) – were still stranded in Estonia at the beginning of July. Frustrated, Lomonosov elected to return to Moscow with Krasin when the latter reached Tallinn en route to obtain approval for the British government's conditions for a trade agreement. It was when Krasin and Lomonosov both returned from Moscow to Tallinn in mid-July, after the British had made further trade talks conditional upon a Polish–Soviet cease-fire and the Soviet government had indignantly refused, that the two men's differences over their responsibilities first came to a head. Genuinely worried, Lomonosov was prepared to answer for the technical condition of the engines being purchased only if he had, firstly, the final word concerning the choice of locomotive type and materials, and secondly, Russian engineers as quality inspectors at the factories – a job for which he had employed up to 300 people in the USA. According to Lomonosov, Krasin dismissed the creation of any such large establishment as 'madness' and objected that even if foreign governments gave Russian engineers visas, which was unlikely, the latter would simply take bribes and drink. Furthermore, Krasin maintained that, since he formally still headed the NKPS, he retained ultimate responsibility for the whole operation. Finally, Krasin was determined to continue conducting all commercial negotiations himself.[94]

Deep as their divisions were, a *modus operandi* did nevertheless emerge. This achievement, encapsulated in two special directives of 20 July from Krasin (as NKPS head) to Lomonosov, was possible mainly because Krasin gave ground.[95] Firstly, he conceded Lomonosov's demands concerning technical choices and quality control, on the understanding that this would represent the full extent of Lomonosov's government mandate. Secondly, perhaps realising that he would have to concentrate on Anglo-Soviet relations, he also accepted that one person – Lomonosov – should handle all the technical and commercial aspects of locomotive orders. All this, however, was on condition that Lomonosov kept Krasin fully briefed about all developments, sought his permission for each proposed commercial decision and did not interfere in non-locomotive issues.

That same day Krasin sent explanatory telegrams to Kopp and Martens, who were involved in locomotive negotiations in Germany and the USA respectively. They were told that Lomonosov had been appointed as a Sovnarkom plenipotentiary for technical matters and for concluding, in conjunction with Krasin, all agreements for locomotives and other railway materials, and they were therefore requested to give Lomonosov every assistance.[96]

But there was still considerable mutual distrust between Krasin and the professor. On the day that Krasin signed the two directives, Lomonosov found further fuel for his doubts. Encountering an old pre-war friend, Ludwig Bamberger, who was now an agent for the famous German company Friedrich Krupp AG, Lomonosov learnt that on 24 June Krupp had officially offered to build 1,000 German-type 2–10–0s for Russia and that Krasin had recommended this proposal to the Politburo only to have it rebuffed.[97] Convinced that Krasin had kept this offer secret from him, and having obtained a copy of the document from Bamberger, Lomonosov confronted Krasin on 21 July. In his embarrassment Krasin agreed to send a special telegram to Chicherin, Trotskii and Lezhava (recently appointed a deputy commissar for foreign trade) to ensure that such a 'lack of coordination' would be avoided henceforth:

> It is essential to concentrate orders and negotiations about steam locomotives in one place, that is, with Lomonosov. Otherwise there will be complete confusion: one and the same locomotives are being offered to different Soviet representatives, as a result of which the price is being inflated. I have already given appropriate instructions to Kopp and Martens, but it is essential that you, too, maintain contact with foreign locomotive builders only through Lomonosov, otherwise he will be powerless to do anything. For example, he knew nothing about the fact that you had rejected the Krupp proposal.[98]

Thus, amidst a flurry of sharp words, did a new personality appear on the stage. The next phase of the Russians' activity would establish Lomonosov in a leading role.

4 Approaches to Britain and Germany

If Krasin had a motto when he arrived in London in late May 1920, doubtless it was 'Everything for the Trade Agreement!' But though the Anglo-Soviet negotiations dominated his attention until an agreement was signed in March 1921, Soviet endeavours to agree commercial contracts did continue. Railway business took much of this effort, these ten months seeing not only Lomonosov's appointment, Solomon's Estonian contract and the commencement of work by Nohab, but also discussions with Austrian, Czech, Italian and other firms together with numerous fruitless meetings with trading companies about American decapods. The most important projects were negotiations with British and German engineering companies held by Krasin and Lomonosov respectively, plus the formation of a unique Soviet foreign trade organisation – the Russian Railway Mission Abroad – specifically for managing railway contracts. It is with Krasin's railway discussions in Britain and Lomonosov's first German negotiations that this chapter is concerned.

The British connection

Accounts of Krasin's negotiations with Lloyd George's government have tended to assume that the British were tempted into signing the Anglo-Soviet Trade Agreement by Krasin's promises of large expenditure. Was this really the case, and if so, how? Probably by far the largest prospective contract concerned railway locomotives, and its history casts new light on the origins of the trade agreement.

By May 1920 there was an important element of consensus between Krasin and the British government: both regarded railway equipment as the first priority for possible Soviet purchases, and believed that, other things being equal (which they were not), payment in gold would bring the quickest results.¹ To quote the record of a British Cabinet conference of 28 May:

> it was felt that if our aim was to encourage the actual Russian producer, better headway would be made if we proceeded in the initial stages to exchange British goods for gold in the hands of the Bolshevist government; and thereby stimulating the improvement of transport facilities. It would be impossible for raw materials to be got out of Russia until much greater transport facilities were available than was the case at present. By exchanging railway material (locomotives and wagons) for gold, a start would be made which might result in the Russians being able to export raw materials. It was, however, generally agreed that an operation which went no further than the exchange of railway material for gold would serve no useful purpose.²

Whitehall officials began considering ways to assist the Soviet transport system within days of the naval blockade's demise in January 1920. Direct sales of railway supplies were not contemplated initially, doubtless because of the Supreme Economic Council's terms for trade. Instead, attention focused on the possible sale to the Russian cooperatives based in Europe of wagons and spare parts, stored in Canada and Hong Kong, which had originally been ordered for Russia during the First World War.³ But by April Krasin's delegation had overshadowed these cooperatives, and when the British envoy, E. F. Wise, met Krasin in Scandinavia on 7 April the latter stressed that he was interested mainly in obtaining new locomotives and workshop tools.⁴ This prompted Cabinet discussion about whether the Ministry of Munitions might supply locomotives, perhaps by regauging its own war-surplus engines or building new ones. But the ministry demurred, possibly from political distaste and doubtless partly because its experiment to build locomotives at Woolwich Arsenal under a government job-creation scheme was proving decidedly unhappy.⁵ Thus, if locomotive orders were the main concern, private companies would have to make the running. Indeed, one of Britain's foremost engineering firms, Sir W. G. Armstrong Whitworth and Company, had already entered the fray by 14 May.⁶

Nonetheless, Krasin had difficulty building on this foundation. The proposed trade agreement was not signed for another ten months, this delay occurring largely because of internal disputes on both sides about how quickly they should proceed, if at all.⁷ Within the British government Lloyd George continued to advocate the rapid expansion of trade as the best means to diminish the appeal of Bolshevism within both Russia and the British Empire, whereas others like Lord Curzon and the Secretary of State for War, Winston Churchill, saw no reason to open trade relations. On the Soviet side Krasin remained keen to place orders quickly, as in Scandinavia, whereas Chicherin in particular prioritised political relations and a full Anglo-Soviet peace agreement. As Chicherin warned in a telegram on 12 June:

> Lloyd George apparently wishes that we should give everything, bind ourselves, put down the revolution in the East and release every British subject, all this for the sake of the problematic benefit of the renewal of trade relations, which is not yet a matter for discussion. However necessary locomotives may be, we must not sacrifice everything for the doubtful possibility of perhaps getting a few of them. To show firmness does not imply the renouncing of results. You must in no wise yield to British blackmailing ... By giving in to Curzon's attitude of blackmail we will do ourselves as much harm as we did by our panicky attitude with Palmstierna ... if we do nothing else but make concessions we will not even get locomotives ... You must believe absolutely nothing and show the greatest firmness.[8]

Despite such rebukes the Tsentrosoiuz delegation continued preparations during June and July for railway orders in Britain. Krasin probably played little part at this stage: he spent much of his first month in London negotiating with Lloyd George's government and establishing a company, the All-Russian Cooperative Society Ltd (Arcos Ltd), to manage all Anglo-Soviet trade, then departed for Moscow in early July, and could not return to Britain until August owing to the Anglo-Soviet dispute over the Polish war. In the meantime Voskresenskii and Ivitskii handled liaisons with British railway engineering firms.

Talks were held with several companies, but the Russians soon focused on Armstrong Whitworth. Founded in 1847 at Elswick (near Newcastle-upon-Tyne), Armstrongs had specialised in armaments and shipbuilding and had supplied icebreakers to Russia.[9] It had chosen locomotive-building as its main postwar civilian production, intending to transform its Scotswood works in Newcastle into 'the largest self-contained locomotive building establishment in the world' and produce 300–400 locomotives a year.[10] Shortly after Scotswood outshopped its first engines in late 1919, the company also decided to convert its armour-plate shops at Openshaw (Manchester) for overhauling up to 400 locomotives a year.[11]

In a report to Krasin about railway contracts on 8 August, Ivitskii enthused at length about Armstrongs, whose Newcastle premises he had visited on 1 July.[12] Much impressed by their focus on mass production, Ivitskii even imagined them working for the NKPS with an American firm like Baldwin. He calculated that Armstrongs could probably build up to sixty engines a month, and noted that large ships could be docked nearby: engines could thus be shipped fully assembled and ready for traffic. Moreover, product quality would be high: the company's thoroughly mechanised boiler and mechanical shops had first-class equipment, careful attention was paid to detail, technical standards were demanding, the workforce was apparently well qualified, and there was already evidence of customer satisfaction. Finally, Armstrongs would probably meet deadlines more easily than other companies because its plant was well stocked with materials and was largely self-contained with its own sources of supplies.

As for drawbacks, existing orders meant that the first Russian engines could not appear for approximately a year, initially at a rate of only about twenty-five a month. Though the factory seemed keen for a Russian order, it would not reduce this delay. Nor, seemingly, did Armstrongs appreciate the potential economic advantage of working for Russia on a mass-production basis compared to its current work on relatively small orders for nine different types of locomotive. Finally, the firm's prices would probably be high, apparently to recoup the factory conversion costs.

Ivitskii was dubious about having Armstrongs overhaul Soviet engines, however. The Openshaw works was fully occupied, and was poorly situated for delivery by ship; and while the firm was agreeable to overhauling locomotives in Newcastle, it would probably demand a specific quantity to guarantee covering the costs of factory alterations. Also, it was reluctant to quote a price, preferring to proceed on the basis of actual costs plus overheads plus profit. Yet the NKPS could hardly guarantee any quantity without some indication of the cost. Nevertheless, Ivitskii concluded somewhat lamely, it might be possible to reach some arrangement.

Ivitskii was still concentrating on new engines, yet it was for overhauls that Armstrongs' commercial manager, B. Irving, presented an official proposal on 9 August as draft heads of contract. Furthermore, whereas the Estonians hoped to overhaul up to 500 Soviet engines in total, Armstrongs were considering as many as 300 per annum for a minimum of five years, making the staggering quantity of 1,500, and the company added that the annual amount could be increased if extra measures were taken. Their terms involved a non-fixed price of costs plus 15 per cent, with a deposit of £200,000.[13]

Krasin promptly copied the offer to the NKVT in Moscow (for the attention of the NKPS) and to Professor Lomonosov, who had just arrived in Berlin for talks with German locomotive-builders. To Lomonosov, Krasin wrote on 12 August: 'We suggest that the opportunity of arranging the overhaul of steam locomotives for us by Armstrongs is a matter of great importance in general, and as the first contract in this business in England it has a further special significance, given the reputation and influence which this firm enjoys in England.'[14] Writing to the NKPS, Krasin acknowledged an obvious need for major changes to the proposal and requested the commissariat's opinion about several issues. Above all Krasin asked whether the principle would be acceptable and desirable if the cost did not exceed a specific, as yet undetermined sum. He concluded on a positive note, judging the concept reasonable provided that – and this was the crux of the matter, in his opinion – the locomotives could be shipped to England cheaply.[15]

The responses were unenthusiastic. Lomonosov castigated the 'draft contract' as 'monstrous', and predicted that substantial savings could be made by sending only one type of engine, by having only comprehensive overhauls and by standardising the work against a detailed specification (*kharakteristika*), which would also allow a fixed cost to be predetermined. Perhaps mischievously, perhaps just tactlessly, he also offered to meet company representatives to press the terms which he had already provisionally agreed in analogous discussions with German companies.[16] For its part, the NKPS pointedly observed that a complete factory capable of carrying out 300 heavy overhauls per annum could be built in Russia for the same likely cost. But it did approve the principle, and though it preferred a fixed price, it accepted the company's method of pricing provided that the Russians could monitor all costs.[17]

Despite these cautions, Krasin chose, for reasons unknown, to concentrate on this repair scheme rather than on acquiring new engines. He seems to have become convinced that a deal with Armstrongs could help rescue his stalled negotiations with Lloyd George, and he dwelt at length on railway equipment in a letter to the Prime Minister of 4 October. Krasin stated that British industry could certainly help to meet Russia's need for locomotives, which would expand as the economy recovered, and several British companies were interested in overhauling Soviet locomotives in Britain, whilst the Soviet railways would also need up to £10 million worth of other imported supplies per annum, much of which could be bought from Britain.[18]

As Lomonosov could not visit London quickly, Krasin handled the negotiations with Armstrongs himself, obtaining a revised draft contract on 15 December.[19] The terms were little changed, but Krasin's priority was to conclude a contract. He admitted to Lomonosov's deputy, M. Ia. Lazerson, on 15 December that the lack of a fixed price would create complications. But 'the political significance of concluding such an agreement precisely at the present moment with such a significant factory as Armstrongs is so great, and so important in the sense that it will facilitate the conclusion of a trade agreement with England, that this circumstance unquestionably outweighs the minuses of calculating the price by costs'.[20] In any case, Krasin believed, Armstrongs were unlikely to make further concessions because they were discussing doing similar work for the Serbian government. Provided that Lomonosov concurred, he would simply sign the agreement and inform Moscow *post factum*.[21]

Again Lomonosov was unhappy. He reiterated his preference for a detailed work specification, as agreed with Estonian and German factories, and he compared quotes from these countries at 29 and 30 per cent of the price of a new engine (inclusive of transport) with a minimum of 41 per cent from Armstrongs. That figure could be reduced if the Russians sent just one type of engine and if Armstrongs dropped their assumption that a quarter of the engines would need new boilers. However, given Krasin's political concerns, Lomonosov acquiesced provided that certain technical details were amended.[22]

Ivitskii visited Stockholm with Armstrongs' commercial manager, Irving, and the firm's Works Board Manager, R. B. McCall, together with a company agent named J. R. Glass, for technical meetings with Lomonosov on 8 and 10–11 January 1921. Apparently Krasin told Ivitskii to insist that terms be settled with Armstrongs at all costs. But Lomonosov did at least win a few concessions: only one type of engine would be sent, Armstrongs would use the Nicholas Railway's stringent pre-war overhaul specifications, and only the first 300 engines would be overhauled on a cost basis, the price for the remainder to be fixed by mutual consent. A final contract was to be agreed by 16 February 1921.[23]

According to Lomonosov, both sides signed a special protocol on 11 January; or as Armstrongs' Chairman, Sir Glynn West, told his Finance Committee on 19 January, the Russian representatives signed a 'draft Contract'.[24] Krasin then wrote to Armstrongs specifying two important additional clauses. One declared that the contract would 'become operative only upon the signing of a separate agreement between the Delegation and the Contractors regarding the means of realisation of the gold'; the other stated that:

> the Delegation has the right not to deposit the indemnity sum of £150,000 until such time as the British government will give to the Russian Government the necessary guaranty of immunity of the funds and property of the Russian Soviet Government. The Contractors have no right to raise any claims against the Delegation for not depositing the indemnity sum until this guaranty is obtained.[25]

If these changes were accepted, Krasin continued, 'the contract in question will be signed upon my return to London'.[26]

Was the Armstrong contract a 'payment' for the Anglo-Soviet Trade Agreement, as Krasin insisted to Lomonosov shortly after that long-awaited document was signed in March 1921?[27] The available evidence suggests that the situation was not so clear-cut. The existence of exploratory talks with Armstrongs evidently mattered little in Whitehall's eyes when the Polish crisis deepened in July and August 1920, even though the Russians were already thought to have signed a valuable locomotive contract with a foreign competitor, Nohab. Moreover, Lloyd George replied evasively to Krasin's letter of 4 October, and only in mid-November did the Cabinet eventually produce a draft trade agreement.[28] But the possibility of obtaining Soviet railway orders did influence British policy-making in one important respect: it helped Lloyd George to counter Winston Churchill, Lord Curzon and others who were campaigning for the Soviet delegation's expulsion.

During the summer and autumn of 1920 the British Admiralty secretly intercepted and decoded the Soviet delegation's telegrams, and Curzon and Churchill provided their Cabinet colleagues with translations of selected messages.[29] For Churchill these documents unambiguously demonstrated that delegation members were much more interested in propaganda and subversion than trade. At length, on 26 August, Churchill sent a long protest to Lloyd George, who was holidaying in Switzerland. Demanding the delegates' immediate expulsion for their 'treasonable conspiracy', Churchill saw no reason for Britain even to consider signing a trade agreement:

> Why is it necessary to do more than lift the Blockade and authorise British subjects to trade freely if they choose and if they can? Why have we ... got to undertake the role of being the official bear-leaders to these ruffianly conspirators and revolutionaries? A policy of detachment should surely free us from this odious function. All the time they have been here they have been trying to foment a revolutionary movement and intriguing or bribing on every side. They

have done much to render the labour situation more dangerous, whilst so far as the Tory Party is concerned the harm done to our political and party interests is progressive and continuous. Moreover, there is neither food nor trade to be expected from the Russia which the Bolsheviks control.[30]

Other Cabinet members concurred. As the Lord Privy Seal, A. Bonar Law, wrote on 2 September to the King's private secretary, Lord Stamfordham, he and several colleagues had agreed at a special conference that without doubt the Soviet delegation would have to be 'sent away' and that some of the telegrams should be published as justification. He hoped that the Prime Minister would give his approval within a few days.[31]

However, Lloyd George did not concur. Indeed, he may have reached the conclusion that certain of his Cabinet colleagues were attempting to deceive him about the true extent of the Soviet delegation's trading intentions and activities. The point was that very few of the translated telegram intercepts that were circulated to the Cabinet by Churchill concerned details of trade issues, and the Cabinet's attention was not drawn to, for instance, the numerous telegrams exchanged by Krasin and Lomonosov about proposed locomotive orders for Germany and the United States – documents that clearly undermined the case being made by Churchill and Curzon for the Soviet delegation to be expelled.[32] However, if there was a conspiracy to deceive the Prime Minister, it was exposed on about 23 August, when Lloyd George received a personal letter from the German Foreign Minister, Dr Walter Simons, in which details of Russia's trade negotiations with other countries became apparent.

Simons attempted the well-nigh impossible task of persuading the Prime Minister to allow British banks to help Germany resume trade with Soviet Russia even before Britain herself had reopened relations. Choosing his words with extreme care, Simons explained that he had become convinced of Lloyd George's concern not just with Britain's welfare but for the defence of all Europe against the approaching danger of moral and economic ruin. And Simons agreed that although food shortages in Central Europe might seriously threaten European stability, this problem could be solved 'by regaining the food supplies of Russia'. It was in an attempt 'to show a way in this direction' that he enclosed an *aide-mémoire* for the Prime Minister's attention.[33]

This document stated that the key to resuming Russian grain exports was the rapid reconstruction of Russia's transport system. It argued that here 'Germany can do more than any other country, even more than the United States of America who, with an equal or superior industrial capacity, are lacking in the geographical facilities of the German plants.' On these grounds Simons requested British approval for, and assistance in financing, a contract proposed by Lomonosov for Germany to build 1,000 new engines and possibly a further 2,000 at a future date. As Simons somewhat disingenuously explained, hinting at the Swedish breach of the gold embargo and studiously not mentioning the Treaty of Versailles and German war reparations:

> The question of the Russian guarantees for payment can be settled through neutral banks; but the German government, who are not directly concerned in the affair, would prefer to see these guarantees consolidated by a collaboration of English banks instead of neutral ones. Certainly that could only be done with the consent of the British government; and it is in order to secure this consent that these lines are written.[34]

Finally, Simons suggested that such a locomotive contract would also have other important benefits for Europe. It would contribute to 'securing the inner peace of Germany', where business was slack and unemployment serious, and where Bolshevism was such a great danger that every European nation should come to the rescue. Also, it would enable Germany to help ensure that normal import–export trade with Russia could resume within a year of peace being established.

Lloyd George, however, was not beguiled by these arguments. He briefly acknowledged receipt of the letter and its 'most interesting enclosure' on 24 August, and promised to reply within a few days.[35] He then drafted a firm rejection of the German request. Noting that he could not give a definite response until after consulting his Chancellor of the Exchequer, he identified two fundamental difficulties. Firstly, there was an atmosphere of suspicion about Germany's attitude towards the Treaty of Versailles and reparations, and this 'impedes any transaction of this kind'; in general, gestures of German good faith were needed. Secondly, peace had not yet been made with Russia, and the first step had to be a Polish–Soviet armistice.[36]

In early September Lloyd George sent his Cabinet colleagues a special memorandum on the subject of whether or not to expel the Soviet delegation, and he specifically cited this approach from Germany, even attaching copies of the documents.[37] The Prime Minister acknowledged that there was a good case for expulsion, in that delegates were guilty of 'a flagrant breach of the conditions under which they were permitted to enter England'. But, he insisted, the disadvantages of expulsion were considerable, and on balance it was preferable to resume the trade talks. Firstly, the benefit of monitoring Soviet telegrams would be lost if any intercepts were published. Secondly, Soviet propaganda was not dangerous, it was merely crude and violent and displayed a complete ignorance of facts and British working-class psychology, and the expulsion of the trade delegates would not stop it. Thirdly, other countries, especially Germany, were ready to forge ahead:

> We are in for a period of unemployment and an increase in unemployment is a far more formidable peril than all the lunacies of Lenin. Germany has already received an order for thousands of locomotives. Dr Simons sent me a memorandum which I forwarded to the Chancellor and a copy of which I enclose, which shows the extent to which Germany is prepared to trade. An order has been given in Sweden; another in America; and the President of the Swiss Republic informed me that orders were being placed in Switzerland. Mr Beneš, the Foreign Minister of Czecho-Slovakia, informed me that orders had been given there for agricultural implements. This is apart from the concessions [schemes] which have been offered.[38]

And, revealing perhaps his real reason for rebuffing Simons, the Prime Minister concluded bluntly: 'I strongly urge that trading relations should be prosecuted and that we should not allow trade to pass to other countries when it is so essential to the well-being of our own population.'[39]

Simons's *aide-mémoire* resurfaced at least twice in Cabinet discussion during the next few months. It merited a special report to the Cabinet on 14 September, and Sir Robert Horne and Lloyd George both mentioned it in the crucial Cabinet debate of 17–18 November, when it was at last decided to resume talks with Krasin. Horne had declared on 2 September that 'the damage which was being done by the Russian agitators was of so grave a nature that it was most important to get them out of the country immediately', but he now strongly favoured reopening trade, not least because this trade would otherwise go to Germany, the USA and elsewhere. Lloyd George recalled agreeing with the Chancellor of the Exchequer in the summer that Britain could not help to provide work in Germany, but he complained that now 'the gold is passing to Sweden and there [the Russians] are giving orders. Germany, Sweden and the USA will be getting orders and we shall be denounced for refusing to sanction the trade agreement.'[40]

If the prospect of railway contracts, or rather fear of foreign competition, thus helped Lloyd George to win support for resuming negotiations with Krasin in the autumn of 1920, there is no evidence yet to suggest that the British government treated the Armstrong contract as 'payment' for the trade agreement. Nor is there anything to support Krasin's assertion in September 1921 (and on subsequent occasions) that the British were probably bustled into signing the trade agreement by the news of a Russian order for 600 locomotives from Germany – a claim which, as chapter 6 will show, was really to do with domestic Soviet politics.[41] That said, however, any British worries about German competition were well founded: in Germany, Lomonosov found a much warmer welcome than did Krasin in Britain.

The road to Berlin

The first half of 1920 has been seen as a time of gradual thaw in Soviet–German relations, with hopes for further improvement seemingly strengthened in July through a change of government in Berlin and Simons's appointment as Foreign Minister. But, it has been believed, German second thoughts were prompted by Russia's defeat in Poland at the Vistula in mid-August and by Soviet refusals to make further recompense for the murder of the German Ambassador, Wilhelm von Mirbach, in Moscow in 1918. According, for example, to Debo:

> The retreat from Poland quickly destroyed the economic, as well as the political, foundations of the agreement [proposed agreement about Soviet–German relations]. When it appeared as if the Polish barrier to Soviet–German trade would be smashed Moscow had rushed a commission to Berlin to buy a thousand locomotives. An agreement was quickly reached and still further purchases were made to relieve other shortages, but rapidly advancing Polish troops quickly severed the only railways by which these commodities could be sent to Russia.[42]

Thus, 'Moscow had little to show for its almost ceaseless effort to improve relations with Germany' by late 1920. The agreement on prisoners of war, Russia's low-level representation in Germany, and the 'trickle of trade' were overshadowed by mutual suspicion and contradictory aspirations.[43]

It is difficult to disagree with this view concerning political relations. But the history of the railway negotiations reveals that the trade question was much more complicated – and Soviet expenditure commitments in Germany much greater – than has been thought. Not least, the German government was actively supportive from August onwards.

The end of the Allied naval blockade stimulated German state and private interest in trade with Russia. True, the German authorities described trade operations as a purely private matter and deferred to the Entente's political position concerning Russia, not least because the Allies could confiscate Soviet gold and other goods supplied as payment for German exports. But the government did take important steps to encourage trade. For instance, it gave Kopp semi-official recognition as a Soviet trade representative on 20 February. As the British Ambassador to Berlin, Lord Kilmarnock, reported apprehensively to London, the German Foreign Minister had virtually admitted in private conversation that German–Soviet negotiations about prisoners of war would be extended to commercial matters.[44]

The Soviet side, prioritising locomotive contracts, approached the German Verband of locomotive-builders through several intermediaries. One was the Chairman of the Allgemeine Deutsche Gewerkschaftsbunde (German General Federation of Trades Unions), Karl Legien, who was also associated with the Deutsche Ökonomie GmbH, where Olof Aschberg was a director. Kopp made the initial contact in about March, Krasin wrote formally on 6 May, and on 15 May Kopp gave Legien a warrant authorising Deutsche Ökonomie to order 1,000 freight locomotives from German factories.[45]

Krasin also approached an old Swedish acquaintance, the prominent publisher Tor Bonnier. Bonnier contacted the Krupp firm's Stockholm representative, Harald Berg, who was also a director of the Stockholm-based Victor Berg company, and Krupp headquarters in Essen was informed by 12 April.[46] One of Krupp's principal directors, Otto Hagemann, represented the company in a rapidly assembled delegation, and he was introduced to Krasin in Copenhagen on 23 April by an associate of Bonnier, a certain Herr Lion. Krasin provided written confirmation that the Tsentrosoiuz wanted to purchase 2,200 engines of three different types, together with large quantities of spare parts such as springs, tyres, couplings and buffers, and Hagemann promised to brief the Verband.[47]

The Verband was additionally contacted by various Western companies on their own initiative. For instance, the Copenhagen-based

United Railway Equipment Company and the Metallgesellschaft of Frankfurt jointly proposed forming a special company to handle Russo-German trade, whilst Briske & Prohl, the Berlin firm which had helped Lomonosov in 1919, wanted to manage railway orders on the grounds that it was already working closely with Krasin.[48] Generally the Verband dismissed these advances, but it vacillated over whether to deal with Bonnier and Krasin, or Legien and Deutsche Ökonomie, until, on 8 May, Krasin himself suggested placing his order through Krupp.[49]

As for making an offer, the Verband proceeded cautiously, assessing the risk as high. On 15 May it decided to continue negotiations and convene a special policy-making commission. Only then was an offer drafted for a maximum of 1,200 2-10-0 freight engines at 227,000 gold rubles (5 million marks) each. A 50 per cent deposit on the whole contract was to be followed by a further 25 per cent for each locomotive against its boiler tests, and the balance upon the engine's delivery for shipping.[50]

Once Krasin had signed the Nohab contract, and the Verband's commission was informed about it on 25 May, the Soviet delegation itself began talking about ordering only 1,000 rather than 2,200 engines. A modified German-type 2-10-0 was specified, almost certainly to ensure quick delivery. The Verband responded on 24 June with an offer to supply 1,000 German Class G-12 engines for 3.3 million marks each at the German-Polish frontier or the ports of Lübeck or Stettin. The payment schedule was again 50:25:25 with an international bank guarantee, and delivery was to be completed within twelve months.[51]

Krasin, evidently feeling that agreement was near, now supplied Bonnier with a large emolument. Berg informed Essen on 2 July that Krasin was sending a representative to Stockholm to close the deal with Bonnier and Krupp, notwithstanding the Verband's readiness to bypass intermediaries. A week later, on 9 July, Bonnier and Lion signed a provisional agreement with Krupp whereby Bonnier would obtain the Soviet contract at a commission of 1.5 per cent, or less if the factories had to lower their price again.[52]

However, the Politburo rejected the Verband's proposal as too expensive and, ironically, because (as requested) it involved German-type engines.[53] Kopp, too, was unhappy. Shunned by the Verband and, like Lomonosov, not consulted by Krasin, he had only heard rumours about the offer, and he sent a worried letter to Krasin on 11 July. Kopp reckoned that the Verband was refusing to keep him informed in the belief that he could understand their calculations, could influence their prices and was cooperating with the trades unions. To avoid confusion, it was essential for all negotiations about German engines to be conducted exclusively in Germany, by either Kopp himself or 'someone else'. Further, he said, a price of 1.8 million marks for each locomotive was realistic, inclusive of 15 per cent profit for the builders; and it was important to cooperate with the trades unions, both as a matter of principle and to avoid strikes.[54]

Kopp also explained that in order to avoid being 'caballed' by the Verband he had contacted a German organisation called the Reichsbetrieb. This was apparently a state-owned operation which had vast railway workshops, 70,000 workers and empty order books. Hitherto it had merely repaired locomotives, and so Kopp planned to associate it with companies outside the locomotive Verband or potential defectors from it – Borsig, Henschel and Hartmann were likely candidates – and thereby generate competition to force down what he regarded as the Verband's high prices.[55]

It was at this juncture that Lomonosov became involved. Possibly, without yet having been briefed, he was the Soviet representative travelling to Stockholm whom Berg had mentioned in his report to Essen on 2 July. Be that as it may, Lomonosov acquainted himself with the Verband's June offer courtesy of Bamberger on 21 July and, having embarrassed Krasin over it (as mentioned in chapter 3), was ready for action. Significantly, he viewed negotiations with the Verband as the quickest and best course, regarding the Reichsbetrieb and Deutsche Ökonomie primarily as means to pressure the Verband.

On 22 July the Lomonosov mission sailed with Krasin from Tallinn to Stockholm for talks with Nohab and to confront the Verband.[56] The first main German–Soviet conference, attended on 24 July by Krasin, Lomonosov, Bonnier, Hagemann, Berg, Bamberger and two other Germans, identified four principal issues. One was finance: Krasin offered gold, but it was unclear how to avoid antagonising the Entente. Next was the price: Moscow had rejected 3.3 million marks for each locomotive, Alco had quoted less than half this sum – approximately $46,000 – for comparable Class Ye decapods, and the internal German price was 'known' to the Russians to be under 2 million marks. The third problem was quality control: Hagemann refused to consider admitting Russian engineer-inspectors to the factories. The final question was the locomotive type: Lomonosov provided a set of Class E drawings, and the Germans promised to reply on 28 July about whether they would supply the Russian Class E as opposed to a German type.[57]

Krasin then departed for London, leaving Lomonosov in charge. The result of intense haggling from 29 to 31 July was a draft protocol which would commit the Soviet government to order 400 Class E engines subject to agreement about price and finance, with a 30-day option to decide on a total of 1,000 or 2,000 engines. Delivery was scheduled for nine, twelve or nineteen months depending on the quantity, and a German firm such as Briske & Prohl would handle quality inspection under Russian supervision. The first 1,000 engines would each cost a maximum of 2.4 million marks, with payment in instalments: 25 per cent of the total cost against the contract, 25 per cent of the cost of each batch of engines upon delivery of the materials for them, 25 per cent of each engine's price against its boiler tests, 20 per cent upon the preliminary acceptance of each engine, and 5 per cent after each engine's final acceptance test in Russia. Finally, the Verband was to start preliminary work immediately, and the Soviet government would reimburse expenses up to 100,000 marks in total if the contract was not confirmed.[58]

This draft document left only the final price and finance unresolved; but it represented a major change of Soviet policy in allowing a maximum price which was 400,000 marks above the original target. The trouble was that, having requested but not received Krasin's approval by the evening of 31 July, Lomonosov signed the document on his own initiative. And Krasin's response, when it did arrive shortly afterwards, was a firm insistence that the price could be driven below 2 million marks. The overall conjuncture was becoming more favourable, he told Lomonosov, and it was therefore important not to rush into obligations, the more so because the main problem of finance would depend on the general situation.[59]

Lomonosov's unilateral ratification of the protocol must have alarmed Krasin. Surprisingly, though, Krasin avoided recriminations: on 3 August he merely reiterated his objections of 31 July and added that 'there are no special political considerations in this matter at the moment' – a sign, incidentally, that he was not expecting to frighten the British government with this affair.[60] But Krasin must have been all the more disturbed by the professor's response to these objections: an hysterical telegram offering his resignation and requesting a transfer to the Red Army.[61]

At this point a two-week lull ensued in the German negotiations, allowing Lomonosov to concentrate on three other important issues in

Sweden. Firstly, he met the Prime Minister, Branting, and had two encounters with Palmstierna. As Chicherin had hoped, the professor was permitted to use diplomatic couriers and ciphers as temporary head of the Tsentrosoiuz mission in Sweden. But Palmstierna was dismayed that the Swedish embassy and general consulate buildings in Russia remained in Soviet control, and he was also annoyed that the Russians had not delivered the correct amount of gold to Sweden that was required by the contracts already signed. Lomonosov promised to convey the first complaint to Moscow, observed that the gold was awaiting collection in Tallinn, agreed to sign himself 'Représentant du Tsentrosojuz Russe', and, on 12 August, found himself formally accredited as acting head of the Tsentrosoiuz mission in Sweden.[62]

The second issue was Nohab. Lomonosov was favourably impressed by the Trollhättan factory, except for its annual capacity of only forty boilers. However, Gunnar Anderson proposed to order the shortfall in Germany, an expedient which Krasin had in any case probably expected.[63] Lomonosov also considered the possibility of ordering Nohab water turbines. This idea had been broached by Anderson on 26 July, partly because Nohab was contractually obliged to devote all its attention to Russian orders and would otherwise have to close or mothball its turbine shops. Lomonosov suggested to Krasin that Nohab might supply turbines for the River Volkhov dam-construction project (Volkhovstroi) and the similar Svir project. These contracts could be funded with the Swedish Concern's credit, and by reducing Nohab's overheads they would also lower the cost of the locomotives.[64]

Finally, Lomonosov investigated other possible contracts. In conjunction with Professor E. F. Ion, a technical adviser whom Krasin had appointed to manage the Tsentrosoiuz's dealings with the Swedish Concern, he clarified what the Concern could supply for the NKPS and sent approximately 100 inquiries about locomotive tyres and boiler tubes to various Swedish, British and German companies. Also, he met six different groups about American-built Class Ye decapods, identifying two possible contenders: Aschberg's Deutsche Ökonomie, which was reportedly backed by Baldwin and the Guaranty Trust Company, and a Tallinn-based import–export company headed by a businessman named Gordin. Eventually Aschberg agreed to supply 450 decapods at $59,000 each at a US port, whereas Gordin offered 2,000 engines at $46,000 in the USA or approximately $52,000 in full working order at the Soviet–Estonian border. Neither Lomonosov nor Krasin was impressed, and both offers were rejected by 14 August.[65]

By this time the German locomotive producers were ready to resume the negotiations. Lomonosov decided to travel to Germany, desiring to inspect the German factories, and this change of location enabled the German government to become deeply involved.[66]

The German questions

It required a further two months to resolve the issues of price and finance. The former proved much less problematic despite an inauspicious start. On 16 August Lomonosov met the Verband's commission for the first time since 31 July and demanded a significant reduction from 2.4 million marks per engine. When the Verband declined to drop the price below 2.35 million marks, Lomonosov adjourned the discussion until 19 August. This time Krasin telegraphed his approval, repeating his instruction not to hurry because the financial problem remained and German prices were gradually falling.[67]

Adolf Maltzan, head of the Russian desk in the German Foreign Ministry's Fourth Department, attended the meeting on 16 August and talked with Lomonosov at length; he provided an interesting pen portrait of the professor in action:

> The heavy, thickset figure of Lomonosov and his calm easy-going manner is in no way reminiscent of the hitherto more or less chauvinistic and hysterical appearances of the Soviet representatives known here or passing through. He represented far more the nuances of the good, bourgeois, experienced and realistic merchant of the old Russia. His general impression is in short bourgeois, positive and cunning.[68]

Identifying strong antipathy between Lomonosov and Kopp over the price question, Maltzan reported that after Lomonosov had agreed to 2.4 million marks, German trades union representatives had offered to secure a much lower figure. This move evidently stemmed from 'machinations' by Kopp, who was seeking influence over the German labour movement and saw Lomonosov as a rival. Lomonosov was embarrassed: as a Soviet representative he could not ignore the gesture, but he justified his avoidance of the unions by citing instructions from Lenin not to interfere in German internal affairs. However, Maltzan continued, Lomonosov thought that an authoritative statement by the Verband and an expert German source like the Ministry of Trade and Industry about the offer price would reassure his government.[69]

Pursuing this idea, Maltzan arranged an expert commission to scrutinise the Verband's price for Lomonosov.[70] Also, within hours he conducted Lomonosov to an unofficial meeting with his superior, Gustav Behrendt, head of the Fourth Department, where it transpired that the ministry's State Secretary for political affairs, Edgar K. A. Haniel von Haimhausen, had approved the idea of checking the price. Haniel received Lomonosov the next day, 17 August, and at a meeting with Privy Counsellor Hermann Bücher on 18 August Lomonosov was authorised to use diplomatic ciphers.[71]

The price commission convened on 17 August. It comprised the engineer, Professor Fren, for the Soviet side, Bücher for the Foreign Ministry and, in the chair, an iron and steel specialist from the Ministry of Trade and Industry, Dr Könemann – an appointment which might have raised eyebrows but which Lomonosov obviously encouraged. First the commission derived a base cost of 1,785,000 marks for the Class E from the similar but slightly lighter German Class G-10. Next, it allowed for various extra costs, like the E's additional features, the different materials, the higher prices which German firms had to pay to subcontractors in export contracts, and the cost of transport. The result, including a modest contingency against cost rises, was 2,631,000 marks, leading the commission to describe the offer price as 'completely appropriate'.[72]

Hagemann later described Könemann's verdict as favourable for the Verband.[73] Lomonosov was dubious, telling journalists that whilst the German government was most courteous, his own government could not afford to squander its money and might have to look to North America instead.[74] Privately he tried to convince Krasin of the Germans' good faith by noting that the price of $46,037 for an American decapod at the factory ready for shipment equated to 2.35 million marks, which was very close to the Verband's offer.[75] In short, it would seem that Lomonosov tried to use the special price-review as a means to undermine Kopp's allegations of gross overpricing by the Verband, and that either he was surprised by the resulting figure of over 2.6 million marks or he was perhaps anticipating such a high figure, compared to which a price of 2.3 or 2.4 million marks would appear very reasonable.

The problem was solved on 20 August, basically by deleting several expensive elements from the contract price. The protocol of 31 July was amended so that the Soviet government would order a minimum of 500 engines for delivery within 10 months, subject to the same deadline of 30 August for signing the final contract. There was to be a minimum, not maximum, price of 2.25 million marks at the factory, which would exclude packing and transport, and the factories were to deliver the engines to the German border at their own expense and risk. Finally, because the German mark was falling, each factory could choose to be paid in foreign currency.[76]

This accord was quickly approved by Kopp, Krasin and Moscow.[77] Thus, once Legien and Aschberg had renounced their claim to negotiating rights after having several heated meetings with Lomonosov, the only major problem still to be resolved was the means of finance.[78] Both sides had already begun to look for a way forward. The Verband, for instance, had sought advice from Bücher at the German Foreign Ministry after signing the protocol of 31 July. The Germans recognised that the proposed deal was so large as to need a consortium of prominent banks capable of guaranteeing the full sum unconditionally and that this consortium would need to cooperate with banks in neutral countries, especially Sweden. Bücher himself contacted the Deutsche Bank and Disconto-Gesellschaft, whilst Hagemann and Prohl briefed Mendelssohn & Co. Significantly, the hitherto anti-Russian German banks mostly began to show 'striking interest', only Mendelssohn holding back somewhat.[79]

On the Soviet side, Lomonosov asked Krasin on 10 August whether he should begin financial discussions, pointing out that he would need the secondment of Krasin's financial adviser, S. K. Bel'gard, if authorised to proceed.[80] But Krasin merely instructed Lomonosov to negotiate in conjunction with Kopp, using the latter's connections, and reminded him not to sign any agreements without consent.[81] Somewhat irritated, Lomonosov specifically requested a financial adviser on 18 August, at the same time enquiring whether he should prioritise the major banks and whether Mendelssohn could participate at a commission of some 2 or 3 per cent.[82] Krasin confirmed his preference for the bigger banks, but wanted the very high fee reduced and an earlier dispute with Mendelssohn dating from 1918 resolved. As for a financial assistant, Krasin recommended M. Ia. Lazerson, for whom the People's Commissar of Finances, N. N. Krestinskii, could vouch.[83]

Kopp, however, was pessimistic about the major German banks, as became clear during a 'fairly stormy' meeting between himself, Lomonosov and Lazerson on 23 August.[84] He expected that, as had happened in Sweden, it would be necessary to involve smaller banks which, for a price, would risk handling Soviet gold. To that end he had already contacted Otto Markevich, whose bank had a capital of some 200 million marks and was an important force in communal loans, and these talks had generated proposals for a credit agreement and gold sales.[85] Eventually, though, Kopp and Lomonosov agreed to continue their respective bank negotiations separately. As they informed Krasin, they would have no further use for 'speculators' like Markevich if the larger banks made an acceptable offer.[86]

With Lazerson appointed as his financial adviser and commercial deputy by 21 August, Lomonosov informed the Germans of his readiness to begin financial discussions. The Foreign Ministry then tried two initiatives, both of which involved the British.[87] One was its unsuccessful *aide-mémoire* of 22 August to Lloyd George. The other was a two-hour conference at Mendelssohn's headquarters on 23 August between Lomonosov, Lazerson, the Deutsche Bank, Mendelssohn and Disconto. This established that the chief obstacle to getting the bank guarantees was the fear of Allied intervention. Certain Swedish and Dutch banks were eager to participate as intermediaries, but the meeting unanimously agreed that, with the Foreign Ministry's blessing, the Germans should approach British banks first, and so the contract deadline was deferred to 3 September.[88] However, this brief postponement proved insufficient because the German Foreign Ministry prevented Mendelssohn from contacting London banks until 2 September.[89] Probably the ministry was waiting for Lloyd George's reply to Simons. Whatever the cause, no further progress could be expected for some days, and this explained the further extension of the deadline to 30 September.

The idea of involving British banks was greeted with scepticism by both Krasin and Litvinov, who was now based in Scandinavia whilst retaining his position as Deputy People's Commissar of Foreign Affairs.[90] But Lomonosov was more confident, and he even conceived a further scheme to tempt them. Bearing in mind that the Allis Chalmers Company, the well-known Toronto-based agricultural manufacturing concern, had given Krasin a detailed proposal for 500 freight engines within 21 months on 20 August, and that Krasin regarded a Canadian order as very desirable reinsurance (*perestrakhovka*) to avoid concentrating Soviet orders in one country, Lomonosov wondered whether British financial support might be obtained by promising a locomotive order for Canada. But again Krasin was doubtful, and nothing was done. In fact, by December 1920 Krasin was convinced that Canadian orders might be useful precisely because the Canadians wanted to trade without waiting for the British Trade Agreement, and because the British regarded them as rivals like the United States. Unfortunately for the Canadians, however, this Russian interest did not crystallise into a locomotive order.[91]

The response of the British banks eventually arrived on about 18 September.[92] It was negative, and consequently the leading German banks would not risk handling Soviet gold. However, as both Lomonosov and the Germans were perfectly aware, the transaction could still be arranged by banks in neutral countries. Lomonosov began recasting the project along these lines on 17 September, and the stage was soon set for the final and most dramatic phase of these negotiations.

The idea was to persuade Nohab to subcontract a large part of its order to the German Verband in exchange for some financial compensation. This would greatly speed up the five-year Swedish contract without precluding further orders for Germany, which could also be placed through an intermediary if necessary. The key question was whether Anderson and the Swedish government would cooperate. Whereas the purchase of specific parts such as boilers was already expected, complete engines were a different matter, implying the loss of much work from the Trollhättan plant.[93] Sure enough, Anderson refused to relinquish any part of his order. But he did agree to act as an intermediary for a new order of up to 800 engines from the Verband, which would be backed by major Swedish and German banks. The Verband voiced its support, and once more the deadline for signing a final German contract was postponed, this time until 31 October.[94]

Needless to say, events did not follow this plan precisely. Lomonosov did obtain Krasin's authority to proceed, but it proved impossible to arrange a consortium of major Swedish banks: the Enskilda Bank echoed French objections against breaking the gold embargo, whilst the Skandinaviska Bank insisted on using firms which it had vetted, a condition firmly rejected by Lomonosov.[95] However, an alternative scheme arose whereby Nordiska Handelsbanken – the small Swedish bank which had backed Anderson in the spring – would finance 500 engines. This was obviously a pale imitation of Lomonosov's original intention, but it became very attractive when the Svenska Riksbank agreed to support Nordiska. As Lomonosov wrote in his memoirs, the Riksbank's involvement was a success beyond his dreams.[96]

This idea was developed into definite proposals by 8 October. The Riksbank would earn some 400,000 Swedish crowns by buying 2 tonnes of Soviet gold at the low price of 2,600 crowns per kilogram, though it would pay a near-market rate of 2,800 crowns per kilogram for a further 8 tonnes. Nordiska would guarantee 116 million crowns against a deposit of 46 tonnes of gold and would guarantee a minimum sale price of 2,600 crowns per kilogram, the sales being subject to Tsentrosoiuz control. As for terms, Nordiska wanted a commission of 0.5 per cent and a guarantee that Swedish industry would have new orders worth 30 million crowns. The Russians baulked at this demand because German prices were much lower, and they whittled the sum down to 10 million crowns. Nordiska thereupon demanded an additional Russian deposit of 15 million crowns to cover costs already incurred by Nohab, and permission to lend this money to Nohab for materials and factory improvements. Lomonosov accepted these terms provided that the Tsentrosoiuz could vet any expenditure proposals.[97]

This complicated arrangement required six agreements: first, between the Tsentrosoiuz and Anderson, cancelling the May contract for 1,000 engines; second, between the Tsentrosoiuz and Nohab, for delivery of 1,500 engines, of which 1,000 would be built at Trollhättan; third, between the Tsentrosoiuz and Nordiska, about guarantees for the gold; fourth, between Nordiska and the Riksbank; fifth, between Nordiska and Nohab; and sixth, between Nohab and the Verband, for 500 engines. Once the Russians and Nordiska had reached agreement the whole package was swiftly approved by the Riksbank, Palmstierna intimated that he would guarantee the security of the gold, and on 8 October Lomonosov despatched a jubilant telegram to Krasin describing the offer and requesting permission to complete immediately.[98]

Speed was indeed vital for success. As early as 9 October Lomonosov warned Krasin that the Swedes were anxious to seal the deal quickly because of a 'ministerial crisis'.[99] But Krasin did not receive the crucial communication of 8 October until over a week later. Ironically, this hitch occurred because of the Russians' close cooperation with the Germans: as both he and Kopp had been doing occasionally for some months, Lomonosov sent his telegram by German diplomatic channels, the message first being sent in German cipher to Berlin and thence to Krasin. Unfortunately, because of a delay in Berlin – which was presumably unintentional – Krasin did not receive the report until about 16 October.[100] And by that time, needless to say, the whole scene had changed radically yet again.

By 11 October there were rumours of British and French protests against the proposal.[101] At first Lomonosov was not unduly concerned and even assured the Verband that the Entente would not intervene: Sweden had already received gold worth 85 million crowns and rejected Entente protests. The Riksbank's Director, Victor Moll, was also reassuring.[102] However, by 13 October, when Lomonosov had still not received a reply from Krasin, he was sufficiently anxious to tell Krasin that he would sign the contract on his own responsibility if he received no instructions.[103] Then, on 15 October, the Swedish government withdrew its support, Palmstierna complaining that the Russians had ignored Krasin's earlier undertakings.[104] And, as if adding insult to injury, Krasin's eventual reply of 17 October presented two further objections: firstly, Krasin was unclear whether the Verband had accepted Nordiska's guarantee and the proposed reduction to 500 engines; and secondly, he opposed the sale of gold at a fixed price of 2,600 crowns per kilogram. To Krasin the whole arrangement was even less attractive than a separate offer by Markevich to Kopp. [105]

Yet still Lomonosov persisted. Firstly, Palmstierna had left his door ajar by hinting that his government could still give the same guarantees concerning gold as Krasin had already received, and Branting confirmed this curious position in a personal interview with Lomonosov on 16 October.[106] Secondly, Lomonosov felt that Krasin's worries were founded on misunderstandings, for the Verband had obviously indicated its consent, only 2 tonnes of gold would be sold at 2,600 crowns per kilogram, and the Riksbank's guarantee made the combination far better than anything Markevich or Aschberg could possibly offer.[107] Krasin's doubts were duly allayed, and his authorisation, conditional upon some minor changes, was sent on 19 October.[108] But by then, of course, the scheme had collapsed, this time allegedly because of British pressure on the Swedish government. The Riksbank had withdrawn on 18 October following a Swedish Cabinet meeting, and Lomonosov at last began to acknowledge defeat.[109]

One glimmer of hope remained, however. The Riksbank did at least confirm that Nordiska could cope alone with an agreement for up to 60 tonnes of gold – enough, in theory, for about 600 engines. The risk, though, was greater, and so Lomonosov decided on 19 October to commit just 20 tonnes of gold, comprising 10 tonnes to finance 100 German engines, 6 tonnes for Nohab products and 4 tonnes for Swedish industry. The sum could be increased by a further 40 tonnes at a later date, if appropriate, allowing 400 more engines. Furthermore, Lomonosov also decided, apparently in consultation with Lazerson and Hellberg, who was now acting as his legal adviser, that it was pointless to consult Krasin before signing any such agreement: the final decision rested in Moscow, and Lomonosov had already determined to leave for Russia on 21 October.[110]

The climax of the affair came on the day scheduled for Lomonosov's departure. The first key event was the signing of two contracts which, although not for locomotives, were nonetheless significant in their own right. On 13 October the representatives of Krupp and Henschel had suggested that the Russians place an order for locomotive tyres without waiting for the financial problem to be resolved: the factories would take Lomonosov's word as sufficient guarantee. Lomonosov naturally needed no further encouragement and offered each company an order worth 7.5 million Swedish crowns, paying the necessary 15 per cent deposit from the 2 million crowns provided by Trotskii for initial maintenance expenses. A group headed by the Mannesmann company then offered boiler tubes, and although at first it wanted an irrevocable letter of credit it apparently withdrew this demand, probably because the Victor Berg company agreed to act as intermediary. Three contracts thus resulted: one with Krupp on 18 October for 7,000 tonnes of tyres; a similar one with Henschel on 21 October; and one with Victor Berg for boiler tubes, also signed on 21 October.[111]

The highlight of 21 October naturally concerned locomotives. Granted a verbal blessing by the Swedish Minister of Finance, Lomonosov's decision of 19 October to commit 20 tonnes of gold at last produced the long-awaited Soviet order for German engines, albeit via Nohab for just 100.[112] Of the three requisite contracts two were signed that day: one between the Tsentrosoiuz and Nordiska, and one between the Tsentrosoiuz and Nohab for the latter to supply 100 German-built engines; the third agreement, between Nohab and Krupp, followed on 29 November.[113] As was now also agreed for the main Nohab order, the price was provisionally specified as 230,000 crowns per locomotive, making a total of 23 million crowns for the 100 German engines. At Lenin's insistence the order was to be shared among no less than seventeen factories, a dilution of effort which would help to popularise Russian trade but would raise unit costs and present a logistical nightmare in transporting the engines across Germany. Delivery of all 100 engines was to be completed by 1 November 1921.[114]

This result of the Russians' protracted German negotiations was a far cry from Krasin's first inquiry about 2,200 engines, and even from the recent talk of 500. Yet Lomonosov's first major contracts for 100 locomotives and various quantities of spare parts were still an important achievement. They mean, for instance, that the total value of Soviet contracts signed in 1920 for deliveries from German firms was much greater than has been supposed. Whereas the combined value of all the contracts concluded by Kopp in 1920 – of which few, if any, concerned railway equipment – has been reported by Himmer as 160 million marks, Lomonosov's contract for 100 locomotives was alone worth some 225 million marks at the price agreed in August 1920, or more at the year's end due to the subsequent fall in the German mark's value.[115] Lomonosov's contracts showed that the German questions of price and finance could now have affirmative answers, albeit with caveats, and that the German authorities would go far to ensure success in Soviet–German economic relations even after the Soviet retreat from Poland. It was thus ironic that awkward new problems now arose on the Soviet side, as Lomonosov would soon discover. Objections were heard from Krasin, who was appalled at not having been consulted, and there were also rumblings of discontent in Moscow, not least because of second thoughts about the imports strategy formulated at the start of the year.

5 Second thoughts

In mid-September 1920 Chicherin informed Lomonosov that the national imports policy was under review.[1] The result included Sovnarkom's confirmation, on 5 October, of a revised NKPS programme for 1920 worth 294 million gold rubles.[2] Superficially this decision involved just a minimal reduction of the gold allocation of the previous March. But closer investigation of railway policy, imports planning and the decision-making process reveals that the NKPS was losing its earlier precedence for investment and imports. Second thoughts were emerging about the whole strategy of railway-led reconstruction and especially the NKPS imports programme.

The underlying issue was the deterioration of the economic crisis to the point where it threatened the regime's survival in the winter of 1920–1. Not only did the 'shock' tactic of prioritising transport fail to break the circle of decline, but a rapid breakthrough in transport reconstruction seemed less likely and less relevant. Moreover, controversy over Trotskii's leadership of the NKPS put the transport commissariat politically on the defensive. At the same time competition for gold resources intensified as Krasin's achievements in Europe spurred hopes among other commissariats of using imports to solve their own immediate shortages of equipment, fuel and food. Insofar as the issues of reconstruction and modernisation remained live amidst the deepening crisis, the NKPS found itself no longer able to compete when, to Lenin's delight, the GOELRO commission finally delivered its visionary electrification plan in the late autumn. That the railway imports policy would nonetheless produce a further large locomotive contract in early 1921 would in fact be due mainly to the persistence of Lomonosov himself.

Trotskii, railway reconstruction and imports planning

During the course of 1920 and early 1921 the methods of War Communism proved inappropriate for peacetime economic recovery and reconstruction. Economic administration remained chaotic, food and fuel shortages worsened, industrial output continued to fall, the Polish invasion and the white offensive in the south led by General Vrangel further restricted civilian production by prolonging the demand for military supplies, and whilst the threat to the regime of the locomotive shortage did recede, railway traffic decreased to what would be its nadir. Food requisitions caused serious peasant riots and resistance which, like the Antonov rising in Tambov, could paralyse whole provinces. Thus, whilst the ratification of the GOELRO plan by the Eighth Congress of Soviets in December 1920 reaffirmed modernisation as the regime's aim, the primary concern by this time was survival.[3]

Back in the spring of 1920, however, Trotskii appeared to be having a positive impact on the NKPS.[4] A dramatic increase in the number of operable locomotives was registered in March–June: the total virtually doubled from about 4,000 at the beginning of 1920 to about 7,700 in June and approximately 7,500 two months later. (See table 2.2 on p. 00.) And this change was enough to defuse the immediate danger. True, the proportion of 'sick' stock still hovered around 60 per cent and the railway network was larger, but healthy engines could be transferred from quiet peripheral areas to vital lines at the centre. Though locomotive shortages did remain serious in some areas, nationwide sclerosis was no longer likely. Indeed, by December 1920 over 400 steamable engines were recorded as stored, mainly for want of fuel – a figure which would rise to over 1,000 by February 1921.[5]

But to what extent did Trotskii solve the railway crisis? Policies which he advocated for the economy, especially mass labour mobilisation and martial law, were certainly among the reasons cited by an NKPS official for the March improvement, which also included better organisation, warmer weather and the NKPS Collegium's new policy of prioritising engines which needed only minor repairs.[6] But the main reason, not stressed at the time, was clearly the capture of engines from the Whites. Whereas the total Soviet locomotive stock grew marginally from 9,170 engines in October 1919 to 9,963 by March 1920, it jumped suddenly to 12,155 in April and 18,750 in June, before falling slightly to 18,086 in August. (See table 2.2.) In short, the locomotive crisis effectively resolved itself.

It has been argued that Trotskii had little time to devote to the NKPS.[7] But he certainly made his presence felt in setting an agenda for reconstruction and modernisation. A wide-ranging long-term strategy was already emerging by the end of April. The aim of mass-producing new equipment and spare parts, already approved by the Ninth Party Congress, was linked to such characteristic objectives as a radical overhaul of NKPS propaganda, reform of the transport trades unions, and the militarisation of labour, and these were coalescing into a determined attempt to achieve the transport breakthrough within a framework of long-term planning. As Trotskii's supporters happily mused, the revolution's transport crisis and railway development were being tackled with revolutionary ideas and methods.[8]

An early and enduring result was the resurrection of the national newspaper for railway workers, *Gudok*. Much more ambitious was the immediate elaboration of long-term plans to drive reconstruction and modernisation. The first steps were taken as early as April 1920 when the commissariat began developing comprehensive programmes for overhauling all the surviving locomotives and wagons as quickly as possible. For instance, an NKPS Collegium meeting chaired by Trotskii on 19 April instructed the acting head of the Technical Directorate, M. E. Pravosudovich, to prepare a detailed report about locomotive overhauls for the next meeting.[9] By the beginning of May preliminary conclusions had been put to Sovnarkom's council for coordinating economic policy, the Council of Labour and Defence (STO), and the STO had convened a working party or commission to discuss the mass production of locomotives and spare parts. When this group reported on 28 May, it was reformed as a permanent and powerful planning organ called the Basic Transport Commission (OTK).[10]

Subordinated directly to the STO, the OTK was chaired by Trotskii and comprised of representatives from the NKPS and VSNKh. Its main task was to organise a joint NKPS–VSNKh offensive to penetrate the 'front of destruction'. It had to formulate, coordinate and monitor an overall plan for the 'rebirth of transport', which would encompass the reconstruction of transport and its general development and improvement. The OTK thus had a wide-ranging brief which included long-term planning, encouraging mass production, championing modernisation and assessing requests for imports.[11] So important was this commission that Trotskii reportedly concentrated his own energy on it, whilst one of his NKPS deputies, V. M. Sverdlov, stated in July that the OTK would have as much responsibility as the NKPS in the battle to repair transport.[12]

Within weeks the OTK approved a long-term plan for overhauling the locomotive stock. It was published on 22 May 1920 as NKPS Order No. 1042 and scheduled to commence on 1 July for completion by 1 January 1925 at the latest.[13] The repair work was to be done mainly by NKPS workshops with VSNKh support. Seventeen of the most important VSNKh enterprises were designated as 'shock' factories and given priority for supplies of food and materials, and they would supply most of the requisite spare parts and undertake a limited number of heavy overhauls.[14] Significantly, as Trotskii himself noted with satisfaction, the planners counted only on resources available within Soviet Russia.[15] In other words, reflecting Trotskii's position that imports were desirable but unlikely, they treated foreign supplies simply as a possible bonus.

NKPS Order No. 1042 has been recognised as perhaps the first Soviet long-term economic plan, pre-dating the GOELRO plan by over six months. In fact, there were several other contemporaneous plans for the transport sector with an emphasis on reconstruction and modernisation. Order No. 1157 was a plan for overhauling the wagon stock by 1925, and there was a five-year plan for the restoration and expansion of the fleet of inland waterway steamers and barges. By September 1920 a long-term programme was being formulated for upgrading the railways' track, and targets were set for restoring and modernising buildings, bridges and the communications system. Also, a department was established within the NKPS Technical Directorate to consider the improvement and development of the transport system as a whole.[16]

These ideas earned the NKPS kudos in at least some quarters. The editor of *Ekonomicheskaia zhizn'*, G. Krumin, even called for analogous plans to be drafted for other parts of the economy which could eventually be unified as a national economic plan.[17] And the OTK was sufficiently encouraged by the first results from the rolling-stock plans that it raised the targets by 28 per cent in the autumn.[18] But there were problems, too, which soon threatened to bring the whole project into disrepute and indeed provided a foretaste of future Soviet central planning. Vitriolic exchanges appeared in the press about the quantity and quality of the work. For instance, shortages of spare parts in NKPS workshops were blamed on administrative chaos in the VSNKh Department of Metal rather than on labour, fuel and food shortages.[19] Other reports defended the VSNKh enterprises, and some implicitly attacked the NKPS workshops, alleging that repaired engines often failed upon returning to traffic and that many statistical reports were flawed or fabricated.[20] Feelings ran so high that Trotskii felt obliged to intervene, praising the locomotive overhaul programme in a long article in *Pravda* in early September.[21] But the attacks continued, and coupled with criticism of other aspects of NKPS strategy they helped to goad Trotskii into offering his resignation, unsuccessfully, at the end of September.

The modernisation of the locomotive stock became one of those targets for criticism. As survival became the regime's priority, and the locomotive crisis eased, immediate problems like the fuel shortage were advocated as more worthy of resources. The NKPS countered by stressing that many locomotives were obsolete and underpowered: only 30 per cent of the stock was aged under 15 years, the old Class O 0–8–0 freight locomotive of the 1890s still comprised roughly half of the stock, whilst passenger locomotives of that vintage were suitable merely for suburban, light freight and maintenance trains.[22] However, in contrast to the previous winter, such pleas for railway priority and modernisation elicited little sympathy.

Also part of this uproar was the famous trades union controversy, with A. G. Shliapnikov and the so-called Workers' Opposition leading the attack against Trotskii's proposals to reform and control the trades unions during the autumn of 1920. Generally regarded as a battle between different conceptions of state and society, and for influence within the party leadership, the debate can also be seen as a product of Trotskii's transport reconstruction strategy, and his defeat was logically a statement against that strategy. For the NKPS, then, the controversy represented unwelcome additional pressure. And it was probably no coincidence that, with both Trotskii and the NKPS on the defensive politically by September 1920, Stalin's Commissariat of Workers' and Peasants' Inspection (NKRKI) chose precisely this moment to deliver a blistering indictment of NKPS planning and problem-solving.[23] The NKPS did try to refute the NKRKI charges by quoting expert reports, and Fomin wrote to *Pravda* in Trotskii's defence.[24] But the opposition was determined, and further attacks would force Trotskii's departure from the NKPS in December.

That reconstruction and modernisation remained on the agenda was confirmed by the enthusiastic adoption of the GOELRO programme as official state policy by the Eighth Congress of Soviets. There were still attempts to stress the leading role of transport in the economy: Trotskii praised electrification as the way to socialism within the context of a reconstructed transport system, and planners like Miliutin, a deputy chair of the VSNKh, wanted to prioritise transport, fuel and industry. But Lenin and most congress delegates preferred electrification as an alternative to the railway vision. The Politburo member L. B. Kamenev enthused that it would serve as 'the base for Soviet proletarian power … to open the road to a new conquest by technology, which will mark the greatest gigantic victory by mankind over the elemental forces of nature'.[25] Stalin, too, supported the change of direction, praising the GOELRO programme against the 'wretchedness' of Trotskii's vision.[26]

Over the course of 1920, then, the NKPS and railways gradually lost political support as the vanguard of reconstruction to the point where electrification would easily seize that priority in December. This was partly because of the continuation of the economic crisis, which hindered and postponed reconstruction projects and demanded first call on the available resources. It was partly also because the sector-by-sector approach to reconstruction, with a breakthrough on the 'front of destruction', simply overstretched the military analogy and underestimated the economy's complexity. Lenin's backing for GOELRO was undoubtedly influential, whilst the railway cause may have suffered from the controversy surrounding Trotskii.

That said, the GOELRO planners were at a real disadvantage compared to the NKPS ten months earlier. Not only had most of the optimism about rapid reconstruction and modernisation disappeared, but so too had much of the regime's gold. A large portion of the initial NKPS allocation had already been committed to the Swedish and German locomotives, other commissariats were demanding more resources, and foreign credit remained very scarce. Significantly, though the NKPS was in retreat, its gold allocation remained basically intact until about February 1921. Thus, although the GOELRO plan was based on the assumption that large-scale foreign investment and equipment imports would be available, its political triumph over the railways could not be backed by real resources. If foreign loans failed to materialise, the GEOLRO plan could not be implemented quickly. Indeed, the Bolsheviks now had to conserve their gold, work with a limited budget, and rethink their approach to imports – harsh reality which anticipated the trauma of domestic budgetary discipline to come with the NEP from 1921.

Interest in foreign trade grew considerably in Moscow during 1920. Initially there was little sense of urgency about creating the proposed foreign trade bureaucracy. A VSNKh Committee for Foreign Trade was formed on 10 March to analyse the country's needs for imports, but not until 19 April did the Central Committee's Organisational

Bureau (Orgburo) establish a special interdepartmental commission to monitor foreign trade issues.[27] However, Krasin's Swedish contracts were followed by a sudden burst of organisational activity in late May and early June. The reform of the NKTiP into the NKVT was completed, and a Council of Foreign Trade was instituted to coordinate the imports plan.[28] The VSNKh committee then produced a new imports plan which was ratified by Sovnarkom at the end of June.[29] Next, during the summer and early autumn, the potential economic role of foreign trade was debated in a spate of newspaper articles amidst a mood of greater interest and confidence.[30] In October Lenin himself resurrected the idea of granting economic concessions to foreigners, a proposal which Sovnarkom had earlier accepted in principle but which had been neglected since Krasin's departure in March.[31]

Given a limited budget, this increasing interest in imports threatened the NKPS predominance. Under Trotskii the commissariat based its planning on domestic resources, but naturally had no intention of relinquishing its advantage should imports become possible. Unsurprisingly, then, its relations with the VSNKh Committee for Foreign Trade were sour almost from the outset. The committee's draft imports plan, which the VSNKh Presidium discussed on 17 May, dismissed most of the original NKPS proposal as 'clearly exaggerated', and Sovnarkom had to intervene on 27 May by requesting special reports.[32] Though these reports have not been located, it would seem that the VSNKh committee wanted to limit NKPS gold expenditure to the initial priorities identified by Voskresenskii and Ivitskii: namely 2,000 locomotives and limited supplies of certain spare parts, tools and machinery.[33] But the NKPS stuck to its guns and even ignored further meetings of the VSNKh committee on 25 June and 5, 6 and 9 July, although, as mentioned in chapter 3, it did forward a copy of its own reassessment, still insisting on all 5,000 proposed locomotives.[34]

This self-confidence was to some extent well founded. Sovnarkom apparently continued to give the NKPS imports plan special treatment, and opened a credit of 124.7 million gold rubles on 27 June as the first instalment of the 300 million approved in March, with 100 million for the 1,000 Nohab engines and 24.7 million for spare parts.[35] Meanwhile it was proposed to increase the sum available for all other commissariats from 100 to 177.75 million gold rubles for the year, of which nearly 50 million was allocated to the People's Commissariat for Agriculture, 29 million for chemical products, 30.9 million to the Department of Metal, and 26.35 million for assorted other purposes.[36]

Thus the NKPS was still receiving by far the largest share of the money allocated.

Apparently Sovnarkom agreed the sum of 329,500,985 gold rubles as the imports budget for 1920 on 29 June.[37] This plan most likely comprised the special NKPS credit of 27 June, the allowances agreed for all other Soviet organisations, and some 25 million gold rubles as a reserve or payment for earlier non-NKPS contracts. If so, the NKPS had some 41 per cent of the budget for 1920, not to mention any other railway-related proposals (such as for rails) which may well have been incorporated in the metal industry's programme. Additionally, of course, the NKPS expected a further credit of 175.3 million gold rubles as the remainder of its allocation of 16 March.

However, the NKPS did review its requirements again in late August. One reason for this was Voskresenskii's return from Europe. A conference of heads of NKPS directorates was convened on 23 August to hear him report on his European trip. After explaining how he and Ivitskii had compiled a plan of first priorities, he suggested that the main European suppliers of railway equipment were likely to be Britain and Germany. But he also noted that British factories had enough work for twelve months, that the Germans could not begin deliveries for four to six months, and that Italy and Poland were importing engines from the United States. On this basis Voskresenskii argued, firstly and probably incorrectly, that Europe was hard-pressed to meet its own demand for railway equipment; and secondly, that the USA was still the only hope if all the desired NKPS orders were to be placed. In the meantime, he concluded, it was essential to determine the most urgent priorities.[38]

The minutes of the NKPS managers' next conference, on 27 August, imply that the NKPS now intended to use 70 million gold rubles of its June credit for locomotives, and 54 million for spare parts. Further, it was agreed to remind the STO that 70 million gold rubles would not buy nearly enough engines and that part of the Swedish order would have to be cancelled unless more money was provided. The NKPS also wanted control of 104 million gold rubles which it believed had been allocated to the VSNKh – possibly in addition to the June plan – for imports of rails (70 million gold rubles), non-ferrous metals (12 million) and various construction and other materials (22 million).[39] In other words, there were probably two other reasons for the reassessment. One was the supply problems being encountered with the overhaul plans, which prompted the idea of importing larger quantities of spares; the other was to obtain the early release of more gold. That there was no intention of reducing the number of locomotives in the imports plan was confirmed when the new plan was finalised by an NKPS commission a few days later. There were increased figures for basic parts like tyres and boiler tubes, whilst the claim for 5,000 broad-gauge locomotives remained intact.[40]

The head of the NKPS Directorate of Economics and Materials, A. L. Kolegaev, duly applied to the Council of Foreign Trade for more gold on 15 September.[41] He wanted control of the VSNKh railway-related gold credits totalling 104 million gold rubles, a further 230 million gold rubles to guarantee the delivery of 2,000 locomotives by December 1921, and an additional 142 million gold rubles for workshop equipment and supplies, as well as transfer of the Nohab order to Germany so as to quicken delivery. As these demands, added to the credit of 124.7 million gold rubles, totalled some 600 million gold rubles, he had to agree that full acceptance was unrealistic. But at the very least the NKPS wanted the Nohab contract reassigned to Germany, unless political considerations made this impossible; a moratorium on new contracts until all gold allocations had been clarified; a three- or five-year trade plan, based on the exchange of goods, with export earnings to help pay for locomotives; and recognition that, as Trotskii had always maintained, foreign credit should not be expected.

Scandalised, the Council of Foreign Trade tried to assert its authority. It not only rejected the pitch for the VSNKh funds and for a general review of gold allocations but also imposed a moratorium on new NKPS contracts and declined to discuss the Nohab contract pending a reassessment of all the decisions about releasing gold to the NKPS.[42] Accordingly, Lezhava informed Trotskii of a decision to cease ordering locomotives until Sovnarkom's confirmation of a new NKPS imports plan, whilst Chicherin warned Lomonosov not to sign any contracts for about two weeks pending completion of this reappraisal.[43]

The outcome was a decision, some two weeks later, that locomotive orders would be restricted to the 1,000 Swedish engines and the proposed 1,000 from Germany, and that the NKPS would submit a claim for imports of spares worth 300 million gold rubles for 1921.[44] This high priority for spares is undoubtedly explained by the difficulties with VSNKh supplies and confidence that imports could cover the shortfall. The change made sense in those circumstances, but it evinced a sharp protest from Krasin, who probably sensed a retreat from the modernisation strategy. Yet the NKPS was still intent on obtaining new locomotives: an internal report of 5 October stressed the importance of getting the maximum possible number of new engines from Soviet and foreign suppliers.[45] The point was that the commissariat now wanted imports to cover much of its requirement for spares and materials as well as locomotives, and given the changed domestic circumstances it was content to see the new engines delivered over a longer period than optimists like Mikhailov had hoped. Reconstruction and modernisation were still firmly in the mind of the NKPS, but a slower pace was envisaged.

Treating these decisions as a setback rather than a defeat, the NKPS resumed the attack with a statement by Sverdlov to the Council of Foreign Trade on 4 October.[46] Through a canny reworking of the figures the NKPS now claimed 414 million gold rubles for 1920–1, comprised of 158 million for spare parts and rails (to be ordered in 1920); 142 million for spares and materials (1921); 100 million for the 1,000 German locomotives (delivery by December 1921); and 14 million for the first 100 Swedish engines (delivery by December 1921). In other words, the NKPS had dropped its demand for the delivery of 2,000 locomotives by the end of 1921 but reinstated the Nohab order (which meant further expenditure after 1921, not mentioned in this report); and it had repackaged its failed bid for the VSNKh gold to produce a bigger, seemingly new and strictly NKPS spares claim for 1920.

Again, however, the NKPS was rebuffed. One exchange in particular revealed a telling lack of precision in its argument: when asked how many locomotives really needed to be imported, Sverdlov carelessly cited a figure of 5,000–7,000, depending on the amount of gold available. Alive to the NKPS ruses, the Council of Foreign Trade declined to release more money and carefully budgeted for the entire Nohab order. Thus, in approving NKPS expenditure of 294 million gold rubles using the gold already allocated on 16 March, it designated 140 million gold rubles for the Nohab locomotives, 100 million for the projected German order (1,000 engines) and 54 million for spare parts under the 1920 imports plan – a decision that was ratified by Sovnarkom the next day.[47] The Council also referred the balance of the bid for 158 million gold rubles in 1920 (104 million) back to the VSNKh Committee for Foreign Trade, and refused to prioritise the bid for 142 million gold rubles for supplies in 1921, simply passing it to the VSNKh committee for consideration as part of the national imports plan for 1921. Nor was there any question of further locomotive orders.

With some 205 million gold rubles allowed the previous June for non-NKPS orders in 1920, these decisions implied total planned orders for the year worth about 500 million gold rubles. This represented approximately two-thirds of the gold available in March, and the NKPS share was still an impressive 59 per cent. But the days of virtually unquestioned NKPS priority had obviously passed, and in fact cuts would follow during the winter.

Moscow and the Russian Railway Mission Abroad

Having arrived back in Russia, Lomonosov found that Moscow's response to his German contracts was mixed. Lenin was apparently satisfied, telling the professor that the imports would help Russia recover. Trotskii, though still sceptical about the overall prospects, supported the contracts and felt that at least fifty tonnes of gold could be used. Lezhava even suggested moving sixty tonnes immediately, the maximum sum of the contract. Further encouragement came from Rykov and the People's Commissar for Agriculture, S. P. Sereda. As for objections, there were worries about the risks of exporting more gold, and as a matter of principle Chicherin, the People's Commissar for Foreign Affairs and Litvinov, his deputy, both wanted diplomatic relations established before Soviet–German trade was expanded. Chicherin further complained that, as with Krasin in Sweden, this was another *fait accompli* and that his commissariat was effectively being deprived of influence in Soviet–Western relations. He wanted a Central Committee warning that it was 'unacceptable' to sign large contracts overhastily – in short, without first obtaining his commissariat's support.[48]

Sovnarkom duly forwarded the contracts to the Council of Foreign Trade for comment. There the attendance on 27 October was larger than usual, and it included L. P. Serebriakov from the Central Committee. Lomonosov's report was followed by a lively debate, with considerable attention given to his contracts for spare parts. The final resolution was drafted in a 'closed' session after the main meeting and was apparently favourable, though evidently it accepted the view of Khinchuk, representing the People's Commissariat of Food Procurement, that the Tsentrosoiuz should be allowed to dissect the agreements.[49]

It is interesting that the Tsentrosoiuz board took this task seriously, even though the Soviet government originally involved the organisation in foreign trade merely as a front to outmanoeuvre the Allies, and its session on 28 October was a rigorous test for Lomonosov. In particular, whilst acknowledging the financial agreement with Nordiska as exceptionally important, the board insisted that because Soviet–Swedish relations were still unstable, it was essential to have a formal guarantee that the Swedish government would not prevent sale of the gold on the world market.[50]

These two meetings coincided with new reservations about imports policy, and indeed Sovnarkom instigated another re-evaluation of the national imports plan on 30 October.[51] But the NKPS budget of 5 October was probably not questioned at this juncture. Sovnarkom ratified the German contracts on 28 October subject to the amendments demanded by the Tsentrosoiuz, and the Tsentrosoiuz gave Lomonosov a new warrant covering financial negotiations. Chicherin tried to block the contracts but was successfully opposed by Lezhava. Thus, Lomonosov could devote the rest of his brief visit to organising the first gold shipment and arranging the appointment of engineer-inspectors.[52]

The question of gold policy for the contracts was settled at the Council of Foreign Trade on 1 November. To judge by Lomonosov's memoir account, opinion was divided. Lezhava, chairing the session, now favoured sending only twenty tonnes to Sweden as an experiment. Khinchuk, citing the instability of the gold market, preferred to try for gold-guaranteed loans even though a high interest rate of 10 per cent might be demanded. Lomonosov reportedly noted that at least some sales would be necessary and that a loan would take time to arrange, whereas payments for his first orders were already due. In any case, ten tonnes of gold had been committed for the German engines, and ten more tonnes could support a loan of only about 20–25 million Swedish crowns, which was insufficient for the necessary payments.[53] The compromise decision was to send the requisite twenty tonnes of gold for deposit and sale plus a further ten tonnes as partial cover for the locomotives. However, there was to be no question of a minimum price in sales of this supplementary consignment and the final optional thirty tonnes. Lastly, the NKVT was to organise a suitable procedure for selling gold through its own foreign-based representatives, though it was desirable to avoid sales and instead use the gold as collateral for loans.[54]

The second of Lomonosov's concerns, quality control, was part of the broader question of managing the railway orders, and it brought him into conflict with the NKPS, which had its own ideas about placing this business on a more formal footing. Having persuaded the reluctant Krasin that Russian engineers should be responsible for technical quality control, Lomonosov asked the NKPS several times during the summer to appoint suitably qualified engineers. But his demands provoked irritation at the commissariat, which was short of these vital personnel, and as of mid-October few, if any, had been sent.[55]

The problem partly derived from personal antagonism between Lomonosov and I. N. Borisov, head of the NKPS Main Directorate. Like the professor, engineer Borisov had attained high rank in the tsarist MPS, becoming a deputy minister (*tovarishch ministra*) in 1916. After the October Revolution Borisov had left the railways, but he reappeared as Lomonosov's deputy at the NKPS Technical Directorate in the winter of 1919–20, surprisingly at the professor's request though their relations had long been strained. When Lomonosov returned fom south Russia in May 1920 he was appalled to find Borisov happily installed as head of the newly created Main Directorate, holding in effect the most senior technical position on the railways.[56]

Borisov and the NKPS were concerned to create a whole system for planning and implementing NKPS foreign contracts. This concept was probably developed by the head of the Directorate of Economics and Materials, Kolegaev, after the ad hocery of the June review, and it was discussed by NKPS directorate chiefs on 9 July. They agreed that the Directorate of Economics and Materials and the Technical Directorate should draft a special statute based on four main principles. Firstly, a so-called Special Technical Conference for Foreign Orders (*Osoboe tekhnicheskoe soveshchanie po zagranichnym zakazam*) should be formed under Borisov, comprised of the heads of the Directorate of Economics and Materials, Technical Directorate and Communications Directorate, plus a representative from the Main Directorate for Waterways. Secondly, the technical merits of proposed orders should be evaluated by the Technical Directorate, whilst the Directorate of Economics and Materials should handle all clerical work; a special 'cell' (*iacheika*) should be formed within each directorate for these purposes. Thirdly, NKPS directorates desirous of importing equipment should present their proposals to the head of the Main Directorate. And fourthly, the special conference should adjudicate all matters of principle, as well as serious disputes between directorates. As for quality control, special technical commissions should be created at some future time, formed of representatives from the various directorates and operating under special statutes.[57]

There were further discussions during the remainder of the summer. On 2 August, for instance, the NKPS decided to form an Information and Technical Bureau in Tallinn, presumably to assert NKPS control over the various minor orders which Gukovskii placed there on his own initiative. On 3 September the Directorate of Economics and Materials told Borisov's commissar, Fomin, that its secretariat had approved an organisational system suggested by the NKVT for inspecting, storing and dispatching NKPS imports and exports. And on 7 September the same directorate sent the Main Directorate a draft statute for the proposed technical conference, now known as a special technical council. Meanwhile, a special secretariat was mooted for the Directorate of Economics and Materials to manage NKPS foreign orders. Expected to have a staff of ten, it would identify NKPS priorities for purchase abroad, liaise with the VSNKh and other organisations, organise quality control for the imports, monitor expenditure, and distribute the imports upon delivery to Russia.[58]

It seems likely that the proposed technical council was never created and that its responsibilities were simply handled informally by Borisov. The proposed secretariat excited some opposition, but Kolegaev trenchantly defended it when forwarding the draft statute to Borisov on 18 September, and it was approved.[59] In fact the most controversial question was the appointment of NKPS engineers abroad. The acting head of the new secretariat, L. V. Filippov, completed a detailed proposal for creating NKPS delegations in Germany and Sweden, which was approved in principle by Borisov and his fellow heads of directorate on 18 October, and a revised version helped to foment a furious row in late October about technical inspectors and the legal status of Lomonosov's mission.[60]

Filippov's document argued that, in line with a recent NKPS–NKVT agreement, NKPS imports should be managed within the NKVT framework like those of any other commissariat.[61] An NKVT trade delegation was being created in each country, headed by a trade representative who would be responsible to the NKVT in Moscow and control all Soviet commercial activity within the given country. In Filippov's opinion, the NKPS should imitate other commissariats by appointing its own representatives to these delegations. The matter was urgent because orders were already being placed, and the decision needed to be systematic to guarantee best use of the credits and quick delivery.

At the same time, Filippov continued, it was important to remember that conditions differed between countries. In Sweden the Soviet order was concentrated at just one factory, and so only one NKPS organisation would be needed; to make Nohab work as cheaply as possible without sacrificing quality, only very experienced engineers should be sent there – a tactic which would also allow new Nohab contracts for spare parts and machinery. But contracts in Germany would be spread across numerous sites throughout the country, and so a series of regionally based NKPS organisations would be needed, as indeed Lomonosov was proposing.

Thus, Filippov suggested, it was advisable, firstly, to base two NKPS plenipotentiaries in Berlin with responsibility for operations in both Germany and Sweden, supported by their own staffs; one, Lomonosov, should manage all technical matters, the other – Filippov tactfully volunteered Kolegaev – should control all commercial activity, including the use of NKPS credits, and monitor the speed of the work. Secondly, there should be seven regional groups in Germany, each having a staff of up to seven people: a group monitor, one or two assistants, one or two secondary agents, a clerk and a typist; the monitor, clerk and typist should be Russian, but the other personnel could be hired locally. And there should be one further NKPS representative in Germany – possibly V. V. Romanov, from the Technical Directorate – concentrating on spare parts and other supplies, aided by two assistants. Thirdly, in Sweden there should be seven Russians at Nohab, including an NKPS area representative (Filippov nominated himself), three inspectors, a clerk, a typist and a 'political commissar', a post for which the appointment of a former Sormovo engineer, V. S. Zernov, from the Directorate of Economics and Materials was 'extremely desirable'; as in Germany, other personnel should be hired locally if needed.

In conclusion, Filippov urged that Shchukin and another highly respected locomotive designer be sent to Nohab to check and ratify the locomotive drawings, so as to avoid further alterations during the actual construction of the engines. Somewhat piously, he also voiced the hope that people posted abroad would not view their position 'egotistically' but would strive to acquire and disseminate technical information being published there. Finally, he pleaded for his report to be discussed immediately so that work could be started quickly.

This report, with its direct challenges to Lomonosov's position and pride, was effectively a time bomb. The explosion duly occurred at a conference of directorate chiefs and commissars chaired by Borisov on 27 October. The minutes indicate that Lomonosov delivered a report which ranged from renewed requests for engineer-inspectors to complaints about Moscow's tardiness in correspondence, and they show that this report was accepted, the engineers appointed, and a promise given to process correspondence more quickly.[62] Lomonosov's memoir account is more colourful and claims that the meeting ended in chaos over the question of organisation. Borisov reportedly favoured centralisation, whereas the head of the Communications Directorate, K. N. Chekhovskii, objected that that would require vast improvements in the international telegraph system if it was to function at all. Lomonosov accused Borisov of intriguing against him – doubtless to many NKPS minds a classic case of pot and kettle – and Kolegaev castigated Lomonosov for shooting across Europe like a comet without actually achieving anything.[63]

Be that as it may, the organisational problem still had to be solved urgently. Significantly, Lomonosov is coy about what happened next. Most probably, he raised the matter with Lenin during one or both of his long audiences on 29 and 31 October.[64] This could explain why, in the professor's account, Lenin issued instructions on 31 October for Lezhava, Litvinov and Lomonosov to discuss the legal status of Lomonosov's mission and draft an appropriate instruction (*nakaz*) which, to avoid arguments, should subordinate the professor not to the NKVT or NKPS but directly to Sovnarkom. This new document was duly produced as a supplement to Lomonosov's government mandate of 17 June, was approved by Sovnarkom on 5 November and was signed by Lenin, Trotskii, Lezhava and a member of the Collegium of the Commissariat of Foreign Affairs, L. M. Karakhan.[65]

The reasons for this surprising outcome, so contrary to NKPS and NKVT thinking, remain unclear apart from one comment by Lomonosov that Litvinov was supportive.[66] Presumably Lenin in effect imposed it on the NKPS and NKVT in the belief that, given the urgency of the situation and possible delay in the creation of NKVT delegations, it was the only practical option for the time being.

Whatever the explanation, Lomonosov now had a legal basis to create a new trade organisation outside the parameters of the NKVT. Reminiscent of the wartime technical mission in the USA, his Russian Railway Mission Abroad would dominate the management of NKPS imports for over two years. Crucially, it was probably unique among Soviet foreign trade organisations of the early 1920s in that its chairman, Lomonosov, was a Sovnarkom plenipotentiary and handled commercial as well as technical affairs. Immediately beneath Lomonosov were his commercial and technical assistants, who were initially Lazerson and Fren respectively. There was a Main Office, with a secretariat, business directorate and accounts department, which was located in Stockholm because of Sweden's role as a clearing area for Soviet gold; and there was a subsidiary office in Berlin, which included several technical departments responsible, among other things, for inviting and evaluating tenders. A network of regional offices was created roughly along the lines of those in Filippov's ill-fated report, a total of fifteen being in operation in early 1922 at the height of the mission's inspection activity. Most were in Germany, but one was in Sweden, another covered Austria and Czechoslovakia, and there was even one in Canada, created in 1921 to monitor an order there for 500 oil-tanker wagons.[67]

The results of Lomonosov's Moscow visit thus extended far beyond confirmation of his October contracts, and they represented a considerable personal triumph for the professor. Yet his tactics left him vulnerable to the accusation, already heard from Chicherin and soon from Krasin too, that he had bamboozled the Soviet government into a major financial commitment. Moreover, though Lomonosov possibly did not realise it at the time, only a few months remained until the demise of the grandiose imports policy as conceived at the beginning of 1920.

Locomotive swan song

Lomonosov's next sojourn abroad lasted until May 1921. It commenced badly in Tallinn with an organisational problem concerning Sweden. Palmstierna had been refusing visas for new personnel to the trade delegation since the previous July, pending fulfilment of Krasin's promise to return the Swedish state property in Russia. The Soviet side, for its part, was annoyed that the Swedes were adhering firmly to the limit of fifteen delegates, insisting on Tsentrosoiuz affiliation and rejecting Litvinov, Vorovskii and F. A. Rotshtein as candidates to head the trade mission. The two sides were still deadlocked when, on 12 or 13 November, Chicherin forbade Lomonosov to send gold to Sweden pending a Central Committee decision about whether to scrap the Nordiska agreement in protest.[68]

The underlying issue was Chicherin's annoyance at Krasin's prioritisation of trade over diplomatic relations. As he explained to Lezhava on 24 November, he had opposed Krasin's Swedish agreement because he felt that once orders had been placed and gold sent there, the Soviet side would not have any leverage to obtain better terms except by threatening cancellation. Further, he believed that more orders would worsen the situation. Trade negotiations required caution: the Swedish case demonstrated that signing contracts did not necessarily yield more rights and privileges.[69] Arguably, Krasin came round to this view during the year. At any rate, he could not sign contracts in Great Britain, his main target, because Lloyd George's government would not give any property guarantees before signing the trade agreement. But Lomonosov's perspective was different, reflecting his single-mindedness for locomotives and the financial implications of the commitments already made. Appalled at Chicherin's stance, he warned that cancellation would also destroy his German orders and that Sweden would break off relations, stranding gold there worth 27 million Swedish crowns. Also, the placement of future orders would be more complicated because bank guarantees would be demanded for the full cost.[70]

Chicherin was unimpressed, reiterating his arguments to Lomonosov in a letter of 15 November and accusing Stockholm of breaking its commitments of May 1920 to Krasin.[71] The same day he sought Politburo approval for the annulment of Lomonosov's agreement about moving gold to Sweden. Curiously, however, his stratagem backfired: he was told to release the gold and was censured for delaying the shipment without permission and – quite unfairly – for not voicing his objections whilst Lomonosov was in Moscow.[72] Consequently, Lomonosov was permitted on 17 November to inform the Swedes that his government would ship some of the gold as a goodwill gesture. The next day he informed Stockholm that he was bringing twenty tonnes of gold but leaving ten tonnes in Tallinn in protest against Swedish policy, and added that he was empowered to negotiate about the appointment of a Soviet trade representative.[73] The railway contracts were thus saved, and, thanks partly to meetings between Lomonosov and the Swedish authorities in December 1920, an Old Bolshevik from the Commissariat of Foreign Affairs, P. M. Kerzhentsev, arrived in Stockholm in late January 1921 as ambassador and head of the trade delegation.[74]

Lomonosov's most serious organisational problem during this winter involved Krasin, and it was perhaps largely of his own making. Krasin had at least four strong grievances.[75] Firstly, the professor had not consulted him before signing the German locomotive order for 100 engines even though, by lacking the Riksbank's participation, the scheme differed radically from the earlier proposed agreement for 500 engines. Secondly, Moscow had failed to consult him adequately when assessing the agreements. Thirdly, the Council of Foreign Trade had allowed Lomonosov to move a large amount of gold to Europe without (in Krasin's opinion) adequate guarantees for its security and sale. Lastly, Krasin accepted that Lomonosov should have special rights, but was adamant that the professor should work through normal NKVT channels; in other words, by placing orders himself Lomonosov would undermine the NKVT's trade monopoly and cause confusion and disaster.

However, Lomonosov rebelled. He told Moscow that it was impracticable to undertake gold operations only in conjunction with Krasin and the NKVT representative in Tallinn, Georgii Solomon, because he lacked access to codes and because Krasin did not reply to his telegrams. And when Solomon refused to transfer money to him in December, Lomonosov threatened in telegrams to Lenin and Krasin to stop making scheduled payments on 15 December. Also, he complained to Lenin that Krasin had admitted not even reading the contracts and that he was simply relying on tendentious assessments from Bel'gard and Solomon. In short, although there were some objective difficulties in what Krasin wanted, Lomonosov was determined not to become, in his words, merely Krasin's 'errand boy'.[76]

Krasin stubbornly insisted on the principle of prior consultation and the placement of all orders through NKVT channels.[77] But surprisingly, like Chicherin in November, Krasin failed to get his way. For whatever reason he could not persuade the party or government to transfer the Railway Mission's commercial activity to the NKVT offices in Germany and Sweden.[78] Crucially, although he did eventually get Lomonosov subordinated to the NKPS for technical matters and to the NKVT for commercial affairs, he could not get Lomonosov's appointment as a Sovnarkom plenipotentiary rescinded. This meant that, completely against the will of the People's Commissar for Foreign Trade, Lomonosov could develop the Railway Mission into a foreign trade organisation employing well over 300 people by 1922. And, as Krasin feared, individual railways and even non-railway organisations began to see the Railway Mission as a potential alternative to the NKVT system. Medicines and medical equipment were obvious requests; more unusual was a cultural organisation's desperate plea in June 1921 for musical-instrument strings.[79]

So far as new contracts were concerned, Lomonosov had a busy winter. He first used the latest NKPS lists to devise his own 'shock programme' of priority orders from West European firms. It included the remaining 900 locomotives, which he hoped to buy quite quickly, as well as more than 50,000 tyres and 250,000 boiler tubes, wagon spare parts worth 5 million Swedish crowns, 2,000 tonnes of springs and spring steel, nearly 150,000 brakepipes, fire hoses and oil pipes, 1,500 tonnes of tin, 3,500 tonnes of lead, 1,000 tonnes of copper sheet, and tools to the value of 3 million crowns along with 100 motorised trollies, hundreds of pumps and thousands of gauges and carriage lamp bulbs. Together with a further 250,000 boiler tubes requested by the NKPS in March 1921, most of these items had already been ordered by 1 May 1921.[80]

But, as before, the main business was locomotive negotiations. Frustratingly, there was much correspondence about American decapods but no progress, and indeed the Revalis contract had had to be renegotiated by Martens in October 1920 given the US government's intransigence.[81] More encouragingly, various companies and banks in Austria, Czechoslovakia, Switzerland, Finland and Italy expressed keen interest in supplying locomotives, as did the German Verband. By late January 1921 Lomonosov was hoping to order 600 Class E locomotives from Germany and 300 from Austria or Czechoslovakia or, again, Germany. However, for various reasons only his contacts with the Verband got much beyond an exploratory stage.[82]

Discussions with the German Verband recommenced in December 1920. Since all technical issues had long since been resolved, the main question was finance. One obvious possibility was to use Anderson as an intermediary, and again a price of 230,000 Swedish crowns per engine was quoted. A second idea was to reconsider direct cooperation with German banks, especially after Bücher hinted on 8 December that this might now be possible (though not with Mendelssohn).[83] But no real progress was made until an intriguing proposal was tabled by one of Krupp's agents, Ludwig Bamberger, and the Deutsche Bank's Stockholm representative, Herr Steinbach, on about 13 January. As Lomonosov explained in his memoirs, the essence of their idea was an international debt-swap: Soviet gold could be transferred to Sweden, the Swedish authorities could treat this gold as part-payment of the German war debt to Sweden, and the German government could guarantee all the payments owed to the Verband. In other words, the Soviet government would continue to channel its gold through Sweden whilst enjoying the lower German prices.[84]

It was soon agreed that 500 locomotives could be financed. However, a dispute about the Deutsche Bank's proposed fee appears to have prompted a modification whereby the engines would be ordered through the Victor Berg company, with which the Krupp agent Harald Berg was associated. This scheme would still involve the leading banks, but the price would be set in gold rubles and Victor Berg would be paid in Tallinn. With each locomotive priced at 125,000 gold rubles (approximately 246,000 Swedish crowns), the cost of 500 engines was thus 62.5 million gold rubles, representing a colossal overspend of 12.5 million gold rubles against the budget approved by Sovnarkom the previous October.[85]

Nonetheless, Lomonosov was encouraged to pursue this idea by Krasin, Litvinov and Solomon on 22 January.[86] A few days later Berg offered to increase the order from 500 to 600 engines, and there were reports on 27 January that the banks would finance as many as 900. But Lomonosov preferred to discuss no more than 600 locomotives with Berg, hoping to acquire the remaining 300 more cheaply through Anderson or, if circumstances allowed, in Austria, Italy or Czechoslovakia.[87] The main reason for favouring Berg was probably to guarantee the involvement of top Swedish and German banks. Anderson was linked only with the small Nordiska Handelsbanken, and Lomonosov was in any case quarrelling with Nordiska over gold sales: with the price of gold falling, the bank wanted to sell immediately – it was contractually obliged to sell 7.5 tonnes by 1 March 1921 – whereas Lomonosov wanted to wait, both to allow a price recovery and to keep this gold supporting a loan of 48 million Swedish crowns.[88] Most worrying for Lomonosov was the fact that Nordiska was acting within its rights under the Tsentrosoiuz–Nordiska accord of October 1920 and a supplementary agreement of 18 December, and was in any case entitled to sell at its own discretion after 1 March.[89]

To complicate matters further, Lomonosov unceremoniously sacked his financial adviser, Lazerson, on 15 February. Since Lazerson was accused of scheming to lower the price of Soviet gold – a charge which Krasin had begun to level at the Railway Mission – it may be that Lomonosov was seeking a scapegoat, and they may well have clashed over Nordiska's demand for gold sales. Equally, it is quite possible that, as Lazerson hints in his own memoirs, this departure really stemmed from personal acrimony between Lazerson and Lomonosov's wife, Raisa Nikolaevna, who had recently arrived in Europe from the United States and was installed as her husband's personal secretary. Whatever the reasons, Lomonosov could hardly have lost his financial adviser at a worse time.[90]

Given this background, Lomonosov very possibly had a personal incentive to conclude a new locomotive order quickly. If Nordiska unilaterally sold a large amount of gold, he would be open to more criticism from Moscow, whereas a new locomotive contract would force fresh gold sales to cover the deposit and other payments. On 8 February Lomonosov warned Moscow that German industrial capacity was reportedly being bought up by British and other interests so as to force prices higher for the Russians; he declared that it was better to lose money on gold sales now than suffer much higher prices later. To be fair, Lomonosov may have had good reason for fearing such British intervention, but equally he may have hoped to extract himself from a potentially ugly situation through a new contract.[91]

Lomonosov's insistence certainly disturbed Krasin. Writing to Lenin on 12 February, Krasin agreed that there was some danger of British interference, but he recommended a sensible negotiating strategy and a campaign to exploit conflicts of interest between major British and German companies. Also, he was worried about using Sweden as an intermediary: there were no guarantees against losing the gold, the price of Soviet gold would be undermined, and the price was no different to that of a German–British combination. In any case it might be possible to place the order in Canada if the Germans insisted on high prices. In general, Krasin wrote, Lomonosov's urgency was worrying and his policy a case of jumping out of the frying pan into the fire.[92]

Nonetheless Krasin participated in the final negotiations in Berlin in late February. There the main problems were the price and the enmity between Krasin and Lomonosov. After a preliminary meeting between Lomonosov and the Verband on 24 February produced a draft contract for 600 locomotives and probably also an agreed price, Krasin insisted on various amendments to the text.[93] Then the Germans reportedly raised their price on 26 February, and when Lomonosov provisionally agreed a figure of 122,000 gold rubles per locomotive and tender, Krasin intervened again. Virtually accusing Lomonosov of selling out to the Germans, he met the Verband alone on 27 February and achieved a reduction to 119,400 gold rubles. He then summoned Lomonosov to check the technical clauses, and only when Krasin initialled the agreed price was a precarious peace re-established between the two men.[94]

The final contract was signed on 28 February, just a few days before the abortive German revolution that would become known as the 'March Action' and on which the Comintern unavailingly pinned such hope. A total of 600 Class E locomotives was subcontracted through Victor Berg and would cost nearly 72 million gold rubles excluding commission fees and certain shipping costs. Payments were to be made through Berg in Tallinn or Stockholm, and the Soviet side had to deliver 10 million gold rubles by 13 March, 26 million by 25 March and the remainder (up to 46 million gold rubles) during the summer of 1921, the precise date depending on when the factories prepared the materials for the boilers and frames.[95]

The irony was, however, that whilst this contract increased the total number of Soviet locomotives on order in Europe to 1,700, only 300 short of the revised target of 2,000, most policy-makers in Moscow no longer wanted more locomotive contracts by this time. Their prime concern was to avert the complete disintegration of the economy, and insofar as economic recovery and modernisation remained the longer term aim, the railways were now playing second fiddle to the GOELRO plan. Even the NKPS had its attention elsewhere: there was political disarray as Trotskii was hastily and temporarily replaced in December by A. I. Emshanov, who had recently been drafted to the NKPS Collegium from the Perm' Railway. Also, the locomotive and wagon repair plans were degenerating into chaos, crippled by the food and fuel shortages and by the Soviet metal industry's failure to supply spare parts. The plan targets were lowered in April 1921 and were eventually quietly forgotten.[96]

Furthermore, in late January 1921 a scandal erupted over the principle of having locomotives overhauled abroad. The NKPS was never particularly keen on the concept, and after Solomon's contract for 230 locomotives to be overhauled in Estonia had caused some concern among directorate chiefs in the autumn, the commissariat was dismayed to hear of a preliminary contract with Armstrong Whitworth. Thus it was unsurprising that, when asked by the OTK to review the whole question of foreign overhauls with particular reference to Armstrongs, the NKPS Technical Directorate responded with a condemnatory paper.[97] It commenced by doubting the feasibility of sending engines to Britain and Germany: the shipment operation would be difficult, time-consuming and expensive. The purchase of spare parts and materials was preferable because, in the authors' opinion, shortages of these were the main cause of disruption at Russian workshops. And the Armstrong proposal was also problematic in that it lacked an overall fixed price, was likely to have high basic cost, and required a large deposit.

The OTK took an even dimmer view. Apart from preferring to support Russian workshops, it felt that this scheme would not significantly quicken the restoration of the railway system. The venture was extremely risky, too, for in the event of any complications the deposit and engines might be lost. The OTK thus firmly opposed such projects, and soon had its conclusion endorsed by Borisov's commissar, Fomin: 'Fully sharing the OTK sub-commission's view about the overhaul of locomotives abroad, I suggest that the [Armstrong] deal is not merely disadvantageous but dangerous'.[98]

This scandal coincided with a sense of crisis about expenditure abroad. By 14 February 1921 Sovnarkom had authorised expenditure of 551,848,049 gold rubles on imports, equivalent to some 75 per cent of the gold reserve available the previous spring. Some of this total may have been covered from other sources like export earnings and the Swedish Concern's credit, but without large foreign credits this rate of expenditure was simply unsustainable. Reporting on 14 February, a Sovnarkom commission therefore recommended cutting the budget for 1920 and early 1921 to 309 million gold rubles, this time including curtailment of NKPS commitments, and it also supported the calls to create a new organisation for producing a single national economic plan. This report thus contributed to the birth of the State Planning Commission (Gosplan) the next day, a fresh review of the imports plan being among its first priorities.[99]

These discussions seemed increasingly liable to abort Lomonosov's locomotive negotiations. Krasin told Lomonosov on 23 February that no further contracts were permitted except for locomotives.[100] The next day a Central Committee commission comprising Kamenev, A. D. Tsiurupa and N. Osinskii recommended increased imports of machinery at the expense of food purchases. If this verdict meant factory and workshop equipment rather than locomotives, it may explain why Lezhava warned Lomonosov by telegram that day not to conclude locomotive contracts because the policy was being reconsidered.[101]

Since Lezhava apparently sent no further messages on this matter, the key question is why his telegram of 24 February failed to prevent the signing of the second German locomotive contract. One possibility is a transmission delay: telegraph contact between Moscow and Europe was generally difficult and slow, and 'urgent' telegrams commonly took three days. It is also conceivable that Lomonosov kept Lezhava's message secret from Krasin. As yet the only certainty is that the contract was signed, and if the Central Committee was perhaps aggrieved, the first payments were nevertheless sent more or less on schedule, the Kronshtadt rebellion and German revolutionaries notwithstanding.

Thus, the main achievements of the railway imports policy by 1 March 1921 were firm contracts for 1,700 Class E locomotives for delivery by 1926, plus a draft contract for overhauling 1,500 locomotives in Britain, and an order for 230 locomotive overhauls in Estonia. Also, Gukovskii had signed a few small contracts in the early summer, and Lomonosov and his new Railway Mission had placed twenty-seven minor orders for various spare parts and other supplies by 21 February 1921, including some contracts using the credit from the Swedish Concern.[102] This represented a substantial expenditure commitment in excess of 200 million gold rubles. However, the second German locomotive contract was really the swan song of the original grandiose imports policy. The NKPS had lost its absolute priority for reconstruction investment and imports, and indeed March 1921 would bring not only the New Economic Policy, the Kronshtadt rebellion and the Anglo-Soviet Trade Agreement, but also more soul-searching about the country's gold expenditure priorities. The idea of rapid sector-by-sector reconstruction and modernisation was discredited, and the heroic period in the history of Soviet foreign trade had ended.

1 Class Ye 2–10–0 decapod, Canadian Locomotive Company, 1915.

2 Belgian-built 'Flamme' locomotive in 'cemetery' condition, *circa* February 1920.

3 Iu. V. Lomonosov and R. N. Lomonosova.

4 On the Tallinn–Stockholm ferry, 23 July 1920: seated, from right: L. B. Krasin, A. N. Shelest, unidentified; standing: L. Bamberger, V. N. Fren, C. H. Lindhagen? W. Hellberg? N. P. Shelest.

5 The Nohab factory, Trollhättan, *circa* 1922.

6 M. Billing and colleagues at Nordiska Handelsbanken, *circa* 1921.

7 Iu. V. Lomonosov (second right), G. W. Anderson (second left) et al., Trollhättan, August 1921.

8 The Russian Railway Mission: Lomonosov and colleagues, *circa* 1921.

9 The Railway Mission's second anniversary party, November 1922.

10 The Railway Mission at work, *circa* 1922.

11 G. W. Anderson, the owner of Nohab, and Iu. V. Lomonosov.

12 William Hellberg, a socialist Swedish lawyer and occasional legal adviser to Krasin and Lomonosov.

13 Otto Hagemann, the chief negotiator of Friedrich Krupp AG.

14 V. N. Fren, deputy head of the Railway Mission.

15 A. I. Emshanov, deputy People's Commissar of Ways of Communication, 1921–1923.

16 The Railway Mission's Berlin premises, *circa* 1921.

17 F. F. Perno, the Railway Mission's chief accountant.

18 Academician A. N. Krylov, head of the Railway Mission's shipping department.

19 The steamship *Odin* in the Kiel canal, *circa* 1922.

20 Nohab locomotives delayed at Trollhättan, 1922.

21 E^{SH}-4151 on test in Russia, October 1922.

22 A locomotive of the type overhauled in Estonia, 1921–1924.

23 Canadian-built tanker wagon, 1921.

24 Armstrong boilers awaiting shipment, 1922.

25 The Avanesov commission, 30 November 1922.

26 Sovnarkom meeting with Lomonosov seated at extreme right, October 1922.

27 E^{SH}-4131 in Soviet service, *circa* 1975.

PART III

Retreat, 1921–1924

6   The new order

After a brief visit to Russia in May 1921, William Peters, shortly to become Assistant Agent at the British government's Trade Mission in Moscow, reported to the Department for Overseas Trade that 'the past two months have been marked by a complete change in the Soviet internal economic policy'. It was principally the work of Lenin, who was arguing that Russia's salvation depended on improving the peasants' lot by allowing them to trade surplus produce. This meant, explained Peters, that the Soviet government was encouraging some measure of capitalism, though in specific forms amenable to state control.[1]

This New Economic Policy, which was launched by the Tenth Party Congress in March 1921, represented a momentous and controversial change. Only reluctantly did Lenin and his Politburo colleagues concede its necessity, fully realising how unpopular it would be among rank-and-file party members. Trenchant opposition had to be overcome both within the Central Committee and at the Congress, especially from the Commissar of Food Procurement, A. D. Tsiurupa. One Congress delegate bitterly assessed the new grain policy as 'capitulation before the petite bourgeoisie'.[2] Abroad, there were some correspondingly cheerful verdicts. In Britain, for example, Lloyd George described the NEP as 'an admission of the complete failure of the Communist system'; the *Review of Reviews* assessed it as 'the abandonment of Communism'; and the *New Statesman* proclaimed in the autumn that the 'Communistic experiment had failed'.[3]

Two key issues discussed at the Congress were the pace of recovery and the role of foreign trade and investment. Some party members feared the possibility of economic dependence and political enslavement, but Lenin disagreed. Delivering the Central Committee report on the first day of the Congress he defended the proposed trade agreement with Britain as an urgent requirement. Further, he argued the economic necessity of encouraging foreign capitalists to invest in Soviet industry as concessionaires, for this would bring income and modern technology. Even with such assistance, he cautioned, general recovery would take 'many years, no less than a decade and – in view of our devastated condition – probably even more'.[4] And towards the end of the Congress he also asserted that the reconstruction of heavy industry would rely mainly on foreign capital.[5] Gone, then, was the expectation of rapid progress, whilst cooperation with foreign capitalism seemed essential.

In the West the new strategy certainly fuelled optimism about the prospects for Soviet–Western economic relations. For instance, William Peters reported to London that 'the change in internal policy is naturally accompanied by a change in external policy. In particular as regards concessions, the Soviet Government seem to be prepared to go a considerable way.'[6] Less restrained, *The Economist* cheerily declared in November 1921 that there were 'undoubtedly big possibilities' in Russia for the businessman.[7] But how did Soviet imports policy actually change under NEP? With so much of the gold reserve already committed, the scope for new expenditure commitments was obviously small unless and until substantial export earnings and foreign credits appeared. In the meantime retrenchment, not new contracts, was the order of the day, and the railway imports policy became a prime target.

Change and continuity under the New Economic Policy

The NEP initially aimed to assist the peasantry by substituting taxation in kind for food requisitions. It necessitated a partial legalisation of private trade, and soon brought change to non-agrarian sectors of the economy. The nationalisation of small-scale industry was abandoned in May 1921, and individuals and cooperatives were permitted to open small private businesses. The state retained control over the 'commanding heights' of the economy such as heavy industry, transport, foreign trade and banking, and indeed strengthened its grip with Gosplan. Yet soon even these sacrosanct sectors faced upheaval as self-financing was introduced and state subsidies were cut.[8]

On the railways the spring of 1921 saw the appointment of the much feared 'Sword of the Revolution', F. E. Dzerzhinskii, as People's Commissar. He was to stay at the NKPS for nearly three years, providing its first experience of sustained strong leadership since

1917. His main contribution in 1921–2 was to launch several major policy initiatives and represent NKPS interests to the Politburo and Central Committee, whilst routine management was left to Emshanov, Borisov and Fomin. Among Dzerzhinskii's early concerns were campaigns against theft from wagons and to improve discipline among transport workers. However, his principal task was to establish strict financial discipline and eliminate the railways' need for a huge subsidy, which he achieved through efficiency campaigns, sweeping staff cuts and even the temporary closure of minor routes. Indeed, partly because of this stringency, and partly because of industrial and agricultural problems, railway freight traffic scarcely increased in 1921 compared with 1920, and recovered only very slowly thereafter.[9]

Heavy industry remained in crisis for months, still crippled by every conceivable shortage. The metal industry in particular faced a cruel paradox. Ideally reconstruction of the transport system would generate demand for metal products, which would help revive Soviet industry; industry's revival would spur demand for transport, which would in turn require more industrial products. But in practice a catastrophic nationwide shortage of working capital helped turn this virtuous circle into an extremely vicious one. Soviet industry urgently needed large orders and advance payments, yet could not guarantee contract deadlines; the NKPS had no funds for large-scale orders and no interest in paying deposits for products which it might never receive.[10]

On the agricultural front the NEP came too late to avert an horrific famine. The scale of the disaster was evident by July 1921, and by December the Volga basin had been devastated, with over 20 million people in need, according to official estimates. In February 1921 the Central Committee intended to cut food imports, but in early March Sovnarkom allocated 10 million gold rubles for new purchases, and by the summer food imports were an urgent priority. So appalling was the catastrophe that in August 1921 the Soviet government signed an agreement for famine relief with Herbert Hoover's American Relief Administration. The aid lasted into 1923.[11]

Hoover's involvement notwithstanding, Soviet–American diplomatic relations were not established until the 1930s.[12] In Europe, by contrast, the Anglo-Soviet Trade Agreement was followed by agreements with other countries and diplomatic recognition in most cases by the mid-1920s. A trade accord with Germany was signed in May 1921, and an NKVT delegation was established in Berlin under B. S. Stomoniakov and a former luminary of the Workers' Opposition, Iu.

Kh. Lutovinov, whilst N. N. Krestinskii arrived as ambassador. The Norwegian government displayed particular interest in normalising relations, and recognised the local Soviet delegation in September 1921. In Italy Vorovskii became ambassador in March 1921 and was joined by A. Naglovskii as the NKVT plenipotentiary, with a trade agreement concluded in December. The Czechoslovak government signed a trade agreement in 1922 after the collapse of the Genoa conference on European reconstruction. Ironically, relations with Sweden developed slowly: on 1 March 1922 the Swedish parliament rejected an agreement negotiated with Kerzhentsev, the Soviet political and trade representative, and an accord was not signed until 1924.[13]

In the meantime, slow progress was recorded in the realms of concessions policy and foreign loans. Relatively few concession agreements were finalised because Western companies remained chary and the Russians assessed proposals cautiously. Indeed, contradicting Peters's enthusiasm, Krasin complained in May 1921 that an ironical attitude towards concession projects had become fashionable in Russia.[14] As for loans, the NKVT Collegium was sufficiently optimistic that on 7 May 1921 it decided to consult the NKPS and Gosplan about compiling a new programme for major railway imports.[15] But though various relatively small loan proposals were considered, no large-scale credit appeared, and by January 1922 Moscow's main hopes, such as they were, lay with the upcoming Genoa economic conference. However, this gathering in April 1922 saw disagreement between Russia and the Entente countries over political recognition, Russia's abrogated foreign debts and Allied compensation for war damage, and then over the Russo-German Treaty of Rapallo of 16 April 1922. The prospect of massive international credit faded.[16]

In these circumstances the NKVT control of the state monopoly of foreign economic relations came under intense scrutiny.[17] In both Russia and the West the NEP raised expectations of increased freedom to trade, and whilst the state monopoly had always been detested abroad, many Soviet functionaries were also criticising it by late 1921. The Eleventh Party Conference and the Ninth Congress of Soviets, both held in Moscow in December 1921, reasserted the principle of the monopoly but did permit state trusts and cooperatives to engage in import–export operations under overall NKVT supervision. Crucially, Lenin continued to back the NKVT monopoly as an essential barrier against Western economic imperialism, and a VTsIK decree defended it on 13 March 1922. Nonetheless, the NKVT's domestic opponents, who included Bukharin and the Commissar of Finances, G. Ia. Sokol'nikov, maintained their pressure. Thanks to a combination of Lenin's absence through illness, and support from the Stalin–Kamenev–Zinov'ev triumvirate, they achieved a significant loosening of the monopoly by a Central Committee Plenum on 6 October 1922. However, Lenin then persuaded Stalin, Kamenev and Zinov'ev to change sides, and the resolution of 6 October was countermanded by another Plenum on 18 December – a decision which, as O'Connor has observed, signalled an important victory for the proponents of planned industrial development over advocates of a much greater role for market forces.[18]

It should thus be no surprise, given the Railway Mission's anomalous character, that relations between Lomonosov and his senior foreign-based colleagues were usually very strained after 1920. The Krasin–Lomonosov rift became a chasm by 1922, whilst the Lomonosov–Kerzhentsev relationship was extremely tense from their first meeting on 12 February 1921, again over the Railway Mission's relative autonomy.[19] In Germany Stomoniakov and Lomonosov were frequently at odds about, for instance, the procedure for placing contracts and the shipment of the locomotives to Russia, and this atmosphere deteriorated further after Krestinskii's arrival. So exasperated did Krestinskii become that, asked by the professor for instructions one day in July 1923, he sardonically recommended Lomonosov to die so that a statue of him could be erected in Russia and his colleagues could at last work in peace.[20]

Kerzhentsev was so outspoken about the Railway Mission in reports in April and early May 1921 as to force the Central Committee to intervene. He felt that the 'complete, at least in practice, autonomy of Professor Lomonosov's railway mission' was shattering his own mission's prestige and causing organisational confusion, and that a total reorganisation of the situation was essential 'to establish political control', involving the Railway Mission's incorporation into the NKVT apparatus.[21] The Orgburo therefore appointed Stalin to chair an investigation into the interrelationship between Lomonosov's mission and other Soviet departments and representatives based abroad. A Central Committee secretary, V. M. Mikhailov, was appointed as deputy chairman of the investigating commission, the NKPS was represented by Emshanov, and Lomonosov was the other member.[22]

V. M. Molotov deputised for Stalin and Mikhailov when this commission convened on 12 May, and Litvinov and Lezhava were included at Chicherin's insistence. Lomonosov later claimed that he deflected complaints from Lezhava about the Railway Mission's financial affairs by reporting that special arrangements had just been agreed with the NKVT. Yet, of course, Lezhava's objections stemmed from the mission's unusual status, and debate about this more fundamental issue could not be avoided. The main question, indeed, was whether the mission was really necessary.[23]

This question was answered affirmatively, though the mission's status was modified. Lomonosov's mandate and instructions were confirmed, but his autonomy was reduced slightly by making his staff responsible ultimately to the Soviet ambassador in their country of employment. Lomonosov himself was subordinated jointly to the NKVT (commercial matters) and NKPS (technical matters). Also, the mission's Main Office was transferred to Berlin – a measure probably intended to defuse the confrontation with Kerzhentsev but which left Lomonosov anticipating equally bitter trouble with Stomoniakov. Indeed these reforms were essentially meaningless because Lomonosov retained his authority as a Sovnarkom plenipotentiary with commercial as well as technical responsibilities, which meant that in practice he could continue placing orders without involving NKVT personnel.[24]

Why, then, did the Railway Mission survive, and indeed exist for two more years despite continued opposition? One important reason for this was the influence of Lenin. Though he sided with Krasin over the trade monopoly, he had played perhaps the key role in creating the mission, and he continued to value Lomonosov's opinions about transport until his final illness and retirement in late 1922. Lenin intervened on Lomonosov's behalf on several occasions in 1921–2, as will be shown below, and he may well have contributed informally to the commission's deliberations in May 1921. Equally, Lenin's poor health during 1922 deprived Lomonosov of a valuable ally at a time when the railway contracts were attracting intense criticism.

Stalin, too, was inclined to be supportive, at least until mid-1922, to judge by one of his memoranda to Lenin in March of that year.[25] Here Stalin's remarks were a subtle salvo in the campaign against the NKVT monopoly, trying to break Lenin's support for Krasin by playing on his sympathy for Lomonosov. Krasin was said to be waging 'a mad (*beshenuiu*) battle' against Lomonosov, 'not so much because of the interests of the job as of glory in Europe'. Until recently, Stalin remarked, Krasin had been regarded in Europe's business world as 'the only intelligent and business-like representative of

Soviet Russia'. However, 'the appearance of Lomonosov with his practical approach to the job and massive contracts has undoubtedly shaken the "position" of comrade Krasin'. Whereas Krasin had concluded scarcely any agreements over the previous year, Lomonosov had lots to his name: evidently the business world preferred him. Thus Krasin probably feared that he would be 'conclusively shamed' if Lomonosov managed to do his job smoothly in London – 'God forbid, he-he! ...' According to Stalin, 'filth' (*griaz'*) was probably the key to Krasin's campaign, for it was otherwise impossible to understand 'how a person who has the "shameful" contract with Armstrongs behind his back can stammer on about the drawbacks (*nevygodnost'*) of comrade Lomonosov's contracts'.

As O'Connor has remarked, Krasin was also despised and distrusted by Kamenev and Dzerzhinskii. Significantly, Lomonosov had enjoyed a close friendship with Kamenev and his family since the autumn of 1919, increasingly regarding Kamenev as his political patron, and Lomonosov remained a welcome visitor to the Politburo member's Kremlin apartment and country dacha until persistent controversy eventually made Kamenev distance himself in late 1922.[26]

NKPS leaders also afforded the Railway Mission valuable support, perhaps partly from Dzerzhinskii's antipathy towards Krasin but mainly because they felt that NKPS interests would be better served by a powerful experienced railwayman than by the NKVT bureaucracy. The potential value of this arrangement was illustrated just a few days after the above-mentioned investigation. On 20 May 1921 the STO declared a moratorium on new foreign contracts for all commissariats pending Gosplan's first reassessment of imports policy, and this threatened a proposed new NKPS 'shock' imports programme. But Lomonosov was able quietly to assure NKPS leaders that the most crucial items – workshop tools and fire-resistant brick – could still be purchased using interest earned on bank deposits and other monies accumulated by the Railway Mission. As Lomonosov later commented, a close friendship began between him and the NKPS Collegium at this juncture despite his rivalry with Borisov.[27]

Needless to say, the decisions taken by the Central Committee commission failed to improve the mission's relations with other Soviet representatives in Europe. For example, a further tussle occurred between Lomonosov and Kerzhentsev as early as June 1921.[28] Much more serious, and quite typical, was an almighty row between Krasin, Stomoniakov and Lomonosov in Berlin on 27 May. The issues were the negotiation of railway contracts in Germany and the shipment of the German locomotives to Russia. Krasin argued that it was vital to coordinate Railway Mission and NKVT activity, and whilst he apparently did not demand that the mission be abolished, he did insist that all railway orders be placed through Stomoniakov. But Lomonosov refused to be sidelined as a mere 'errand boy', and he reportedly suggested liquidating the mission as the easiest option. After the meeting, however, one of Lomonosov's deputies persuaded him to remain in post until at least the autumn, and by 30 May Lomonosov was writing in his diary of his readiness to take on the world.[29] Doubtless he had required little persuasion.

When Lutovinov arranged a meeting on 31 May to effect a reconciliation, Lomonosov proposed a strange compromise whereby NKPS orders would be defined in three categories: firstly, purely railway contracts, like those for locomotives, wagons and spare parts; secondly, orders for machines, tooling, electrical equipment and special materials; and thirdly, orders for general materials. The first category would be the exclusive prerogative of the Railway Mission, the second type would be handled jointly by the mission and the NKVT, and the last category could be managed solely by the NKVT. According to Lomonosov, Stomoniakov agreed to this suggestion, presumably very reluctantly. But because Stomoniakov still demanded to be consulted before any contract was signed, Lomonosov appealed to Sovnarkom. And ultimately the NKVT representatives were frustrated once again: with Lenin's support Lomonosov not only retained control over all NKPS orders but also, in early 1922, won responsibility for shipping the locomotives to Russia.[30]

This fracas between Lomonosov and the NKVT also helped to delay the movement of the first Swedish locomotives to Russia, even though output had fallen well behind schedule. As a temporary measure the first engines were sent overland via Finland in the autumn of 1921, but unfortunately they coincided with the Karelian uprising, and this route was abandoned after eighteen engines had been despatched. All the remaining engines, both Swedish and German, were sent by ship, normally in batches of about ten and with only a few minor parts dismantled for safe-keeping. They travelled either directly to Petrograd or through the Baltic ports of Tallinn, Riga or Ventspils, and underwent their acceptance trials after checks at NKPS workshops in Petrograd or Velikie Luki. Ships had to be specially modified to hold the locomotives, for which task Lomonosov employed the highly respected shipping expert Academician A. N. Krylov, who also took over the Railway Mission's shipping department.[31]

It is curious that although Lomonosov often voiced agreement that his mission should be incorporated into the NKVT trade delegations in Sweden and Germany, he stubbornly resisted any measures to achieve this end. Perhaps he did genuinely believe that Krasin, Kerzhentsev and others were mainly pursuing personal vendettas against him. Perhaps, too, he feared for his comfortable (not to say extravagant) lifestyle and the kudos of negotiating with major foreign banks and companies. Almost certainly he hoped that his responsible position would help him return to the NKPS Collegium, from which he had been removed in the autumn of 1920; as late as the autumn of 1922 he still hoped to become People's Commissar of Ways of Communication or, bizarrely, Soviet ambassador to Sweden, notwithstanding all the controversy and his non-membership of the Party.[32]

There were countless altercations between Lomonosov and representatives of the NKVT and Commissariat of Foreign Affairs before the mission was eventually abolished in April 1923. Topics ranged from individual contracts, gold sales and the salaries of Lomonosov's personnel, to responsibility for repairing and maintaining the ships bought or hired for the movement of NKPS goods to Russia. They even prompted Lomonosov's resignation in January 1922, only for this to be opposed by Lenin and refused by the Politburo; and they may have influenced Lezhava in his similarly unsuccessful resignation from the NKVT Collegium a few days later.[33] And it was in this rather sordid context as the NEP was consolidated that a series of rows unfolded in Moscow concerning NKPS foreign expenditure, culminating in a major confrontation between the NKPS and VSNKh during the first half of 1922.

Retrenchment

The NKPS remained anxious to obtain imports of spares and materials for its immediate needs throughout the winter of 1920–1. Typical was a statement from the OTK to the STO on 3 December that deliveries of foreign-made boiler tubes and tyres ought to be the NKVT's first priority.[34] Similarly, the railway newspaper *Gudok* complained in January 1921 that VSNKh factories were supplying only about 40 per cent of the transport system's requirement for metals and metal products, and stressed that Lomonosov's imports were helping to ease a very difficult situation.[35] Several months later Emshanov and the OTK's secretary, A. I. Grinshtein, warned the STO that the imported tyres and boiler tubes were proving vital, and that more imports would be essential if even a scaled-down version of the repair programme was to be implemented, let alone the original plan.[36] And shortly before Dzerzhinskii was appointed People's Commissar, Emshanov approved the statute of an NKPS secretariat for foreign affairs. It is not clear whether this office with its staff of seven was new or derived from the special secretariat of the Directorate of Economics and Materials, but its appearance certainly reaffirmed NKPS interest in imports.[37]

Nor did Dzerzhinskii dampen this hunger for imports, his reputed aversion to foreign capital notwithstanding. An NKPS meeting which he chaired on 9 May 1921 defined the supply issue as one of the most acute problems, and imports as one of the main solutions.[38] At this time, too, the NKPS submitted a fresh 'shock programme' for imports, emphasising tools, wagon spare parts, nails, roofing iron, telegraph equipment and a vital component for oil-burning locomotives, fire-resistant brick.[39]

By now, however, the government had little room for manoeuvre over new foreign expenditure. The Gosplan Sub-Commission for Foreign Trade and Concessions began reassessing the national imports plan in April 1921, and its interim report, approved by the STO on 20 May, recommended a moratorium on new contracts pending more detailed investigation. There was painstaking discussion of the plan, covering all previously approved expenditure as well as recent applications, and by 1 June Gosplan had authorised expenditure totalling 511,183,976 gold rubles. This total was only about 40 million rubles less than the sum authorised by 14 February, but it disguised a big cut of some 155 million rubles to 397,161,162 rubles and the addition of 113,992,814 rubles for military needs.[40] With the uncommitted gold reserve thus likely to be under 240 million rubles, Gosplan recommended that only about 20 million gold rubles be available for all new contracts for the second half of 1921, including famine relief, and the STO concurred on 15 July, albeit with a slightly higher figure of 29,957,610 gold rubles.[41]

Inevitably the NKPS suffered badly in this retrenchment. As of 1 June its share was set to drop from 315,438,850 to 182,986,859 gold rubles (46.1 per cent of the total), though its existing contracts were worth 222,234,319 gold rubles. Ignoring the original aim of rapid reconstruction, Gosplan sharply rebuked the NKPS for buying many more foreign locomotives and planning far more overhauls than could be justified for the traffic now expected in 1921. There could be no question of ordering the final 300 of the 2,000 engines authorised in

October 1920. Future NKPS contracts, the planners insisted, should be restricted to spare parts and materials. Yet here too there was trouble. It will be recalled that on 4 October 1920 the NKPS had sought 158 million gold rubles for spare parts and rails under the 1920 imports plan, and a further 142 million gold rubles for spares and materials in the 1921 imports plan, but that the Council of Foreign Trade had released only 54 million gold rubles as part of the 1920 plan. Now, in early May 1921, Gosplan imposed a limit of only 41,066,910 gold rubles for railway-related spare parts and materials in 1921, and then came big cuts as a result of the STO's general retrenchment in June and July.[42]

The NKPS and OTK did win a morale-boosting victory on 18 May when the STO endorsed the latest NKPS 'shock programme' of imports as an act 'of least resistance' to support a 'minimal' programme of overhauls.[43] But then came the moratorium on placing new orders, which included the NKPS plan, despite the OTK's insistence that the proposed railway imports were absolutely essential. Subsequently, the NKPS pared its claim for new contracts to 17 million gold rubles, complaining that any further cut would be extremely harmful, only for Gosplan to stipulate on 5 July a maximum of just 9,338,750 gold rubles. Nor did the agony end there: a special commission then set the NKPS share for the rest of 1921 at just 3 million gold rubles, and the STO ratified this figure on 15 July.[44]

In short, with the objective of economic reconstruction becoming more distant, both Krasin's and Trotskii's strategies for the railways had fallen into disfavour. Discussions about modernisation and technological innovation did continue in the press and within the NKPS, but subsistence was the priority. As for imports, the only ways to circumvent the expenditure limit were by using Lomonosov's savings and persuading the STO and Sovnarkom to authorise extra credits for special purposes. However, as the NKPS would soon discover, this tactic risked causing more harm than good by antagonising Gosplan, Sovnarkom's standing commission for gold affairs, and rival claimants.

It was perhaps in an attempt to outrun the impending budget storm that on 11 March 1921 the NKPS asked Lomonosov to try to buy up the elusive American decapods.[45] Since the summer of 1920 discussions about Class Ye locomotives had been continuing in somewhat desultory fashion with six or more trading companies, covering both the US War Department's stock and possible new construction. But terms could not be agreed, especially the price, and the US authorities still appeared hostile, forcing the renegotiation of the Revalis contract during the autumn. Now, however, the Railway Mission and Krasin reconsidered the War Department engines, including one offer dated 21 March with a unit price as low as $22,000.[46]

Ironically, it is possible that a Soviet order for new locomotives might have been placed successfully. A scheme for 100 new Baldwin decapods was devised by the British Baltic Commercial Corporation, with the locomotives to be shipped as kits for reassembly in Göteborg or Helsingfors, and in April 1921 the US State Department decided not to oppose the idea given that Baldwin was on half-time working and there would not be any direct American involvement with the Bolsheviks.[47] But the Soviet side concentrated on the War Department's engines, and here the State Department veto was firm despite the use of intermediary companies. The only difference from 1920 was the reason now cited: retaliation for the imprisonment of several American citizens in Bolshevik Russia.[48]

However, even before these nuances could be investigated the Railway Mission began rejecting the intermediaries' offers. Officially the Russians blamed 'political reasons' and the lack of diplomatic relations, but the real cause was a shortage of money.[49] Only with Revalis did Krasin and Lomonosov continue to show any interest, and that was through fear of losing their deposit of some $117,520. At length, in mid-June, Lomonosov accepted a Revalis offer of 40 locomotives at $16,500 each, but a few days later he was informed that the War Department had sold its last engines.[50] Indeed, all 200 of the War Department engines found homes on US railways, and the Revalis contract was eventually annulled.[51]

Thus ended the attempts to place major railway contracts in the USA. There were reportedly some 7,290 tonnes of minor railway imports in 1921–3 which have been valued at 2.67 million gold rubles (in pre-war prices) and which may include deliveries against Gukovskii's contracts of 1920 for rails and boiler tubes. Not until Lend-Lease deliveries of several thousand Class Ye locomotives during the Second World War would there be any American imports on the scale of the German and Swedish contracts of 1920–1.[52]

While the decapod saga reached its conclusion the rationale and cost of several existing and intended railway contracts came under attack in Moscow. The most important talking points were proposed orders for modern oil-tanker wagons and fire-resistant brick, and especially the locomotive overhaul contracts. The biggest items of expenditure – the Swedish and German locomotives – did attract some criticism during 1921, but the cost of shipping them to Russia caused much greater consternation, which only later extended to the locomotives themselves.

The purchase of modern oil-tankers was mooted by Krasin in early 1921 to facilitate exports of oil. The OTK acquiesced on 10 May to a maximum of 3,000 tankers and associated spare parts, but Gosplan's drastic revision of the imports plan badly delayed the project. The NKPS therefore had to request a special credit, and Gosplan set a limit of only 1,700 tankers in July, presumably for financial reasons. Even so the expected cost was approximately 10 million gold rubles – one-third of the amount just finalised for the national imports plan for the remainder of 1921.[53] Meanwhile Krasin, impatient at the delay, personally authorised Lomonosov to begin placing orders immediately. Thus, 500 four-axle tankers with a 38-tonne capacity were ordered from the Canadian Car and Foundry Company (Montreal) on 25 June. Then, this time with authorisation from Gosplan and Sovnarkom, a further 1,000 identical tankers were agreed with an Anglo-German partnership involving the Leeds Forge Company and the Linke-Hofmann company of Breslau on 25 August.[54] However, there were complaints about the apparently cavalier manner in which Krasin and Lomonosov handled this whole project. The VTsIK overruled Sovnarkom's approval, and Sovnarkom's permanent commission for gold affairs, chaired by a deputy head of the NKRKI and Cheka, V. A. Avanesov, undertook a hostile investigation. But both contracts gained STO assent in early November, and all 1,500 tankers were delivered to Novorossiisk by December 1922.[55]

Not just cost but the revival of Soviet industry seemed at stake in the proposal to import fire-resistant brick. As a classic example of the way in which the NKPS–supplier relationship had disintegrated, it would provoke months of soul-searching. The railways wanted to convert locomotives to burn oil, which was more plentiful than coal and wood in certain areas, and this brick was essential for the fireboxes in oil-burners, but the one Soviet factory that produced the brick was at a standstill. The NKPS saw imports as the only solution, whilst the VSNKh wanted priority assistance for its factory, and this time the domestic option prevailed. The NKPS was allowed to import only a tenth of its requirement, for which it was allocated 189,000 gold rubles from its already minimal allocation of 3 million gold rubles at the expense of other supplies in November 1921. In fact even this credit was axed in early 1922 before it could be used fully, and because the domestic output of the brick remained insignificant the conversion programme collapsed.[56]

As for the overhaul of locomotives abroad, the NKPS had always had misgivings about the concept and cost. Neither the commissariat nor Lomonosov was involved in the final negotiation of Solomon's Estonian contract for repairing Class O locomotives, and almost immediately the commissariat suspended delivery of engines in protest at certain clauses. Lomonosov took over responsibility for supervising the work several months later and drafted a new contract on 12 August 1921. The NKRKI and its NKPS filiation, the Inspectorate of Ways of Communication, condemned the whole enterprise as unnecessary, but Gosplan allowed Lomonosov to proceed on condition that no Soviet expenditure would be required, and following STO approval on 16 November a replacement contract for 200 overhauls was sealed on 20 December 1921.[57]

The Armstrong affair was much more problematic.[58] Though prevented by the OTK from signing a final contract for 1,500 locomotive overhauls upon his return to London in March 1921, Krasin was unrepentant. However, a compromise emerged on 10 May when the OTK heard reports by Krasin, Lomonosov and the NKPS Head of Traction, P. I. Krasovskii. The deal was narrowly approved in a four-three vote, but Krasin was to try to change the object of the contract from locomotive overhauls to either new locomotives or spare parts, and Moscow's policy of overhauling engines abroad would be reviewed urgently.[59] Thus, when Armstrongs pressed Krasin to sign the contract for overhauls in mid-June, he declined. Not only had the legal test cases about Soviet property not been settled, despite British government assurances, but conditions in Russia had improved 'radically', and Finnish and Estonian companies had offered to overhaul engines on much better terms. Nevertheless, Krasin said, he would do everything possible for a contract with Armstrongs. The company could help by easing its terms or agreeing to make either Russian-type locomotives or spare parts, and as a gesture of goodwill he would accept prices up to 10 per cent above other quotations.[60]

This last statement would have sparked outrage in Moscow had it become known there. The 1921 gold budget was being drastically cut at precisely this time, and the NKRKI and Inspectorate of Ways of Communications were beginning to scent scandal in the whole business of NKPS foreign orders. Investigations were being launched into the tanker scheme and other projects, and the NKRKI and Inspectorate of Ways of Communications submitted a critical report about the

Armstrong business to Sovnarkom only a few weeks later.[61] So strong was this ill feeling that in early August Krasin warned the newly appointed British representative to Russia, R. M. Hodgson, that it would be impossible to conclude the Armstrong contract on financial grounds. The company was infuriated, and, unusually, the British Foreign Office even tried to intervene.[62]

Sovnarkom debated the affair on 23 August. According to Lomonosov's memoirs, there was much opposition to the conclusion of a contract with Armstrongs, but Lenin's support ensured a majority for a resolution tabled by Krasin:

> the negotiations with the Armstrong firm, which concern the repair of Russian locomotives and were started in order to speed up the diplomatic negotiations about a Russian–English agreement, have reached such a stage (the signing by comrade Lomonosov in January 1921 of preliminary terms with Armstrongs) that at the present time rejection of this contract would be understood in England as the breaking of promises given by the Plenipotentiary Representative of the Government of the RSFSR, which could be unfavourably reflected in the business credit of the republic.[63]

A five-year contract was to be signed for 1,500 overhauls, and 5.25 million gold rubles were assigned for the first payments.[64] Apparently it was also decided, though not recorded in the protocol, that Lomonosov should immediately try to reduce the order or, if possible, renegotiate it for new engines or spare parts, as the OTK had instructed some months earlier.[65]

As with the tankers, the VTsIK objected to Sovnarkom's decision on 8 September. But Krasin seemed determined to conclude a contract at all costs. Apparently he appealed to the Politburo, and he convened a meeting of his London delegation on 30 September which instructed Lomonosov to finalise a text with Armstrongs.[66] Two fraught sessions with the company followed, Armstrongs giving way almost completely on 3 October and settling for just 200 new boilers.[67] Worth £797,500, the final contract was signed in Berlin on 15 October 1921, the Russians supplying the cash deposit and technical drawings immediately. At the same time Lomonosov arranged to use 50 of these boilers in the Russian engines being built at Trollhättan, selling them to Anderson for about 60,000 Swedish crowns each and writing down the resultant loss to 'the liquidation of Krasin's political agreement'. The other 150 boilers were earmarked for existing Soviet Class O and Shch locomotives.[68]

Krasin was probably quite satisfied with this relatively inexpensive outcome. By contrast, Armstrongs felt betrayed: having signed the contract for the company, Sir Walter Preston even refused Lomonosov's invitation to a commemorative dinner.[69] There was disgust in Moscow, too, the contract being attacked particularly at STO meetings on 28 October and 4 November 1921. However, Fomin strongly defended Lomonosov – thanks to his clever work 'this whole Armstrong adventure' would cost only 5 million gold rubles instead of 60 million – and Lomonosov's actions were approved. The full sum of gold was allocated on 9 November, and the boilers were delivered during 1922.[70]

Such, then, were the main contracts which drew fire during the summer of 1921. There were, however, two further important issues which, in conjunction with these arguments, brought the main locomotive contracts into disrepute by 1922. The first was the cost of shipping the Swedish- and German-built locomotives to Russia; the second was the state of NKPS–VSNKh relations.

The dispute over shipping costs arose because these costs were excluded from the locomotive contracts to reduce the unit price and were subsequently overlooked in Moscow. Sovnarkom thus had a nasty surprise when, on 23 August 1921, Lomonosov requested a large special credit to fund the movement of the 700 German and first 250 Swedish locomotives. As he later explained to the Gosplan Sub-Commission for Foreign Trade and Concessions, he had covered the preliminary costs partly by using funds allocated for the locomotives themselves and partly by loans at 8 per cent interest, and he was now hiring ships for 1922–3 at a cost of roughly 4,700 gold rubles per locomotive. The sum required to move 950 locomotives in 1921–2 was 4,465,000 gold rubles, of which half was needed by 1 January 1922 and the remainder by 1 July 1922.[71]

Sovnarkom responded to this virtual ultimatum by instigating yet another Gosplan review of the national imports programme. The foreign trade sub-commission duly reported that the only possible source of cash among existing allocations was the remnant of a credit opened for the paper industry, and deadlock ensued when the NKVT objected without indicating any alternative. As was to be expected, Grinshtein of the NKPS and OTK proposed asking the STO for a special credit, but the Gosplan sub-commission backed a counter-suggestion to take an advance from the NKPS share of the as yet undetermined 1922 gold expenditure programme.[72]

The issue of finalising a plan for all 1922 imports would prove difficult too. Applications for imports in 1922 totalled 496 million gold rubles (excluding any military request), and the NKPS claim was modest compared to previous years. The two biggest bids came from the commissariat of food procurement (187 million) and VSNKh (136 million), followed by the agriculture commissariat (66 million) and, in lowly fourth place, the NKPS (41 million); the remainder (total 66 million) was sought by four other commissariats and the Ugol' coal-mining trust. The trouble was that, allowing for existing commitments, the state's reserve of gold and precious metals was under 200 million gold rubles. A certain amount of foreign credit was becoming available for famine relief, but there was little for the likes of the NKPS and VSNKh. The total cash available for non-famine imports during 1922 could hardly be much more than the sum allowed for the second half of 1921, roughly 30 million gold rubles.[73]

Thus, the situation was tense when the Gosplan sub-commission reassembled on 2 December 1921 to consider the NKPS bid for 1922.[74] The introductory report, delivered by P. S. Ianushevskii of Gosplan's Transport Section, outlined the main elements: 5,955,647 gold rubles for urgent requirements which could not be produced in Russia; 4,465,000 gold rubles for the locomotive shipments; and 23 million gold rubles for scheduled payments for the new locomotives – a sum which 'may lie as a heavy burden on the imports plan for 1922'. The subsequent discussion was relatively short, not least because the bid seemed like another ultimatum. Surprisingly, the bid for nearly 6 million gold rubles was approved without any recorded objection; more significantly, the sub-commission wanted Sovnarkom or the STO to launch a special investigation into the payments needed for existing and new railway orders so as to forestall any more NKPS or Railway Mission ultimatums in 1922. And this request went to the STO on 15 December with the blessing of the Gosplan Presidium.[75]

One can see, then, that the NKPS made a spirited effort to circumvent the retrenchment of 1921. At the end of that year its tactics must have seemed reasonably successful in that the tanker and Armstrong projects – both, ironically, initiated by Krasin – had been approved outside the national imports plan, and approval of its bid for 1922 seemed probable by force of circumstances. But at what cost to the NKPS? Gosplan and the Sovnarkom gold commission had been seriously antagonised, and indeed Gosplan's call on 2 December for an investigation into NKPS foreign expenditure commitments would lead to the idea of cancelling the locomotive contracts. Perhaps not before time, NKPS chickens were beginning to come home to roost, and when the VSNKh intervened at precisely this juncture, the feathers really began to fly.

Politics of scarcity: a conflict of interests

In early 1920 the notion of importing railway equipment had evinced mixed feelings within the VSNKh. Rykov, the chairman, had supported Krasin's foreign trade strategy, including railway-related imports, whereas at least one official of the Department of Metal, Al'perovich, had been outspokenly opposed to locomotive imports. This basic divergence of opinion probably persisted during the remainder of 1920 and early 1921, for Rykov continued to support Krasin. But a major dispute did not ensue within the VSNKh, to judge by the lack of further comment about it in the press and the meetings of the VSNKh Presidium during 1920 and early 1921. Doubtless this was partly because the Department of Metal became preoccupied with other issues: war with Poland and the campaign against General Vrangel' meant more demand for armaments, whilst the long-term locomotive and wagon overhaul programmes looked set to occupy the Soviet factories for years, albeit with work normally despised by the locomotive-builders and production crippled by shortages in the short term.[76]

However, VSNKh attitudes towards imports were hardening by mid-1921 under the influence of the NEP. By the end of May the Department of Metal's Chairman, P. A. Bogdanov, had replaced Rykov as VSNKh Chairman, whilst the Department of Metal was reorganised as Glavmetall in June and placed under L. K. Martens, recently returned from the United States. And if commissariats like the NKPS placed great hopes on imports, so too did the VSNKh, Glavmetall and their factories. Indeed, the new policy of financial discipline encouraged the VSNKh to complain about commissariats placing contracts abroad just when its own factories urgently needed new orders. Clearly dissatisfied with the limited influence of the VSNKh Committee for Foreign Trade, the VSNKh and Glavmetall sought the right to veto the foreign expenditure proposals of other commissariats on the grounds that most orders typically placed abroad could be successfully completed more cheaply in Russia. They also wanted to have their own office in Europe to purchase metals, tools and other goods for VSNKh departments and enterprises, a demand which directly challenged NKVT control of the trade monopoly.[77]

The campaign waged by the VSNKh and its engineering factories was in some ways reminiscent of the final pre-war decades. Tsarist ministers had tried to force the growth of the heavy-engineering industry and protect it from foreign competition, one of the principal objectives being to avoid economic and political dependence on the West. The VSNKh now played upon precisely these fears of dependence, also raising the spectre of deindustrialisation for good measure. If the Soviet government failed to protect Russian industry in its hour of crisis, the quick and inevitable result would be counter-revolution and Russia's political enslavement.

This VSNKh campaign inevitably meant direct conflict with other commissariats. Three interrelated disputes developed with the NKPS in particular towards the close of 1921, highlighting the complex interaction between domestic and foreign economic policy under the NEP. With both organisations facing a small domestic budget and chronic lack of working capital, the first problem concerned mutual payments for services rendered: the railways demanded payment for shipments to and from VSNKh factories, whereas the VSNKh objected that the NKPS failure to pay its bills was crippling heavy industry's finances. The second issue followed directly from the first: the factories wanted contracts so as to boost their income, and they needed investment to enable completion of those contracts, whereas the NKPS predicted catastrophe if it was forced to rely on Soviet industry for boiler tubes, tyres, springs, fire-resistant brick and other essential spares.

With justice on both sides, compromise was clearly needed. Above all an overview was required which prioritised not one or another commissariat but the economic links between them. However, the lack of resources restricted the scope for manoeuvre, and neither the NKPS nor VSNKh could operate in that spirit. For them, survival implied scrambling for absolute priority treatment, and this in turn generated their third issue of dispute: gold. For both organisations gold was the means with which to break the vicious circle, above all by funding imports of their most urgent requirements, be they spare parts or food. In such circumstances, therefore, it would fall to Gosplan, Sovnarkom and, ultimately, the Politburo and Central Committee to arbitrate and impose a solution. Significantly, that task would prove easier said than done.

An early indication of the VSNKh's determination came in August 1921 with a sweeping attack against the NKVT in *Ekonomicheskaia zhizn'*. A member of Glavmetall's Collegium, B. Stiunkel', complained that commissariats routinely requested imports of products without first clarifying whether these goods could be produced in Russia. He offered NKPS imports as a sobering example:

> Transport needs components, items of equipment, spare parts. With the actual resources at their disposal our factories cannot meet orders at the customer's request, and the latter follows the line of least resistance and orders everything abroad. In this way locomotives have been ordered at a time when we have about 2,000 locomotives idle in store owing to a shortage of fuel. A factory is being built abroad to enable completion of part of the [locomotive] order ... on which the gold reserve is being spent, whilst our industry is in a state of paralysis. Meanwhile, this gold would produce a definite and real effect if it was used for our factories on the purchase of the most essential machines to mechanise the preparation and delivery of fuel, the purchase of parts, raw materials, fuel, clothing and food.[78]

For Stiunkel' a fundamental reorganisation of Soviet foreign trade was vital. The NKVT should be restricted to currency regulation and the supervision of purchasing activity abroad, and VSNKh production departments should be consulted about all imports requested by other commissariats and should control the credits allocated.

Stiunkel' was obviously reluctant to distinguish himself by fair criticism and factual accuracy. There had not been any 'healthy' engines in store when the policy was formulated, and there were about 1,000 in store by February 1921; to cite a later statistic here was tendentious misrepresentation. Equally, his claim about funding a foreign factory was garbled. In reality, Lomonosov obtained Krasin's permission in early 1921 to give Nohab a commercial loan to expand the Trollhättan boiler shop. Next, Lomonosov made several loans to Nohab against a guarantee for delivery of all 1,000 engines by 31 December 1925, and the annulment of certain previous financial commitments, including the Tsentrosoiuz's obligation to provide a 10 per cent return on Nohab's share capital. These loans were secured against all of Nohab's property and would be repaid through reductions in the price of locomotives, the whole arrangement being formalised on 13 March 1921 by a new edition of the Nohab locomotive contract.[79]

But there was no denying the pertinence of two of Stiunkel''s comments. Commissariats obviously found it far easier to obtain equipment and materials abroad if they had sufficient gold or foreign credit; indeed, the concept of 'least resistance' had even been quoted in May 1921 with regard to the latest NKPS 'shock programme'. Also, there can be little doubt that many Soviet factories could have increased their production if given imported supplies.

The NKPS and NKVT both resisted such attacks vigorously. For example, *Gudok* reminded readers on 13 September of how imports were easing the difficult supply situation on the railways.[80] Similarly, Krasin condemned the VSNKh desire to operate independently in foreign markets. Indeed it was at this juncture that, as mentioned already, he praised the second German locomotive order for helping him to win over the British government, and he also lauded the Nohab and Armstrong contracts.[81] Interestingly, too, Krasin stressed in *Ekonomicheskaia zhizn'* that although the NKPS in effect had its own organisation abroad, the Railway Mission did operate under NKVT control.[82] Since this did not really happen in practice, it may be that Lomonosov's relative autonomy was encouraging the VSNKh to think in similar terms.

Such controversy developed over the whole complex issue of NKPS supplies during the autumn of 1921 that the STO commissioned a special report from the OTK. Unfortunately for Soviet industry, the OTK sided with the NKPS. Basically, the commission could not foresee any rapid improvement in VSNKh output and warned of imminent catastrophe on the transport system.[83] Apparently, the commission's final report advised allowing the NKPS to make purchases on the domestic free market and allocating enough gold to import all the most vital items. The OTK also wanted VSNKh factories to cease overhauling locomotives and wagons as soon as practicable – an idea already endorsed by Gosplan in August 1921 – possibly because it believed that NKPS workshops were better equipped for this work and could do it more cheaply. As for the metal factories, the OTK merely called for urgent measures to restore the industry, including reorganisation and new production plans.[84]

Needless to say, Stiunkel' was unimpressed. In his opinion, the factories' problems would not be solved with 'bureaucratic' measures like reorganisation and planning, but with adequate food, fuel and materials.[85] However, he did not disagree about the proposed cessation of locomotive and wagon overhauls, even though this recommendation presented the VSNKh with arguably its most important decision: if these contracts were abandoned, the locomotive- and wagon-building plants would be left without rolling-stock work unless they could get new construction orders – an option which the OTK report seemingly ignored or simply rejected.

Never particularly enthusiastic about the unglamorous repair business, and fully supporting its flagship enterprises, Glavmetall concentrated on winning contracts for new stock. It offered to build Class E engines to the same deadlines as the foreign companies for only 65 per cent of their price, and it thereby presented the transport commissariat with an awkward dilemma. Whereas the NKPS wanted as many new modern engines as possible, it did not actually need them immediately and could not afford them if they were built in Russia. The point was that the Swedish and German contracts were being financed from the gold reserve, whereas orders for Soviet industry would have to be funded from the NKPS domestic ruble budget. Yet the NKPS regarded its domestic budget for 1922, which equated to 48 million gold rubles, as woefully inadequate for providing even a minimal service, let alone investment in capital equipment.[86]

Reluctantly, the NKPS declined Glavmetall's offer, but it did pledge to support any Glavmetall application to the STO for funding for new contracts.[87] The problem was clearly financial, but this proof that the NKPS would welcome Soviet-built rolling-stock was enough to spur the metal industry into battle. Led, ironically, by Martens, and later by P. I. Sudakov, Glavmetall and the metal industry began a determined campaign against stubborn NKPS resistance for the cancellation of the foreign locomotive contracts and their transfer to Soviet factories.

Protectionism resurgent

Lenin himself informed the Ninth Congress of Soviets on 23 December 1921 that the first fifty German and Swedish locomotives had reached Russia.[88] But whilst he treated this news as welcome evidence of a trade revival, Glavmetall disagreed. In an old-style call for priority treatment, Martens warned the congress that imports would undermine Russian industry and that the state's independence was at stake. In Glavmetall's opinion the country had to concentrate on food, fuel and metal.[89]

Significantly, the OTK moved in this direction on 26 December by accepting, doubtless in the teeth of NKPS objections, the recommendation of a special commission that NKPS foreign contracts be transferred to the Soviet metal industry.[90] Then, on 9 January 1922, the OTK went further by calling for a locomotive construction plan for VSNKh factories.[91] A week later Glavmetall's A. S. Chernov reiterated Stiunkel''s criticisms of the recent OTK report and added that Soviet industry could benefit enormously from even a fraction of the NKPS gold.[92] And the same stance was taken by a vituperative report, which was probably produced by the GOMZA machine-building group in early 1922 and which is worth considering at length as much for its tone as its arguments.[93]

The report commenced by observing darkly that although the recovery of the metal industry was a designated national priority, a 'strange situation' prevailed. The major factories needed contracts, yet GOMZA lacked orders for its main products, locomotives and wagons, and was even unsure whether it could meet existing commitments for other products owing to its almost total deprivation of working capital. Indignantly the report complained:

> How is one to explain such an attitude on the Centre's part towards the factories, which justifiably consider themselves among the principal factories of our Russian industry? The issue is extremely simple. It is not known why our supreme government bodies placed large orders for rolling-stock abroad. 1,000 0–5–0 engines have been ordered in Sweden and 700 in Germany. Large orders for tank wagons have also been issued abroad. We do not know whether orders have been made for wagons and other goods which can easily be produced by our factories, since it is naturally very difficult for us to obtain full data of this nature. Thus, because of orders placed abroad, our factories completely lose their usefulness. And at the same time the locomotives which are currently being imported are not actually being used owing to the objective circumstances of the life and work of the Commissariat of Ways of Communication, and there has been talk at the NKPS, notably in a report by citizen Puzanov, of stopping the construction of new engines at the factories of central Russia because such locomotives are completely unnecessary.[94]

This was not to say that imports should be banned. Rather, the report wanted planners to address six issues when compiling imports plans: the feasibility of producing the given items at Soviet factories; the urgency of the proposed order; price; political considerations; financial aspects, such as the availability of credit; and the quality of production. And it declared that in this light the NKPS contracts for rails, tyres, boiler tubes, locomotives, tankers and other metal goods had no justification whatsoever.

By way of illustration the authors focused on the locomotive orders, primarily the Nohab contract. They were adamant that GOMZA's three locomotive factories (Briansk, Kolomna and Sormovo) could have managed to produce the full quantity in three years, half the time actually agreed. There had not been any urgency as justification: the NKPS had long been storing thousands of serviceable locomotives for want of traffic and had begun disputing the need for more contracts, whether at home or abroad. Concerning price, it was wrong to negotiate long-term orders when prices were falling and could be below pre-war levels within five years; in any case GOMZA's maximum price for the Class E would not exceed 75,000 gold rubles, whereas the Swedish price was 'undoubtedly' at least 140,000 gold rubles and probably much more because the Swedes were recording fictitiously high costs. Furthermore:

> Even if political considerations force us to place orders abroad, even at high prices (usually it is the other way round, for political reasons orders are given to domestic factories even at a high price), one can surely place orders which the supplier-country wants and for goods which, firstly, this country needs, and secondly, cannot be made at domestic factories. Yet we do not need steam locomotives, we could make them ourselves, and finally they are hardly desirable for Sweden, since Sweden is not a locomotive-building country and must construct a factory for this order, this being evident from the fact that she will deliver only 60 engines in the first year, 200 in the second, and will not start supplying at an annual rate of 250 until the third year. Yet for the same money a mass of products could be bought which used to be imported into Russia from Sweden and which are that country's speciality, such as tools, tool steel, machine tools, ships and ship machinery, oil engines, separators and so forth.[95]

There was no financial advantage either: the Swedes required a multi-million ruble deposit, payments were being advanced to cover the cost of materials, and fixed capital was also being provided to complete the factory. Finally, the technical specifications had if anything been eased, so the quality of the engines would not be superior. It was even possible that, since the foreigners might maliciously work slowly, the Soviet railways could find themselves in a few years' time still taking delivery of foreign-built engines which had long since been technologically superseded.

In the metal industry's opinion, the conclusion was plain. Reiterating that similar criticisms could be levelled against all the other NKPS contracts, the report asserted that if just some of the resources were redirected to Soviet factories, all these orders could be tackled successfully in Russia. Since Soviet factories were disrupted by nothing more than a shortage of resources, it was certain that the hundreds of millions of gold rubles earmarked for imports could restore the metal industry to its full strength.

The tendentious character of this report did not augur well for an informed debate. Apart from everything else, its allegation about the technical specifications was quite false, and it utterly failed to justify the prices which it quoted. But its deep indignation was obviously genuine, and there was of course no doubt that the industry could benefit from the gold. The key problem, then, was to determine the best use of the country's gold, or for that matter whether non-expenditure represented the best option.

The first indication of serious doubt about the locomotive contracts at the level of Sovnarkom and the Central Committee came in early January 1922, and stemmed from the potent combination of Gosplan's anxiety, Avanesov's anger and the metal industry's lobbying. Gosplan's request for an investigation of anticipated railway expenditure had not been granted as such: on 16 December the STO merely instructed the Sovnarkom gold commission to brief Gosplan about the credits which had been opened for the Railway Mission.[96] However, Avanesov's gold commission was no less concerned than Gosplan, and, given also the OTK's change of policy, it was probably no coincidence that a crucial STO resolution was signed on a day, 4 January 1922, when Avanesov was acting as the council's chairman. According to this resolution, which was seemingly not discussed at a council session, the NKPS was granted the 23 million gold rubles needed for the foreign locomotives but was required to consider whether any engines could be cancelled.[97]

As usual the NKPS was less concerned with charity for Soviet industry than with Western assistance for its own needs. As preparation for the Genoa conference gathered momentum, it hoped, for example, to attract vast foreign investment for reconstruction, provided that it retained its sovereignty over the railways.[98] Characteristically, it displayed no enthusiasm for an Anglo-American scheme whereby foreign banks would back a 'railway ruble' and fund equipment worth £200 million, also having some control over this expenditure.[99] But the NKPS did favour a national foreign loan, happily reviving its plans for a network of new supermainlines and valuing its requirements at a massive 6,500 million gold rubles.[100] It also warmed to several modest foreign initiatives, one of which envisaged the completion and operation of the Mozherez factory by concessionaires, and another the leasing by the Paris-based Compagnie Internationale des Wagons-Lits of Russian sleeping cars formerly owned by the firm.[101]

The proposed cancellation of the foreign contracts was thus given short shrift. Lomonosov told Emshanov and Fomin on 24 January that most of the engines were already being assembled, and cancellation was thereupon dismissed as impracticable, the more so because the cash loss would be large and relations with Sweden badly damaged. Indeed, this triumvirate was more interested in future orders. For example, wagon spare parts were urgently wanted to facilitate the spring 'seed campaign' shipments; it was hoped that the Sovnarkom decree of 16 January 1922, whereby the NKPS became a self-financing organisation, would enable some 6 million gold rubles to be raised through sales of NKPS scrap metal in Europe. Also discussed, surprisingly, was a Lomonosov proposal to order 100 more locomotives abroad 'without burdening our budget' (*ne obremeniaia nashei smety*); virtually disregarding VSNKh ill feeling, they decided to seek Central Committee approval once Lomonosov had consulted the relevant commissariats.[102]

This last proposal – soon abandoned, needless to say – was all the more curious because Lomonosov hoped to divert some of his gold to it.[103] Possibly it stemmed from negotiations which he and Kerzhentsev had been conducting with Anderson and the Swedish government since October 1921, whereby the Soviets would place a lot of new contracts in Sweden in exchange for a Soviet–Swedish trade agreement, de jure recognition and a special loan. In October 1921 Kerzhentsev apparently suggested trying to pressure the Swedes by threatening to cancel part of the Nohab order.[104] In the event the two sides came close to agreement without such dramatic gestures, only for the talks to collapse in late November, partly through NKVT objections that there was nothing worth purchasing in Sweden. Nevertheless, negotiations were resumed early in January 1922, and more talks would follow in February and March, by which time Lomonosov hoped to spend much of the planned loan on machinery for the Mozherez and its sister project, Sazherez. But the loan idea eventually died, not least because on 1 March 1922 the Swedish parliament refused to ratify the draft Soviet–Swedish trade agreement.[105]

An NKPS meeting to review the Railway Mission's affairs, chaired by Emshanov on 30 January, reaffirmed the commissariat's desire for imports. First, the 'catastrophic situation' with essential supplies prompted a decision to ask Sovnarkom for an advance of 6 million gold rubles pending the proposed scrap metal sales. Further, because of long delays the NKPS wanted the mission to have responsibility for shipping NKPS goods to Russia, as well as the appointment of an

NKPS representative to the board of the German–Russian shipping company Derutra. The cancellation of locomotives was mentioned only in the sense that Lomonosov was permitted to order three experimental mainline diesel locomotives in place of three steam engines.[106] And ten days later Emshanov instructed Lomonosov to begin ordering the most essential goods immediately so as to avert disaster with the impending spring shipments of seed and grain.[107]

This typically pugnacious NKPS response was, however, ineffective. With regard to minor orders, the Railway Mission signed contracts worth about 3.5 million gold rubles by early April, but the STO refused to advance the money and indeed cut the NKPS shopping list from 6 million to only 2.57 million gold rubles irrespective of the planned scrap sales; and only 1.1 million gold rubles were actually released by the Sovnarkom gold commission. Moreover, the scrap sales generated far less income than expected. Nevertheless the signing of small contracts continued during the summer and early autumn, and the discrepancy between gold allocation and expenditure seems to have been covered gradually by scrap sales and savings made by the mission.[108]

Beyond this tale of railway adversity was the much more expensive question of the locomotive orders and, beyond that, the broader issues of NKPS–VSNKh relations and use of the gold reserve. In fact, the Central Committee and Politburo were now being drawn into the affair. Oddly enough, the immediate reason for this was less the VSNKh lobbying – though that was an indirect cause – than two other developments. One was Kerzhentsev's latest salvo against the Railway Mission, which was a telegram of 20 January to the STO calling for the Nohab locomotive order to be reworked into one for agricultural machinery and other metal products. The Sovnarkom Secretariat redirected the missive to the Central Committee Secretary Molotov, who in turn sought comment from Bogdanov at the VSNKh.[109] True to form, Bogdanov lambasted the whole gamut of NKPS orders, and this time the Politburo accepted his views on 22 February.[110]

Probably the main reason for this change of heart was the second, parallel development. The machinations of December 1921 over NKPS gold expenditure provoked a comprehensive survey of the country's hard currency reserve and commitments by the Commissariat of Finances, and the resultant report, sent to Lenin on 4 February, revealed a crisis. On 1 February 1922 the total reserve of gold, silver, platinum and foreign currency was only about 280 million gold rubles, including the equivalent of 19 million gold rubles held abroad as foreign currency by the NKVT and 512 poods (8.3456 tonnes) of gold antiques worth an estimated 10 million gold rubles. Existing foreign commitments would require well over half of this sum: some 174 million gold rubles for contracts already signed in 1920–2 (including the 23 million recently requested for the locomotives and 64 million due on railway contracts in 1923–5) plus further (unspecified) sums to cover shipments of NKPS imports in 1923–5 and Russia's obligations to Poland under the Treaty of Riga.[111] In short, the so-called 'free remnant' of the reserve was now probably around 100 million gold rubles whereas the 1922 bids for 'essential' imports were valued at nearly 500 million.

Since the prospects for compensation and loans through the upcoming Genoa conference were considered poor, the Politburo concentrated on stopping the rot. On 22 February it withdrew all unused gold credits and restricted overall expenditure in 1921 and 1922 to 52,857,717 gold rubles, with a maximum of 30 million gold rubles to be available for 1922 – figures which evidently excluded the money needed for the locomotives; Gosplan was to draft the new programme within one week. Also, the NKVT was to present a full report about all costs incurred in 1920–1, especially its overheads, whilst Tsiurupa and Sokol'nikov were to check all the gold credits opened in 1920 and 1921. As for the railway imports, the Politburo demanded three reports: firstly, the VSNKh, GOMZA and the Metalworkers' Union were to discuss completing the orders at Russian factories, comparing Russian and foreign costs; secondly, the NKPS and NKVT were to clarify the cost of cancelling or modifying the orders for 'locomotives being built by Lomonosov at Swedish factories'; and thirdly, the NKRKI was to assess the quality of Lomonosov's imports and the 'disadvantageous character' (*nevygodnost'*) of his contracts.[112]

Opponents of the railway contracts needed no further encouragement. For instance, Avanesov sent a bitter essay on the NKRKI's behalf on 17 March.[113] Typical was a report received in early March from representatives of Glavmetall, GOMZA and the Metalworkers' Union. Needless to say, the new Glavmetall head, Sudakov, and his colleagues berated the locomotive contracts and also the orders for tyres, rails, boiler tubes, tank wagons and, inevitably, the infamous Armstrong boilers. Discussing each of these cases at length, they alleged that the foreign contracts involved huge overpayments compared with Soviet prices, amounting to 110 million gold rubles for the locomotives alone.[114]

The Sovnarkom Secretariat also sought opinions, circulating Kerzhentsev's telegram and Bogdanov's comments to Fomin, G. M. Krzhizhanovskii (the head of Gosplan) and Krasin on 6 March. Somewhat impudently Fomin responded simply with a copy of NKPS report No. 38/s, which Emshanov had sent a few weeks earlier in reply to the STO resolution of 4 January and which opposed cancellation of the locomotives because of the likely cash loss and rupture of Soviet–Swedish relations. By contrast, Krzhizhanovskii and the Gosplan Transport Section favoured cancelling the locomotives and resuming overhauls at VSNKh factories provided that relations with Sweden were not harmed. Krasin had no qualms about cancellation, but suggested sending an investigatory commission to Sweden first.[115] Consequently, on 14 March Tsiurupa asked Krzhizhanovskii to take charge and report within three days, and the latter met Krasin, Dzerzhinskii and Litvinov on 16 March to thrash out a compromise. For once, moreover, it did prove possible to do this because Dzerzhinskii evidently gave way. Cancellation of the Swedish locomotives was recommended because they were unduly expensive, with two caveats: the locomotives must be reordered elsewhere, and the final decision should be made in Berlin by a special commission.[116]

It was the Politburo which, on 20 March, approved these recommendations and appointed Krzhizhanovskii to lead the proposed Berlin commission. Interestingly, Stalin sent his denigration of Krasin to Lenin at this juncture, on 22 March, and though he did not argue specifically against cancellation, his memorandum might be indicative of some dissent within the Politburo as well as an anti-NKVT statement. Be that as it may, a Central Committee plenum confirmed the Politburo's decision on 25 March, additionally requiring the Berlin commission to investigate all the complaints against the Railway Mission.[117] There was deep embarrassment, however, when the subject arose at the Eleventh Party Congress just two days later. Shliapnikov, the head of the Metalworkers' Union and former leader of the Workers' Opposition, had obtained a copy of Sudakov's submission to the Politburo, and he incorporated the whole text in his Congress speech to underline his allegation that the Party leadership was divorced from the Soviet working masses. Since, to judge by the published transcript, Lenin avoided mentioning the NKPS imports in his reply, there is little doubt that Shliapnikov had touched a very raw nerve. Ironically, it was left to Trotskii to admit on his colleagues' behalf that a mistake had perhaps been made, without giving any indication that the matter was being addressed.[118]

With the iron obviously hot, and with supportive articles in *Pravda* and *Ekonomicheskaia zhizn'*, the impecunious metal industry was quick to strike again.[119] In early April GOMZA demanded the replacement of the foreign locomotive contracts with an 18-month plan for 804 new engines from Soviet factories.[120] This programme would not only save almost 42 million gold rubles of scheduled gold expenditure but would also spur the factories' recovery, directly benefit their 20,000 workers and assist a further 40,000 workers (and their families) in auxiliary plants. Interestingly, GOMZA attacked the Petrograd-based Putilov and Nevskii factories for being dependent on foreign coal and far removed from the main centres of the Soviet metallurgical industry. Instead, the trust wanted its own factories to build 461 engines at a unit cost of just over 85,000 gold rubles, and the Khar'kov and Lugansk plants of the Iugostal' machine-building trust to complete 343 new engines at an eventual rate of 27 per month.

Characteristically, GOMZA stipulated wide-ranging conditions, including some that were distinctly reminiscent of the prerevolutionary epoch. Firstly, once approved the production plan was not to be modified. Secondly, the trusts were to be paid in hard currency and entitled to realise this currency themselves and import food and materials themselves. Thirdly, the Briansk factory was to be relieved of its contracts for armouring trains. Fourthly, the factories were also to receive various other orders so as to improve their viability. Lastly, but not least, there was to be no interference by trades unions or other bodies in factory operations, especially concerning wages.

The NKPS, equally penniless, did not respond immediately. It was preoccupied with getting its domestic budget increased and resolving the critical shortages of spare parts, as well as with sweeping staff cuts demanded by Gosplan, and the need for a general NKPS–VSNKh understanding about procedures for settling their mutual routine bills.[121] But when the VSNKh chairman, Bogdanov, recommended the GOMZA plan to the STO on 2 May 1922 and Rykov sent it to Stalin for the Politburo on 6 May, the NKPS was stung into producing a scathing counter-report.[122]

The NKPS naturally regarded the cancellation question and domestic locomotive construction as two financially distinct matters. Taking the foreign issue first, it asserted that virtually all of the 700 German engines were complete or under construction, but admitted that part of the Swedish order could be cancelled. However, the saving predicted by the metal industry was unlikely to materialise because there would be large cancellation costs and because GOMZA had exaggerated the foreign prices whilst underestimating its own. As for the domestic issue, the NKPS envisaged two options. Resources could be concentrated on building new engines or on overhauling locomotives and making spare parts. For the NKPS it was 'obvious' that the second option was preferable and that domestic locomotive construction should be minimal or perhaps even stopped completely. After all, some 13,500 existing engines could have an intermediate overhaul for the cost of 804 new locomotives, and the proposed building programme would also disrupt the output of vital spare parts, wagons and agricultural equipment – completely unacceptable when about 60 per cent of the locomotive stock was unserviceable. In short, the NKPS saw no reason to treat locomotive building as a matter of national significance. The metal industry was simply ignoring transport's real interests and the paucity of state resources.

This position matched government policy to minimise costs and repair existing equipment, and the NKPS did at least consider GOMZA's viability by proposing contracts for overhauls and much needed spare parts. But still the commissariat failed to discredit the cancellation campaign, so pronounced was the ill feeling. True, the Berlin commission had not convened, probably because Krasin and Litvinov were seconded to the Genoa conference. But instead two new commissions were formed to carry the review forward. On 19 May the STO instructed Gosplan to reassess the supply situation and, in consultation with the NKVT, VSNKh, NKRKI and NKPS, the practicability of transferring the Railway Mission's orders to Russia without increasing the overall cost or delaying deliveries – a signal that, whilst the Soviet factories' cause was recognised as just, their sums and schedules remained in question.[123] Secondly, on 26 May the Politburo replaced the still-born Berlin commission with a new group under Dzerzhinskii; perhaps also prompted by a Lomonosov statement to the Politburo revealing Krasin's links with Bonnier, this commission would review the locomotive orders and especially the complaints against the Railway Mission.[124]

Stubborn persistence was one reason why cancellation became acceptable, as perhaps was shock at the apparent absurdity of importing foreign equipment whilst Soviet factories cried out for work. Less directly, the unremittingly acrimonious disputes between the NKVT and Lomonosov may also have contributed, even if just by souring the atmosphere around the imports. Doubtless a further factor was the collapse of the Genoa conference, which dashed any remaining hopes for massive Western financial and other assistance.

Contradicting Lenin's statements to the Tenth Party Congress a year earlier, articles in *Pravda* declared that Russia had to restore her industry without relying on Western help and that it was vital, for strategic reasons, to maintain Russian industry independently of the West.[125] And whilst the Treaty of Rapallo with Germany presumably rendered the cancellation of NKPS orders in Germany politically unthinkable (except, of course, to the Soviet metal industry), no such restrictions applied in Sweden, where trouble might be blamed on the rejection of the draft Swedish–Soviet trade agreement.

The Gosplan Presidium formed a commission from representatives of its industry and transport sections. Meetings were held on 31 May, 1 June and 10 June before the Presidium discussed the findings on 13 June. Delegates from the VSNKh, GOMZA, NKVT and NKPS also attended the sessions, as on the final occasion did Professor Lomonosov, recently arrived in Moscow on his first visit since early February.[126]

The cancellation of locomotives was the principal topic for 10 June. After the chairman of the Gosplan Section for Industry, R. Ia. Gartvan, made the opening report, a GOMZA representative, S. A. Khrennikov, repeated the allegation that Nohab locomotives were costing 144,000 gold rubles and claimed that many German factories had not even started work on their engines. Lomonosov apparently did not oppose curtailment of the Nohab order, but he did dispute the possibility of cancelling German engines. At length the commission decided that the Swedish order should be reduced by at least the 650 engines scheduled for construction in 1923–5, and recommended that a member of Gosplan's Presidium, A. G. Kogan, should visit Germany to assess the situation there – a compromise which Lomonosov took, correctly, as a sign of collective distrust.[127]

In the same meeting the revised Estonian contract for 200 locomotive overhauls had a narrow escape, having already been criticised on 1 June. Lomonosov records that the head of the NKPS Department for Traction, Krasovskii, described these overhauls as 40 per cent cheaper than at VSNKh factories. But Gosplan had permitted this contract only on condition that no gold was spent, and perhaps because Lomonosov did divert some gold to it, the commission roundly condemned the whole business as 'disadvantageous' and prohibited similar orders henceforth. However, the Estonian contract was reluctantly left in force, provided that the prices were not increased.[128]

These decisions were accepted by the Gosplan Presidium on 13 June, as were the other recommendations. In particular, the NKPS was to transfer various small orders and associated credits to the VSNKh, such as 150 tonnes of spring steel and 700 kilograms of mercury. Also, the NKPS was to import ferrous metals and ferrous metal products only when unavailable from VSNKh suppliers. However, although this outcome indicated that the VSNKh had largely won its way, there were also signs that Gosplan was trying to forge an NKPS–VSNKh compromise on the home front. Specifically, the Presidium required VSNKh to resume overhauling locomotives and supplying spare parts, presenting detailed output plans within a fortnight. Furthermore, the Commissariat of Finances would be instructed to recognise the importance of restoring transport by allocating credits to cover all the plans for domestic locomotive and rolling-stock construction.[129]

Meanwhile, the Dzerzhinskii commission covered much of the same ground to much the same effect.[130] Its results were then accepted by the Politburo on 15 June, though not without controversy. A special commission comprised of Lomonosov, Litvinov and a VSNKh representative was mooted to organise the actual reduction in Sweden, but because Litvinov wanted to concentrate on the forthcoming Hague conference, Kerzhentsev was nominated as his alternate. Trotskii thereupon objected that Lomonosov would effectively be in charge, 'which does not give any guarantee of success in the matter' – provoking Dzerzhinskii into an equally outspoken defence of Lomonosov.[131] Ultimately Trotskii's objection was dismissed. As Litvinov explained in a letter of 16 June to Kerzhentsev, the cancellation was required primarily for economic reasons, and Lomonosov had suggested it could be achieved if Anderson received some 'personal compensation'. However, success was unlikely without Lomonosov's involvement, and so Kerzhentsev's task would be to monitor Lomonosov's activity without upsetting him.[132]

Further controversy was caused by the NKPS: clearly the fact that Dzerzhinskii had chaired the Politburo commission did not imply full NKPS acquiescence to the recommendations. While the transport commissariat did reconcile itself to losing some of its foreign locomotives, it remained vehemently opposed to funding new orders in Russia and was not mollified by Gosplan's insistence on overhauls and the promise of cooperation by the Commissariat of Finances. As Krasovskii implied in reports to the NKPS Collegium on 14 and 30 June, the commissariat wanted to use the resources released by the Nohab annulment primarily to fund heavy overhauls. On 30 June Krasovskii even opined that the railways would not need any new locomotives for two or three years given traffic growth at an annual rate of 20 per cent, the resuscitation of some 286 'sick' modern engines and the arrival of 600 German and Swedish engines during the year.[133]

Making a stand, the NKPS submitted a draft STO resolution on 15 June which envisaged the resumption of heavy overhauls by the VSNKh without any orders for new engines. Once again Gosplan was summoned to arbitrate, and a familiar train of intemperate events ensued. On 29 June the special Gosplan commission was resurrected, and once again the NKPS clashed with the Gosplan Section for Industry, this time so acrimoniously that the Presidium had to create a second commission under the chairmanship of A. A. Neopikhanov from its Transport Section. Not until 18 July was a result secured and supported by the Presidium: the same compromise of building new engines and overhauling existing ones. Specifically, the VSNKh was told to compile plans for 650 new engines and 1,800 overhauls for 1923–5, whilst the NKPS was to provide a preliminary plan for locomotive construction between 1923 and about 1930.[134]

However, developments in Sweden rendered Gosplan's figures obsolete before detailed plans could be drafted. Compared to the protracted intrigues in Moscow, the negotiations with Nohab proved remarkably trouble-free, but they produced a smaller reduction than many in Moscow had anticipated and thus freed less money than planned for VSNKh orders. Indeed, the cancellation commission made a sorry start when Litvinov, Lomonosov and the candidate VSNKh representative, Khrennikov, gathered in Moscow on 17 June. His pride already injured by the commission's very existence, Lomonosov was so outraged by the terms of reference proposed by his two colleagues that he refused to leave for Sweden, the more so because the Dzerzhinskii commission had still to exonerate him from the accusations made by Krasin and others. On 22 June Lomonosov appeared before the Politburo to explain his strike, and he did not relent until informed by Stalin that a decision on his case was due on 29 June and, in effect, that by creating a whole commission to cancel the contract the Politburo had merely been trying to forestall gossip.[135]

Accordingly the Dzerzhinskii commission reconvened on 28 June to consider the complaints against Lomonosov amidst a new offensive by Krasin. On 19 June, for instance, Krasin publicly accused the Railway Mission of making elementary commercial mistakes which not even the most lowly NKVT functionary would commit.[136] He repeated his argument in a written submission to the Dzerzhinskii commission as well as at the hearing itself, where evidence was also taken from Stomoniakov and Lomonosov, among others. Needless to say, battle was soon joined, especially over the locomotive orders, with Krasin downplaying his own involvement during 1920. For instance, he maintained that he had ordered only 100 locomotives in Sweden in 1920, the other 900 not being definitely contracted, and that Lomonosov had transformed this into a contract for a full 1,000 engines; but the professor countered this with a copy of the first contract. As for the German locomotives, Krasin claimed that he had supported the price – which, he further declared, was entirely Lomonosov's responsibility – solely for political reasons; but he also had to acknowledge his statements that the second German contract did help him secure the Anglo-Soviet Trade Agreement. Allegations were also made against Lomonosov's integrity, notably of collusion with foreign businessmen to steer orders through intermediaries rather than directly to manufacturers. But Krasin's primary grievance was that Lomonosov had usurped the NKVT's rights, a statement which was true in spirit even if Lomonosov could wave his Sovnarkom mandates in response, and which hinted at Krasin's anxiety about the domestic threat to the NKVT monopoly.[137]

The Krasin–Lomonosov feud was now so bitter that Dzerzhinskii's chances of defusing it were almost nil. One of the recommendations – for a full investigation of Lomonosov's commercial activity – had been sought by both sides, but other findings inevitably offended one side or the other. On the one hand, the commission rejected the accusations against Lomonosov's integrity and against the technical aspects of his mission's contracts. But on the other hand, it recommended that the mission be abolished from 1 January 1923 and, to Lomonosov's intense dismay, it refused to condemn his adversaries for slander.[138] These recommendations were accepted by the Politburo and Sovnarkom on 29 June and 3 July respectively.[139]

Feeling defeated, Lomonosov departed for Stockholm on 1 July; if nothing else, he wanted a few more months of Western comfort.[140] There he ascertained that Nohab had completed 137 engines and purchased the materials for 350 more, which effectively limited the total possible reduction to 513. It also emerged that Nohab was in financial trouble, partly because Anderson had acquired a bankrupt Swedish metallurgical factory earlier in the year. The fact that the Russians had not been consulted about this deal gave them a pretext for creating a scandal, as did Nohab's inability to provide a long-overdue detailed statement of its costs. Also, the firm had begun delaying the departure of completed engines to Russia because of cancellation rumours, and, ironically, this obstructiveness provided a further pretext for cancellation.[141]

Nevertheless, when the cancellation commission held its first meeting in Sweden on 14 July, with Kerzhentsev deputising for Litvinov, it was accepted that the annulment should preferably be by amicable mutual agreement with Anderson. But it was also agreed that the order had to be reduced at all costs. In Lomonosov's memoir account the strength of Kerzhentsev's feeling, for instance, was shown by his readiness to delay his general negotiations with the Swedish government if the latter tried to forestall the cancellation by offering de jure recognition and long-term credits.[142]

Lomonosov confronted Anderson with a 'reduction' on 19 July. Evidently spotting an opportunity to revive his company's finances, Anderson intimated his consent provided that Nohab was protected from lay-offs and received a large advance of 6 million Swedish crowns. The next day he told Lomonosov that he was even ready to ignore protests which, he claimed, the Swedish government was making. By 27 July Anderson had accepted a figure of 500 engines, and after Lomonosov's colleagues had given their assent, a revised contract was signed on 28 July.[143]

Under this new contract Nohab would supply a total of 500 Class E engines by the end of 1924, including those already supplied since 1920. One important new benefit was that all the engines would be sold at fixed prices, which would greatly simplify the accounting process for all concerned. Thus, whereas the March 1921 edition of the contract had specified 230,000 Swedish crowns as a maximum price, now the first 350 engines (including those already delivered) would cost 230,000 crowns each, with the final 150 at 160,000 crowns. Moreover, Nohab was to discount these prices in order to pay off its various Soviet loans, including a new advance of 5.75 million crowns proffered under this latest version of the contract.[144]

All told, this exercise apparently cost the Russians about 18.5 million Swedish crowns. This sum included a secret payment to Anderson of 4 million crowns, which was provided in sterling and US dollars through the London Joint City and Midland Bank and which represented the 'personal compensation' suggested by Lomonosov in June. In his memoirs Lomonosov presents the payment as purely a bribe.[145] But equally it may have been linked to Anderson's original financial commitment of May 1920 and designed quite legitimately to ensure that he did not suffer any personal loss as a result of his borrowing in 1920, irrespective of the revised terms negotiated in March 1921.

Other participants in the affair received payments totalling 287,000 crowns, probably without Litvinov, Kerzhentsev and Khrennikov being aware of them. Ironically, given Lomonosov's recent protestations of his integrity, this figure included a sum of 50,000 crowns to his own wife, in addition to 35,000 crowns which she had already banked some months earlier. Even though, or perhaps precisely because, many of the persistently recurrent accusations against Lomonosov and his mission were unfounded or muddled, not to say ridiculous in some cases, the deepening controversy had prompted the couple to start making contingency plans for a life in emigration.[146] Fortunately for Lomonosov, his inquisitors did not suspect this embezzlement.

In the light of the Nohab cancellation the STO reconsidered Gosplan's recommendations on 4 August, approving the plan for 1,800 overhauls but objecting that the Republic could not afford 650 new engines. Gosplan's industrial section therefore proposed a contract for 508 new engines, 1,800 heavy repairs and 135 so-called reconstruction overhauls (*vosstanovitel'nyi remont*). These figures were approved by the Gosplan Presidium on 15 August and endorsed by an STO resolution nine days later, and the following December the NKPS and VSNKh signed this new order.[147]

7 Denouement

By late August 1922 the Soviet leadership seemingly had good reason to consider its problems with the railway contracts more or less resolved. The Nohab order had been curtailed, there was a new VSNKh locomotive-building plan, and it remained simply to investigate the Railway Mission's commercial activity, abolish the mission and agree the NKPS–VSNKh contract. But in fact these issues would fester for up to three more years, and they raised awkward and far-reaching questions about policy-making responsibility, central authority, resources and economic recovery. Not one but several investigations would ensue, each basically treating Lomonosov as a scapegoat for the railway imports policy. Also, the mission's death agony was several months longer and rather more eventful than planned, including a final flurry of minor contracts and bureaucratic confusion. And Gosplan's compromise policy for locomotive construction collapsed disastrously amidst more retrenchment and expectations of very slow economic recovery.

The Avanesov commission

If several more months of Western comfort, with an opportunity to emigrate if necessary, were among Lomonosov's reasons for returning to Sweden in July 1922, another was his desire to be present in Berlin and Stockholm when the mission's commercial activity was audited. He expected vindictive vilification, and his worst forebodings seemed confirmed on 18 July when Sovnarkom appointed comrades Avanesov, Iaroslavskii and Medved'ev as the investigatory team, for he regarded Avanesov of the NKRKI and Cheka as one of his worst slanderers.[1] That said, Lomonosov was perhaps less fearful of the Cheka than many because Dzerzhinskii, its head, still seemed supportive.

The Avanesov commission investigated various NKVT delegations, evidently taking a few days over each one, but spent nearly two months on the Railway Mission. The audit commenced in Berlin in late September and moved to Stockholm after several weeks.[2] Interviewing staff and examining the mission's accounts and correspondence, the investigators were especially curious about the staff profile and salaries, including some hard-currency bonus payments celebrating the mission's first anniversary in October 1921. The commission also dwelt on several contracts, including the renegotiation of the Nohab order in March 1921 and July 1922, the Armstrong and Estonian repair contracts, and an order in March 1922 for ten water-turbines from Nohab for Volkhovstroi.[3]

Data supplied to the investigators showed that the Railway Mission's payroll, having peaked at over 300 people, was shrinking as the workload declined. On 15 September 1922 there were 200 full-time and 14 part-time staff, of whom 92 were based in Berlin, 31 at German factories, 56 in Sweden, 15 in Britain, 3 in Czechoslovakia and Austria, 10 in Estonia, 4 in Latvia and 3 in Moscow. The political and national profile reflected heavy reliance on non-Party specialists and foreigners: the communist contingent totalled just 22, including 10 members of the Russian Communist Party. The 81 Soviet citizens accounted for just over one third of the staff; the remainder comprised 75 Germans, 26 Swedes, 10 Latvians, 8 Estonians, 6 Britons, 4 Poles, 2 Lithuanians, 1 Austrian and 1 Persian.[4]

With regard to contracts, the turbine order was a revealing example of how a simple idea could become entangled in bureaucratic confusion. Its origins lay in Krasin's stipulations in May 1920 that Nohab should work exclusively for Russia and that the locomotive price would be based on the factory's actual costs. As mentioned in chapter 4, Lomonosov recommended in August 1920 that because Nohab could reduce its overhead costs by building water-turbines, an order should be placed immediately for the Volkhov and Svir dams using the Swedish Concern's new credit.[5] This proposal was duly discussed by the VSNKh foreign trade committee.[6] But because Lomonosov did not receive any reply before his arrival in Moscow in October, he asked Lenin to intervene.[7] Lenin promptly gave his blessing, and the appropriate VSNKh department, Elektrostroi, instructed Lomonosov to place an order. Meanwhile, however, the NKVT asked its temporary representative in Stockholm, Professor Ion, to approach various other companies, and when Lomonosov queried this instruction, Lezhava confirmed that the two professors should merely forward the quotations to Moscow. Ion accordingly sent offers from Nohab and four other Scandinavian companies, whilst Lomonosov made an exasperated protest. Then, as silence ensued, Lomonosov sent further telegrams requesting instructions in April, May and June 1921, by which time Nohab's turbine shop had been idle but kept open (with Krasin's approval) for nearly a year at a cost of 100,000 gold rubles.[8]

After the VSNKh civil construction agency, Komgosor, replied in July that turbines could not be ordered in 1921 because 'the question of Volkhovstroi is unclear', Lomonosov appealed to Sovnarkom on 23 August. Apparently Lenin intervened again, this time to support the transfer of the project from the seemingly dilatory NKVT to the Railway Mission.[9] On 2 November Gosplan's Section for Energy recommended ordering turbines from Nohab immediately, the Sovnarkom gold commission under Avanesov's chairmanship approved preliminary expenditure of 500,000 gold rubles on 5 November, and the STO confirmed this decision on 21 November. A month later Volkhovstroi's chief engineer, Professor G. O. Graftio, travelled to Sweden, hoping for a deal by mid-January 1922.[10] But more misunderstandings caused further delay. For instance, Krasin tried to block the order because there had not been competitive tendering.[11] Not until 10 March 1922, over 18 months after Lomonosov's first telegram, was an appropriate contract signed, for 10 turbines at a total cost of 4,200,570 Swedish crowns (as of April 1923).[12] However, even this did not end the confusion: Krasin lodged an objection in Moscow, and Sovnarkom instructed Krzhizhanovskii, Krasin and Lomonosov to reconsider the contract's necessity. Then, on 24 March, Sovnarkom unjustly rebuked Lomonosov for spending money on his own initiative to keep the Nohab turbine shops open. Ultimately, though, the contract was left in force.[13]

Unfortunately, it is unclear what Avanesov and his fellow investigators made of this peculiarly convoluted, yet in some ways typical, episode. Overall, however, they evidently felt that their work was worthwhile. They reportedly told Lomonosov that the Railway Mission's technical apparatus and accounting procedures were superior to those of the NKVT delegations, but considered that salaries were excessively high and that the anniversary bonuses had been illegal. Also, there were financial irregularities concerning payments on account (*podotchetnye*).[14]

Characteristically combative, Lomonosov hardly helped his case by issuing a further round of bonuses just a few days later. Ostensibly to mark the mission's second anniversary, he insisted that their main justification was to support his foreign specialists because their pay was low by local standards. Not surprisingly, Krestinskii was outraged and protested to Moscow, with the result that Sovnarkom publicly reprimanded the professor.[15]

Submitted in late February or early March 1923, the Avanesov commission's final report was the first thorough analysis of the Railway Mission's affairs. Apparently it made numerous complaints. At the most general level, it does seem to have questioned the principle of importing locomotives, though it did so by making a personal attack on Lomonosov instead of investigating Lenin, Krasin, Sovnarkom or the NKPS. Thus, according to Lomonosov, the report alleged that the professor had hypnotised the Politburo and Sovnarkom, ordering locomotives at very high prices whilst aware that the railways did not actually need them. The contracts had impossible delivery schedules, and intermediaries were used without good reason. Moreover, it claimed, Lomonosov had constantly overstepped his authority and interfered in the work of Soviet ambassadors. He was keeping 'fictitious' accounts and maintaining a den of White guards and dubious foreigners.[16]

Lomonosov could certainly be criticised for, above all, his determination to continue ordering locomotives in the winter of 1920–1 and maintain his autonomy from the NKVT. But it was grossly unfair to blame him for the whole policy. In general, so far as one can judge, some of the accusations were just, but many were half-baked or ridiculous. It was simply nonsensical, for example, to complain that boilers were ordered from Armstrongs without competitive tendering. Particularly important was the accusation that the quality of the locomotives was poor, a charge persistently repeated despite numerous denials by both Lomonosov and the NKPS leadership. Certainly various faults were found, but the problems were neither serious nor unusual for new locomotives. Indeed, engines delivered from Soviet factories in 1922 and 1923 experienced similar troubles.[17] Most likely, the issue in this instance was not poor quality but demagogy.

That Avanesov and his colleagues failed to confront the underlying issue of the policy's origins is intriguing. It seems inconceivable that they were unaware of the initial decision making of early 1920 and especially the roles of Lenin and Krasin. Copies of the Sovnarkom resolution of 16 March existed in the Railway Mission files, and in any case Avanesov must have been aware of that document in his capacity as chair of Sovnarkom's gold commission. Also, a copy of Krasin's locomotive contract with Anderson was provided for the investigators.[18] One might speculate, then, that they wanted to gloss over Lenin's ultimate responsibility for a policy that was increasingly seen as a costly blunder. Lomonosov was an ideal scapegoat because he was widely regarded as a high-handed bourgeois 'spets' (specialist), his lifestyle in Europe was extravagant and, unlike Krasin, he made no effort to distance himself from the policy, being genuinely proud of his work.

The party leadership, too, was evidently unwilling to confront this question of ultimate responsibility. The Central Committee formed a commission under Rykov to consider Avanesov's report, but of course Rykov had publicly supported Krasin in 1920, and his commission's main conclusions were accordingly limited. Firstly, the Railway Mission was to be abolished by 15 April and its affairs transferred to Emshanov as NKPS plenipotentiary; secondly, only absolutely essential items could be imported henceforth; thirdly, there was insufficient cause to put Lomonosov on trial, and his proposed appointment as head of the NKPS Technical Committee could be confirmed; fourthly, Emshanov, Stomoniakov and Krestinskii should study the possibility of transferring the mission's remaining contracts to Russia; and finally, the NKRKI should conduct a comprehensive investigation of the mission for the Central Committee.[19]

This verdict, generally similar to that of Dzerzhinskii the previous summer, can hardly have cheered either Avanesov or Lomonosov. One senses that Avanesov, Krasin and others had become firmly convinced that Lomonosov was somehow concealing atrocious irregularities and misdeeds such as collusion with foreign firms and intermediaries, and that to their immense frustration they could not expose this. Indeed, they did fail to convict him over the genuine instance of embezzlement, and, more importantly, it took them two years to eliminate the institutional confusion caused by the parallel existence of the NKVT apparatus and the Railway Mission. For his part, Lomonosov felt exonerated on many counts, but he was concerned about the proposed NKRKI investigation, specifically with regard to questions about certain payments made to various individuals, his wife included (although embezzlement, if alleged, was not proved). He was especially concerned about some secret payments, including one of 20,000 Swedish crowns, which was described intriguingly as a 'bribe' for the Swedish Minister of Justice.[20]

A comprehensive investigation was begun after Lomonosov submitted his own report in the autumn of 1923, and it took about two years. But again the initial policy-making was ignored. Concentrating on Lomonosov and his mission, the investigators regurgitated many of the hoary old allegations about locomotive faults, the 'incomprehensible' Armstrong boilers, high contract prices and so forth. They even accused Lomonosov of criminal negligence towards the gold in his care, and concluded by recommending Sovnarkom to reject his report.[21] However, the matter was allowed to drop. Perhaps this was because, as will be shown below, Lomonosov was now undertaking other railway work for the Soviet government in Germany. Perhaps there was a cover-up out of fear of political embarrassment if the original policy decisions were broached in some sort of public trial. Perhaps the decision reflected the high degree of secrecy maintained about the gold reserve. Or perhaps it was simply despair at ever getting to the bottom of this whole business.

Demise and results

The issue of whether and how to abolish or reform the Railway Mission was live virtually from the outset. The tide eventually turned against Lomonosov in the summer of 1922, probably because Dzerzhinskii became persuaded of the need for change. Even in retreat, though, Lomonosov haggled. Asked by Dzerzhinskii on 16 June for suggestions about what should be done, he mentioned Krasin's desire to incorporate the mission offices into NKVT delegations, and put forward two ideas of his own: for the mission to become a purely technical NKPS delegation, or for it to be a commercial-technical organisation under an NKPS plenipotentiary.[22] Lomonosov recounts that he personally favoured transforming the mission into an NKPS technical delegation, but that Dzerzhinskii preferred subordinating it to an NKPS plenipotentiary; if that was so, Dzerzhinskii perhaps hoped that the NKPS could retain some independence from the NKVT apparatus without the inconvenience of Lomonosov's scandals. Be that as it may, the Dzerzhinskii commission recommended the third variant, the Politburo concurred and Sovnarkom followed suit on 3 July. The change was to happen once the Nohab order had been cancelled, and Dzerzhinskii and Lomonosov were instructed to determine the procedure.[23]

There the matter rested until October 1922, when the professor next visited Moscow and another squabble ensued. Lomonosov claims that on 19 October he agreed with one of the deputy commissars of foreign trade, M. I. Frumkin, to make the Berlin and Stockholm offices self-standing by 1 January so that they could each then place their orders through the local trade delegation. Afterwards, however, Frumkin allegedly began insisting that the mission's future structure was none of Lomonosov's business. The latter thereupon told Fomin and L. P. Serebriakov (a new appointee to the NKPS Collegium from the Central Committee Secretariat) that the NKVT was rejecting the NKPS plan for winding up the mission, and the NKPS officials agreed that if their proposals were rejected, the status quo should be preserved until 1 April 1923.[24]

This description may suggest that Lomonosov was acting disruptively, or at least disingenuously. If that was the case, Lenin for once firmly put him in his place on 31 October. Lenin was already alarmed at the Central Committee's recent decision to loosen central control over foreign trade operations, and he would shortly seek an alliance with Trotskii to re-establish this control. On this occasion he supported Frumkin by citing a VTsIK decree of 16 October 1922 which permitted commissariats and even individual trusts to maintain their own representatives abroad provided – crucially – that all their trade activity was controlled by the local NKVT delegation. Defeated, Lomonosov could merely respond that the most convenient dates for the change would be 1 February or 1 April 1923, coinciding respectively with delivery of the last of the 700 German engines and the last British materials, and the former date was chosen.[25]

This decision paved the way at last for full NKVT control over NKPS contracts. Yet final victory over the Railway Mission would elude Krasin and the NKVT for another few months. On 9 January Sovnarkom extended the deadline to 1 March, and then by a further two weeks on 26 February owing, ironically, to a delay in the completion of Avanesov's report. On 13 March Sovnarkom approved yet another postponement until 1 April, but only after a further fortnight's delay did Lomonosov finally yield to his successor, Emshanov, in Berlin on 15 April.[26]

Upon Lomonosov's departure the Railway Mission ceased to exist as such, and its various offices were absorbed into the NKVT apparatus, as envisaged under a statute drafted early in March.[27] Emshanov served as an NKPS plenipotentiary based in the NKVT Berlin delegation and basically acted as a coordinator for NKPS affairs, responsible primarily for supervising the remaining technical operations. In fact, he was replaced the following autumn by Iu. V. Rudyi, who had been in communication with the Americans in Siberia in 1920 and who had latterly served as a deputy to Fomin.[28] If nothing else, it seems safe to assume that Emshanov and Rudyi both enjoyed vastly better relations with the NKVT, Kerzhentsev and Krestinskii than Lomonosov ever did.

Following Emshanov's arrival, inspection activity continued much as before and remained quite extensive for over a year because the Swedish locomotive order was not completed until late 1924. Moreover, as of April 1923 Nohab had not finished the Volkhovstroi turbines, and the Estonian repair contract and approximately thirty minor orders needed attention.[29] The most notable happening was a major financial dispute with Nohab during 1924 when the firm's near-bankruptcy cast doubt on the final deliveries, and this was resolved only by the Tsentrosoiuz agreeing to pay 4 million crowns to ensure completion of the order, enabling the last of the 500 engines to leave Sweden in December 1924.[30]

The volume of new NKPS orders was relatively low during the Railway Mission's final year, and probably remained so thereafter. The summer of 1922 witnessed a burst of activity as the mission ordered goods worth over 1 million Swedish crowns in each of July, August and September, funded by the small STO gold allocation, income expected from scrap metal sales and the mission's savings. But new contracts in October and November were worth only 78,442 and 19,158 Swedish crowns respectively, and although December 1922 saw a flurry of 18 orders costing 861,913 crowns, the final expenditure on contracts signed in the first quarter of 1923 was expected (in April 1923) to be a mere 75,681 crowns. As for subsequent orders, it is known that the NKPS applied for imports valued at just over 5.5 million gold rubles for 1 January to 1 October 1923, only for Gosplan to reject most of this plan.[31]

Among the largest of the mission's new projects in the summer of 1922 was a contract worth some 146,000 Swedish crowns for spare parts for the Anglo-German oil tankers. As usual, tenders were obtained from a variety of companies, and two Czechoslovak firms – the Skoda Works of Prague, and the Vitkovice Mining and Foundry Works of Ostrava – greatly undercut their German and British rivals; Skoda won the day, apparently by dropping its prices by over 20 per cent at the last minute.[32] A VSNKh protest was defeated by the NKPS on this occasion, but as opinion hardened against such imports the VSNKh prevailed when Lomonosov sought permission to order spare parts for the foreign-built locomotives in the autumn. Skoda and Vitkovice again undercut their rivals, reportedly by as much as 50 per cent even inclusive of new castings, though the Germans could deliver more quickly. However, Bogdanov protested at the expected cost of 400,000 gold rubles, and Sovnarkom redirected the order to Russia.[33]

Three other contracts also caused trouble for Lomonosov in Moscow during the winter of 1922–3. Misgivings about the Estonian repair contract forced its curtailment from 200 to 150 overhauls in December 1922; indeed, six months later, on 30 May 1923, the STO would instruct Emshanov to cancel the contract altogether, although it would take over a year and much bitter argument with the Estonians to achieve this, the final tally of completed overhauls being approximately 70.[34] A rather different case concerned two ships which, using money allocated for hiring foreign vessels to transport the German and Swedish locomotives, Lomonosov had actually purchased on his own initiative. Whereas he now wanted to sell them so as to balance the mission's books, Rykov and others demanded their transfer to the as yet still tiny Soviet merchant fleet.[35] Also, in another case as confused as the turbine saga, Lomonosov was somewhat unjustly rebuked for selling fifteen locomotives to Latvia at a scrap price of 20,000 gold rubles each, even though all were in appalling 'cemetery' condition with major boiler ailments, if indeed they had a boiler at all.[36]

Equally troublesome in its own way for the professor was a potentially expensive quarrel with Nohab about Armstrong boilers in the summer of 1922. The first difficulty was that the Railway Mission paid approximately 250,000 crowns in customs duties when the fifty boilers were delivered to Sweden, expecting reimbursement from Nohab. But Anderson refused, and Nohab also complained that the boilers were seriously defective. Much horse-trading, including a threat to publicise the recent secret payment to Anderson, was required for a solution, which involved remedial work at Armstrong Whitworth's expense.[37]

The mission's last months also saw some contracts which perpetuated the NKPS interest in modernisation and which would become Lomonosov's next project: the development of experimental mainline diesel locomotives.[38] His interest in diesel traction dated from his time as Traction Superintendent of the Tashkent Railway in 1909–10, and he had included Shelest in his small party in June 1920 precisely because Shelest was a veteran advocate of dieselisation. As early as the autumn of 1920 they had begun using their scarce spare time to design a range of diesel locomotives for comparative evaluation, and Lomonosov deliberately recruited some German engineers already interested in diesel traction when he built up the Railway Mission during the winter of 1920–1. In May 1921 he asked the NKPS for permission to order two mainline diesels (one with electric transmission and one designed by Shelest with a steam–gas turbine combination), and in August he was allowed to order them in place of two steam locomotives. Then, as mentioned in chapter 6, Lomonosov was authorised on 30 January 1922 to order three rather than two prototypes. He duly reached an agreement in principle with Nohab for the first two diesels, but when the part-cancellation of the main Nohab order cast doubt on their future, he obtained extra funds from Sovnarkom to reassign them to Germany separately from the steam orders. He thus ordered the two locomotives from the German locomotive-building company Hohenzollern AG and electrical equipment from the Swiss firm Brown Boveri on 15 December 1922, also buying two ex-submarine diesel engines for them, for a total cost of 542,069 Swedish crowns (as of April 1923).[39]

During 1921–2 Lomonosov and Shelest quarrelled bitterly about the feasibility of the latter's combined steam–gas turbine concept. Shelest eventually left the mission in December 1922, and in 1923 he was permitted to order a locomotive of his own design from Armstrong Whitworth, though the contract was abrogated when Britain broke off diplomatic relations in 1927, and Shelest never managed to complete a prototype.[40] Meanwhile, Lomonosov was appointed to the NKPS Technical Committee in 1923 but was authorised to remain in Germany with a few colleagues to work on his diesels. Needless to say, his relations with Krestinskii remained poor, and he was frequently at odds with Rudyi as well. Yet his team helped to earn the USSR a world lead in this new technology, and the first of his two locomotives, with electric transmission, has been recognised as the world's first operationally successful mainline diesel locomotive. Completed at the Esslingen machine-building works in June 1924, it was tested and modified there during the summer and autumn before being partially dismantled and taken through Poland to Latvia, where, after reassembly in Daugavpils, it hauled its first test trains. After arriving in Moscow in late January 1925, it quickly proved itself in NKPS acceptance trials and was soon at work on an extensive programme of test trains to the Caucasus and elsewhere.[41] The second diesel locomotive was completed by Hohenzollern in 1925. Interestingly, it was designed to run with either European- or Russian-gauge wheels and was tested on German railways for a time. But its mechanical transmission was prone to faults and it was already

Table 7.1. *Quantity and value of Railway Mission orders, 15 October 1920–15 April 1923 (by year in Swedish crowns, as recalculated in source for 15 April 1923)*

Year	Quantity of orders	Value (crowns)
1920	9[a]	36,739,096
1921	172	259,999,244
1922	254[b]	12,642,630
	1[c]	109,112,500
1923	18	75,681
TOTAL	454[d]	418,569,151

Notes:
a. Excludes Nohab order for 1,000 locomotives.
b. Includes renegotiated contract for overhaul of 150 locomotives, at 4,616,220 crowns, which was curtailed in 1924, and one contract for 10 turbines for Volkhovstroi, for 4,200,570 crowns.
c. Renegotiated Nohab contract for 500 Class E locomotives (curtailment of order of May 1920).
d. Excludes seven minor contracts which were cancelled, one minor order of which the value is unknown, and three minor orders for which no charges were levied.
   According to *The Economist* (14 April 1923, p. 811), London exchange rates for sterling on 13 April 1923 were:
   Swedish crowns   17.49–52
   German marks   97,500–98,500
   US$ 4.65 5/8–7/8

Source: Calculated from Lomonosov, *Predvaritel'nyi otchet*, 'Prilozhenie V', pp. 1–11; this source shows a final total of 417,687,515 crowns.

regarded as a problem child when shipped to the USSR in 1927. A troubled symbol of modernisation, it was almost certainly the final delivery on a Railway Mission contract.[42]

The tangible results of the railway imports policy were substantial. Lomonosov and the Railway Mission placed 454 orders between 15 October 1920 and 15 April 1923, including Krasin's Nohab order as renegotiated in July 1922 and the Volkhovstroi turbines. (See tables 7.1 and 7.2.) Most of these orders were completed by April 1923, and the remainder were finished by the end of January 1925, excepting the last turbines, the second diesel locomotive, the cancelled overhauls and several possible though insignificant cancellations. In all, Soviet Russia received 1,200 new steam locomotives, 2 diesel locomotives, 1,500 tanker wagons, 200 Armstrong boilers (including 50 on Nohab

Table 7.2. *Principal Soviet railway contracts with foreign companies, 1920–1923 (value in excess of 1 million Swedish crowns, as recalculated in source for 15 April 1923)*

Date	Item	Company	Value (crowns)
27 Apr. 1920	113 decapod locomotives[a]	Revalis	—
15 May 1920	1,000 class E locomotives[b]	G. Anderson, for Nohab	[max. 275m]
5 Oct. 1920	overhaul of 230 class O locomotives[c]	United Mechanical Factories of Estonia	—
18 Oct. 1920	16,000 locomotive tyres	Krupp	4,064,060
20 Oct. 1920	22,000 locomotive tyres	Henschel	3,575,071
20 Oct. 1920	153,900 boiler tubes	Mannesmann et al.	2,509,381
21 Oct. 1920	100 class E locomotives	Verband, via Nohab[d]	25,741,950
[11 Jan. 1921]	overhaul of 1,500 locomotives[e]	Armstrong Whitworth	—
24 Jan. 1921	5,720 tyres	Krupp	1,056,000
25 Jan. 1921	5,800 tyres	Krupp	1,375,000
21 Feb. 1921	1,350 weights	Holmquist	1,082,527
28 Feb. 1921	600 class E locomotives	Verband, via V. Berg[d]	178,613,400
5 Mar. 1921	100,000 boiler tubes	Mannesmann	1,204,500
9 Apr. 1921	58,510 tonnes, rails and parts	Dortmund Union et al.	13,442,520
13 Apr. 1921	20,000 tonnes, rails and parts	Wolf	4,114,000
13 Apr. 1921	249,470 boiler tubes	Rheinmetall, Wolf, etc.	1,554,773
25 June 1921	500 oil tanker wagons	Canadian Car and Foundry	8,939,242
25 Aug. 1921	1,000 oil tanker wagons	Leeds Forge/Linke-Hofmann	13,027,950
15 Oct. 1921	200 locomotives boilers	Armstrong Whitworth	14,667,620
10 Mar. 1922	10 turbines[f]	Nohab	4,200,570

Notes:
a. Not implemented; value not recalculated in 1923.
b. Reduced to 500 engines on 28 July 1922, for 109,112,500 crowns.
c. Replaced on 20 December 1921 by a contract for 200 overhauls, for 4,616,220 crowns; curtailed in 1924.
d. Sub-contracted as planned to German locomotive-building syndicate.
e. Provisional agreement, not implemented; value not recalculated in 1923.
f. For Volkhovstroi; to reduce cost of Nohab engines.
Source: Calculated from Lomonosov, *Predvaritel'nyi otchet*, 'Prilozhenie V', pp. 1–11.

engines), nearly 80,000 tonnes of rails and fittings, over 50,000 tyres and 500,000 boiler tubes, as well as about 70 overhauled locomotives and numerous other items. The railways may also have received some minor supplies from Gukovskii's contracts of 1920, Arcos orders and other sources.

An indication of the place of these deliveries in overall Soviet imports is given in the main official compendium of interwar Soviet foreign trade statistics, which is based on customs data.[43] Unfortunately, NKPS imports are not disaggregated, and so table 7.3 shows only principal headings with definite or possible railway content, together with steam turbines (presumably including or comprising the Volkhovstroi order) and, for comparison, food imports and total imports; such headings as 'Other transport resources' and 'Tubes/pipes' undoubtedly include, or consist of, non-NKPS imports. Also, the source gives gold ruble values in average 1913 prices until 1923/4, and so for ease of comparability table 7.3 excludes later imports, which comprised about sixty-five Nohab locomotives, the two diesel locomotives and part of the turbine order. According to table 7.3, then, the peak of the imports policy was the 1921/2 financial year, with principal railway and possible railway imports worth nearly 43 million gold rubles, or some 15.7 per cent of the year's total value. Total possible railway expenditure on these main headings in 1920–3/4 was 90,754,210 gold rubles, or some 10.2 per cent of total imports by value. By contrast, the 1,303,710 tonnes of food imports in the famine period of 1921–2/3 alone were worth 149,333,200 gold rubles, or about 16.7 per cent of total imports for 1920–3/4.

However, there are serious problems with this source. An understandable omission is the Estonian overhaul contract, which was not supposed to involve gold expenditure and did not involve imports as such. More serious is the absence of locomotive boilers, tyres and wheelsets, to name the most important items, and Lomonosov's diesel locomotives are not shown in later years either. Nor, one suspects, is all the rolling-stock shown: the tonnage figures for locomotive imports seem broadly accurate, but the wagon tonnages suggest an improbably low tare weight of about 11 tonnes for the 1,500 tankers. Curiously, there is no heading for rolling-stock spare parts, yet there is a heading for automobile spares.

Also problematic are the valuations and the source of funding. Because of changing price patterns and exchange rates, the use of pre-war prices makes it difficult to relate the recorded railway expenditure to other products, and especially to the depletion of the gold reserve.

Table 7.3. *Value of total Soviet imports and selected products, 1920–1923/4 (average 1913 prices, thousand gold rubles)*

Item	1920	1921	1921/2	1922/3	1923/4	TOTAL
All imports	28,724.9	210,725.1	271,099.0	148,631.0	233,531.9	892,711.9
of which:						
Steam boilers, equipment	—	—	—	—	—	—
Steam turbines, equipment	—	—	—	—	818.1	818.1
Steam locomotives	119.9	3,552.0	35,677.9	9,894.1	11,461.9	60,705.8
Diesel locomotives	—	—	—	—	—	—
Wagons	—	—	3,516.1	3,735.9	17.8	7,269.8
Other railway equipment	—	—	—	—	—	—
Other transport resources	—	2.9	11.8	200.9	23.81	239.41
Rails	—	8,439.9	1,496.9	47.1	29.0	10,012.9
Tyres	—	—	—	—	—	—
Wheelsets	—	—	—	—	—	—
Tool steel	—	—	—	—	—	—
Tubes/pipes	64.0	2,704.1	2,050.2	2,861.9	4,028.0	11,708.2
Points	—	—	—	—	—	—
Materials for food products	42.8	9,126.0	36,209.3	3,628.3	16,883.6	65,890.0
Food products	1,102.0	24,716.7	57,722.9	17,930.0	18,761.9	120,233.5

Notes: Includes principal statistical headings under which Railway Mission imports may be recorded; some headings may include or consist fully of non-railway imports, especially 'other transport resources' and 'tubes/pipes', whilst the turbines are presumably for Volkhovstroi; the locomotives reportedly imported in 1920, weighing only 183 tonnes, are unknown. The rules evidently indicate a zero return, but as this book shows, at least some of these items were definitely imported.

Source: Calculated from *Vneshniaia torgovlia SSSR za 1918–1940gg.*, pp. 204, 210–11, 213–14, 237, 243–4, 246–7, 269, 275, 278–9.

For instance, a unit price of 119,400 gold rubles was agreed for the 600 German locomotives ordered in February 1921, making 71,640,000 gold rubles in total; yet the compendium shows 60,705,800 gold rubles for total deliveries in 1920–3/4 of 109,276 tonnes (approximately 1135 engines if one takes the official NKPS weight of locomotive and tender). As for funding, a large proportion of the food imports in 1921–3 was in fact donated by foreign agencies for famine relief, one American source putting the volume of the 'American donation' at about 540,000 tons (489,780 tonnes). Their inclusion in these statistics distorts the overall picture of trade revival and, logically, the place of the railway imports in that revival.[44]

If one considers the railway imports in contemporary prices as calculated by the Railway Mission's accountant, F. F. Perno, a different picture begins to emerge. Perno recalculated and standardised prices in Swedish crowns for 15 April 1923 for virtually all 454 mission contracts, excepting only a handful of small cancellations. (See table 7.1.) Evidently excluding overheads like the mission's maintenance costs, transportation and the cost of the Nohab curtailment, his list gives a total value of 418,569,151 crowns, or some £23,918,237 at the then exchange rate of 17.50 crowns per pound sterling. It is possible that some of the outstanding minor orders may have been cancelled by Emshanov or Rudyi, but the termination of the Estonian overhaul contract in 1924 was the only significant change. The amount of hard currency expenditure on this contract and the final tally of repaired engines are not known precisely, but a rough sense of the change can be given by a pro rata reduction of the contract value from 4,616,220 Swedish crowns (150 engines) to 2,154,236 crowns (for 70 overhauls). This would give an overall total value, excluding overheads, of some 416,107,167 crowns, equating to approximately £23,777,550 sterling.

Unfortunately it has not yet been possible to confirm the exchange rate used by Perno for gold rubles. However, two other sources have been found which give reasonably detailed valuations in gold rubles. One is from Gosplan, which collected information in early 1922 about Soviet expenditure on contracts signed in 1920–1, showing contemporary prices and including special extra commitments and outstanding contractual obligations. (See table 7.4.) NKPS contracts were valued at nearly 250 million gold rubles as of 1 January 1922 and were responsible for virtually 50 per cent of the total expenditure and outstanding commitment, probably including overheads like transportation costs. Next, interestingly, were military contracts at just under 20 per cent and, at only 11.53 per cent, food and related

Table 7.4. *Values of Soviet contracts for imports, April 1920–1 January 1922 (contemporary gold rubles)*

Purchasing authority	Apr. 1920–1 Nov. 1920	1 Nov. 1920–1 June 1921	1 June 1921–1 Jan. 1922	TOTAL	Percentage of all contracts
NKPS	13,258,246	222,234,319	14,409,855	249,902,420[a]	49.85
VSNKh	20,552,812	6,084,912	6,774,313	33,412,637[b]	6.67
Glavtop[c]	6,855,471	385,812	4,839,738	12,081,021	2.41
NKZem[d]	10,287,162	19,113,442	6,044,940	35,445,544	7.07
NKProd[e]	1,843,429	4,050,124	51,889,886	57,783,439	11.53
Military	—[f]	96,985,269	2,695,044	99,680,313	19.88
Other	81,207	5,809,633	6,563,260	12,954,100[g]	2.58
TOTAL	52,878,327	354,663,511	93,717,636[h]	501,259,474[i]	100

Notes:
a. The NKPS figures include the Nohab contract as renegotiated in March 1921 (rather than for May 1920).
b. Total as given in source, but actual total is 33,412,037.
c. The Fuel Department.
d. The People's Commissariat of Agriculture.
e. The People's Commissariat of Food Procurement.
f. No value is given for the military in 1920.
g. Total as given in source, but actual total is 12,454,100.
h. Total for 1 June 1921–1 January 1922 as given in source, but actual total is 93,217,036.
i. Overall total as given in source, but actual overall total is 500,758,974.
Source: Rossiiskii gosudarstvennyi arkhiv ekonomiki, 4372/11/62/296.

imports. However, these statistics predate the curtailment of the Nohab contract, and gold expenditure on food imports additional to foreign donations may have been much higher in 1922.

The other source is a set of statistics compiled by the Railway Mission in contemporary gold rubles for 20 November 1922. (See table 7.5.) This gives the total value of completed and outstanding NKPS contracts for that day as 202,448,338 gold rubles, including the Nohab order as revised to 500 engines, and the Volkhovstroi turbines, but probably excluding overheads; if the Estonian figure is reduced pro rata to 1,251,250 gold rubles for 70 overhauls, a total of 200,124,588 gold rubles would result. If, furthermore, one allows for the remaining minor orders to April 1923 and overheads, particularly maintenance of the mission, transportation costs and the cost of the Nohab curtail-

Table 7.5. *Value of Railway Mission current and completed contracts at 20 November 1922 (contemporary gold rubles)*

Item	Value	Comprising	Value
1,200 locomotives	147,750,000	700 German	95,500,000
		500 Swedish	52,250,000
Tyres	4,707,633		
Smoke tubes	4,294,175		
Springs, copper tubes etc.	3,671,536		
Coloured metals	1,224,560		
1,500 oil tankers	11,281,250	500 Canadian	4,906,250
		1000 Anglo-German	6,375,000
Rails and fittings	8,800,680		
200 locomotive boilers	6,778,750		
Spare parts	3,900,355		
200 locomotive overhauls	3,575,000		
Workshop equipment	2,878,919		
Water turbines	1,913,708		
Miscellaneous	1,671,772		
TOTAL	202,448,338		

Note: The locomotive overhaul contract was curtailed to about 70 in 1924, the final value is unknown; almost all of the remaining expenditure was made: see table 7.1.
Source: Leeds Russian Archive, G. V. Lomonossoff Collection, MS 716.6.1.9, photograph album 'Russian Railway Mission', pp. 1, 28.

ment, the final bill conceivably exceeded 220 million gold rubles, mostly paid with gold. That figure would equal about 30 per cent of the gold reserve of March 1920, and is all the more striking given that the reserve did not exceed 445–540 million gold rubles for the rest of the decade.[45] From this perspective, the railway imports represented a very substantial portion of early Soviet gold-funded imports. Unfortunately, given the evident unreliability of the published compendium, it is impossible to be more precise without considerable further research, including access to the archive of the People's Commissariat of Finances gold commission.

As far as the NKPS was concerned, the imports of spare parts and raw materials were vital for the railways' day-to-day operations in 1921–2. It seems impossible to clarify how the commissariat calculated its bids for resources, but even allowing for a degree of exaggeration, it appears probable, to judge by the figures in tables 7.6 and 7.7, that imported tyres and boiler tubes did play a crucial role in sustaining

Table 7.6. *Deliveries of selected products to the NKPS, 1 January 1920–1 November 1922 (aggregated figures, tonnes)*

Item	NKPS demand	Deliveries	Percentage of demand
Roofing iron	67,791.7	25,558.4	37.70
Spring steel	12,469.5	2,184.2	17.52
Nails	36,772.8	9,877.8	26.86
Tin	1,283.6	642.2	50.03
Lead	3,846.8	3,276.3	85.17
Babbite	11,165.5	3,194.8	28.61
Tyres	52,551.2	24,352.2	46.34
Axles	8,247.8	2,749.8	33.34
Boiler tubes	19,723.0	13,333.4	67.60
Rails	324,370.0	162,364.3	50.06

Notes:
Annual figures added to give an overall aggregate.
The relatively high levels of many delivery figures suggest that imports are included.
There is no indication of how NKPS 'demand' was calculated.
Source: Calculated from Fomin, *Piatiletie Sovetskogo transporta*, pp. 34–5.

the railways during 1921 and 1922. The quantity of imported rails was not particularly large by normal standards, but may well have represented a vital supplement to domestic production for track repairs. As for the wagon stock, imported nails and roofing iron probably contributed significantly to its overall health, and though no information about the service of the tankers has been found, their arrival doubtless made oil shipments in the Caucasus much easier as production resumed. However, the Estonian repair contract was probably more trouble than it was worth.

But most of the expenditure comprised investment in new locomotives. Comparison of the locomotive stock on 1 October 1925 with the last full pre-war year, 1913, shows that the Soviet imports helped to alter the overall profile significantly.[46] There was superficial stability in that the absolute quantity of locomotives increased by less than 100 to 20,143 in 1925.[47] But the health of the stock became much worse with just over 50 per cent of the locomotives undergoing or awaiting overhaul in 1925 compared to an average of 16.8 per cent in 1913.[48] Also worse was the age profile, with 50.3 per cent aged thirteen or less in 1913 compared to only 32.7 per cent aged fifteen or less in 1925. On the other hand, deliveries of new locomotives did continue

Table 7.7. *Deliveries of selected products to the NKPS, 1 October 1921–1 October 1922, including imports (tonnes)*

Item	NKPS demand	Domestic deliveries	Imported deliveries	Total deliveries	Total percentage of demand
Cast iron	37,604.1	20,538.0	—	20,538.0	54.62
Profiled iron	86,487.8	17,359.5	—	17,359.5	20.07
Roofing iron	23,309.0	8,378.2	2,542.8	10,921.0	46.85
Wire	6,145.1	554.2	—	554.2	9.02
Nails	14,621.1	2,037.5	1,206.2	3,243.7	22.19
Nuts and bolts	11,866.4	2,282.0	—	2,282.0	19.23
Tin	293.4	44.01	203.75	247.76	84.44
Lead	766.1	114.1	1,890.8	2,004.9	261.70
Babbite	5,167.1	603.1	163.0	766.1	14.83
Tyres	9,176.0	1,630.0	2,656.9	4,286.9	46.72
Axles	260.8	141.81	—	141.81	54.38
Boiler tubes	6,699.3	570.5	3,080.7	3,651.2	54.50
Parts for copper fireboxes	423.8	244.5	—	244.5	57.69
Locomotive spare parts	5,868.0	554.2	130.4	684.6	11.67
Wagon spare parts	5,721.3	391.2	—	391.2	6.84
Iron castings	11,899.0	945.4	—	945.4	7.95
Wagon springs	4,580.3	635.7	16.3	652.0	14.23
Rails	96,023.0	—	23,031.9	23,031.9	23.99

Notes:
Data supplied by the NKPS Directorate of Economics and Materials, to some extent reflecting orders placed before October 1921, especially for rails.
There is no indication of how the NKPS 'demand' was calculated.
The rules indicate a zero return, which is probably inaccurate for such items as wagon spares.
Source: Iz opyta sostavleniia plana material'nogo snabzheniia transporta na 1922–23 god, p. 14.

throughout the period, albeit somewhat erratically, so that by October 1925 the Soviet railways possessed 5,095 freight and 698 passenger engines dating from 1913–25. The average of about 448 deliveries per year was considerably below the peak Russian output in 1906 (1,266) but was respectable compared to production in 1880–1913. True, 3,907 of these engines (67 per cent) were built in 1913–17, but as many as 1,916 were constructed during the civil war and 'reconstruction period', an annual rate of nearly 240, which is strikingly high in the circumstances and relies on the 1,200 German and Swedish imports.[49] Moreover, the majority were so-called 'powerful' types like the E (2,709), Ye (744) and S (600), and they boosted the quantity of 'powerful' engines to 7,646 in October 1925.[50] Finally, because fewer 'powerful' locomotives were needed to haul a given amount of traffic, many obsolete engines could be scrapped: 2,186 engines were condemned in 1920–4 and over 1,000 more in the year commencing 1 October 1925. Whereas 4,522 locomotives dating from 1857–90 were recorded in 1913, only 842 remained in October 1925, and 398 a year later.[51]

Admittedly, locomotive deliveries during the period 1914–25 fell well short of the MPS plans of early 1914 and the NKPS plans of 1919–20, and the Class E did not represent, in world terms, the latest technology. But the deliveries of 1920–5 ensured that the 'reconstruction period' of 1921–5, usually defined as merely the maintenance and repair of existing equipment, meant far more for the railways. Intended as 'interim modernisation' and forming nearly two-thirds of all deliveries between 1918 and October 1925, the 1,200 imported locomotives thus helped to place the railways in a much less shaky position on the eve of the First Five-Year Plan than might otherwise have been the case.

It is conceivable that Soviet locomotive production might have increased to this level given the same gold resources from 1920, and a case might be made that the imports delayed domestic industrial recovery. As has been shown, industry representatives passionately took that view. Also conceivable, however, is a repeat of the failure to increase production of fire-resistant brick, which helped to make the NKPS so cynical about VSNKh promises. Moreover, large VSNKh foreign orders to assist domestic locomotive production would presumably also have become vulnerable to cancellation so as to save gold. Indeed, the gold released by the Nohab curtailment in 1922 was not redirected to the locomotive-building industry, the reality being three more years of NKPS–VSNKh argument over resources. Dashing hopes that the Gosplan compromise would ameliorate their relationship, the battle recommenced as early as January 1923 with the usual vehemence. A full account is beyond the scope of this book, but a brief overview may help to place the NKPS imports in the context of longer-term economic recovery and growth.[52]

Epilogue: towards Stalinist industrialisation

Following the Gosplan and STO decisions of August 1922 concerning locomotive construction and overhauls at Soviet factories, the NKPS and VSNKh signed final contracts on 20–1 December 1922 for the construction of 148 locomotives in 1923, 180 in 1924 and 180 in 1925, together with 585 locomotive overhauls in 1923, 600 in 1924 and 750 in 1925. The contracts included all locomotives built after 1 March 1922 or the date when the factories ceased to receive state supplies. As for deadlines, the autumn of 1922 was treated as a preparatory period and completion was scheduled for December 1925 during the 1925–6 financial year.[53]

However, P. S. Ianushevskii of Gosplan's Transport Section unwittingly sowed the first seeds of this programme's disruption in September 1922 when he attempted to calculate the railway system's requirement for metal products. Having inevitably identified a huge discrepancy between NKPS demand and actual VSNKh output, he recommended pruning the transport system's reconstruction plans, though he accepted the locomotive-building plan as sacrosanct. Then, in November, Ianushevskii and several NKPS planners produced an important treatise about the railway economy's prospects to 1925 and beyond. Aligning with Gosplan's forecasts for the economy's other main sectors, they predicted an annual increase in traffic of only 5–15 per cent for some years, and, allowing for the final imported engines plus the deliveries under the new VSNKh programme, they calculated that no other new locomotives would be needed until about 1930.[54]

No sooner were the December contracts signed than the railways rebelled on the basis of these Gosplan forecasts. In January 1923 Dzerzhinskii was told that no additional new locomotives would be needed for between five and ten years, and that it was important to concentrate on resurrecting the existing stock. Similarly, a conference chaired by Fomin expected no demand for new engines during the next three to four years.[55] Dzerzhinskii reported these findings to the STO on 7 February, and after the latter commissioned the first of many reviews of the 1923–5 locomotive-building plan, successive NKPS analyses went further than ever. For instance, a report of 17 February calculated that there might not be any need for new engines until 1929, 1932 or even 1941, depending on the rate of traffic recovery.[56] And by April 1923 it was even admitted that the Mozherez repair factory – still under construction as a prime symbol of the railways' recovery and expansion – was no longer needed urgently.[57]

Needless to say, the railway lobby had not lost its traditional predilection for new equipment. Rather, this was a severe case of short-term penny-pinching. Indeed, Krasovskii continued researching new locomotive designs, delivering a report about a proposed passenger type to the Thirty-Third Congress of Traction Engineers on 18 June 1923.[58] In short, NKPS–VSNKh relations were essentially little changed since late 1921, though perhaps now the VSNKh had the upper hand. However, as with the NKPS a year earlier, Soviet industry's response arguably lacked imagination and sensitivity. The VSNKh simply refused to halt locomotive construction even temporarily, or to overhaul rolling-stock on the scale demanded by the NKPS, and, unsurprisingly, the result was stalemate.

Despite Ianushevskii's comments Gosplan failed to support the NKPS.[59] However, in the autumn of 1923 the NKPS found an unexpected new opening in the so-called 'scissors crisis', when urban–rural trade was threatened as prices for metal goods rocketed whilst agricultural prices slumped in relative terms. The commissariat lambasted VSNKh pricing policy and alleged gross inefficiency in the metal industry's use of fuel, and it did not restrict its venom to rolling-stock contracts.[60] Two months, several long pamphlets, a host of newspaper articles and many speeches later the NKPS had won, at least as far as reducing the locomotive-building plan was concerned. Again asked to arbitrate, Gosplan had again sought compromise, suggesting that the metal industry should produce the same number of engines in 1924 as in 1923. But, as ever, the conflict was a duel to the death, and the final decision was to cut the 1924 programme to just twenty engines.[61]

If this NKPS victory was not quite absolute, the difference was insignificant in the circumstances. Or at least it would have been so, had the triumph not been short-lived. Lenin's death on 21 January 1924 prompted a government reshuffle which took Dzerzhinskii to the VSNKh, whilst Ia. E. Rudzutak took charge at the NKPS. A new position with new advisers transformed Dzerzhinskii's outlook, and he was soon master-minding the metal industry's counter-campaign against the NKPS. As early as March 1924 he persuaded the Central

Committee to establish a special government commission for the metal industry, and this gathering produced a plan for 161 new locomotives in 1924, which was confirmed by the STO on 7 May.[62]

The NKPS appealed, using a new Gosplan forecast that traffic would not regain its 1913 level until 1941, and the quarrel continued. For instance, in January 1925 Dzerzhinskii condemned NKPS policy at a Central Committee plenum but only won new investigations instead of a final decision in the VSNKh's favour. In fact 'life' finally forced the issue by revitalising NKPS interest in new locomotives. During 1925 traffic began growing very rapidly as economic activity revived much faster than predicted, and a potential shortage of serviceable engines began to loom. One obvious option was to concentrate on repairing the many stored locomotives, mostly of older types. But with traffic now approaching its pre-war levels, NKPS thoughts turned again to modernisation. The result was an NKPS–VSNKh truce in November 1925 whereby both sides accepted a plan to expand production to 450 engines in 1926/7 and 1,200 in 1929/30.[63]

Needless to say, as gold and foreign credit remained scarce and the concept of 'Socialism in One Country' took hold, there could be no question of more large-scale locomotive imports. Indeed, neither railway development nor imports would serve as driving forces of interwar Soviet industrialisation. It is true that the Turkestan–Siberian (Turksib) Railway became a symbol of the First Five-Year Plan, modern locomotives adorned propaganda posters, and money was invested in automatic couplings, several new locomotive designs and new railways.[64] But as Westwood remarks:

> In the Stalinist scheme of things, railways were simply means, an unwelcome necessity to be exploited for the benefit of production but benefiting as little as possible from that production. Under the five-year plans the USSR made a unique contribution to the history of railway transport, by carrying to extremes the policy of limiting investment whilst increasing traffic. The result of this under-investment may have been the faster development of industry, but certainly bequeathed to Stalin's successors a ramshackle transport system that remained a burden in the 1990s.[65]

This represented a fundamental change from the Vitte model. As in other sectors, investment fell behind requirements during the First World War.[66] But the railway reconstruction strategy of 1920, and especially the gold allocation for imports, show that the railways retained their predominant place in thought about socioeconomic development up to and including 1920, only to lose it through a combination of the crisis of War Communism, a redefinition of 'reconstruction' in more modest terms emphasising just recovery to pre-war norms, and the GOELRO alternative. It would never return.

As for interwar foreign trade, the overall turnover barely recovered to half its pre-war level. By contrast, the structure was basically similar to pre-war patterns. Exports continued to be dominated by raw materials and agrarian products, though with much less grain than earlier, whilst imports included machinery and metal goods together with semimanufactured and agrarian products. However, imports of consumer goods were now minimal, and machinery and metal products would account for roughly 60 per cent of imports by 1938 compared to just over 20 per cent in 1913. As before the revolution, scarcely any rolling-stock or rails were imported, and so the railway-related deliveries of 1915–24/5 appear as a distinct exception on the broad canvas of late tsarist and interwar Soviet industrialisation.[67]

In the meantime, Lomonosov remained mired in controversy. In December 1925 he was obliged to relinquish most of his diesel responsibilities to another one-time member of the NKPS Collegium, P. N. Kirsanov.[68] Just over a year later, in January 1927, he disobeyed a recall to Moscow and became an émigré in the West. However, he did not mix with White emigrants, even priding himself on his Soviet citizenship until the execution of his former friend and patron Kamenev shocked him into taking British citizenship in the late 1930s. He died in retirement in Montreal in November 1952 at the age of seventy-six.[69]

The professor's emigration proved timely. The following year, 1928, his fellow traction 'spets' Krasovskii was arrested in the NKPS version of the 'Shakhty' affair, accused, in phrases menacingly reminiscent of those perennial accusations against Lomonosov, of ordering unnecessary equipment from foreign firms and negotiating poor contracts; Borisov was perhaps fortunate to die the same year from natural causes.[70] By the mid-1930s the NKPS preached that the so-called 'Lomonosov school' had retarded Russian traction development, and Lomonosov's son-in-law and erstwhile Railway Mission colleague, N. I. Dobrovol'skii, was imprisoned for several years, as were many other NKPS locomotive engineers.[71] Needless to say, whereas Krasin and Dzerzhinskii died of natural causes in the mid-1920s, most of Lomonosov's communist colleagues were purged in the 1930s, including Emshanov, Lezhava, Krestinskii and Kerzhentsev; Fomin reportedly died in 1942 aged about fifty-eight.[72]

The imported locomotives were initially allocated mainly to the industrial heartland of north-west Russia, the Ukraine and south Russia. Most gave at least three decades of useful service – a far cry from the 'interim modernisation' of 1919 – and some survived in railway stock until the 1980s. One such example was Class E^{SH} No. 4444, shipped from Sweden to Leningrad in September 1924.[73] After final assembly and tests it joined the North Western Railway, first in the Leningrad area and from 1927 at Dno, before returning to Leningrad in 1930 to work on the October (formerly Nicholas) Railway. Evading capture during the Nazi invasion in 1941, No. 4444 moved to Moscow (Western Railway) in early 1942 and was incorporated in the Third Column of the NKPS Special Reserve on 1 July 1943. Demobilisation in 1946 left the engine based at Polotsk in Belorussia, and after one further reallocation it arrived at Dnepropetrovsk in February 1955. The following year it was placed in store, having travelled about 1.25 million kilometres, and there it remained until it was withdrawn from stock by the Dneiper Railway in 1989. Miraculously it survived to be rescued in 1991 for possible preservation, and together with about six of its German and Swedish fellows it should thus serve as a tangible reminder of the birth of Soviet–Western trade and the first great but misconceived and ill-fated Soviet leap towards economic reconstruction and modernisation.

Conclusion

The railway imports policy was part of a general strategy to kick-start rapid economic reconstruction and modernisation in 1920 by concentrating resources on the transport sector, primarily the railways. Though the prospects for foreign trade were uncertain, the NKPS imports plan had unprecedented targets of 5,000 new locomotives and 100,000 wagons, and it won a staggering 40 per cent of the gold reserve for initial orders. Its grandiosity epitomised the tremendous but naive optimism with which the Bolshevik leadership addressed economic policy at the beginning of 1920, when Lenin spoke of overcoming the economic crisis and beginning to build a modern socialist industrial economy within only a few months. This general strategy collapsed by 1921, but the allocation of so much gold did ensure that, despite later financial cutbacks, the railway imports policy played a major role in the expansion of Soviet–Western trade in 1920–1, and in the revitalisation of the Soviet railways.

The complex roots of this policy included decisions made before and during the First World War as well as planning during the civil war. But little would have happened without the Soviet government's willingness to assign 300 million gold rubles for it in March 1920. This book has argued that this unique decision is explained by – and dramatically demonstrates – the Bolshevik leadership's determination to embark immediately on rapid economic recovery, modernisation and development within the framework of War Communism. The tactic was to concentrate resources on one priority sector – echoing the Bolsheviks' successful civil war military tactics – and the first target was not GOELRO but the transport system. This effectively meant the railways, not just because the railway crisis posed the most immediate threat to the regime's survival but also because the recovery and expansion of the railway system were seen as the prerequisite for new industrial development, including nationwide electrification. The reconstruction process was to involve substantial modernisation as well as repair work, including the acquisition of thousands of new locomotives, and it would pave the way for the resumption of industrialisation. Thus the leadership's slogan 'Everything for Transport!' was really much more than mere reaction to crisis: it emphasised the urgent character and initial direction of their postwar economic strategy.

Railway planners hoped that, as in the tsarist era, the railways would continue to have a pre-eminent place in national socioeconomic development. But the Bolshevik prioritisation of the railways in early 1920 only superficially resembled tsarist strategy. Even by 1914 the economy's increasing sophistication was beginning to reduce the role of railway development in stimulating economic growth, and new technologies like electrification were soon to appear as potential alternative motors of growth. Moreover, far fewer resources were available in Russia in 1920 compared to the 1890s, and the prospects for large foreign loans were at best uncertain. Whereas Vitte prioritised industry over agriculture, the Bolsheviks resorted to a 'front-by-front' tactic. Also, as the railway imports plan shows, whilst Vitte supported protectionism, the Bolsheviks were open to imports. Captivated by their military success and enthusiasm for rapid modernisation, they deemed speed of delivery more important at this juncture than restoring the economic links between the railways and the railway-engineering industry.

The potential place of foreign economic relations in national development was debated during the civil war but especially from December 1919. The Bolsheviks recognised a danger of subjugation by foreign powers, but they were confident of averting it through state control of foreign trade and investment, and in the absence of international revolution the desirability of foreign economic relations with capitalist countries was scarcely doubted. The issue was their probability. Trotskii, on one side, argued that Soviet Russia would have to rely on its own internal resources – including labour conscription – because the capitalist world would continue to isolate the revolutionary country as a political pariah. By contrast, Krasin contended that the regime needed rapid economic progress to retain popular support, for which foreign economic resources would be essential, and that capitalist countries could soon be tempted into economic relations despite the ideology of international revolution.

The outcome of this debate was a compromise. Soviet economic planning was to be based on Trotskii's analysis, but imports and loans would also be sought. Furthermore, the transport commissariat would have precedence for domestic resources and imports, which would primarily be new locomotives and wagons. Significantly, technology transfer was not an issue concerning locomotives: the most modern existing Russian types were preferred to ensure speedy delivery and entry into service. In short, genuinely interested in imports for the economy, the Soviet leadership tried to keep its planning options open by treating imports as a potential bonus which, if they appeared, would quicken the pace of interim railway modernisation.

This compromise over foreign trade policy cannily satisfied both camps. But the wisdom of the overall economic strategy must be questioned. Entranced by grandiose visions of socialist development, the Bolshevik leadership ignored the rising spectre of famine whilst badly underestimating the economy's complexity and the depth of the economic crisis. As the next twelve months would show, the 'front-by-front' approach was simply unworkable and naive. And as potentially a key part of this strategy, the railway imports policy must equally be regarded as ill-conceived. Its emphasis on new locomotives and wagons embodied the idea of a rapid breakthrough in the reconstruction and modernisation of the railways, whereas the more pressing need in this area was restoration of the basic economic relationships between the railways and Soviet industry.

Seen in this light, the traditional view of 1921 as the beginning of the so-called 'reconstruction period' seems inappropriate. In fact the Bolsheviks were very much concerned with reconstruction during 1920. Starting with the railways, they made a determined attempt to embark on this process. But by the spring of 1921 they were forced to redefine reconstruction much more modestly in terms of gradually restoring the economy to its pre-war position. The transition from War Communism to the NEP was thus not only a compromise with the peasantry but was unequivocally a retreat from the grand objective of rapid economic reconstruction established only a year earlier. Indeed, though it encouraged hopes of greater opportunities for foreign economic relations, it actually revived and stimulated traditional protectionist attitudes when foreign investment failed to appear, and those attitudes foreshadowed and perhaps help to explain the popularity of 'Socialism in One Country' within a couple of years.

Never again after 1920 would railway development have the highest priority as both end and means for economic growth. The GOELRO plan replaced it as the would-be driving force of modernisation by December 1920, although, because the gold reserve was already badly depleted by that time, it did not enjoy similar large-scale imports during the NEP. Then, when the industrialisation debate of the mid-1920s was followed by the human tragedy of Stalinist industrialisation and collectivisation, heavy industry was the main beneficiary of investment. The modernisation and expansion of the Soviet railway system did continue to a degree, but chronic underfunding and gradual progress were the order of the day, especially in the 1930s.

The railway imports plan may have been poorly conceived, but its implementation was the one really substantial, tangible achievement of the ill-fated strategy of 1920. The crucial factor was the swift approval of so much gold for the NKPS. Whereas the GOELRO experts missed their moment by not submitting their plan until December 1920, the NKPS produced its imports plan within a couple of weeks. Not only did the gold decision confirm the commitment to economic modernisation, but, once Sweden ignored the gold embargo, it enabled real progress in Europe. By March 1921 the spectacular result was a series of railway contracts and draft contracts worth several hundred million gold rubles in total, in what this book has presented as the heroic period of Soviet foreign trade. Above all, no fewer than 1,000 Russian-type locomotives were ordered in Sweden and a further 700 in Germany.

Still more locomotives would have been bought had funds continued to be available. But it soon became clear that, because the gold reserve was limited and the large foreign loans predicted by Krasin did not appear, gold expenditure would need to be restricted. Tight budget limits quickly became a feature of imports planning during 1920, months before such financial discipline hit the domestic Soviet economy under the NEP in 1921. In fact the autumn and winter of 1920 saw cuts in the national imports plan and a ceiling of 240 million gold rubles imposed on NKPS foreign expenditure on locomotives, and the introduction of the NEP was even accompanied by a general moratorium on new gold commitments. Also, as the overall crisis deepened, the emphasis on importing new capital equipment was overshadowed by demands for food imports and, so far as the railways were concerned, for spare parts and raw materials to cope with immediate shortages.

Thereafter, the NKPS could never realistically hope for more gold for new equipment on the scale of 1920, and the prospect of further locomotive orders died. The commissariat was allowed a mere 3 million gold rubles for new contracts under the national imports plan for July–December 1921, and its basic budgets for 1922 and 1923 were smaller still. It did obtain several other special gold allocations, but most of this was necessary because of earlier activity, particularly to pay for the Armstrong boilers and the shipment of the locomotives to Russia. Indeed the quantity of locomotives on order was actually reduced from 1,700 to 1,200 in July 1922, mainly so as to conserve gold stocks and accommodate the Soviet metal industry's protectionist response to the financial reforms of the NEP.

The railway imports policy yielded substantial results: 1,200 new Russian-type steam locomotives, which reached Russia between October 1921 and December 1924; 1,500 new tanker wagons, delivered in 1921–2; 150 spare boilers; and several hundred thousand tonnes of rails, tyres, boiler tubes and other spare parts and raw materials, mostly delivered between late 1920 and 1922. It also included some 70 locomotive overhauls and the 2 diesel locomotives ordered in 1922, which reached Russia in 1925–7 and helped to give the country a world lead in this technology. In general, of course, these supplies were much less than was originally planned, but they still represented a huge quantity of equipment by any standards. Their overall cost was probably in the region of 220 million gold rubles, or about 30 per cent of the Soviet gold reserve as of March 1920. Most of this sum was probably paid from the reserve in 1920–2, and thus represents a major part of the reserve's depletion in the early 1920s.

The history of this unique policy suggests several conclusions about the way in which early Soviet–Western trade relations developed. Whereas the official statistics show an exponential growth curve for the turnover in the early 1920s, this study reveals an erratic pattern of growth by focusing on expenditure commitments and highlighting the time lag between the dates of contract and delivery. In terms of commitments to expenditure, there was far more Soviet trade activity in 1920 than has been realised: the contract value of the 1,100 locomotives ordered that year was, at roughly 123 million gold rubles, over four times greater than the recorded turnover of some 30 million gold rubles. By the same token, contrary to the impression given by the turnover statistics, the NEP probably did not spur an increase in Soviet expenditure commitments. The release of gold for new contracts was drastically reduced in 1921 and 1922 because of the general lack of resources, and though other commissariats may have gained special extra allocations in the same way that the NKPS had done, it seems impossible that total new commitments repeated the volume of 1920 and early 1921, even allowing for possible foreign loans. The

NEP's impact on the most valuable NKPS contracts, those for locomotives, is seen more clearly from the absence of new orders after February 1921 and the reduction of the Nohab order in 1922 than from the large deliveries in 1921–4.

According to Gosplan, approved expenditure on imports totalled over 550 million gold rubles by mid-February 1921, including the NKPS share of some 315 million. This sum was small compared to that of the prerevolutionary period, but it was huge in the circumstances, equalling about 75 per cent of the gold reserve. It would seem that, far from having minimal trade during 1920, the Bolsheviks committed gold at a rate which could be sustained for only a few more months. Thus, their financial position was probably already weak when the seriousness of the famine became apparent in 1921. What, then, was actually spent on contracts agreed in 1920 and early 1921? Were contracts abrogated, thus undermining the process of building trade confidence? There is a need for detailed research into the plans, contracts and actual expenditure for other commissariats, which would reveal not only the extent of special extra gold allocations and Gosplan cuts, but also the overall significance of imports in the depletion of the gold reserve. It would also confirm whether, as seems likely from this study, gold was primarily spent on imports, including military supplies in 1921, rather than on subsidies to promote international revolution. Further, it might clarify how much gold was really available for famine relief in 1921, and the importance for the currency reserve of the seizure of Church wealth in 1922.

In terms of the types of products purchased, the pre-war pattern of imports of metal goods took longer to re-establish than has been thought. Contemporary Soviet reports stressed that, as before the World War, manufactured and metal goods already formed a large proportion of imports by 1921 and remained prominent thereafter. But it can now be seen that whereas pre-war imports of railway equipment were minimal owing to protectionism, they represented a large proportion of early Soviet manufactured imports by weight and value. In general terms, the pattern was quickly restored, but in terms of actual products imported, the early 1920s must be seen as an aberration.

As for the development of Soviet foreign trade policy, this study shows how Krasin, as People's Commissar for Foreign Trade, found himself fighting on two fronts. On the one hand, he faced an uphill struggle to secure foreign support, which he attempted both by offering large orders and by exploiting his old business contacts, to the point of involving them, like Bonnier, as intermediaries. On the other hand, he had to win over sceptical comrades in Moscow, and this imperative may well be the main reason why he took the extraordinary step of ordering so many locomotives from Anderson in Sweden. This contract was basically a political move, for there was no question of rapid delivery, and whilst its huge scale clearly did help Krasin to break the gold embargo in Sweden, it could be seen as a very expensive option for which Krasin must bear responsibility.

Also worthy of note are the differing reactions of foreign governments and companies. Perhaps the most intriguing finding here is the considerable extent of the German government's involvement and the relatively close relations which Lomonosov was able to develop with the German Verband and government. The British government and Armstrong Whitworth, by contrast, leave the impression that they felt, as it were, rightfully entitled to a large Soviet railway order, for which complacency they paid accordingly. Relations between the Russians and Armstrong Whitworth were never particularly warm, and it was a relief for Krasin when the proposed Armstrong repair contract, which was in any case largely a political gesture, was abandoned in 1921.

The organisation of Soviet foreign trade also appears in a novel light. The central office of the Tsentrosoiuz in Moscow clearly took its foreign trade responsibilities seriously in the autumn of 1920, and its dismissal as a mere front organisation to circumvent the Allied restrictions may need reassessment. But more important are the existence and activity of the Railway Mission. Admittedly, Lomonosov was subordinated jointly to the NKPS (technical issues) and NKVT (commercial issues) from 1921, but because he kept his status as Sovnarkom plenipotentiary, he and his Railway Mission effectively continued to enjoy virtual autonomy from the NKVT, much to the annoyance of Krasin, Kerzhentsev and Stomoniakov in particular. While Sovnarkom did maintain an overall state monopoly of Soviet foreign trade, the operation of that monopoly was not solely controlled by the NKVT.

This conclusion re-emphasises the scope for a forceful individual to influence policy. Lomonosov was not responsible for the NKPS imports policy in late January and February 1920, having left Moscow for south Russia after his speech of 23 January, yet he became its most ardent defender. Almost single-handedly, it would seem, he managed to bring the Railway Mission into being against the wishes of the NKVT and, initially, probably the NKPS as well. Furthermore, admittedly with the support of Lenin and the NKPS, he successfully resisted repeated calls by Krasin, Kerzhentsev and others for the mission to be abolished, and even after abolition was scheduled for January 1923, Lomonosov still managed – with the help of circumstances – to delay the process for some months.

A further example of how an individual could shape policy is Krasin's reluctance to delegate full authority to Lomonosov in 1920. This stance may be explained by Krasin's passionate belief in the trade monopoly and the coordination of planning, his strong sense of responsibility for the gold and, above all, his apprehension about what Lomonosov might do on his own initiative. But it clearly rendered the negotiating process slower and more bureaucratic than would otherwise have been the case. It also demonstrated how much the smooth operation of the NKVT depended on personal trust between Krasin and his principal subordinates in Moscow and the various European countries.

Conversely, the controversies which surrounded the railway contracts suggest a deficit of authority in the economic bureaucracy over institutional lobbies like the NKPS and VSNKh. The decision-making process was bedevilled by prolonged and often bitter cycles of appeal and counter-appeal against supposedly final decisions. In particular, the twists and turns of the Armstrong affair and the NKPS–VSNKh dispute over locomotive-building policy testify to the bureaucracy's difficulty in identifying policy priorities and generating authoritative final decisions when the interests of two or more commissariats clashed. Even a personal intervention by Lenin failed to resolve the Armstrong affair in August 1921, and neither Gosplan nor the party-state leadership as a whole necessarily possessed sufficient authority to put a firm end to these disputes. Whereas similar problems within the Party bureaucracy were addressed at the Tenth Party Congress with the restrictions on discussion, no such discipline was enforced in relation to these economic decisions.

What of the vexed question of Bolshevik ideology as a factor in foreign trade decision making? Although international revolution was obviously a major Bolshevik concern, it did not significantly impinge upon the origins and implementation of the railway imports policy. At most, the People's Commissariat of Foreign Affairs sometimes prevented the placement of railway orders or threatened to cancel contracts in order to attain diplomatic objectives. Thus, most notably, the Comintern did not feature in debates about railway policy, and the process of negotiating with the German locomotive builders in 1920–1

Conclusion 233

was kept separate from any support for the eventual 'March Action' in Germany. Also, contrary to the German Verband's fears, there is no evidence that the Railway Mission's army of technical workers was engaged in systematic political subversion: the inspectorate was created through Lomonosov's personal insistence on Russian supervision of quality control, it had relatively few communists, and if it did cause disruption, that was probably mainly due to the internecine battles between Lomonosov and his colleagues.

But ideology did make an important contribution in other senses. For example, through their attachment to technical and technological innovation and their sense of railway transport as the first key to growth, Bolshevik leaders were very receptive to the schemes and dreams of railway engineers in the same way that they later supported the GOELRO programme. This, combined with immense Bolshevik self-confidence, encouraged both the priority for railway needs in early 1920 and the astonishing expansiveness of the NKPS planning. Ideological preconceptions also guided the Soviet leadership in the crucial dispute about the prospects for foreign economic relations in 1920. Similarly, it may be argued that although the debate about the NKPS imports in late 1921 and 1922 was dominated by financial issues, Soviet industry played on fears of economic enslavement which, whilst in some respects traditional, were also ideologically motivated.

So was the railway imports policy a costly blunder, as Soviet industry claimed, or a major success? The basic strategy of prioritising the railways for a reconstruction breakthrough was ill-conceived and overoptimistic. It naively overstretched the analogy with military tactics and underestimated the economy's complex character and problems. The same must be said of the basic idea for rolling-stock imports and, ultimately, Lenin's consent to release the gold. Retention of the gold as a means to support possible foreign loans might have represented a more appropriate policy, as was being suggested by the autumn of 1920. Equally, if this gold was to be spent abroad, it could be argued that other options such as larger-scale imports of spare parts as well as supplies for VSNKh factories might have represented better value in the circumstances. Also dubious were important aspects of the policy's implementation, especially Krasin's locomotive contract with Anderson in May 1920 and his proposal to overhaul locomotives in Britain. The Class E was chosen for speed of delivery, familiarity and standardisation, but may be seen as technically a step backwards from the American-built decapod. In any case, the NKPS imports plan was deprived of its main rationale – rapid reconstruction – long before the first German- and Swedish-built locomotives reached Russia in the autumn of 1921, by which time such imports appeared increasingly incongruous as Soviet industry languished in need of orders. And, given his determination to keep ordering locomotives in the winter of 1920–1 when the problems of famine, economic crisis and limited gold resources were already becoming very clear, Lomonosov must be blamed for reducing the gold reserve to a lower level than would otherwise have been the case.

On the other hand, if gold was to be used for imports in 1920, at least the choice of railway equipment struck a chord with foreign governments, who agreed with the definition of transport difficulties as the key priority. It thus underlined the seriousness of the Russians' interest in trade relations, and may therefore have significantly helped Krasin in overcoming foreign hostility. As for the actual NKPS orders, it is hard to believe that, as things turned out, they did any great harm to the Soviet locomotive-building industry, whilst imported spare parts and raw materials usefully took the edge off some of the most critical shortages. And though the 1,200 Class E locomotives were technically not an ideal investment, they did still represent a valuable and relatively modern resource for the future trial of forced industrialisation. At a time when railway transport was almost symbolised by the rusting hulks of sick locomotives, the imports policy did at least lend practical and lasting, if faintly ironic, meaning to the rallying cry, 'Our Locomotive, Fly Forward!' All things considered, that was no mean achievement.

Notes

Abbreviations

Archive collections

ADM	Admiralty papers, PRO
AVP	Arkhiv vneshnei politiki Rossiiskoi Federatsii
AW	Sir W. G. Armstrong Whitworth & Co. papers, Tyne and Wear Archives Service
BT	Board of Trade papers, PRO
CAB	Cabinet papers, PRO
FO	Foreign Office papers, PRO
GARF	Gosudarstvennyi arkhiv Rossiiskoi Federatsii
GFM	German Foreign Ministry microfilms, PRO
HIA	Hoover Institution Archives
HLRO	House of Lords Record Office
IISG	Internationaal Instituut voor Sociale Geschiedenis
LG	Lloyd George papers, HLRO
LRA	Leeds Russian Archive
NARG	National Archives Record Group, United States National Archives
PRO	Public Record Office
RGAE	Rossiiskii gosudarstvennyi arkhiv ekonomiki
RGIA	Rossiiskii gosudarstvennyi istoricheskii arkhiv
RTsKhIDNI	Rossiiskii tsentr khraneniia i izucheniia dokumentov noveishei istorii
SRA	Svenska Riksarkivet
UD:1920	Utrikesdepartamentets arkhiv, 1920 års dossiersystem, SRA

Publications

ADAP	*Akten zur Deutschen Auswärtigen Politik, 1918–1945: Serie A, 1918–1925*
BDFA	Cameron Watt, D. (ed.), *British Documents on Foreign Affairs: Reports and Papers from the Confidential Print, Part II, Series A: The Soviet Union, 1917–1939*

DBFP	Woodward, E. L. and Butler, R. (eds), *Documents on British Foreign Policy, 1919–1939, First Series*
DSV	*Dekrety Sovetskoi vlasti*
DVP	Gromyko, A. A. et al. (eds), *Dokumenty vneshnei politiki SSSR*
FRUS	*Papers Relating to the Foreign Relations of the United States*
PPG	Rogovskii, N. I. et al. (eds), *Protokoly Prezidiuma Gosplana za 1921–1922 gody*
PSS	Lenin, V. I., *Polnoe sobranie sochinenii*

Full details are given in the Bibliography.

Introduction

1 See, for example, Nove, *Economic History*, pp. 46–159.
2 Malle, *Economic Organisation of War Communism*, especially pp. 1–25.
3 Davies (ed.), *From Tsarism to NEP*, pp. 23–6.
4 Coopersmith, *Electrification*, pp. 1, 147; see also Remington, *Building Socialism*, especially pp. 3–22, 113–45.
5 Coopersmith, *Electrification*, pp. 174–8; Rassweiler, *Generation of Power*, pp. 12–13.
6 Steklov, *V. I. Lenin i elektrifikatsiia*, p. 494.
7 Coopersmith, *Electrification*, pp. 251–7.
8 See, for instance, Nove, *Economic History*, pp. 68, 89; Dohan, 'Foreign Trade', pp. 217–33; Lewis, 'Foreign Economic Relations', pp. 200–6.
9 *Vneshniaia torgovlia SSSR za 1918–1940gg.*, p. 14; Shtein, *Vneshniaia torgovaia politika*, p. 3.
10 General works include Ioffe, *Organizatsiia interventsii*; Kennan, *Russia and the West*; Sutton, *Western Technology*; Uldricks, *Diplomacy and Ideology*; Shishkin, *Sovetskoe gosudarstvo*; Dongarov, *Inostrannyi kapital*; Debo, *Revolution and Survival*; and Fischer, *Soviets in World Affairs*. Among studies of Soviet relations with specific countries are: Ullman, *Anglo-Soviet Relations*; C. White, *British and American Commercial Relations*; Haigh et al., *German–Soviet Relations*; and Fithian, 'Soviet–American Economic Relations' (unpublished PhD dissertation).
11 For example, Sonkin, *Okno vo vneshnii mir*, pp. 134–99; Shishkin, *V bor'be s blokadoi*, pp. 108–11.
12 Typical is Lewis, 'Foreign Economic Relations', p. 205.
13 C. White, *British and American Commercial Relations*, passim.
14 See Gromyko and Ponomarev (eds), *Istoriia vneshnei politiki*, Vol. I, p. 197.
15 Kennan, *Russia and the West*, pp. 182–3, 197–8.
16 Carr, *Bolshevik Revolution*, Vol. II, pp. 244–5 and Vol. III, pp. 182–3.
17 For example, C. White, *British and American Commercial Relations*, pp. 160–9; O'Connor, *Engineer of Revolution*, pp. 170–2; Phillips, *Between the Revolution and the West*, pp. 41–5.
18 *DSV*, Vol. VII, pp. 564–5.
19 The value of the gold reserve was probably about 738 million gold rubles.

See Novitsky, 'Fate of the Russian Gold Reserve', pp. 346–57; Iurovskii, *Denezhnaia politika sovetskoi vlasti*, pp. 33–9, 83–7; Smele, 'White Gold', pp. 1317–47.
20 On the history of Russia's railways to 1920 see Westwood, *History of Russian Railways*, pp. 17–198.
21 Examples are: *Ekonomicheskaia zhizn'*, 19 September 1920, p. 1, and 12 June 1921, p. 2; *Gudok*, 27 March 1921, p. 3, 30 March 1921, p. 1 and 6 September 1921, pp. 3–6; *Deiatel'nost' Russkoi* [sic] *zheleznodorozhnoi missii*; Lomonosov (ed.), *Perevozka parovozov*; Lomonosov, *Predvaritel'nyi otchet*; Lomonosov, *Parovozy 0-5-0*.
22 *Pravda* duly recorded this cinematic collaboration: Iakhontov, 'Tysiacha parovozov dlia Lenina'.
23 The statistics are discussed in chapter 7.
24 A curious exception during the Stalin years is Krylov, *Moi vospominaniia*, pp. 277–318, especially 297–8. Lomonosov is absent from Rakov's seminal *Lokomotivy zheleznykh dorog* of 1955, but figures briefly in Iakobson, *Istoriia teplovoza v SSSR*. The main Soviet comments about him during the 1960s and 1970s are within Lovtsov, 'Iz istorii bor'by Kommunisticheskoi partii', pp. 100–33 and 'Leninskii printsip', pp. 161–75; and Shishkin, *Sovetskoe gosudarstvo*, pp. 225–6, whilst the Railway Mission is scarcely mentioned in Zvezdin et al., *Zheleznodorozhnyi transport v vosstanovitel'nyi period*, pp. 98, 255 (note 24). Lomonosov was problematic as late as the mid-1980s: note the careful omission of his name in Erokhin, ' "Spetsial'no sledit' za etim delom . . ." '
25 Norman, 'Teplovoz professora Lomonosova', pp. 116–25. Subsequent Soviet publications were: Kuz'mich, 'Pervye sovetskie', and 'Tovarishchu Lomonosovu . . . ', and Suboch, 'Gorenie', pp. 40–42, which is basically an unacknowledged transcription of Norman's publication. See also Sosnovskii and Zenzinov, *Otechestvennye uchenye-zheleznodorozhniki*, pp. 124–5.
26 For example, Warburg–Lomonosov, 20 June 1938: LRA, MS 716.4.35.3.
27 Johnsson, *Nydqvist & Holm: 100 År*, pp. 213–61.
28 For instance, Shishkin, *Sovetskoe gosudarstvo*, pp. 225–6; Rakov, *Lokomotivy zheleznykh dorog*, p. 175.
29 Nove, *Economic History*, pp. 89–90.
30 Examples are: Le Fleming and Price, *Russian Steam Locomotives*, pp. 39–40; Rakov, *Lokomotivy zheleznykh dorog*, pp. 175–7; Shadur, *Razvitie otechestvennogo vagonnogo parka*, p. 70; Westwood, *Soviet Locomotive Technology*, pp. 8–9, and *History of Russian Railways*, p. 221; Lovtsov, 'Leninskii printsip', pp. 161–75; Shishkin, *Sovetskoe gosudarstvo*, pp. 166–8, 225–6; S. White, *Britain and the Bolshevik Revolution*, pp. 17, 24; Sutton, *Western Technology*, Vol. I, pp. 168–73; Åhlander, 'Staat, Wirtschaft und Handelspolitik', pp. 223–33; Carlbäck-Isotalo, 'Pengar eller politik', pp. 203–8; Himmer, 'German–Soviet Economic Relations' (unpublished PhD dissertation), pp. 235–44; Pogge von Strandmann, 'Grossindustrie und Rapallopolitik', pp. 284–9.

31 Archival sources are listed in the Bibliography; Lomonosov's unpublished 'Vospominaniia' and 'Dnevnik' are at LRA, MS 716.2.1 and MS 716.3, and the final classification of the Nohab papers may differ from the provisional arrangement used at the time of my visit to the Landsarkivet, Gothenburg.

1 Prologue

1. Marks, *Road to Power*, p. xi.
2. On Vitte and his strategy see Von Laue, *Sergei Witte*, *passim*.
3. For a good short overview see C. White, *British and American Commercial Relations*, pp. 4–24.
4. Geyer, *Russian Imperialism*, p. 268.
5. Falkus, *Industrialisation of Russia*, p. 69.
6. Gatrell, *Tsarist Economy*, pp. 225–7.
7. Geyer, *Russian Imperialism*, pp. 44, 164. See also Dohan, 'Foreign Trade', pp. 321–8, and Gatrell, *Tsarist Economy*, pp. 223–7.
8. Lewis, 'Foreign Economic Relations', p. 199; C. White, *British and American Commercial Relations*, p. 9.
9. Westwood, 'Transport', p. 158.
10. For instance, Haywood, *Beginnings of Railway Development*, pp. 64–5.
11. Fadeev et al. (eds), *Istoriia zheleznodorozhnogo transporta*, pp. 76–7.
12. Haywood, *Beginnings of Railway Development*, pp. 229–30 confirms that this wider gauge was chosen as a compromise between two differing engineering viewpoints rather than for military reasons.
13. See Westwood, *History of Russian Railways*, p. 304. These figures exclude industrial feeder lines, Finnish railways and (for 1913) the Chinese Eastern Railway. There were approximately 2,760 km of industrial lines in 1917: ibid., p. 305.
14. Falkus, *Industrialisation of Russia*, p. 55; Westwood, *History of Russian Railways*, p. 137; Page and de Pater, *Russian Locomotives*, p. 229; *Statisticheskii sbornik Ministerstva putei soobshcheniia (vypusk sto sorok pervyi): Zheleznye dorogi v 1913g. Chast' I*, table IIIA, p. 8.
15. Westwood, *History of Russian Railways*, pp. 306–7; Davies (ed.), *From Tsarism to NEP*, p. 312.
16. Gatrell, *Tsarist Economy*, p. 151.
17. Argenbright, 'Russian Railroad System' (unpublished PhD dissertation), p. 30.
18. Gatrell, *Tsarist Economy*, pp. 151–3, 174.
19. Fadeev et al. (eds), *Istoriia zheleznodorozhnogo transporta*, p. 77.
20. Hurt, 'Russian Economic Development', pp. 156–7.
21. Westwood, *History of Russian Railways*, pp. 74–8.
22. See Haywood, *Beginnings of Railway Development*, pp. 46–62, 65–134, 234–7; Blackwell, *Beginnings of Russian Industrialization*, pp. 279–314.
23. Gatrell, *Tsarist Economy*, p. 150; Hurt, 'Russian Economic Development', pp. 87–93. Some import duties may have been intended primarily to raise revenue, and were not protectionist: Gatrell, *Tsarist Economy*, p. 166.

24 Westwood, *History of Russian Railways*, pp. 91–3; Page and de Pater, *Russian Locomotives*, p. 13.
25 Gatrell, *Tsarist Economy*, p. 154.
26 Rakow, *Russische und sowjetische Dampflokomotiven*, p. 298.
27 Page and de Pater, *Russian Locomotives*, p. 229.
28 Gatrell, *Tsarist Economy*, pp. 172–3; Falkus, *Industrialisation of Russia*, p. 77.
29 Gatrell, *Tsarist Economy*, pp. 177–8. On the formation of the locomotive-builders' cartel see Kubitskaia, 'Stanovlenie parovozostroitel'noi monopolii', pp. 134–58.
30 Pogrebinskii, 'Komitet po zheleznodorozhnym zakazam', pp. 233–43; Gatrell, *Tsarist Economy*, pp. 180–1.
31 Westwood, *History of Russian Railways*, pp. 157–9.
32 See, for instance, Davies (ed.), *From Tsarism to NEP*, pp. 1–23 for the debate.
33 Falkus, *Industrialisation of Russia*, pp. 51–2; Nove, *Economic History*, pp. 12–13.
34 Falkus, *Industrialisation of Russia*, p. 46; Nove, *Economic History*, pp. 12–16.
35 For instance, Sidorov, 'Zheleznodorozhnyi transport', pp. 3–18.
36 For Russian locomotive output in 1881–1917 see Rakov, *Lokomotivy otechestvennykh zheleznykh dorog*, p. 127.
37 See Westwood et al., 'The Railways', pp. 169–78.
38 Westwood, *History of Russian Railways*, pp. 131–2.
39 See, for instance, Rakov, *Lokomotivy otechestvennykh zheleznykh dorog*, pp. 183–90, 238–43; Westwood, *History of Russian Railways*, pp. 154–5; and Nikol'skii, 'Sozdanie i ekspluatatsiia parka parovozov serii S', pp. 38–49. The Russian railways described their locomotives by axles: for example, a 2–10–0 was a 1–5–0 or a 5/6.
40 *MPS, Inzhenernyi sovet: Zhurnaly Komissii podvizhnogo sostava i tiagi* (henceforth *MPS, Inzhenernyi sovet*), No. 8 (19 April 1914), p. 158.
41 *MPS, Inzhenernyi sovet*, No. 4 (8 February 1914), p. 67; No. 5 (26 February 1914), pp. 91–2; No. 8 (19 April 1914), pp. 153–7, 175; Shchukin, *Istoricheskii ocherk*, pp. 9–10; Council of Representatives of Locomotive-Building Factories, Protocol No. 7 (30 April 1914): RGIA, 120/1/31/34–ob.
42 Gatrell, *Tsarist Economy*, pp. 151–4.
43 Detailed accounts of Russia at war include Lincoln, *Passage through Armageddon* and Stone, *Eastern Front*.
44 For analyses of the wartime railways see, for example, Shmukker, *Ocherki finansov*, pp. 21–137; Vasil'ev, *Transport Rossii v voine*; Westwood, *History of Russian Railways*, pp. 167–77; Sidorov, 'Zheleznodorozhnyi transport', pp. 18–64; and Westwood et al., 'The Railways', pp. 176–8.
45 Vasil'ev, *Transport Rossii v voine*, pp. 65–82.
46 Pogrebinskii, 'Popytki regulirovaniia', p. 246.
47 Sidorov, *Istoricheskie predposylki*, pp. 31–2; Westwood et al., 'The Railways', pp. 176–8.
48 *XXXIII soveshchatel'nyi s"ezd inzhenerov podvizhnogo sostava*, pp. 342, 344; Pogrebinskii, 'Popytki regulirovaniia', p. 261.

49 Report about main workshops (January 1914–June 1918): RGAE, 1884/43/593/91–4; figures quoted by Pogrebinskii: 'Popytki regulirovaniia', pp. 251, 261.
50 Afonina, *Kratkie svedeniia*, pp. 86–91.
51 Bogdanovich et al., *Ministry i Narkomy*, p. 111; 'Komissiia Tovarishcha Ministra Borisova', [n.d.]: RGIA, 247/1/1/11–ob.; and *The Russian Government's Plan of Future Railroad Construction* (English translation of an MPS submission to the State Duma dated 10 June 1916).
52 For an overview see C. White, *British and American Commercial Relations*, pp. 24–32.
53 Sidorov, *Ekonomicheskoe polozhenie Rossii v gody pervoi mirovoi voiny*, pp. 252–332, 628–33; Dohan, 'Foreign Trade', pp. 217–18; Stone, *Eastern Front*, pp. 144–64. The blockade is also discussed in, for instance, Mitchell, *History of Russian and Soviet Sea Power*, pp. 284–6; and Emets, *Ocherki vneshnei politiki Rossii*, pp. 109–48.
54 See Neilson, *Strategy and Supply*, passim; List of contracts on orders by the Russian Supply Committee in America to 20 January 1918: HIA, Russia: Posol'stvo (U.S.), box 328, file 328–7. This list commences in 1915 and shows a small amount of railway equipment ordered for non-MPS use, which is not discussed below. Further research is needed to clarify the full extent of Russia's wartime foreign expenditure.
55 Danilevskii–Briansk Machine-building Factory, 26 August 1914: RGIA, 120/1/271/270; Lomonosov, *Parovozy 0–5–0*, p. 8; *MPS, Inzhenernyi sovet*, No. 21 (20 September 1914), pp. 489–90; Council of Representatives of Locomotive-Building Factories, Protocol No. 14 (17 September 1914): RGIA, 120/1/31/65ob.; and Rakov, *Lokomotivy otechestvennykh zheleznykh dorog*, p. 193.
56 Vauclain, *Steaming Up!*, pp. 233, 236. Vauclain, who was also associated with the Remington company, was not the only American to scent business in Russia: C. White, *British and American Commercial Relations*, pp. 29–32.
57 Vauclain, *Steaming Up!*, pp. 237–45; Lomonosov, 'Vospominaniia', Vol. 5, pp. 751–2.
58 Rukhlov–Council of Ministers, 30 July 1914: RGIA, 120/1/45/122–7; [Danilevskii]–Rukhlov, 20 August 1914: RGIA, 120/1/45/128–9; Council of Representatives of Locomotive-Building Factories–Chairman of Council of Ministers, 20 October 1914: RGIA, 120/1/45/131; and Pogrebinskii, 'Komitet po zakazam', pp. 237–9.
59 For example, Council of Representatives of Locomotive-Building Factories, Protocol No. 12 (12 August 1914): RGIA, 120/1/32/21–ob.; No. 13 (3 September 1914): RGIA, 120/1/31/63–ob.; [Danilevskii]–War Minister, 15 January 1915: RGIA, 120/1/304/9.
60 Danilevskii–Briansk Machine-building Factory, 26 August 1914: RGIA, 120/1/271/120; Council of Representatives of Locomotive-Building Factories, Protocol No. 14 (17 September 1914): RGIA, 120/1/31/65ob.–66; Protocol No. 1 (10 January 1915): RGIA, 120/1/35/1ob.-2ob.

61 Pogrebinskii, 'Komitet po zakazam', p. 239.
62 Draft report to Council of Ministers, April 1916: RGIA, 247/1/3/4ob.
63 Pogrebinskii, 'Popytki regulirovaniia', p. 258.
64 Sidorov, 'Zheleznodorozhnyi transport', p. 43. Part or much of the shortage was caused by the military authorities hoarding wagons, according to a report to the Tsar in April 1915: ibid., p. 23.
65 Shmukker, *Ocherki finansov*, pp. 89–90.
66 Lipets, *Parovozy tipa 'dekapod'*, pp. 1–2.
67 Sidorov, 'Zheleznodorozhnyi transport', p. 58; Pogrebinskii, 'Komitet po zakazam', p. 239.
68 Sidorov, 'Zheleznodorozhnyi transport', p. 44.
69 *MPS, Inzhenernyi sovet*, No. 5/454 (4 April 1915), pp. 2–4.
70 Pogrebinskii, 'Komitet po zakazam', pp. 239–40.
71 Report about locomotive and wagon construction, [May 1916]: RGIA, 247/1/1/24–ob.
72 Pogrebinskii, 'Popytki regulirovaniia', pp. 258–60; Vasil'ev, *Transport Rossii vo voine*, p. 102.
73 Marginally different figures are given in Production of locomotive-building factories in 1916, 4 February 1917: RGIA, 120/1/67/192–3.
74 NKPS list of orders abroad during WWI: RGAE, 4038/1/45/210–17; Lipets, *Parovozy tipa 'dekapod'*, p. 7.
75 Report on the Activity of the Russian Supply Committee and its Liquidation Commission, Vol. 2, Part 3, 'Commission of Ways of Communication': NARG 261, entry 26, box L37.
76 Since the letter designation of this locomotive class, which is normally transliterated as 'E' in the Latin alphabet, is sometimes confused with the native Russian class E 0–10–0, the American engines are described henceforth as Class Ye or decapods. On these engines see, for example, Lipets, *Parovozy tipa 'dekapod'*, especially pp. 1–7; Edson, 'Russian Decapods', pp. 64–75; Rakov, *Lokomotivy otechestvennykh zheleznykh dorog*, pp. 192–8; and Page and Nurminen, *Russian Locomotives*, pp. 233–40.
77 Lipets, *Parovozy tipa 'dekapod'*, pp. 2–3; Ianush, *Russkie parovozy*, p. 57; the general problems are raised in Sidorov, *Ekonomicheskoe polozhenie Rossii v gody pervoi mirovoi voiny*, pp. 252–332.
78 *XXXIII soveshchatel'nyi s"ezd inzhenerov podvizhnogo sostava*, pp. 167–77; Rakov, *Lokomotivy otechestvennykh zheleznykh dorog*, p. 194. See also, for example, Vauclain–Willard (Council of National Defense), 9/22 June 1917: NARG 62, entry 1–A1, box 9, file F-1-2-2 'Russia: Equipment and Material'; and correspondence in NARG 261, Russian Supply Committee, box K138, file 719.
79 *MPS, Inzhenernyi sovet*, No. 23/494 (2 September 1916), pp. 7–8.
80 Design changes were discussed by the Shchukin commission on numerous occasions in 1915–17; see, for example, *MPS, Inzhenernyi sovet*, No. 17/488 (15 July 1916) and attached list. The later eulogy and recommendations are in *XXXIII soveshchatel'nyi s"ezd inzhenerov podvizhnogo sostava*, p. 172, and *Trudy XXXIV soveshchatel'nogo s"ezda inzhenerov podvizhnogo sostava*, p. 192.

81 *MPS, Inzhenernyi sovet*, No. 26/497 ([25] September 1916), pp. 14–16, and No. 5/503 (8 February 1917), pp. 6–14; *Vestnik putei soobshcheniia*, No. 2 (1918), p. 21. Also interesting is 'Shortcomings of American Wagons, 5/18 June 1917', in NARG 43, entry 833, box 1, file 2.
82 Sidorov, 'Zheleznodorozhnyi transport', p. 58. See also Lebedev, *Russko-amerikanskie ekonomicheskie otnosheniia*, pp. 190–3.
83 Sidorov et al. (eds), *Ekonomicheskoe polozhenie*, Vol. II, pp. 541–5. See also: Credit operations during the war, and Information about foreign indebtedness on 8 October 1917: HIA, M. V. Bernatskii papers, documents III, IX.
84 See C. White, *British and American Commercial Relations*, p. 27; Neilson, *Strategy and Supply*, pp. 111–14; Financial Agreement between the British and Russian Government Supplementary to the Agreement of September 30, 1915, 27 October 1916: FO 371/2750/402–18.
85 Financial Agreement between the British and Russian Government Supplementary to the Agreement of September 30, 1915, 27 October 1916: FO 371/2750/402–18.
86 See Sidorov, 'Zheleznodorozhnyi transport', pp. 58–60; Report on the Activity of the Russian Supply Committee and its Liquidation Commission, Vol. 2, Part 3, 'Commission of Ways of Communication', pp. 62–3: NARG 261, entry 26, box L37.
87 Sidorov, 'Zheleznodorozhnyi transport', pp. 58–60; Buchanan–Foreign Office, 4 May 1916: FO 371/2846/149; C. White, *British and American Commercial Relations*, pp. 27–8. Concerning Aschberg see Ganelin, *Rossiia i SShA*, pp. 54–6; biographical details are in Grew (Copenhagen)–State Department, 4 January 1921: NARG 59, 1910–29 decimal series, file 661.1115/254. Finland was regarded as a separate country in railway terms, despite being within the Russian Empire.
88 For example, Council of Representatives of Locomotive-Building Factories, protocol No. 7 (16 March 1916): RGIA, 120/1/37/10–ob.
89 Buchanan–Foreign Office, March 1916: FO 371/2846/130–1.
90 Buchanan–Foreign Office, 8 April 1916, and copy of Russian report: FO 371/2846/135–41.
91 Buchanan–Foreign Office, 4 May 1916, and note from Russian Ministry of Finances: FO 371/2846/149, 152–58. See also Sidorov, 'Zheleznodorozhnyi transport', pp. 58–61. These demands (with 300,000 tonnes of rails) were reiterated at a conference in mid-July: Neilson, *Strategy and Supply*, pp. 197–8.
92 Buchanan–Foreign Office, March 1916: FO 371/2846/130–1. The tonnage problem is considered in Neilson, *Strategy and Supply*, pp. 176–81.
93 Buchanan–Foreign Office, March 1916 and 8 April 1916: FO 371/2846/130–1, 149. See also Neilson, *Strategy and Supply*, p. 184.
94 War Office–Foreign Office, 21 April 1916: FO 371/2846/145.
95 Vernon (Ministry of Munitions)–Foreign Office, 18 May 1916: FO 371/2846/162.
96 Bradbury (Treasury)–Foreign Office, 10 June 1916: FO 371/2846/172–5. See also Neilson, *Strategy and Supply*, p. 190.

97 Foreign Office minute: FO 371/2846/171.
98 Sidorov, 'Zheleznodorozhnyi transport', pp. 58–61.
99 Buchanan–Foreign Office, 20 June 1916 and July 1916: FO 371/2846/170, 188–9.
100 Buchanan–Foreign Office, July 1916: FO 371/2846/188–9; Bradbury–Foreign Office, 22 July 1916: ibid., p. 204; Buchanan–Foreign Office, 1 August 1916: ibid., p. 209; and Bradbury–Foreign Office, 4 August 1916: ibid., p. 211. Also Neilson, *Strategy and Supply*, pp. 190–1, 205–7.
101 Lebedev, *Russko-amerikanskie ekonomicheskie otnosheniia*, pp. 192–3; Sidorov, 'Zheleznodorozhnyi transport', pp. 61–2; List of WWI orders: RGAE, 4038/1/45/210–17; Foreign Office–Buchanan, 13 January 1917: FO 371/3108/259. Approximately forty-two 'Flamme' locomotives were taken into stock: Rakov, *Lokomotivy otechestvennykh zheleznykh dorog*, pp. 191–2.
102 See Levi, *Rasstroistvo zheleznodorozhnogo transporta*, pp. 33–9; and Ostapenko, *Transport i voina*.
103 Sidorov, 'Zheleznodorozhnyi transport', p. 56. Possibly it was expected that a lot of second-hand equipment could be obtained quickly: General Mikhel'son gave that impression to a visiting American delegation a few months later: Transcript of Proceedings of Conference between General Manikovsky, Assistant to the Minister of War, and Officers, and General Scott, Chief of Staff, and Officers, 5/18 June 1917: NARG 39, Country Series, box 179, file 'Russia 9'.
104 Sidorov et al. (eds), *Ekonomicheskoe polozhenie*, Vol. I, pp. 370–6. Whether or not these proposed contracts were signed has not been ascertained.
105 Excerpt from MPS report to Provisional government, 31 March/13 April 1917: NARG 261, Russian Supply Committee, box K57, file 'May–Dec 1917'. See also Shcheglovitov and Karelin, *Transport*, p. 17; and Volobuev, 'Vremennoe pravitel'stvo', p. 264.
106 See *Trudy XXXII-go soveshchatel'nogo s"ezda inzhenerov sluzhby tiagi*, p. 67.
107 St John, 'John F. Stevens' (unpublished PhD dissertation), pp. 230–1; Diary of W. L. Darling, entry dated 17/30 September 1917: HIA, W. L. Darling papers.
108 Sidorov et al. (eds), *Ekonomicheskoe polozhenie*, Vol. II, pp. 453–4.
109 Paraphrase of Francis–Secretary of State, 18/31 March 1917: NARG 39, Country Series, box 176, file RS-200 'Russia: General'; Secretary of State–Francis, 3 April 1917, in *FRUS*, 1918, Russia Vol. III, p. 1; Francis–Secretary of State, 6 April 1917, in *FRUS*, 1918, Russia Vol. III, pp. 2–3; McAdoo–Woodrow Wilson, 15 May 1917: NARG 39, Country Series, box 176, file RS-200 'Russia: General'. See also Francis, *Russia from the American Embassy*, p. 124, though the sum is inaccurately indicated as $100 million.
110 Sidorov et al. (eds), *Ekonomicheskoe polozhenie*, Vol. II, pp. 453–4 and 534–5.
111 Protocol of meeting of Provisional government, 1/14 April 1917: GARF, 1779/1/7/6–10ob.; Francis–Secretary of State, 20 April 1917: *FRUS*, 1918, Russia Vol. III, pp. 3–4.

112 Secretary of State–Francis, 7 May 1917: *FRUS*, 1918, Russia Vol. III, pp. 7–8.
113 A copy of the instruction to Shulenburg, dated 25 April 1917, is at NARG 59, 1910–1929 decimal series, file 861.51/137. For the delegation's composition, see Sidorov et al. (eds), *Ekonomicheskoe polozhenie*, Vol. II, p. 578, note 568/1; on the proposed railway commission see ibid., pp. 477 and 579, note 591/1.
114 For a brief biography of Lomonosov see Aplin, 'Iurii Vladimirovich Lomonosov', pp. vii–xx, on which this paragraph is based.
115 Lomonosov's memoir about the February revolution was published as *Vospominaniia o Martovskoi revoliutsii 1917 goda*.
116 Aplin, 'Lomonosov', pp. x–xi.
117 The two men had their first contretemps even before leaving Petrograd: Lomonosov, 'Vospominaniia', Vol. 6, pp. 8–10.
118 The preliminary negotiations are described in Vauclain–Baruch (Council of National Defense), 26 May 1917: NARG 39, Country Series, box 177, file 212.21(b) 'Baldwin Locomotive Works'. For the exchange of correspondence see Bakhmet'ev–Crosby, 2 July 1917, and Crosby–Bakhmet'ev, 6 July 1917: both in ibid., file RS-212.21(b) 'Locomotive contracts'. The mission kept numerical and alphabetical lists of its contracts: see, for example, Contract Record: NARG 261, Russian Supply Committee, box K34. The final talks are described by Lomonosov: 'Vospominaniia', Vol. 6, pp. 151–2, 156–9.
119 On the MPS mission see, for example, Lomonosov, 'Vospominaniia', Vol. 6, pp. 173–6, 335–46, 716–30; Lipets, *Parovozy tipa 'dekapod'*, p. 7.
120 Memorandum of conversation between Lomonosov, Zach, Vauclain and Willard, 15/28 June 1917; Vauclain–Willard, 3 July 1917; and Baker–Willard, 6 July 1917: all in NARG 62, entry 1–A1, box 9, file 1–2–2 'Russia: Equipment and Material'. See also Sidorov et al. (eds), *Ekonomicheskoe polozhenie*, Vol. II, pp. 508–9; Lomonosov, 'Vospominaniia', Vol. 6, p. 262. The credits are listed in: Information about Russian state credit operations in the USA during the war: HIA, M. V. Bernatskii papers, document IV, p. 1.
121 Sidorov et al. (eds), *Ekonomicheskoe polozhenie*, Vol. II, pp. 508–9.
122 Ibid., p. 554.
123 McAdoo–Baker, 1 August 1917, and Baker–McAdoo, 1 August 1917: NARG 39, Country Series, box 177, file RS-212.21(b) 'Locomotive contracts'.
124 See McAdoo–Lansing, 23 August 1917: NARG 39, Country Series, box 176, file RS-200 'Russia: General'. Baker asserted priority for the AEF in July with the proviso that the Russian needs would take precedence over all other work: Baker–Willard, 8/21 July 1917: NARG 62, entry 1–A1, box 8, file F-1–2 'Equipment for Allies'; Crosby–Bakhmet'ev, 14/27 July 1917: NARG 39, Country Series, box 177, file RS-212.21(b) 'Locomotive contracts'.
125 St John, 'John F. Stevens', p. 74.

126 Ibid., p. 150.
127 For example, Sidorov et al. (eds), *Ekonomicheskoe polozhenie*, Vol. II, pp. 476–8. The question of an advisory commission was probably raised in late March (New Style), and the Provisional government authorised it on 26 March/8 April: GARF, 1779/1/6/134ob. The Russians' reluctance is stressed in Francis–Secretary of State, 29 March/11 April 1917: *FRUS*, 1918, Russia Vol. III, p. 185. See also Ganelin, *Rossiia i SShA*, pp. 200–3.
128 On Stevens's work, and the Railway Service Corps in 1917 and during the Russian civil war, see St John, 'John F. Stevens', pp. 84–5, 127–237, 252–4, 293–4; Reitzer, 'United States–Russian Economic Relations' (unpublished PhD dissertation), pp. 26–35, 197–220; and Popova, 'Missiia Stevensa', pp. 31–85.
129 Quoted in Reitzer, 'United States–Russian Economic Relations', p. 220. This colourful comment must be heavily qualified, however. Different practice was not necessarily bad practice, and indeed Russia followed the smaller European stock norms. At that time British railways had thousands of relatively small nineteenth-century engines in service and small 16–20 tonne wagons were predominant; wholesale automatic braking of freight trains did not become a British policy aim until 1955.
130 Actual maximum capacity is usually understood as about 80 per cent of the theoretical maximum of 100 per cent, to allow time for maintenance. It is unclear whether Stevens is indicating a percentage of the theoretical maximum.
131 Account of activities in Russia and Siberia (by Stevens), p. 2: HIA, John F. Stevens papers, box I, folder I.
132 The impact of the food shortage is noted in: Diary of W. L. Darling, entry for 10/23 September 1917: HIA, W. L. Darling papers.
133 St John, 'John F. Stevens', pp. 122, 130–7, 230–1.
134 Sidorov et al. (eds), *Ekonomicheskoe polozhenie*, Vol. II, pp. 495–7.
135 Reitzer, 'United States–Russian Economic Relations', pp. 26–7. See also, for instance, Sidorov et al. (eds), *Ekonomicheskoe polozhenie*, Vol. II, pp. 243–4.
136 Quoted in Reitzer, 'United States–Russian Economic Relations', p. 30. Darling commented that the most difficult part of the commission's work was getting its recommendations put into effect: Diary of W. L. Darling, preface, p. 3 (dated 1921): HIA, W. L. Darling papers.
137 Stevens–Nekrasov, 3 July 1917: NARG 43, entry 833, box 1, file 4.
138 Stevens–Secretary of State/Willard, 2 July 1917; 'Message to the People of Russia from the United States Railway Commission, 4 July 1917'; and Stevens–Willard, 7 July 1917: all in NARG 39, Country Series, box 177, file RS-212.20(b) 'US Railway Commission to Russia'.
139 Worry about the steel shortage is clear in: Material Situation at Car Building Plants and Effect on Output [July 1917]: NARG 62, entry 1–A1, box 4, file C-2. For examples of annoyance at Stevens's conduct see Willard–Baker, 3 August, 1917: NARG 39, Country Series, box 177, file RS-212.21(c) 'Car contracts'; and Crosby–McAdoo, 15 August 1917:

NARG 39, Country Series, box 177, file RS-212.20(b) 'US Railway Commission to Russia'.
140 Baker–McAdoo, 5 July 1917: NARG 39, Country Series, box 177, file RS-212.21(c) 'Car contracts'; McAdoo–Bakhmet'ev, 18 July 1917: NARG 39, Country Series, box 177, file RS-212.11 'Machinery purchases'; Crosby–McAdoo, 21 July 1917: NARG 39, Country Series, box 176, file RS-200/17–3 'General'; US–Russian agreement, 24 August 1917: NARG 39, Country Series, box 177, file RS-212.11 'Machinery purchases'.
141 Memorandum for Crosby, 17 July 1917 (by McAdoo): NARG 39, Country Series, box 177, file RS-212.21(c) 'Car contracts'.
142 McAdoo–Lansing, 25 July 1917: NARG 39, Country Series, box 176, file RS-200 'Russia: General'. The sum requested by Bakhmet'ev was in addition to the total credit of $175 million already opened, but included $325 million of the $500 million loan authorised in the spring. Full details are in Crosby–McAdoo, 21 July 1917: ibid.
143 Willard–Baker, 3 August 1917: NARG 39, Country Series, box 177, file RS 212.21(c) 'Car contracts'.
144 Crosby–McAdoo, 15 August 1917: NARG 39, Country Series, box 177, file RS 212.20(b) 'US Railway Commission to Russia'.
145 McAdoo–Lansing, 23 August 1917: NARG 39, Country Series, box 176, file RS-200 'Russia: General'.
146 See Minutes of Russian Supply Committee, 3 October 1917: NARG 261, Russian Supply Committee, box K138, file 721; memorandum for Willard, 5 October 1917 (by Vauclain): NARG 62, entry 1–A1, box 9, file F-1-2-2 'Russia: Equipment and material'; Crosby–Willard, 9 October 1917; and Willard–Crosby, 11 October 1917: both in NARG 39, Country Series, box 177, file RS-212.21(c) 'Car contracts'. The only serious contenders for the locomotive contracts were Baldwin and Alco, whose quotes are in: NARG 261, Russian Supply Committee, box K138, file 722.
147 Lomonosov, 'Vospominaniia', Vol. 6, pp. 436, 439.
148 Ibid., pp. 440–1.
149 The two protocols (one each for the locomotives and the wagons) are in: NARG 261, Russian Supply Committee, box K138, file 722.
150 Lomonosov–Bakhmet'ev, 10 November 1917: NARG 261, Russian Supply Committee, box K57, file 'May–December 1917'.
151 Lomonosov–Vauclain, 15 November 1917; Vauclain–Willard, 16 November 1917; Baker–McAdoo, 23 November 1917; and McAdoo–Baker, 27 November 1917: all in NARG 39, Country Series, box 177, file 212.21(b) 'Locomotive contracts'; Lipets–Vauclain, 16 November 1917, and [Russian representative]–US Treasury, [draft, 20 November 1917]: NARG 261, Russian Supply Committee, box K138, file 722; Lomonosov, 'Vospominaniia', Vol. 6, pp. 452–9.
152 The State Department's reasoning for this tactic was explained to a House of Representatives committee in 1921: *Conditions in Russia*, pp. 221, 229. The disposal of the railway supplies, including further shipments to Russia, is detailed in two reports by the MPS mission: Reports about the

activity of the mission of the Ministry of Ways of Communication, 1 January 1918 to 30 June 1919, and 1 July 1919 to 1 May 1920: HIA, Russia: Posol'stvo (U.S.), box 102.

153 See Leffingwell (Treasury)–Polk (State Dept), 31 January 1918: NARG 59, 1910–1929 decimal series, file 861.77/285.

154 Memorandum concerning component parts of about 976 Russian freight cars: NARG 39, Country Series, box 177, file RS-212.21(c) 'Car contracts'; Report about the activity of the MPS mission, 1 July 1919 to 1 May 1920, pp. 4–6: HIA, Russia: Posol'stvo (U.S.), box 102.

155 In mid-January 1918 the State Department was still permitting the shipment of railway materials in the belief that their practical use in Russia outweighed the risk of aiding the German war effort. See Polk–Baker, 22 January 1918: NARG 59, 1910–1929 decimal series, file 861.77/260.

156 Concerning the delivery of the decapods see Page and Nurminen, *Russian Locomotives*, pp. 233–40; Report about the activity of the MPS Mission, 1 January 1918 to 30 June 1919, p. 6: HIA, Russia: Posol'stvo (U.S.), box 102; and Lipets–Sample (Baldwin), 28 May 1920: NARG 261, Russian Supply Committee, box K138, file 720.

157 Report about the activity of the MPS Mission, 1 July 1919 to 1 May 1920, pp. 4–6: HIA, Russia: Posol'stvo (U.S.), box 102.

158 See, for instance, ibid., pp. 4, 14–18. Most of the 'Mallets' were sold to the British, but some were kept in store for years. The sale contract for the final nine engines (to the Anglo-Chilean Nitrate Corporation) in July 1926 is in: HIA, Russia: Posol'stvo (U.S.), box 153, file 2.

159 For example: Lipets, *Parovozy tipa 'dekapod'*, p. vii; Lebedev, *Russko-amerikanskie ekonomicheskie otnosheniia*, pp. 321, 323; Gaworek, 'Allied Economic Warfare' (unpublished PhD dissertation), pp. 86–9, 94–102.

2 The revolutionary railway vision

1 For a detailed account of this collapse see, for instance, Carr, *Bolshevik Revolution*, Vol. 2, pp. 28–268. Economic management is covered in Malle, *Economic Organisation of War Communism*, passim. On the civil war in 1917–19 see Mawdsley, *Russian Civil War*, pp. 3–215.
2 Stites, *Revolutionary Dreams*, pp. 3–4, 36–40, 46–7.
3 Coopersmith, *Electrification*, p. 121.
4 See ibid., pp. 121–50.
5 Trotskii, *Sochineniia*, Vol. XVII, p. 335.
6 See Krasin, *Zadachi zheleznodorozhnikov*, pp. 4–7; Lenin, *PSS*, Vol. XL, p. 86.
7 The text is in Naporko, *Zheleznodorozhnyi transport*, pp. 78–80.
8 Lenin, *PSS*, Vol. XL, pp. 123–4.
9 On the railways during the civil war see Westwood, *History of Russian Railways*, pp. 177–98, and Argenbright, 'Russian Railroad System', pp. 69–290.
10 Shmukker, *Ocherki finansov*, p. 239.
11 Report by Fomin [March 1920]: RsTsKhIDNI, 17/112/14/38.

12 *Svedeniia i materialy*, p. 19.
13 Trotskii, *My Life*, pp. 462–3.
14 *Vestnik putei soobshcheniia*, No. 9–10 (1919), p. 2.
15 Carr, *Bolshevik Revolution*, Vol. II, pp. 394–7.
16 Westwood, *History of Russian Railways*, pp. 182–8.
17 Quoted in Golopolosov, *Obzor zheleznodorozhnogo transporta*, p. 109.
18 A list of all People's Commissars and (Soviet) Ministers of Ways of Communication is in *Gudok*, 14 July 1989, p. 4, albeit with incorrect dates for Krasin and his immediate successor, Trotskii.
19 Destruction on the railway network, 1 January 1917–1 April 1920: RGAE, 1884/42/1097/440, 445ob.–6.
20 Concerning military orders see *Ekonomicheskaia zhizn'*, 14 March 1920, p. 1; *Narodnoe khoziaistvo*, No. 9–10 (1919), p. 55; and *Gosudarstvennye mashinostroitel'nye zavody*, pp. 14–15.
21 *Svedeniia i materialy*, pp. 45–8. Created in November 1918, GOMZA was based on the recently nationalised Sormovo–Kolomna group (formed in 1913) and Briansk locomotive factory: *Protokoly prezidiuma VSNKh*, pp. 270–1.
22 Sarab'ianov, *Metallopromyshlennost' Rossii*, pp. 34–5, 56. For alternative production statistics see, for example, Il'inskii and Ivanitskii, *Ocherk istorii parovozostroitel'noi promyshlennosti*, p. 108. NKPS workshops handled most locomotive overhauls: *Protokoly prezidiuma VSNKh*, p. 231.
23 *Vestnik putei soobshcheniia*, No. 9–10 (1919), p. 2.
24 *Ekonomicheskaia zhizn'*, 20 May 1919, p. 3, and *Krasnyi put' zheleznodorozhnika*, No. 19 (1919), pp. 19–20. The M. A. Lomov mentioned in the source was presumably the left-communist G. I. Lomov (Oppokov), also known as A. Lomov.
25 *Krasnyi put' zheleznodorozhnika*, No. 28 (1919), p. 26.
26 Report by P. I. Krasovskii, 23 March 1923: RGAE, 1884/43/594/24.
27 *Krasnyi put' zheleznodorozhnika*, No. 7 (1920), p. 8.
28 Grinevetskii, *Poslevoennye perspektivy*, especially pp. 108–17. The broader significance of this publication for Soviet economic reconstruction and planning is discussed in Smolinski, 'Grinevetskii and Soviet Industrialisation', and Nove, 'Soviet Planning and Grinevetskii – A Comment'.
29 See Westwood et al., 'The Railways', pp. 170–8. Also, for instance, Arskii, 'Bor'ba s transportnoi razrukhoi', in *Vestnik Narodnogo komissariata torgovli i promyshlennosti*, No. 3–4 (1919), pp. 5–11; Mikhailov, *Transport: Ego sovremennoe sostoianie*, passim; Boublikoff, *The Necessity for Russo-American Co-operation*.
30 See Coopersmith, *Electrification*, pp. 140–1.
31 Grinevetskii, *Poslevoennye perspektivy*, p. 117.
32 Ibid., pp. 107–8, 117–37. See also his *Problema teplovoza i ee znachenie dlia Rossii*.
33 *Krasnyi put' zheleznodorozhnika*, No. 20 (1919), pp. 6–7.
34 See, for example, Goriacheva and Shelest, *Aleksei Nesterovich Shelest*,

pp. 31–44; *Vestnik putei soobshcheniia*, No. 11–12 (1918), pp. 31–2; and *Krasnyi put' zheleznodorozhnika*, No. 20 (1919), pp. 6–7.
35 *Krasnyi put' zheleznodorozhnika*, No. 19 (1919), inside front cover; protocol of meeting of NKPS Supreme Technical Council, 16 April 1918: RGAE, 1884/4/6/19. Similarly, Mikhailov, *Raschet oborudovaniia magistral'nykh zheleznykh dorog v tiagovom otnoshenii*, passim.
36 *Zheleznodorozhnaia tekhnika i ekonomika*, No. 2 (1919), pp. 12–18.
37 See Lomonosov, 'Vospominaniia', Vol. 7, pp. 651–2.
38 *Vestnik putei soobshcheniia*, No. 3 (1919), p. 22; *Krasnyi put' zheleznodorozhnika*, No. 17 (1919), p. 25.
39 Report by N. V. Gammel'farb, 15 December 1921: RGAE, 1884/43/600/19–ob.
40 *Krasnyi put' zheleznodorozhnika*, No. 21 (1919), p. 20.
41 *Ekonomicheskaia zhizn'*, 23 February 1919, p. 3.
42 *Vestnik putei soobshcheniia*, No. 14–15 (1919), p. 10. See also p. 5.
43 *Zheleznodorozhnaia tekhnika i ekonomika*, No. 1 (1919), p. 6. In 1920 this journal became *Tekhnika i ekonomika putei soobshcheniia*.
44 *Krasnyi put' zheleznodorozhnika*, No. 37 (1919), pp. 3–4.
45 Aplin, 'Lomonosov', pp. xiii–xv.
46 Lomonosov, 'Vospominaniia', Vol. 7, pp. 648, 653.
47 Ibid., pp. 648–58; *Krasnyi put' zheleznodorozhnika*, No. 47 (1919), pp. 8–9.
48 Lomonosov, 'Vospominaniia', Vol. 7, pp. 654–7.
49 Electrical engineers also avoided costing their dreams: Coopersmith, *Electrification*, p. 94.
50 Buharin and Preobrazhensky, *ABC of Communism*, pp. 159, 272–3.
51 Day, *Leon Trotsky*, pp. 6–16.
52 Quoted in ibid., p. 9.
53 Ibid., p. 9.
54 Ibid., pp. 15–16.
55 For instance, Debo, *Revolution and Survival*, pp. 45–194; Shishkin, *Sovetskoe gosudarstvo*, pp. 21–33.
56 On the establishment of the state monopoly of foreign trade see Shishkin, *Sovetskoe gosudarstvo*, pp. 87–92.
57 *Vestnik putei soobshcheniia*, No. 25–26–27 (1918), p. 21.
58 See Lubov Krassin, *Leonid Krassin*, pp. 19–79; Glenny, 'Leonid Krasin', pp. 192–221; Siegelbaum, *Politics of Industrial Mobilisation*, pp. 56–7; O'Connor, *Engineer of Revolution*, pp. 99–120, 123–33, 156.
59 Krasin–Krasina, 25 May 1918: in IISG, Krasin papers, file 1b; also quoted, with a slightly different translation, in Lubov Krassin, *Leonid Krassin*, p. 83.
60 Lubov Krassin, *Leonid Krassin*, pp. 88–9.
61 O'Connor, *Engineer of Revolution*, pp. 156–60; Karpova, *L. B. Krasin*, pp. 46–7; Shishkin, *Sovetskoe gosudarstvo*, pp. 95–6.
62 *Vestnik putei soobshcheniia*, No. 5 (1919), p. 8.
63 *Ekonomicheskaia zhizn'*, 1 January 1919, p. 1.
64 Ibid., 14 January 1919, p. 1.
65 Ibid., 30 March 1919, p. 1.

66 Ibid., 11 April 1919, p. 1.
67 Carlbäck-Isotalo, 'Sweden and Russia in Dissolution', pp. 221, 227–8. See also Krasin–Krasina, 14 March [1919] (dated by contents): IISG, Krasin papers, file 1b.
68 Report by A. Belonozhkin, 22 February 1919: SRA, UD:s arkiv, 1902 års dossiersystem, Vol. 277.
69 Krasin–Belonozhkin, 28 February 1919: SRA, UD:s arkiv, 1902 års dossiersystem, Vol. 277. For another example, see *Vestnik Narodnogo komissariata torgovli i promyshlennosti*, No. 7–8 (1919), p. 35.
70 Shishkin, 'Stanovlenie sovetsko-skandinavskikh ekonomicheskikh otnoshenii', pp. 167–71, 179–82; Carlbäck-Isotalo, 'Pengar eller politik', p. 198. It is interesting that Krasin sent a private letter to his family via Hellberg: Krasin–Krasina, 18 May 1919: IISG, Krasin papers, file 5.
71 *Ekonomicheskaia zhizn'*, 19 September 1919, p. 2.
72 Krasin (comp.), *Narodnyi komissariat putei soobshcheniia za dva goda revoliutsii*, p. 26.
73 See, for example, *Protokoly prezidiuma VSNKh*, pp. 48, 58–60, 68, 316 (note 42); report of VSNKh meeting of 15 February 1918: NARG 59, 1910–29 decimal series, file 861.77/387; Martens–Secretary of State: NARG 59, 1910–29 decimal series, file 861.77/807; Litvinov–Martens, 27 May 1919: *DVP*, Vol. II, pp. 176–7; Martens–Secretary of State, [June 1919]: *DVP*, Vol. II, pp. 194–7. See also Shishkin, *Sovetskoe gosudarstvo*, pp. 115–17, 130–7; and Gvishiani, *Sovetskaia Rossiia i SShA*, pp. 236–49.
74 Lomonosov, 'Dnevnik', Vol. 4, pp. 21–3, and 'Vospominaniia', Vol. 7, pp. 30–2.
75 Lomonosov, 'Dnevnik', Vol. 4, pp. 37, 39, and 'Vospominaniia', Vol. 7, pp. 43–5, 126–7.
76 Lomonosov, 'Vospominaniia', Vol. 7, pp. 104–5.
77 Report by Lomonosov, 22 September 1919: AVP, 04/46/54073/282/19–20ob. (also LRA MS 716.1.83); Lomonosov, 'Dnevnik', Vol. 5, pp. 39–40, and 'Vospominaniia', Vol. 7, pp. 221–2, 246.
78 Report by Lomonosov, 22 September 1919: AVP, 04/46/54073/282/19–20ob.; Lomonosov, 'Dnevnik', Vol. 5, pp. 22–7, 30, 45–6, 50–6, and 'Vospominaniia', Vol. 7, p. 234.
79 Himmer, 'German–Soviet Economic Relations', pp. 53–5, 90–5, 101–3.
80 Report by Lomonosov, 22 September 1919: AVP, 04/46/54073/282/19–20ob.; Lomonosov, 'Dnevnik', Vol. 5, pp. 45–6, and 'Vospominaniia', Vol. 7, pp. 250–1. The diplomat's precise identity is unclear from Lomonosov's account.
81 Report by Lomonosov, 22 September 1919: AVP, 04/46/54073/282/19–20ob.; Lomonosov–Briske & Prohl, 2 September 1919: AVP, 04/46/54073/282/18; Briske & Prohl–Lomonosov, 2 September 1919: AVP, 04/46/54073/282/17; Lomonosov, 'Dnevnik', Vol. 5, pp. 50–6, and 'Vospominaniia', Vol. 7, pp. 252–7, 269. Himmer reports, by contrast, that Stockhammern was expecting the Bolshevik regime's imminent collapse: 'German–Soviet Economic Relations', pp. 109–11.

82 Himmer, 'German–Soviet Economic Relations', p. 111.
83 Carr, *Bolshevik Revolution*, Vol. III, pp. 148–55; Shishkin, *Sovetskoe gosudarstvo*, pp. 143–52.
84 Deutscher, *Prophet Armed*, pp. 487–95.
85 Stites, *Revolutionary Dreams*, p. 49.
86 Rassweiler, quoting Lenin in *Generation of Power*, p. 18.
87 Ibid., pp. 18–19.
88 For Krasin's speeches see *Vestnik putei soobsheniia*, No. 14–15 (1919), pp. 5–7 and 9–12, and *Krasnyi put' zheleznodorozhnika*, No. 37 (1919), pp. 3–5; on Trotskii see Day, *Leon Trotsky*, p. 5; Dongarov, *Inostrannyi kapital*, pp. 45, 49–50; and Wistrich, *Trotsky*, pp. 109–11. Interestingly, Krasin requested a portrait of Trotskii for his office: NKPS memorandum, 5 February 1920: RGAE, 1884/92/195/126.
89 Day, *Leon Trotsky*, pp. 5, 27–8; Dongarov, *Inostrannyi kapital*, pp. 49–50.
90 Day, *Leon Trotsky*, pp. 48–55; Dongarov, *Inostrannyi kapital*, p. 46; and Shishkin, *Sovetskoe gosudarstvo*, pp. 143–240.
91 For example, in conversation with Lomonosov, 13 November 1919: Lomonosov, 'Vospominaniia', Vol. 7, pp. 700–1.
92 SNK Theses on Foreign Trade, 10 February 1920: *DSV*, Vol. VII, pp. 508–12 (earlier draft at GARF, 130/4/318/2–3ob.).
93 Day, *Leon Trotsky*, p. 26.
94 Trotskii, *Sochineniia*, Vol. XV, pp. 87–8.
95 Ibid., p. 44. It is interesting that, according to Lomonosov, Trotskii berated Krasin on 22 November to a Sovnarkom commission investigating the railway crisis and NKPS: 'Vospominaniia', Vol. 7, p. 726.
96 Day, *Leon Trotsky*, pp. 25–8, 45.
97 Deutscher, *Prophet Armed*, p. 493.
98 *Ekonomicheskaia zhizn'*, 30 December 1919, p. 1.
99 Ibid., 29 January 1920, p. 1; *Izvestiia*, 17 February 1920, p. 1. Of senior Bolshevik leaders Radek, lately released from imprisonment in Germany, had the most recent if not especially happy experience of the West.
100 Day, *Leon Trotsky*, pp. 48–50; *Ekonomicheskaia zhizn'*, 24 January 1920, p. 2. Whether this debate suggests the existence of a Right Opposition early in 1920 is doubtful: a technocratic bias is apparent in Krasin's known support, but Rykov's association with Krasin was probably limited. Lomonosov, enjoying Rykov's patronage at this time, was urged by the latter in November 1919 to exploit an opportunity to attack Krasin: 'Vospominaniia', Vol. 7, p. 724.
101 *Pravda*, 21 January 1920, p. 1; *Izvestiia*, 16 January 1920, p. 1.
102 *Ekonomicheskaia zhizn'*, 22 January 1920, p. 1.
103 Lenin, *PSS*, Vol. XL, p. 88.
104 Ibid., p. 109.
105 Ibid., p. 89.
106 *Ekonomicheskaia zhizn'*, 24 January 1920, p. 2; Lomonosov, 'Dnevnik', Vol. 6, pp. 54–5, 70.
107 Grant Watson (Copenhagen)–Curzon, 27 January 1920: FO 371/4032/174;

Davis (London)–Secretary of State, 7 February 1920: in *FRUS*, 1920, Vol. III, pp. 702–3.
108 Himmer, 'German–Soviet Economic Relations', p. 148. This followed a proposition by Radek a week earlier: Breuning, 'German Foreign Policy' (unpublished PhD dissertation), p. 20.
109 Cuttings from *Stockholms Dagblad*, 31 January 1920 and *The Observer*, 1 February 1920, in SRA, UD:1920, HP32B, Vols 1446/II and 1446/I.
110 Kilmarnock (Berlin)–Curzon, 20 February 1920, in *BDFA*, Vol. II, p. 164; Porter (Tallinn)–Foreign Office, 25 February 1920: FO 371/4032/363; *New York Times*, 27 February 1920, cited in Himmer, 'German–Soviet Economic Relations', p. 233.
111 For the text of the SEC Communiqué see *DBFP*, Vol. II, p. 912.
112 Protocol of Politburo meeting, 19 January 1920: RTsKhIDNI, 17/3/56/1; Day, *Leon Trotsky*, p. 26.
113 Protocol of Politburo meeting, 17–18 January 1920: RTsKhIDNI, 17/3/55/2–3; Protocol of Politburo meeting, 19 January 1920: RTsKhIDNI, 17/3/56/1. See also 'Deiatel'nost' Tsentral'nogo komiteta partii v dokumentakh (sobytiia i fakhty): 3–31 ianvaria, 1920g.', in *Izvestiia TsK KPSS*, No. 8 (1990), p. 191; Golikov et al. (eds), *Lenin: Biograficheskaia khronika*, Vol. VIII, pp. 231, 234. A communist majority had been installed in the Tsentrosoiuz in June 1919: Lezhava–Kuibysheva, 'Na khoziaistvennom fronte', p. 134.
114 Protocol of Sovnarkom meeting, 27 January 1920: GARF, 130/4/1/26; *DSV*, Vol. VII, p. 512.
115 S. White, *Britain and the Bolshevik Revolution*, pp. 4–5; Shishkin, *Sovetskoe gosudarstvo*, p. 218. Krasin's Tsentrosoiuz mandate, authorised in March 1920, is at: RGAE, 413/2/443/1ob.
116 Protocol of meeting of Small Sovnarkom, 13 February 1920: GARF, 130/4/161/46ob.
117 Naporko, *Zheleznodorozhnyi transport*, pp. 88–9.
118 Great demand from other commissariats for imports is clear in a note from Lenin to Krasin in February or early March 1920: *Leninskii sbornik*, Vol. XXXVIII, pp. 305–6.
119 The NKPS calculation is at RGAE, 4038/1/45/120. See also A. A. Postnikov's report to Krasin, 20 March 1920: RGAE, 1884/92/195/297–302; and P. I. Krasovskii's report to Dzerzhinskii, 2 March 1923: RTsKhIDNI, 76/2/76/70–ob.
120 Cutting from *Daily Herald*, 17 February 1920, in: SRA, UD:1920, HP32B, Vol. 1446/II.
121 Interview with Lincoln Eyres: *DVP*, Vol. II, pp. 379–84.
122 Ibid., pp. 380–1.
123 Day, *Leon Trotsky*, pp. 33–4; Arskii, *Sostoianie transporta*, p. 13; Shatunovskii, *Obshchie printsipy organizatsii remonta*, p. 1.
124 *Ekonomicheskaia zhizn'*, 14 April 1920, p. 2.
125 Ibid., 21 March 1920, p. 1.
126 Protocol of meeting of Small Sovnarkom, 13 February 1920: GARF, 130/4/161/46ob.; Protocol of SNK meeting, 16 March 1920: RTsKhIDNI, 19/

1/355/2; SNK resolution, 16 March 1920: *DSV*, Vol. VII, pp. 564–5. That this second allocation was in addition to the money approved in February is clear from the SNK protocol, 27 April 1920: GARF: 130/4/1/104, item 5.
127 *Deviatyi s"ezd RKP(b)*, pp. 404–17.
128 Report to TsK by Fomin [March 1920]: RTsKhIDNI, 17/112/14/39ob.
129 On 21 March Krasin told Lomonosov of his intention to rejoin the NKPS after his European trip: Lomonosov, 'Vospominaniia', Vol. 7, p. 1063. For Trotskii's request that his appointment be temporary, see Meijer (ed.), *Trotsky Papers*, Vol. II, pp. 114–17.

3 Krasin's first results

1 Reitzer, 'United States–Russian Economic Relations', p. 285; C. White, *British and American Commercial Relations*, p. 197.
2 *Ekonomicheskaia zhizn'*, 7 March 1920, p. 1; 18 April 1920, p. 1; and 25 April 1920, p. 1.
3 Chicherin–US government, 24 February 1920: *DVP*, Vol. II, pp. 387–8; Minister in Sweden (Morris)–Acting Secretary of State, 25 February 1920: *FRUS*, 1920, Vol. III, p. 447.
4 Stevens was now President of the Inter-Allied Technical Board, under the Inter-Allied Railway Committee. On the Committee and the Railway Service Corps see, for instance, Reitzer, 'United States–Russian Economic Relations', pp. 197–220.
5 Rudyi–Stevens/Johnson, 23 March 1920: RGAE, 1884/3/41/46. Rudyi and B. M. Sverdlov made the same appeal through Lt Col. F. R. Blunt, an American railway engineer captured by the Bolsheviks in January 1920 and released on 24 March. See Blunt's Report, 3 April 1920: NARG 43, entry 838, box 8, file 1; and also Rudyi–[NKPS?], 25 March 1920: GARF, 130/4/539/12–ob.
6 Sundheimer–Stevens, 24 March 1920: NARG 43, entry 838-A, box 4, file 'Advisory Commission of Railway Experts to Russia/4'. The cited comment was almost certainly by Johnson, who was on Russian territory, as opposed to Sundheimer, who forwarded the telegram to Stevens from Harbin.
7 Stevens–Secretary of State, 26 March 1920: NARG 59, 1910–1929 decimal series, file 861.77/1441.
8 Colby (Secretary of State)–Stevens, 31 March 1920: NARG 59, 1910–1929 decimal series, file 861.77/1441.
9 The disposal of the railway equipment by the Bakhmet'ev mission is detailed in: Reports about activities of MPS Mission, January 1918–June 1919 and July 1919–May 1920: HIA, Russia: Posol'stvo (U.S.), box 102.
10 Martens–Colby, 31 March 1920: *DVP*, Vol. II, pp. 432–4; Reitzer, 'United States–Russian Economic Relations', pp. 258–9. It is unclear why Martens was instructed to order nothing but railway equipment: presumably as a priority but conceivably to minimise expenditure.

11 Martens–US War Department: RGAE, 4038/1/104/197–8.
12 Reitzer, 'United States–Russian Economic Relations', p. 260.
13 Hinger–A. A. Heller, 19 March 1920: RGAE, 4038/1/104/204–5.
14 Vauclain, *Steaming Up!*, p. 282.
15 Martens–Hinger, 25 March 1920: RGAE, 4038/1/104/201–2; see also Martens–Litvinov, 24 March 1920, where he recommends allowing Vauclain to enter Russia: RGAE, 4038/1/104/203. The 'fifteen thousand' engines mentioned by Martens are undoubtedly a misprint for 'five thousand'.
16 Hinger–Martens, [n.d.]: RGAE, 4038/1/104/199–200.
17 Acting Secretary of State–Ambassador in France, 7 July 1920: *FRUS*, 1920, Vol. III, p. 717; Dept of State Press Release, 7 July 1920, copy at: RGAE, 4038/1/104/186–8. It is interesting that Lenin probably did not receive a translation of this crucial statement until early September, to judge by a note from Lezhava: GARF, 130/4/320/2–5.
18 Colby–Minister in Denmark, 17 July 1920: *FRUS*, 1920, Vol. III, p. 718; Announcement by Dept of State, War Trade Board Section, 8 July 1920, copy at: RGAE, 4038/1/104/179–80; Reitzer, 'United States–Russian Economic Relations', pp. 276–7. The restrictions on railway equipment originated in the State Department's Russian Division: Acting Chief, War Trade Board Section–Bennett, 26 July 1920: in NARG 182, entry 235, box 1519, file 'Russia – July 1920'.
19 C. White, 'Prelude to Trade' (unpublished Ph.D. dissertation), p. 234.
20 Gade (Riga)–Secretary of State, 11 February 1920: NARG 59, 1910–1929 decimal series, file 861.77/1349.
21 See Gade–Secretary of State, 16 March 1920: NARG 59, 1910–1929 decimal series, file 661.1115/27; Gade–Secretary of State, [July 1920]: NARG 59, 1910–1929 decimal series, file 860i.77/14; Gukovskii–Chicherin, 27 March 1920: *DVP*, Vol. II, p. 424; memoranda by Coombes, [n.d.], and Poole, 15 June 1921: NARG 59, 1910–1929 decimal series, file 661.1115/330.
22 See report by Henkel (Tallinn)–Foreign Ministry (Berlin), 1 May 1920: PRO GFM 34/4528/frame 504356.
23 See Chicherin–Sheinman (NKVT), [April 1920]: RGAE, 413/2/443/28.
24 The contract is in *DVP*, Vol. II, pp. 631–7. Biographical information about Rabinov is in Hurley (State Dept?)–Winslow (London), 30 August 1920: NARG 59, 1910–1929 decimal series, file 860i.77/16.
25 Bank of Estonia–Gukovskii, 15 May 1920; Revalis–[Krasin?], 17 May 1920; Krasin–Gukovskii, 22 May 1920: all in RGAE, 4038/1/107.
26 For example, Krasin–Gukovskii, 22 May 1920: in ibid.; Colby–Shipping Board, 19 May 1920, and Colby–Secretary of War, 26 May 1920: NARG 59, 1910–1929 decimal series, file 860i.77/8; Secretary of War–Appel, 9 July 1920: NARG 59, 1910–1929 decimal series, file 860i.77/27; Merle–Smith (State Dept)–Secretary of War, 24 July 1920: ibid., file 860i.77/13; Conference with Secretary Baker regarding shipment of locomotives to Esthonia, 18 August 1920 (by Merle-Smith): ibid., file 860i. 77/18; 'Esthonian Locomotives and Gold', 21 March 1921 (memorandum by Packer): ibid., file 860i.77/21.

27 See 'Report on Russian Soviet Bureau in New York', 21 January 1921: NARG 59, 1910–1929 decimal series, file 661.1115/251; and chapter 6.
28 A detailed study of Swedish–Soviet economic relations in the early 1920s is in preparation by Helene Carlbäck-Isotalo, and this may take discussion of this important episode further than is possible here. For an overview of Soviet–Swedish relations in 1920–1, including the locomotive contract, see her 'Pengar eller Politik', pp. 201–14.
29 Barclay–Foreign Office, 24 March 1920: FO 371/4033/318–19; Chicherin–Palmstierna, 1 April 1920: *DVP*, Vol. II, p. 435.
30 Shishkin, *Sovetskoe gosudarstvo*, pp. 165–6; see also Swedish Foreign Ministry report dated 28 March 1920: SRA UD:1920, HP32B, Vol. 1446/III (a discussion of the stance to be taken in talks with Krasin).
31 On British views about whether to inform the neutral countries see, for instance, minutes by Gregory, Harmsworth and Curzon, 19–20 May 1920: FO 371/4035/80–1.
32 Report of discussions on 1 March 1920, [n.d.]: SRA UD:1920, HP32B, Vol. 1446/III.
33 Invitation, 17 March 1920, and minutes of meeting, 20 March 1920: SRA UD:1920, HP32B, Vol. 1446/III.
34 Carlbäck-Isotalo has found that a businessman named Sandström, who negotiated with Krasin in Copenhagen, also supplied Palmstierna with information, bypassing Hamrin: interview with H. Carlbäck-Isotalo, 11 June 1993.
35 Report about negotiations with Russian Trade Delegation 1–6 April 1920, 7 April 1920: SRA UD:1920, HP32B, Vol. 1447/IV.
36 The Swedish government had been expecting the Russians to propose stationing trade representatives in Sweden: interview with H. Carlbäck-Isotalo, 11 June 1993.
37 Report 132/1759a, 7 April 1920: SRA UD:1920, HP32B, Vol. 1447/IV.
38 Hamrin–Palmstierna, 12 April 1920: SRA UD:1920, HP32B, Vol. 1447/V.
39 Hamrin–Palmstierna, 14 April 1920: ibid.
40 Hamrin–Palmstierna, 16 April 1920 and 21 April 1920: ibid.
41 Hamrin–Palmstierna, 17 April 1920: ibid.
42 The question of depositing Soviet gold in Swedish banks is discussed particularly in Hamrin–Palmstierna, 16 April 1920 and 17 April 1920: ibid.
43 For Krasin's criticism see Hamrin–Palmstierna, 24 April 1920: ibid.
44 Hamrin–Palmstierna, 15 April 1920: ibid.
45 Hamrin–Palmstierna, 21 April 1920: ibid.
46 Hamrin–Palmstierna, 24 April 1920: ibid.; Trush, *Mezhdunarodnaia deiatel'-nost'*, *1919–1920*, p. 240.
47 Sveriges Allmänna Exportförening–Hamrin, 27 April 1920, and Hamrin–Palmstierna, 24 April 1920: SRA UD:1920, HP32B, Vol. 1447/V. See also 'Vykort – lok – världsaffärer', in *Göteborgs Handels- och Sjöfarts Tidnings*. I am grateful to Mr B. Thulin for references to local newspapers from Göteborg and Trollhättan.
48 A copy of the provisional locomotive contract is at LRA MS 716.1.99. See

also Krasin–Anderson, 27 April 1920: Nohab papers, Box 'Krasin, Lomonossoff, Litvinov'. The Swedish Foreign Ministry archive contains a document dated 1 April 1920 which reports that Anderson had received 4 million Swedish crowns from Krasin for having arranged a contract with Nohab for 600 locomotives at a price of 240,000 Swedish crowns each; this information is inaccurate, but if the date is correct it indicates that the two men began negotiations very soon after Krasin's arrival in Scandinavia: SRA UD:1920, HP32B, Vol. 1447/IV. See also note 67 below.

49 See Hamrin–Ljungman, 6 May 1920, and Hamrin–Palmstierna, 11 May 1920: SRA UD:1920, HP32B, Vol. 1447/VI.

50 On the importance of exports and the Russian market for the Swedish engineering industry see Kuuse, 'Foreign Trade and the Breakthrough of the Engineering Industry in Sweden', pp. 1–36; Nilsson, 'Foreign Trade and the Breakthrough of the Engineering Industry in Sweden: a comment', pp. 156–63; and Kuuse, 'The Development of the Swedish Engineering Industry: a rejoinder', pp. 164–7. The first engine completed under Krasin's order was allocated works number 1186: Nohab papers, Ånglokomotiv tillverkade vid Nohab, Pärm III, p. 369. All engines built in Sweden are listed in Sundström, Ånglok, passim.

51 Uggla–Hamrin, 23 April 1920: SRA UD:1920, HP32B, Vol. 1447/V.

52 See Anderson–Krasin, 14 May 1920: Nohab papers, Box 'Krasin, Lomonossoff, Litvinov'; and Krasin–Chicherin, 17 May 1920: GARF, 130/4/319/23–4.

53 Minutes of Board Meeting, 31 May 1920: Nohab papers, Protokoll A:1 (1917–1924).

54 [Krasin/Litvinov]–Chicherin, 27 April 1920: RGAE, 413/2/443/45.

55 Krasin/Litvinov–Chicherin, 4 May 1920: RGAE, 413/2/443/49.

56 Krasin/Litvinov–Chicherin, 8 May 1920: RGAE, 413/2/443/73.

57 Protocol of Sovnarkom meeting, 27 April 1920: GARF, 130/4/1/104; Lenin/Stalin/Kamenev/Lalsov(?)/Sheinman–Krasin/Litvinov, 8 May 1920: RGAE, 413/2/443/46 (published in 1945 as a telegram from Lenin and Stalin alone: *Leninskii sbornik*, Vol. XXXV, pp. 123–4).

58 See protocol of Politburo meeting, 11 May 1920: RTsKhIDNI, 17/3/77/3; Golikov et al. (eds.), *Lenin: Biograficheskaia khronika*, Vol. VIII, pp. 544–5; Lenin, *PSS*, Vol. LI, pp. 195–6; Protocol of Politburo meeting, 25 May 1920: RTsKhIDNI, 17/3/82, item 11. Krasin's mandate is at: RGAE, 413/2/443/1ob.

59 Trush, *Mezhdunarodnaia deiatel'nost'*, *1919–1920*, p. 240; extract from Protocol of Politburo meeting, 10 June 1920: RGAE, 4038/1/19/–; Lomonosov, 'Vospominaniia', Vol. 7, p. 1263.

60 See Palmstierna–Krasin (draft), 11 May 1920: SRA UD:1920, HP32B, Vol. 1447/VI; Krasin–Palmstierna, 16 May 1920: *DVP*, Vol. II, pp. 528–30.

61 Krasin–Palmstierna, 16 May 1920: *DVP*, Vol. II, pp. 528–30.

62 The contract's text is in *DVP*, Vol. II, pp. 516–23; see also Shishkin, *Sovetskoe gosudarstvo*, pp. 166–7.

63 For the text see *DVP*, Vol. II, pp. 523–8.

64 Agreement of 21 May 1920: Nohab papers, F1D, Box 2.
65 Minutes of Board Meetings, 29 June and 14 December 1920: Nohab papers, Protokoll A:1 (1917–1924).
66 See *DVP*, Vol. II, p. 760, note 100. Krasin was referring in effect to both contracts, since the Nohab agreement was initially treated as a supplement to the other.
67 Lomonosov, 'Vospominaniia', Vol. 7, p. 1393. The price of 400,000 Swedish crowns is mentioned in a Swedish Foreign Ministry memorandum dated 1 April 1920: SRA UD:1920, HP32B, Vol. 1447/IV (this document's date is queried in note 48 above).
68 An example of support for the publicity explanation is: Debo, *Survival and Consolidation*, p. 249.
69 Åhlander, 'Staat, Wirtschaft und Handelspolitik', pp. 226–7, 403–4.
70 The possibility of subcontracting to other countries is mentioned in Krasin–Lomonosov, 1 July 1920: RGAE, 4038/1/14/195–6.
71 This issue will be discussed in H. Carlbäck-Isotalo's forthcoming study of Swedish–Soviet economic relations.
72 Memorandum by O. O'Malley, 11 June 1920: FO 371/4035/418.
73 Hamrin–Palmstierna, 24 April 1920: SRA UD:1920, HP32B, Vol. 1447/V.
74 See Barclay–Curzon, 15 June 1920: FO 371/4036/363–5. The dearth of information suggests that, despite the Politburo's view, Krasin did not sign the contracts primarily for publicity. Incidentally, the American consul in Göteborg overcame government silence by interviewing Nohab's chief engineer: see Scholes–Secretary of State, 2 August 1920, and enclosed memorandum: NARG 59, 1910–1929 decimal series, file 861.77/1680.
75 On Stol see Lomonosov, 'Vospominaniia', Vol. 7, pp. 1400–1; this spelling is a transliteration from the Russian. For Krasin's requests see: Krasin–Chicherin, 17 May 1920: GARF, r-130/4/319/24; also Lomonosov, 'Dnevnik', Vol. 6, p. 112, and 'Vospominaniia', Vol. 7, p. 1228.
76 Lomonosov, 'Dnevnik', Vol. 6, pp. 54–5, 70, 95, 106–12, and 'Vospominaniia', Vol. 7, pp. 1164–72, 1187, 1207–12, 1217; see also Genkina, *Protokoly Sovnarkoma*, p. 78, note 107.
77 Uncertainty about his future position dominates Lomonosov's diary between May and July 1920. See, for example, 9 June 1920: 'Dnevnik', Vol. 6, pp. 116–17.
78 Extract from protocol of Politburo meeting, 8 June 1920: RGAE, 4038/1/28/–; Lomonosov, 'Vospominaniia', Vol. 7, p. 1245.
79 Lomonosov, 'Vospominaniia', Vol. 7, pp. 1261–5.
80 Ibid., p. 1264.
81 Trotskii–Lomonosov, 11 June 1920: RGAE, 4038/1/28/–; Lomonosov, 'Vospominaniia', Vol. 7, pp. 1252, 1257, 1267.
82 Lomonosov, 'Vospominaniia', Vol. 7, p. 1267; a copy of Lomonosov's Tsentrosoiuz mandate is at RGAE, 4038/1/13/60.
83 Mandate, 17 June 1920: LRA MS 716.1.101.
84 Lomonosov, *Parovozy 0–5–0*, 'Prilozhenie XI'; and 'Vospominaniia', Vol. 7, pp. 1245–6.

85 Lomonosov–Krasin, 30 June 1920: RGAE, 4038/1/14/198; Lomonosov, 'Vospominaniia', Vol. 7, p. 1292.
86 Krasin–Lomonosov, 1 July 1920: RGAE, 4038/1/14/195–6; cited in Lomonosov, *Parovozy 0–5–0*, p. 9. The contract was unquestionably for 1,000 locomotives, so presumably Krasin mentioned 100 because this was the quantity specified as the Swedish Class R. As will be shown below, the order's size would be disputed in 1922.
87 Protocol of meeting in Stockholm, 26 July 1920: RGAE, 4038/1/19/–; Lomonosov, 'Dnevnik', Vol. 6, pp. 182, 188, and 'Vospominaniia', Vol. 7, pp. 1400–1, 1404.
88 Protocols of meetings of KhMU commission, 5 and 9 June 1920: RGAE, 1884/92/204/285–6ob.; protocol of meeting of KhMU commission, 16 June 1920, and copies of the various lists: RGAE, 4038/1/45/192, 116–16a, 120–42, 153–4.
89 Lomonosov, 'Vospominaniia', Vol. 7, pp. 1265, 1272; Goriacheva and Shelest, *Aleksei Nesterovich Shelest*, pp. 47–8.
90 Lomonosov, 'Vospominaniia', Vol. 7, pp. 1287, 1291, 1317, 1355.
91 Copy of preliminary agreement, 25 June 1920: RGAE, 413/10/833/57; Lomonosov, 'Dnevnik', Vol. 6, pp. 128–9, 132; and 'Vospominaniia', Vol. 7, pp. 1280–3.
92 Lomonosov, 'Dnevnik', Vol. 6, pp. 129–30, 132–4; and 'Vospominaniia', Vol. 7, pp. 1212, 1280, 1283, 1288. The Swedish Consulate in Tallinn told Palmstierna on 30 January 1920 of an Estonian offer to repair Soviet engines in Estonia: SRA UD:1920, Vol. 1446/I.
93 A copy of the repair contract is at RGAE, 4038/1/19/–. The history of this affair is the subject of Heywood, 'Estonia's Industrial Policy'.
94 Lomonosov, 'Dnevnik', Vol. 6, p. 169, and 'Vospominaniia', Vol. 7, pp. 1366–82.
95 Krasin–Lomonosov, 20 July 1920: RGAE, 4038/1/14/186, 187.
96 Krasin–Kopp, 20 July 1920: RGAE, 4038/1/44/157; Krasin–Martens, 20 July 1920: RGAE, 4038/1/14/88.
97 Lomonosov, 'Vospominaniia', Vol. 7, pp. 1363, 1378–80. For Bamberger's biography see ibid., pp. 1504–5.
98 Krasin–Chicherin/Trotskii/Lezhava, 21 July 1920: RGAE, 4038/1/13/54; Lomonosov, 'Vospominaniia', Vol. 7, pp. 1381–2.

4 Approaches to Britain and Germany

1 British thoughts about possible railway contracts are discussed in Heywood, 'The Armstrong Affair', pp. 60–7.
2 Conclusions of Conference of Ministers, 28 May 1920: CAB 23/21/198.
3 See, for example, Minutes of Russian Trade Committee, Third Meeting, 18 February 1920: FO 371/4033/229, 231; and Fourth Meeting, 2 March 1920: FO 371/4033/239.
4 Notes of Meeting between Allied Representatives and Delegates of Russian Co-operative Organisations, First Session, 7 April 1920: FO 371/4034/156–7.

5 Conclusions of Conference of Ministers, 28 May 1920: CAB 23/21/200. The disposal of British war-surplus locomotives and the Woolwich scheme are described in Bradley, *Locomotive History*, pp. 87–90, and Jackson, 'The Great Government Locomotive Sales'.
6 Hamrin–Palmstierna, 14 May 1920: SRA UD:1920, HP32B, Vol. 1447/VI; Krasin/Litvinov–Trotskii/Sverdlov, 8 May 1920: RGAE, 413/2/443/73.
7 On the trade agreement negotiations see, for example, Ullman, *Anglo-Soviet Relations*, Vol. III, pp. 89–453; S. White, *Britain and the Bolshevik Revolution*, pp. 3–26; Shishkin, *Sovetskoe gosudarstvo*, pp. 177–91, 249–57; and Glenny, 'The Anglo-Soviet Trade Agreement'.
8 Chicherin–Krasin, 12 June 1920 (intercept 002930): HLRO, LG papers, F12/3/50.
9 For the company's history see Warren, *Armstrongs of Elswick*.
10 Ibid., pp. 11, 197, 205–6.
11 Ibid., p. 205 and illustrative plate 18; Board Minutes, 29 January 1920: AW papers 130/1269 (Board Minute Book No. 4, 1916–26); Lowe, *British Steam Locomotive Builders*, p. 27.
12 Report by Ivitskii, 8 August 1920: RGAE, 4038/1/100/76–82.
13 Irving–Russian Trade Delegation, 9 August 1920: RGAE, 413/2/323/165–6; Draft heads of contract, [9 August 1920]: RGAE, 413/2/323/167–9.
14 Krasin–Lomonosov, 12 August 1920: RGAE, 413/2/323/180–ob.
15 Krasin–NKPS, 17 August 1920: RGAE, 413/2/323/170–1.
16 Lomonosov–Krasin, 22 August 1920: RGAE, 4038/1/14/113.
17 NKPS–Krasin, 7 October 1920: RGAE, 4038/1/45/4. Krasin had sent his letter via the NKVT, which did not forward it until 20 September: NKVT Imports Directorate–NKPS, 20 September 1920: RGAE, 413/2/461/61.
18 Krasin–Lloyd George, 4 October 1920: LG papers, F58/2/1.
19 Lomonosov, 'Vospominaniia', Vol. 8, pp. 19–24; Irving–Krasin, 15 December 1920: RGAE, 413/2/323/139: Draft of heads of proposed contract, [15 December 1920]: RGAE, 413/2/323/140–4ob.; Account by M. Ia. Lazerson of conversation with Krasin on 15 December 1920: RGAE, 4038/1/36/–. Krasin stated that he was trying to tempt the British: see his 'Anglo-sovetskie peregovory', in *Narodnoe khoziaistvo*, No. 1–2 (1921), pp. 3–12.
20 Account by Lazerson of conversation with Krasin on 15 December 1920: RGAE, 4038/1/36/–.
21 Krasin–Lomonosov, 16 December 1920: in ibid.
22 Lomonosov–Krasin, 19 December 1920: RGAE, 413/2/323/137.
23 Minutes of meetings [on 10–11 January 1921]: RGAE, 413/2/323/117; Draft heads of contract: RGAE, 413/2/323/118–26. See also Lomonosov, 'Vospominaniia', Vol. 8, pp. 83, 85; Lomonosov, *Predvaritel'nyi otchet*, pp. 76–7.
24 Minutes of meeting, 19 January 1921: AW papers, 130/1288 (Minutes of Finance Committee, No. 2, 1918–1922); Lomonosov, 'Vospominaniia', Vol. 8, p. 85.
25 Krasin–Armstrong Whitworth, 19 January 1921: RGAE, 413/2/323/114–15.

26 Ibid.
27 Lomonosov, 'Vospominaniia', Vol. 8, p. 314.
28 Lloyd George–Krasin (draft), [October 1920]: LG papers, F58/2/2.
29 Telegrams were intercepted by the Government Code and Cipher School, which was under Admiralty control until April 1922; but use of the telegrams was controlled by the Foreign Secretary: Andrew, *Secret Service*, pp. 259–75. Copies of intercepts circulated to the Cabinet are preserved in the Lloyd George papers and in HLRO, Davidson papers. None appear to survive in the Foreign Office's Russia files at the PRO, but some are kept in Admiralty files at ADM 233/21 (Wireless news, 1918–21); it is unclear whether the latter, most of which do not duplicate those at the HLRO, were shown to the Cabinet.
30 Churchill–Lloyd George, 26 August 1920: LG papers, F9/2/41.
31 Bonar Law–Stamfordham, 2 September 1920: HLRO, Bonar Law papers, 101/4/85; Conclusions of Conference of Ministers, 2 September 1920: CAB 23/22/235–40.
32 Very few of the intercepts preserved at the HLRO and PRO concern trade issues, and none are addressed to or from Lomonosov or Martens. Yet according to Andrew, the British knew most or all of the Russian codes: Andrew, *Secret Service*, p. 268.
33 Simons–Lloyd George, 22 August 1920: LG papers, F53/3/5.
34 Simons, *Aide-mémoire*, [22 August 1920]: LG papers, F53/3/5.
35 Lloyd George–Simons, 24 August 1920: PRO, GFM 34/1433/frame 489940.
36 Lloyd George–Simons (first draft), 26 August 1920: LG papers, F24/3/10(a).
37 Lloyd George, Memorandum on Proposal to expel Messrs Kameneff and Krassin, [2 September 1920?]: HLRO, Davidson papers, file 117.
38 Ibid.
39 Ibid.
40 Conclusions of Conference of Ministers, 2 September 1920: CAB 23/22/237; Cabinet 61 (1920), 17 November 1920: CAB 23/23/97–8.
41 Krasin, *Vneshtorg i vneshniaia ekonomicheskaia politika*, pp. 11–12.
42 Debo, *Revolution and Survival*, p. 308.
43 Ibid., p. 309. For brief discussions of Lomonosov's orders in Germany see, for instance, Himmer, 'German–Soviet Economic Relations', pp. 235–43; and Åhlander, 'Staat, Wirtschaft und Handelspolitik', pp. 223–33. The question of how many locomotives were ordered, and when, has caused particular confusion.
44 See, for instance, Himmer, 'German–Soviet Economic Relations', pp. 153–5, 203; Breuning, 'German Foreign Policy', pp. 21–3; Dernberg et al. (eds), *Sovetsko-germanskie otnosheniia*, Vol. 2, pp. 169–70, 180–1; Shishkin, *Sovetskoe gosudarstvo*, p. 221; Kilmarnock–Foreign Office, 20 January 1920: *BDFA*, Vol. II, p. 164.
45 Niederschrift von Hagemann, p. 5: Historisches Archiv Friedrich Krupp GmbH, Werksarchiv IV 1361; Krasin–Legien, 6 May 1920: RGAE, 4038/1/44/183; statement by Kopp, 15 May 1920: RGAE, 4038/1/44/182;

Lomonosov, *Predvaritel'nyi otchet*, p. 71. Legien is described briefly in *ADAP*, Vol. III, p. 673.
46 Niederschrift von Hagemann, p. 3; Lomonosov, 'Vospominaniia', Vol. 7, pp. 1395, 1575, 1609.
47 Niederschrift von Hagemann, pp. 3–4.
48 Ibid., pp. 4, 6–8, 10.
49 Ibid., pp. 4–6, 11; Åhlander, 'Staat, Wirtschaft und Handelspolitik', p. 227.
50 Niederschrift von Hagemann, pp. 4, 7–8.
51 Ibid., pp. 8–10. A copy of the offer is at RGAE, 4038/1/44/172–7.
52 Niederschrift von Hagemann, pp. 11–12.
53 Lomonosov, 'Vospominaniia', Vol. 7, pp. 1300, 1388–9.
54 Kopp–Krasin, 11 July 1920: RGAE, 4038/1/44/163–6.
55 See RGAE, 4038/1/44/165; Reich–Lomonosov, 26 July 1920: RGAE, 4038/1/44/144–6; Lomonosov, *Predvaritel'nyi otchet*, pp. 72–3. Reich was Kopp's assistant and, according to Lomonosov, his father-in-law: 'Vospominaniia', Vol. 7, p. 1416.
56 Lomonosov, 'Vospominaniia', Vol. 7, pp. 1382–3.
57 Ibid., pp. 1388–90. The two unidentified Germans were probably Herren von Gontard (Henschel) and Hoensch (Linke-Hofmann), who were present on 31 July.
58 Protocol of meeting with Verband, 31 July 1920: RGAE, 4038/1/44/134–7; Niederschrift von Hagemann, pp. 13–15; Lomonosov, 'Vospominaniia', Vol. 7, pp. 1400, 1404, 1411–13, 1416–17, 1422–5.
59 Krasin–Lomonosov, 31 July 1920: RGAE, 4038/1/14/179; Lomonosov, 'Vospominaniia', Vol. 7, p. 1425.
60 See Krasin–Lomonosov, 3 August 1920: RGAE, 4038/1/44/118; Krasin–Lomonosov, 12 August 1920: RGAE, 4038/1/44/117.
61 Lomonosov–Krasin, 31 July 1920: RGAE, 4038/1/44/125–6.
62 See, for instance, Lomonosov–Chicherin, 13 August 1920: AVP, 04/46/54073/282/24–ob.; Lomonosov, 'Vospominaniia', Vol. 7, pp. 1452–6.
63 Lomonosov–Trotskii/Lezhava, [4 August 1920]: RGAE, 4038/1/33/156; Lomonosov, 'Vospominaniia', Vol. 7, pp. 1429–31, 1434–5.
64 Lomonosov–Krasin, 4 August 1920: RGAE, 4038/1/14/172.
65 Lomonosov–Krasin, 8 August 1920: RGAE, 4038/1/14/165; Krasin–Lomonosov, 8 August 1920: RGAE, 4038/1/14/142–3; and 14 August 1920: RGAE, 4038/1/44/131–2. The interested companies are listed at RGAE, 4038/1/104/78.
66 Lomonosov, 'Vospominaniia', Vol. 7, p. 1450; Lomonosov–Krasin, [n.d.]: RGAE, 4038/1/44/116.
67 See Lomonosov–Krasin, 16 August 1920: RGAE, 4038/1/44/89; Krasin–Lomonosov, 17 August 1920: RGAE, 4038/1/44/86; Lomonosov, 'Vospominaniia', Vol. 7, p. 1464. German prices in marks were likely to rise as the mark's value fell.
68 Memorandum, 16 August 1920: GFM 34/3974/frame K096055.
69 Ibid. Lomonosov's account of his first conversation with Maltzan is at:

'Vospominaniia', Vol. 7, pp. 1465–6. He records that it occurred that afternoon at the Foreign Ministry – possibly he mistakenly merges it with a second meeting held later that day. Lomonosov also refers (p. 1465) to the presence of a certain 'Heller'; conceivably, this was Gustav Hilger, who was negotiating with Kopp about prisoners and trade.
70 Memorandum, 16 August 1920: GFM 34/3974/frames K096056–7.
71 Lomonosov, 'Vospominaniia', Vol. 7, pp. 1466, 1472.
72 Bücher–Lomonosov, 18 August 1920: RGAE, 4038/1/44/79. A copy of the judgement is at RGAE, 4038/1/44/77–8. A breakdown of the costs is given in Lomonosov–Krasin, 18 August 1920: RGAE, 4038/1/14/120, and slightly differently in Lomonosov, 'Vospominaniia', Vol. 7, pp. 1472–3.
73 Niederschrift von Hagemann, p. 18.
74 Lomonosov, 'Vospominaniia', Vol. 7, pp. 1473–4; *Ekonomicheskaia zhizn'*, 19 September 1920, p. 1.
75 Lomonosov–Krasin, 18 August 1920: RGAE, 4038/1/14/120, 121.
76 Protocol of meeting on 20 August 1920: RGAE, 4038/1/44/53–5.
77 Kopp/Lomonosov–Krasin, 22 August 1920: RGAE, 4038/1/14/110; Krasin–Lomonosov, 23 August 1920: RGAE, 4038/1/44/43; Niederschrift von Hagemann, p. 18.
78 See Lomonosov–Krasin, 19 August 1920: RGAE, 4038/1/14/106; Lomonosov–Chicherin/Lenin/Trotskii, 19 August 1920: AVP, 082/3/7/2; Krasin–Lomonosov, 20 August 1920: RGAE, 4038/1/14/104–5; Kopp/Lomonosov–Krasin, 22 August 1920: RGAE, 4038/1/14/110; Lomonosov, 'Vospominaniia', Vol. 7, pp. 1474–81, 1524–5.
79 Niederschrift von Hagemann, pp. 17–18. See also *ADAP*, Vol. III, pp. 485–6; Maltzan to Brockdorff-Rantzau, 6 August 1920: GFM 34/3509/frames H237050–1.
80 Lomonosov–Krasin, 10 August 1920: RGAE, 4038/1/44/95.
81 Krasin–Lomonosov, 12 August 1920: RGAE, 4038/1/44/119.
82 Lomonosov–Krasin, 18 August 1920: RGAE, 4038/1/14/118.
83 Krasin–Lomonosov, 19 August 1920: RGAE, 4038/1/14/117, 119. The 1918 affair, in which Lazerson was also involved, has been described by Efimkin: ' "My zaplatili nemetskim imperialistam zoloto ..." ', pp. 147–51.
84 Lomonosov, 'Vospominaniia', Vol. 7, pp. 1496–8.
85 See Kopp–Krasin, 23 August 1920: RGAE, 4038/1/44/39–40.
86 Kopp/Lomonosov–Krasin, 23 August 1920: RGAE, 4038/1/14/57. The negotiations with Markevich collapsed upon the banker's death: Kopp–Lezhava, 8 January 1921: AVP, 082/4/18/1–ob.
87 Lomonosov, 'Vospominaniia', Vol. 7, pp. 1489–90; Memorandum about German–Russian Economic Policy, 23 May 1920: GFM 34/5039/frames L198952–6; Guidelines for German policy vis-à-vis England, [*circa* August 1920]: GFM 34/1433/frames 489943–4.
88 Protocol of meeting on 23 August 1920: RGAE, 4038/1/44/34–8; Kopp/Lomonosov–Krasin, 23 August 1920: RGAE, 4038/1/14/57; Lomonosov, 'Vospominaniia', Vol. 7, pp. 1490, 1495–9.
89 See Lomonosov–Krasin, 4 September 1920: RGAE, 4038/1/14/65.

90 Lomonosov–Krasin, 20 August 1920: RGAE, 4038/1/14/116; Krasin–Lomonosov, 23 August 1920: RGAE, 4038/1/14/109; Krasin–Lomonosov, 26 August 1920: RGAE, 4038/1/14/99; Lomonosov–Krasin, 3 September 1920: RGAE, 4038/1/14/67; Krasin–Lomonosov, 15 September 1920: RGAE, 4038/1/14/63–4; Lomonosov, 'Vospominaniia', Vol. 7, pp. 1506–8.

91 Krasin–Lomonosov, 23 June 1920: RGAE, 4038/1/14/191; Krasin–Lomonosov, 20 August 1920: RGAE, 4038/1/14/107–8; Krasin–Lomonosov, 23 August 1920: RGAE, 4038/1/14/102; Lomonosov–Krasin, 4 September 1920: RGAE, 4038/1/14/65; Krasin–Lomonosov, 15 September 1920: RGAE, 4038/1/14/63–4; account by Lazerson of conversation with Krasin, 15 December 1920: RGAE, 4038/1/36/–. See also Balawyder, *Canadian–Soviet Relations*, pp. 32–7. In 1919 this company offered to supply 250 decapod locomotives from the Davenport (USA) works for the Bakhmet'ev mission: Allis Chalmers–Lipets, 30 September 1919: NARG 261, Russian Supply Committee, box K203, file 745.

92 Lomonosov–Krasin, 18 September 1920: RGAE, 4038/1/14/62; Lomonosov–Krasin, 19 September 1920: RGAE, 4038/1/14/60. See also Lomonosov's report to the Council of Foreign Trade, 27 October 1920: GARF, r-130/4/317/39.

93 Lomonosov, 'Vospominaniia', Vol. 7, pp. 1572–8; Niederschrift von Hagemann, pp. 20–1.

94 Protocol of meeting on 20 September 1920: RGAE, 4038/1/99/–; Lomonosov, 'Vospominaniia', Vol. 7, pp. 1572–9; Niederschrift von Hagemann, pp. 20–2.

95 Niederschrift von Hagemann, p. 22; Lomonosov, 'Vospominaniia', Vol. 7, pp. 1604–5, 1612, 1619–20.

96 Lomonosov, 'Vospominaniia', Vol. 7, pp. 1612–13.

97 Lomonosov–Krasin, 8 October 1920: RGAE, 4038/1/14/23–5; Lomonosov, 'Vospominaniia', Vol. 7, pp. 1619–24.

98 Lomonosov–Krasin, 8 October 1920: RGAE, 4038/1/14/23–5.

99 Lomonosov–Krasin, 9 October 1920: RGAE, 4038/1/14/41. The Branting government fell on 27 October 1920: Carlbäck-Isotalo, 'Ekonomicheskie sviazi Sovetskoi Rossii', pp. 41, 44.

100 Lomonosov, 'Vospominaniia', Vol. 7, pp. 1624, 1633–4.

101 Ibid., pp. 1628–31.

102 Niederschrift von Hagemann, p. 23.

103 Lomonosov–Krasin, 13 October 1920: RGAE, 4038/1/14/36.

104 Lomonosov, 'Vospominaniia', Vol. 7, pp. 1634–7.

105 Krasin–Lomonosov, 17 October 1920: RGAE, 4038/1/14/20–2.

106 Lomonosov, 'Vospominaniia', Vol. 7, pp. 1636–9.

107 Lomonosov–Krasin, 18 October 1920: RGAE, 4038/1/14/26; Lomonosov, 'Vospominaniia', Vol. 7, pp. 1642–3.

108 Krasin–Lomonosov, 19 October 1920: RGAE, 4038/1/14/17–18.

109 Lomonosov, 'Vospominaniia', Vol. 7, p. 1644. In a telegram to Lenin dated 8 November 1920 Krasin blamed British interference for the failure of this combination: RTsKhIDNI, 5/1/1074/4.

110 Lomonosov, 'Vospominaniia', Vol. 7, pp. 1644–6.
111 Ibid., pp. 1632–3, 1644, 1648. For a copy of the Mannesmann contract see HIA, M. Laserson papers, document 18.
112 Lomonosov, 'Vospominaniia', Vol. 7, pp. 1646–7.
113 Niederschrift von Hagemann, pp. 24–5.
114 Contract between Nohab and Krupp, 29 November 1920: HIA, Laserson papers, document 22; Niederschrift von Hagemann, pp. 24–5.
115 Himmer, 'German–Soviet Economic Relations', p. 234.

5 Second thoughts

1 Chicherin–Lomonosov, 22 September 1920: RGAE, 4038/1/33/119.
2 SNK resolution, 5 October 1920: *DSV*, Vol. XI, pp. 292–3.
3 For instance, Nove, *Economic History*, pp. 63–81; Pavliuchenkov, *Krest'ianskii Brest*, pp. 168–273. Concerning modernisation see Remington, *Building Socialism*, pp. 155–62.
4 For a detailed discussion of the railways in 1920 see Argenbright, 'The Russian Railroad System', pp. 328–94.
5 Figures for the 'reserve' may be found in *NKPS v 1920 godu*, p. 24; 'Sostoianie i rabota zheleznykh dorog za pervuiu polovinu 1921 goda', in *Narodnoe khoziaistvo*, No. 8–9 (1921), p. 139.
6 *Izvestiia*, 27 March 1920, p. 1.
7 Argenbright, 'The Russian Railroad System', p. 328.
8 This attitude was encapsulated in the title of Shatunovskii's pamphlet *Vosstanovlenie transporta: Puti soobshcheniia i puti revoliutsii* (*The Reconstruction of Transport: Ways of Communication and Revolutionary Ways*).
9 Protocol of NKPS Collegium meeting, 19 April 1920: RGAE, 1884/28/1/136.
10 STO resolution, 28 May 1920: RGAE, 1884/28/571b/80 (published in *Otchet OTK v Sovet truda i oborony za dekabr' i 2–iu polovinu 1920g.*, p. 3).
11 Sverdlov, *Vse na transport!*, pp. 56–60; Shatunovskii, *Vosstanovlenie transporta*, pp. 20–1; Lomonosov, 'Vospominaniia', Vol. 7, p. 1658.
12 Lomonosov, 'Vospominaniia', Vol. 7, p. 1672; Sverdlov, *Vse na transport!*, p. 60.
13 Shatunovskii, *Vosstanovlenie transporta*, pp. 23, 25–31. Versions for two and a half and three and a half years were also drafted: *Ekonomicheskaia zhizn'*, 9 May 1920, p. 1.
14 Shatunovskii, *Vosstanovlenie transporta*, pp. 21–2, 32–5; *Ekonomicheskaia zhizn'*, 9 May 1920, p. 1.
15 See *Ekonomicheskaia zhizn'*, 29 May 1920, p. 1; and 6 June 1920, p. 1.
16 Sverdlov, *Vse na transport!*, p. 60; Neopikhanov, *Russkii transport*, p. 153; Statement by NKPS Permanent Way Department, 4 September 1920: RGAE, 1884/3/32/248–9. See also protocol of meeting of NKPS directorate chiefs, 8 July 1920: RGAE, 1884/28/3/87; lists of measures for improving transport, August 1920: RGAE, 1884/3/32/17–20 (Technical Directorate), 9–11 (KhMU, Operations Directorate, Finance Directorate, etc.), and *Gudok*, 18 August 1920, p. 2.

17 See *Ekonomicheskaia zhizn'*, 3 June 1920, p. 1; 6 June 1920, p. 1; and 15 September 1920, p. 1.
18 *Pravda*, 12 November 1920, p. 2.
19 See, for example, *Biulleten' Narodnogo komissariata putei soobshcheniia*, No. 99 (1920), pp. 1–2; *Pravda*, 25 August 1920, p. 4; and *Gudok*, 4 November 1920, p. 3. Also *Ekonomicheskaia zhizn'*, 25 August 1920, p. 1; 12 September 1920, p. 1; and 10 October 1920, p. 1.
20 For example, see *Biulleten' Narodnogo komissariata putei soobshcheniia*, No. 66 (1920), pp. 1–2; *Ekonomicheskaia zhizn'*, 12 September 1920, p. 1; 3 October 1920, p. 1; and 22 October 1920, p. 2; *Gudok*, 21 January 1921, p. 4 and 25 March 1921, p. 2; Argenbright, 'The Russian Railroad System', pp. 363, 365.
21 *Pravda*, 8 September 1920, p. 1.
22 *Ekonomicheskaia zhizn'*, 28 August 1920, p. 4.
23 The NKRKI assault is described in Argenbright, 'The Russian Railroad System', pp. 373–9. This link with the trades union controversy seems the more plausible if, like Yoshimasa Tsuji, one sees the debate mainly as a power struggle within the Central Committee: Tsuji, 'The Debate on the Trade Unions', *passim*. See also Day, *Leon Trotsky*, pp. 36–44.
24 Trotskii–Sverdlov/Bumazhnyi, 1 October 1920: RGAE, 1884/3/32/236; Protocol of meeting to discuss Trotskii's communication of 1 October 1920, [5 October 1920]: RGAE, 1884/3/32/204–6; draft resolutions for meeting about locomotive repair chaired by Trotskii, [October 1920]: RGAE, 1884/3/32/216; Fomin–*Pravda*, [n.d.]: RGAE, 1884/3/161/159–60 (Fomin was responding to criticism of Trotskii by Iurii Larin).
25 See Coopersmith, *Electrification*, pp. 174–8.
26 Stalin, *Sochineniia*, Vol. V, pp. 50–1.
27 Extract from protocol of Orgburo meeting, 19 April 1920: RGAE, 3429/1/2104/22; report by VSNKh Presidium to SNK, 21 May 1920: RGAE, 3429/1/2102/72.
28 See Shishkin, *Lenin i vneshneekonomicheskaia politika*, pp. 278–82; also Genkina, *Protokoly Sovnarkoma RSFSR*, pp. 74–5. The reform of the NKTiP into NKVT had been mooted by October 1918. During the civil war NKTiP functioned mainly as a commissariat for trade, including foreign economic affairs. See *Protokoly Prezidiuma VSNKh*, pp. 258, 315 (note 21).
29 Shishkin, *Lenin i vneshneekonomicheskaia politika*, p. 283.
30 See *Ekonomicheskaia zhizn'*, 18 September 1920, pp. 1 and 3; and 5 November 1920, p. 1; *Pravda*, 18 September 1920.
31 On Pilsudski's attack see Mawdsley, *Russian Civil War*, pp. 255–6. The subsequent change is considered in Davies, 'The Missing Revolutionary War', pp. 178–95; and especially Fiddick, *Russia's Retreat*. On the subject of Soviet foreign economic relations see also Day, *Leon Trotsky*, pp. 48–55. Correspondingly, I. I. Stepanova-Skvortsova published eight articles in *Pravda* in the first half of December 1920 explaining and justifying the concept of concession operations. See, for example, *Pravda*, 2 December 1920, p. 1; and also Shishkin, *Sovetskoe gosudarstvo*, pp. 231–9.
32 See protocol of VSNKh Presidium meeting, 17 May 1920: RGAE, 3429/1/

1298/63ob.; report by VSNKh Presidium to SNK, 21 May 1920: RGAE, 3429/1/2102/72; and SNK resolution, 27 May 1920: RGAE, 3429/1/2102/116.
33 Protocol of meeting of VSNKh Committee for Foreign Trade, 29 May 1920: RGAE, 3429/1/2101a/1.
34 Protocols of meetings of VSNKh Committee for Foreign Trade, 25 June 1920: RGAE, 3429/1/2101a/2; 5 July 1920: RGAE, 3429/1/2102/323; 6 July 1920: RGAE, 3429/1/2101a/3; 9 July 1920: RGAE, 3429/1/2101a/4. A copy of the NKPS list is at: RGAE, 4038/1/45/153–4.
35 Resolution of Council of Foreign Trade, 4 October 1920: RGAE, 1884/28/3/150.
36 Protocol of meeting of VSNKh Committee for Foreign Trade, 25 June 1920: RGAE, 3429/1/2101a/2–ob.
37 Shishkin, *Lenin i vneshneekonomicheskaia politika*, p. 283.
38 Protocol of meeting of NKPS directorate chiefs, 23 August 1920: RGAE, 1884/28/3/107; report by Voskresenskii, 23 August 1920: RGAE, 1884/28/3/112–14. A shorter version of the report appeared in *Ekonomicheskaia zhizn'*, 3 October 1920, p. 2.
39 Protocol of meeting of NKPS directorate chiefs, 27 August 1920: RGAE, 1884/28/3/118–ob.
40 Summary list, 27 August 1920: RGAE, 4038/1/45/61, 74; full lists, 31 August 1920: RGAE, 4038/1/45/61ob.–73.
41 Protocol of meeting of Council of Foreign Trade, 15 September 1920: RGAE, 413/2/475a/85–7.
42 Ibid., l. 85.
43 Lezhava–Trotskii, 22 September 1920: *Leninskii sbornik*, Vol. XXXVIII, p. 329; Chicherin–Lomonosov, 22 September 1920: RGAE, 4038/1/33/119.
44 Lezhava–Krasin, 28 September 1920: *Leninskii sbornik*, Vol. XXXVIII, pp. 329–30 (copy at: RGAE, 4038/1/14/52).
45 See protocol of NKPS meeting about imports, 11 October 1920: RGAE, 1884/28/3/148; report to meeting on 5 October 1920 about progress with overhauls under plan No. 1042: RGAE, 1884/3/32/207–9.
46 Protocol of meeting of Council of Foreign Trade, 4 October 1920: RGAE, 413/2/475a/79–84.
47 SNK resolution, 5 October 1920: *DSV*, Vol. XI, pp. 292–3.
48 Lomonosov, 'Vospominaniia', Vol. 7, pp. 1665–71, 1674; Chicherin–Krestinskii, [October 1920]: AVP, 04/46/54073/282/34.
49 Protocol of meeting of Council of Foreign Trade, 27 October 1920: GARF, r-130/4/317/38–40 (no copy of resolution); Lomonosov, 'Vospominaniia', Vol. 7, pp. 1674, 1680.
50 See Extract from protocol of meeting of Tsentrosoiuz Board, 28 October 1920: RGAE, 4038/1/33/91; Lomonosov, 'Vospominaniia', Vol. 7, pp. 1680–1.
51 Protocol of meeting of Council of Foreign Trade, 20 October 1920: GARF, r-130/4/317/35–7; SNK resolution, 30 October 1920: RGAE, 4038/1/28/–.
52 SNK resolution, 28 October 1920: RGAE, 4038/1/19/–; Tsentrosoiuz

warrant, [October 1920]: RGAE, 4038/1/13/29; Protocol of Politburo meeting, 5 November 1920: RTsKhIDNI, 17/3/120, item 10; Chicherin–Krasin, 27 November 1920: RTsKhIDNI, 5/1/2098/88; Lomonosov, 'Vospominaniia', Vol. 7, p. 1681.
53 Lomonosov, 'Vospominaniia', Vol. 7, pp. 1707–8. Lomonosov states that Litvinov supported Khinchuk at this meeting, but the corresponding protocol does not indicate Litvinov's presence: Protocol of meeting of Council for Foreign Trade, 1 November 1920: RGAE, 413/2/475a/74–6.
54 Protocol of meeting of Council of Foreign Trade, 1 November 1920: RGAE, 413/2/475a/74–6.
55 See report by L. V. Filippov, [10 October 1920]: RGAE, 4038/1/13/33–5; Lomonosov–Lezhava/NKPS, 8 October 1920: RGAE, 4038/1/13/36.
56 Borisov's appointment, and its significance for Lomonosov, are described by the latter: 'Vospominaniia', Vol. 7, pp. 1138, 1182–3, 1187–9. For Borisov's biography see Sosnovskii and Zenzinov, *Otechestvennye uchenye-zheleznodorozhniki*, pp. 30–1; Lopukhin, 'Posle 25 oktiabria', p. 90, note 79.
57 Protocol of meeting of NKPS directorate chiefs, 9 July 1920: RGAE, 1884/28/3/88.
58 Protocol of meeting of NKPS directorate chiefs, 2 August 1920: RGAE, 1884/28/3/101–2; Kolegaev–Fomin, 3 September 1920: 1884/3/134/111; Kolegaev–Main Directorate, 7 September 1920: RGAE, 1884/28/3/117; draft statute for KhMU special secretariat, [18 September 1920?]: RGAE, 1884/28/571b/30–ob. A list of Gukovskii's orders to June 1920 is at RGAE, 4038/1/45/111ob.; it has not been ascertained whether these contracts were approved in Moscow and the goods delivered.
59 Protocol of meeting No. 177 of special organisational conference, 16 September 1920: RGAE, 1884/28/571b/28 (chaired by K. K. Khodorovskii); [Khodorovskii?]–Borisov, 17 September 1920: RGAE, 1884/28/571b/27; Kolegaev–Borisov, 18 September 1920: RGAE, 1884/28/571b/25.
60 Report by Filippov, [10 October 1920]: RGAE, 4038/1/13/33–5; protocol of meeting of NKPS directorate chiefs, 18 October 1920: RGAE, 1884/28/3/158; clarificatory note and revised report, [21 October 1920?]: RGAE, 1884/3/169/203–5; Lomonosov, 'Vospominaniia', Vol. 7, pp. 1678–9.
61 Filippov was probably referring to a statute concerning the functions of NKPS representatives based abroad, which was signed by Kolegaev and Lezhava on 20 September 1920. Basically it established NKVT control: NKPS personnel were to work as technical advisers within the NKVT framework and not make any independent purchases: RGAE, 1884/92/203/52.
62 Protocol of NKPS meeting about imports, 27 October 1920: RGAE, 1884/28/3/163–ob.
63 Lomonosov, 'Vospominaniia', Vol. 7, pp. 1676–9.
64 See ibid., pp. 1689–98 for Lomonosov's description of his two main audiences with Lenin.
65 Instruction (*nakaz*) No. 18312, 5 November 1920: LRA MS 716.1.104;

Lomonosov, *Predvaritel'nyi otchet*, pp. 5, 9–10; Lomonosov, 'Vospominaniia', Vol. 7, pp. 1709–11.
66 Lomonosov, 'Vospominaniia', Vol. 8, p. 884.
67 *Deiatel'nost' Russkoi zheleznodorozhnoi missii*, pp. 7–9; Lomonosov, *Predvaritel'nyi otchet*, pp. 17–25.
68 Lomonosov, 'Vospominaniia', Vol. 7, p. 1735; Shishkin, *Sovetskoe gosudarstvo*, pp. 167–8.
69 Chicherin–Lezhava, 24 November 1920: AVP, 140/4/10/63–ob.
70 Lomonosov–Lenin/Trotskii/Chicherin, 13 November 1920: RGAE, 4038/1/94/68; Lomonosov, 'Vospominaniia', Vol. 7, p. 1735.
71 Shishkin, *Sovetskoe gosudarstvo*, p. 168.
72 Protocol of Politburo meeting, 15 November 1920: RTsKhIDNI, 17/3/121, item 1.
73 Lomonosov–Lazerson, 17 November 1920: RGAE, 4038/1/94/79; Lomonosov, 'Vospominaniia', Vol. 7, pp. 1738–44.
74 Lomonosov, 'Vospominaniia', Vol. 7, p. 1744, and Vol. 8, pp. 15, 82, 101; Shishkin, *Sovetskoe gosudarstvo*, pp. 167–8.
75 See Krasin–Lomonosov/Lazerson, 9 November 1920; Krasin–Lomonosov, 11 November 1920: RGAE, 4038/1/36/–; Lomonosov–Krasin, 22 November 1920: RGAE, 4038/1/94/89–93; Krasin–Lomonosov, 21, 22 and 23 November 1920, 16 and 29 December 1920; Lomonosov–Krasin, 22 November 1920, 8 December 1920, (draft letter) 11 December 1920: RGAE, 4038/1/36/–. See also Lomonosov, 'Vospominaniia', Vol. 7, p. 1731, and Vol. 8, pp. 10–14, 35–40, 44–8.
76 For example: Lomonosov–Lezhava/Trotskii/Lenin, 10 December 1920: RGAE, 4038/1/37/11–12; Lomonosov–Lenin, 26 December 1920: RTsKhIDNI, 5/1/1164/1–2. The quoted phrase may be found, for example, in Lomonosov, 'Vospominaniia', Vol. 8, p. 48.
77 See Krasin–Chicherin, 29 December 1920: RTsKhIDNI, 5/1/2126/13; Lomonosov, 'Vospominaniia', Vol. 8, pp. 92–7, 102.
78 Krasin may well have complained about Lomonosov when raising the question of 'essential' personnel changes in Soviet foreign delegations at an Orgburo meeting; the decision was taken to form a commission: Protocol of Orgburo meeting, 9 February 1921: RTsKhIDNI, 137/1/35/1.
79 Kul'tprosvet–Railway Mission, 22 June 1921: RGAE, 4038/1/29/109. On this whole question of requests see, for example, Postnikov–Lomonosov, 22 August 1922: RGAE, 4038/1/38/235–7.
80 See report about implementation of Railway Mission orders as of 1 May 1921: RGAE, 4038/1/6/31–3; Lomonosov, 'Vospominaniia', Vol. 7, pp. 1729, 1737.
81 For example: Gordin–Lomonosov, 20 October 1920: RGAE, 4038/1/104/107; Jorgen Hals AS–Jacob Brunstein [NKVT representative in Norway?], 13 December 1920: RGAE, 4038/1/105/–; American Steel, Engineering and Automobile Products AG (Amstea)–Lomonosov, 14 January 1921: RGAE, 4038/1/104/73; Lomonosov–Amstea, 15 January 1921: RGAE,

4038/1/104/71–2. A copy of the revised Revalis contract, 19 October 1920, is at RGAE, 4038/1/104/113–21. See also Martens–Lomonosov, 3 November 1920: RGAE, 4038/1/104/108–9.
82 See Heywood, 'Reviving Soviet–Western Trade', pp. 192–4.
83 See Lomonosov, 'Vospominaniia', Vol. 7, p. 1730 and Vol. 8, pp. 40, 53.
84 Lomonosov–Krasin/Emshanov/Lezhava, 27 January 1921: AVP, 04/46/54073/282/23 (this copy incorrectly dated 1920); Lomonosov, 'Vospominaniia', Vol. 8, pp. 89–90.
85 Lomonosov, 'Vospominaniia', Vol. 8, pp. 99–100. See also Berg–Lomonosov, 19 January 1921: RGAE, 4038/1/99/–.
86 Krasin/Litvinov/Solomon–Lomonosov, 22 January 1921: RGAE, 4038/1/15/250; Lomonosov, 'Vospominaniia', Vol. 8, p. 110.
87 Berg–Lomonosov, 26 January 1921, and Lomonosov–Krasin/Lezhava/Emshanov, 27 January 1921: RGAE, 4038/1/99/–; Lomonosov, 'Vospominaniia', Vol. 8, p. 112.
88 Lomonosov–Krasin, 5 January 1921: RGAE, 4038/1/15/265; Lomonosov, 'Vospominaniia', Vol. 8, pp. 122–6.
89 See Supplementary Agreement between Tsentrosoiuz and Nordiska, 18 December 1920: RGAE, 4038/1/94/157–9; Lomonosov–Krasin, 5 January 1920: RGAE, 4038/1/94/194; Nordiska–Lomonosov, 4 February 1921: RGAE, 4038/1/94/230–5; Nordiska–Lomonosov, 24 February 1921: RGAE, 4038/1/94/257; Lomonosov–Krasin, 26 February 1920: RGAE, 4038/1/15/237–8; Lomonosov, 'Vospominaniia', Vol. 8, pp. 85, 115, 122–6, 138–9, 208–9.
90 Lomonosov, 'Vospominaniia', Vol. 8, p. 158. Krasin initially accepted Lomonosov's explanation, but later suspected that Lazerson had suffered an injustice: Krasin–Lomonosov, 19 February 1921: RGAE, 4038/1/15/239; and Krasin–Lomonosov, 11 March 1921: RGAE, 4038/1/15/223–4. Lazerson gives an understandably pained account in his memoirs: Larsons, *Na sovetskoi sluzhbe*, pp. 66–7. Elsewhere he offers a somewhat jaundiced portrait of Lomonosov: Larsons, *V sovetskom labirinte*, pp. 115–32. That Lomonosov's wife became a domineering figure in the Railway Mission is also suggested by a former Soviet timber expert who had some official contact with the mission: Libermann, *Dela i liudi*, p. 183.
91 Lomonosov–Lenin/Trotskii/Emshanov/Lezhava/Krasin, and Lomonosov–Lenin, 8 February 1921: RGAE, 4038/1/99/–; Lomonosov, 'Vospominaniia', Vol. 8, pp. 143–4. It is possible that the Germans did try to involve British firms: the British ambassador in Berlin, Lord D'Abernon, informed the Foreign Office on 6 November 1920 that both Vickers and the North British Locomotive Company were fully acquainted with a proposed German–Soviet locomotive contract, though neither was particularly keen to participate; and there were certainly German–British discussions in 1921 about sharing the Russian market. See D'Abernon–Foreign Office, 6 November 1920: FO 371/5444/23, and Davenport–Hines, *Dudley Docker*, pp. 199–200.

92 Krasin–Lenin, 12 February 1921: RTsKhIDNI, 5/1/1077/1–ob.
93 Lomonosov, 'Vospominaniia', Vol. 8, pp. 170–1, 175–9; Niederschrift von Hagemann, pp. 29–32.
94 Lomonosov, 'Vospominaniia', Vol. 8, pp. 183–6, 189–91.
95 Lomonosov–NKVT/NKPS, 1 March 1921: RGAE, 4038/1/15/234–5; Lomonosov, 'Vospominaniia', Vol. 8, p. 192. A copy of the contract is at LRA MS 716.1.107. Maltzan gave Krasin the German Foreign Ministry's verbal blessing for this contract a few days later: Memorandum about meeting with Krasin, 2 March 1921: GFM 34/3974/frames K096205–8.
96 The impact of Trotskii's resignation on the NKPS is discussed in Argenbright, 'The Russian Railroad System', pp. 379–83. Other assessments of Trotskii's NKPS career are Shabunin, 'Vrio narkomputi Lev Trotskii'; and Bogdanovich et al. (eds), *Ministry i Narkomy*, pp. 177–9. On the railways' winter tribulations and revision of plan targets, see *Ekonomicheskaia zhizn'*, 22 January 1921, p. 2; 6 March 1921, p. 2; 6 April 1921, pp. 1–2; 17 April 1921, p. 2; and 24 April 1921, p. 1.
97 See NKPS report to OTK subcommission, [2 February 1921?]: RGAE, 4038/1/46/300–1.
98 See extract from protocol of meeting of OTK sub-commission, 2 February 1921: ibid., l.299.
99 The January review is mentioned in passing in Lezhava–Lomonosov, 21 January 1921: RGAE, 4038/1/34/–. The February one is the subject of Lezhava–Lomonosov, 24 February 1921: RGAE, 4038/1/99/–. See also: Credits allocated in 1920–21: RGAE, 4372/11/62/296; protocol of meeting of Gosplan Foreign Trade Sub-commission, 18 April 1921: GARF, r-130/5/642/32–ob.
100 Lezhava–Lomonosov, 23 February 1921: RGAE, 4038/1/99/–. See also Lomonosov, 'Vospominaniia', Vol. 8, pp. 170–1.
101 Lezhava–Lomonosov, 24 February 1921: RGAE, 4038/1/99/–; Nikitin, 'Razrabotka i osushchestvlenie Kommunisticheskoi partiei vneshneekonomicheskoi politiki', pp. 225–6.
102 Lomonosov, *Predvaritel'nyi otchet*, 'Prilozhenie V', p. 1.

6 The new order

1 Memorandum by Peters, 26 May 1921: *BDFA*, Vol. V, pp. 125–6.
2 For instance, Nove, *Economic History*, pp. 81–2; Service, *Lenin*, pp. 178, 185, 207.
3 Quoted in S. White, *Britain and the Bolshevik Revolution*, pp. 55–6.
4 Service, *Lenin*, pp. 177–8.
5 Ibid., p. 183.
6 Memorandum by Peters, 26 May 1921, and interview with Lomov, 9 May 1921: *BDFA*, Vol. V, pp. 125–6, 129.
7 Quoted in S. White, *Britain and the Bolshevik Revolution*, p. 55.
8 On the introduction of the NEP see, for instance, Carr, *Bolshevik Revolution*, Vol. II, pp. 269–359.

9 See Westwood, *History of Russian Railways*, pp. 199–225; Argenbright, 'The Russian Railroad System', pp. 400–84.
10 Nove, *Economic History*, pp. 87–8. On the problem faced by the NKPS, see, for example, protocol of NKPS Collegium meeting, 1 December 1921: RGAE, 1884/28/7/78.
11 See, for instance, Carr, *Bolshevik Revolution*, Vol. II, pp. 283–7; also *Pravda*, 4 March 1921, p. 2. The Relief Administration's activities are discussed in Weissman, *Herbert Hoover and Famine Relief*. See also C. White, *British and American Commercial Relations*, pp. 178–81.
12 On Soviet–American economic relations in 1921–33 see White, *British and American Commercial Relations*, pp. 170–224, and Siegel, *Loans and Legitimacy*, pp. 62–138.
13 Stomoniakov is the subject of Iordanov, *Krasnyi ekselents*. The development of relations with Germany, Norway, Czechoslovakia and Sweden is detailed in, for instance, Shishkin, *Sovetskoe gosudarstvo*, pp. 258–68, 272–7, 280–2.
14 *Krasnaia gazeta*, 15 May 1921, p. 1.
15 Protocol of NKVT Collegium meeting, 7 May 1921: RGAE, 413/2/242/32.
16 On the role of the Genoa conference and the Treaty of Rapallo in Soviet–Western relations see S. White, *Origins of Detente*. The conference's proceedings are examined in Fink, *Genoa Conference*, pp. 143–280.
17 For an overview of this debate see O'Connor, *Engineer of Revolution*, pp. 173–87.
18 Ibid., p. 185.
19 For example, Krasin–family, 21 January 1921: IISG, Krasin papers, file 5; Lomonosov, 'Vospominaniia', Vol. 8, p. 148.
20 Lomonosov, 'Vospominaniia', Vol. 9, p. 169. Significantly, Kopp also saw himself as a victim of hostile gossip from Stomoniakov: Kopp–Litvinov, 30 June 1921: AVP, 082/4/8/48–9.
21 Kerzhentsev–Chicherin, 17, 26, 29 April, 1, 2 May 1921: RTsKhIDNI, 17/112/168/17–18, 21–2, 27, 29–ob.
22 Orgburo protocol, 5 May 1921: RTsKhIDNI, 17/112/168/1ob.; NKVT–Railway Mission relations were discussed by the NKVT Collegium on 7 May: protocol of NKVT meeting, 7 May 1921: RGAE, 413/2/242/32. The commission is considered in Lomonosov, 'Vospominaniia', Vol. 8, p. 375. Mikhailov has been identified from S. White, *Soviet Leadership*, p. 5.
23 NKID–Molotov, 9 May 1921: RTsKhIDNI, 17/112/168/31; Orgburo protocol, 9 May 1921: RTsKhIDNI, 17/112/170/2ob.; Lomonosov, 'Vospominaniia', Vol. 8, pp. 385–7.
24 Protocol of TsK commission, 12 May 1921: RTsKhIDNI, 17/112/168/32–ob.; Lomonosov, 'Vospominaniia', Vol. 8, pp. 387–8.
25 Stalin–Lenin, 22 March 1922: RTsKhIDNI, 5/2/268/1–2.
26 O'Connor, *Engineer of Revolution*, pp. 133, 138–40. For examples of Kamenev's position as patron see Lomonosov, 'Dnevnik', Vol. 9, pp. 94–5; and 'Vospominaniia', Vol. 8, pp. 1110–12.
27 See Voikov (NKVT)–Lomonosov, 29 June 1921: in RGAE, 4038/1/34/–; Lomonosov, 'Vospominaniia', Vol. 8, pp. 393–4.

28 Lomonosov, 'Vospominaniia', Vol. 8, p. 445.
29 Lomonosov, 'Dnevnik', Vol. 8, p. 21.
30 Lomonosov, 'Vospominaniia', Vol. 8, pp. 425–37; protocol of meeting, 31 May 1921: RGAE, 4038/1/5/25.
31 On the shipment of the locomotives to Russia see Heywood, 'The Baltic Commercial "Bridge"', pp. 63–85. The uprising is discussed in Smith, *Finland and the Russian Revolution*, pp. 192–207.
32 Confirmation of Lomonosov's removal from the NKPS Collegium is in Makhov–Lomonosov, [December 1920?]: RGAE, 4038/1/13/3. With regard to Lomonosov's thoughts about his future during 1921–2, see, for instance, Lomonosov–Lenin, 7 November 1921: RTsKhIDNI, 5/1/1166/1–2; Lomonosov, 'Dnevnik', Vol. 10, pp. 64–5, 69–73, 87–8, 91.
33 See Lomonosov–Sovnarkom, 22 January 1922: RTsKhIDNI, 5/1/1166/4; protocol of Politburo meeting, 2 February 1922: RTsKhIDNI, 17/3/259/5; Lezhava–Lenin, 3 February 1922, and Lenin–Molotov, [n.d.]: RTsKhIDNI, 558/1/2249/–. The immediate reason cited by Lezhava was a VTsIK resolution, but the problem had deeper roots. According to Lezhava, the whole NKVT Collegium felt that 'it was not possible to work whilst there was such a complete absence of any policy line in the party and supreme organs [of government]'.
34 NKPS report to STO, considered 3 December 1920: RGAE, 1884/31/1944/33–4.
35 *Gudok*, 29 January 1921, p. 3 and 13 January 1921, p. 2; *Ekonomicheskaia zhizn'*, 6 April 1921, p. 2; 17 April 1921, p. 2 and 24 April 1921, p. 2; *Izvestiia*, 10 April 1921, p. 4.
36 See Emshanov/Grinshtein–STO (about the situation in March 1921), [late April 1921?]: RGAE, 1884/68/328/5–9.
37 *Biulleten' Narodnogo kommissariata putei soobshcheniia*, No. 68 (256) (14 April 1921), pp. 3, 8.
38 Protocol of meeting about shock tasks, 9 May 1921: RGAE, 1884/28/2/42–64.
39 See Lomonosov, 'Vospominaniia', Vol. 8, pp. 352–4, 387; protocol of meeting on 6 May 1921: RGAE, 1884/28/5/5; protocols of meetings on 9 May 1921 and 13 May 1921: 1884/28/6/47–8.
40 Credits allocated in 1920–1: RGAE, 4372/11/62/296; protocol of meeting of Sub-Commission for Foreign Trade and Concessions, 18 April 1921: GARF, r-130/5/642/32–ob.; *PPG*, Vol. I, pp. 41, 216 (note 9), 42, 45, 217 (note 12). On the origins of Gosplan's involvement see Lezhava-Kuibysheva, 'Na khoziaistvennom fronte', p. 136.
41 Protocol of meeting of Sub-Commission for Foreign Trade and Concessions, 26 July 1921: RGAE, 4372/11/2/68; also Voikov–Lomonosov, 9 June 1921: in RGAE, 4038/1/34/–; Lomonosov–Krasin, 10 June 1921: 4038/1/15/108; Voikov–Lomonosov, 4 July 1921: in 4038/1/34/–; *PPG*, Vol. I, pp. 51–3, 218 (note 26).
42 Credits allocated in 1920–1: RGAE, 4372/11/62/296; protocol of meeting of Sub-Commission for Foreign Trade and Concessions, 13 May 1921: RGAE,

4372/11/2/10–10a; Voikov–Lomonosov, 4 July 1921: RGAE, 4038/1/34/–; and Neopikhanov, *Planirovanie transporta*, pp. 173–216, 487–8.
43 *Ekonomicheskaia zhizn'*, 12 June 1921, p. 2.
44 Protocols of meetings of Sub-Commission for Foreign Trade and Concessions, 14 June 1921: RGAE, 4372/11/2/32; 28 June 1921: RGAE, 4372/11/2/42ob.; 5 July 1921: RGAE, 4372/11/2/53; 14 July 1921: RGAE, 4372/11/2/64; and 26 July 1921: RGAE, 4372/11/2/68.
45 NKPS–Lomonosov, 11 March 1921: RGAE, 4038/1/15/203.
46 Balkoff–Lomonosov, 21 March 1921: RGAE, 4038/1/104/62.
47 Rockwell (Baldwin)–Bliss (3rd Asst Secretary of State), 12 April 1921; Poole (State Dept, Russian Division)–Dearing (Asst Secretary of State), 18 May 1921; memorandum by Poole, 19 May 1921: all in NARG 59, 1910–29 decimal series, file 661.1115/318.
48 See Poole–Dearing, 5 May 1921; memorandum by Poole, 19 May 1921; Poole–Secretary of State, 30 June 1921: all in NARG 59, 1910–29 decimal series, file 661.1115/333; and Secretary of State–Secretary of War, July 1921; memorandum for Asst Secretary of War, 14 July 1921: both in NARG 407, central decimal files 1917–25, file 453.
49 For example, Fren–Balkoff, 29 April 1921: RGAE, 4038/1/104/33; Klodnitskii–Holm, 16 May 1921: RGAE, 4038/1/107/–.
50 Krasin–Lomonosov, 14 March 1921: RGAE, 4038/1/105/111–12; Krasin–Lomonosov, 31 March 1921: RGAE, 4038/1/105/233–4; Krasin–Lomonosov, 6 April 1921: RGAE, 4038/1/15/161; Report about decapod proposals, [May 1921]: RGAE, 4038/1/105/143–4; Lomonosov–Krasin, 13 June 1921: RGAE, 4038/1/105/131; Krasin–Lomonosov, 14 June 1921: RGAE, 4038/1/105/134; Klodnitskii–Rabinov, 16 June 1921: RGAE, 4038/1/105/137; Telson–Lomonosov, 20 June 1921: RGAE, 4038/1/105/138.
51 The eventual homes of the War Department decapods are shown in Edson, 'Russian Decapods', pp. 70–5. The annulment of the Revalis contract is noted in *DVP*, Vol. II, p. 764 (note 113).
52 The role of intermediaries in US–Soviet trade and gold sales is discussed in C. White, *British and American Commercial Relations*, especially pp. 153–7, 160–9, 194–8. For an example of a railway contract undertaken by an American company see 'A report on the Russian Soviet Bureau in New York', 21 January 1921: NARG 59, 1910–29 decimal series, file 661.1115/251. The statistic for 1921–3 is in *Vneshniaia torgovlia SSSR za 1918–1940gg.*, p. 1064. Some 2,000 more Class Ye locomotives, slightly modified from the First World War design, were built for the USSR by Baldwin and Alco during the Second World War: Rakov, *Lokomotivy otechestvennykh zheleznykh dorog*, pp. 339–41.
53 Protocol of OTK meeting, 10 May 1921: RGAE, 4038/1/46/85; protocol of meeting of Sub-Commission for Foreign Trade and Concessions, 1 July 1921: RGAE, 4372/11/2/48–9; NKPS–Lomonosov, 11 July 1921: in RGAE, 4038/1/47/–; Lomonosov, *Predvaritel'nyi otchet*, pp. 87–93.
54 Lomonosov–Krasin, 14 June 1921: RGAE, 4038/1/15/107; Krasin–Lomonosov, 15 June 1921: RGAE, 4038/1/15/106; Lomonosov–Krasin, 17

August 1921, and resolution by Krasin: RGAE, 4038/1/35/206; Lomonosov, *Predvaritel'nyi otchet*, pp. 91–2; *PPG*, Vol. I, pp. 65, 221 (note 50, which mistakenly indicates 17,000 tankers instead of 1,700); protocol of SNK meeting, 23 August 1921: RTsKhIDNI, 19/1/438/3–4. See also report to STO (by SNK gold commission), November 1921: RTsKhIDNI, 5/1/149/39–ob.

55 Lomonosov, 'Vospominaniia', Vol. 8, pp. 756–7; STO resolution, 28 October 1921: RGAE, 4038/1/37/140; STO resolution, 4 November 1921: RGAE, 4038/1/37/120; Lomonosov, *Predvaritel'nyi otchet*, pp. 92–3; and report to STO (by SNK gold commission), November 1921: RTsKhIDNI, 5/1/149/39–ob. Concerning deliveries see, for instance, Fomin–STO, 27 March 1922: GARF, r-130/6/577/98.

56 For example, *PPG*, Vol. I, pp. 67, 69, 85, 101–2, 222 (note 68); STO resolution, 4 November 1921: RGAE, 4038/1/37/124; STO resolution, 15 February 1922: GARF, r-130/6/1247/227–8.

57 NKVT–Lomonosov, 7 March 1921: RGAE, 4038/1/34/–; *PPG*, Vol. I, p. 142; Chicherin–Kerzhentsev, 21 November 1921: RGAE, 4038/1/19/83; protocols of meetings in Reval, 2, [5?], 6 and 10 December 1921: RGAE, 4038/1/19/84–7; Contract, 20 December 1921: RGAE, 4038/1/19/66–74; Lomonosov, *Predvaritel'nyi otchet*, pp. 96–100. This saga is considered in detail in Heywood, 'Estonia's Industrial Policy'.

58 For greater detail see Heywood, 'The Armstrong Affair', pp. 77–84.

59 Protocol of OTK sub-commission meeting, 25 March 1921: RGAE, 1884/31/1944/93–4; protocol of OTK meeting, 10 May 1921: RGAE, 4038/1/46/85; Lomonosov, 'Vospominaniia', Vol. 8, p. 377, and *Predvaritel'nyi otchet*, p. 78.

60 Irving–Russian Trade Delegation, 10 June 1921, and Krasin–Armstrong Whitworth, 21 June 1921: RGAE, 4038/1/15/110–14. Krasin had two test cases in mind. On 12 May 1921, on the basis of the British government's de facto recognition of the Soviet government, the Court of Appeal overturned a High Court decision awarding a load of Soviet timber to a British claimant and thus gave Soviet property protection from claims; on 13 July a High Court ruling extended similar protection to Soviet gold. These decisions, together with the ending of the UK requirement for export licences for goods destined for Russia, meant that there were no further legal hindrances to Anglo-Soviet trade.

61 NKRKI–SNK, 11 July 1921: RGAE, 413/2/323/83–4.

62 Heywood, 'The Armstrong Affair', pp. 79–80.

63 SNK resolution, 23 August 1921: RTsKhIDNI, 19/1/438/56; protocol of SNK meeting, 23 August 1921: RTsKhIDNI, 19/1/438/3. If the argument of this book is correct, the talks with Armstrongs were not started simply to accelerate the governmental talks and did have an economic motivation. Also, Lenin's presence is unconfirmed. The protocol's attendance list does not include him, and the session is not mentioned in Golikov et al. (eds), *Lenin: Biograficheskaia khronika*, vol. XI, pp. 227–32; further, Lomonosov's diary does not record Lenin's presence: 'Dnevnik', Vol. 8, pp. 74, 76.

However, Lomonosov's memoirs are adamant that Lenin appeared unexpectedly for the first half of the meeting, later leaving Krasin in the chair.
64 SNK resolution, 23 August 1921: RTsKhIDNI, 19/1/438/56.
65 Lomonosov, *Predvaritel'nyi otchet*, p. 79. See also Hodgson–Foreign Office, 24 August 1921: FO 371/6929/99; and Hodgson, Report of Interview with Lomonosov, 25 August 1921: FO 371/6929/110–11.
66 See Lomonosov, 'Dnevnik', Vol. 8, p. 102; 'Vospominaniia', Vol. 8, p. 672–4, and *Predvaritel'nyi otchet*, p. 79; protocol of meeting of London Delegation, 30 September 1921: RGAE, 413/2/323/31–2; Lomonosov, 'Vospominaniia', Vol. 8, pp. 672–4.
67 Protocol of meeting, 3 October 1921: RGAE, 413/2/323/16–20; Lomonosov, 'Vospominaniia', Vol. 8, pp. 682–7.
68 Lomonosov, 'Vospominaniia', Vol. 8, pp. 684, 699–700; report to NKVT, [n.d.]: RGAE, 413/2/323/4. A copy of the contract is at RGAE, 413/2/323/6–11.
69 Preston–Lomonosov, 15 October 1921: RGAE, 413/2/323/12; Lomonosov, 'Vospominaniia', Vol. 8, pp. 704–5.
70 Lomonosov, 'Vospominaniia', Vol. 8, pp. 735, 756; STO resolution, 28 October 1921: RGAE, 4038/1/37/152; extract from STO protocol, 4 November 1921: 4038/1/19/–; STO resolution, 9 November 1921: 4038/1/37/172.
71 Extract from protocol of Gosplan Presidium meeting, 27 August 1921: RGAE, 4372/1/16/26; extract from protocol of meeting of Sub-Commission for Foreign Trade and Concessions, 28 October 1921: RGAE, 4372/1/16/94.
72 Protocol of SNK meeting, 23 August 1921: RTsKhIDNI, 19/1/438/3; *PPG*, Vol. I, pp. 96, 118; Gosplan to report to SNK, 18 October 1921: RGAE, 4372/1/16/79; extract from protocol of meeting of Sub-Commission for Foreign Trade and Concessions, 28 October 1921: RGAE, 4372/1/16/94.
73 Gosplan report to STO, [November 1921]: RGAE, 4372/1/16/112. The currency reserves are discussed below.
74 Extract from protocol of Sub-Commission for Foreign Trade and Concessions, 2 December 1921: RGAE, 4372/1/16/150.
75 *PPG*, Vol. I, pp. 160–2; report to STO, 15 December 1921: RGAE, 4372/1/16/173; draft STO resolution: RGAE, 4372/1/16/180.
76 For Rykov's views (especially about foreign trade) in, for example, the autumn of 1920 see 'Itogi sovetskogo stroitel'stva', in *Narodnoe khoziaistvo*, (November 1920), pp. 2–15; 'Polozhenie promyshlennosti i mery k ee vosstanovleniiu', in *Narodnoe khoziaistvo* (December 1920), pp. 4–10. That military work accounted for considerable resources is hinted at in 'Organizatsiia tiazheloi promyshlennosti iuga Rossii', *Narodnoe khoziaistvo*, No. 13–14 (1920), pp. 30–7, and in 'GOMZA v 1920g.', *Narodnoe khoziaistvo*, No. 3 (1921), pp. 95–114.
77 See *Vestnik glavnogo upravleniia promyshlennosti*, No. 1 (1921), pp. 69–71; *Metallopromyshlennost' respubliki i ee nuzhdy*, pp. 122–3; protocol of meeting of Glavmetall Collegium, 28 October 1921: RGAE, 4086/1/2/79.

78 *Ekonomicheskaia zhizn'*, 27 August 1921, p. 1.
79 Lomonosov, 'Vospominaniia', Vol. 8, pp. 101, 126, 138–40, 208–9, 221, 226, 231; Lomonosov–Krasin, 18 January 1921: RGAE, 4038/1/15/257; minutes of conferences at Trollhättan, 31 January 1921, 1–2 February 1921 and 5–6 February 1921: Nohab papers, F1D, Box 5; Nordiska–Lomonosov, 3 February 1921, and Lomonosov–Nordiska, 6 February 1921: Nohab papers, F1C1, Box 11.
80 *Gudok*, 13 September 1921, p. 2.
81 Krasin, *Vneshtorg i vneshniaia ekonomicheskaia politika*, pp. 7–12.
82 *Ekonomicheskaia zhizn'*, 17 August 1921, p. 1.
83 For instance, protocols of OTK meetings on 26 September and 3 October 1921: RGAE, 1884/31/1944/90–1.
84 *Ekonomicheskaia zhizn'*, 21 October 1921, p. 1, and 10 November 1921, pp. 1–2. On Gosplan's thoughts see *PPG*, Vol. I, p. 220 (note 47), and *Ekonomicheskaia zhizn'*, 18 August 1921, p. 2, and 25 August 1921, p. 2. The OTK's report caused the creation of a special commission for the 'painless cessation' of locomotive and wagon overhauls at VSNKh factories, which reported to the OTK on, for instance, 26 December 1921 and 23 January 1922: RGAE, 1884/68/328/30–ob., 35–ob.
85 *Ekonomicheskaia zhizn'*, 26 November 1921, p. 2.
86 See undated report about the locomotive stock: RGAE, 1637/1/509/80; protocol of NKPS Collegium meeting, 3 December 1921: RGAE, 1884/28/6/175.
87 Report about locomotive stock: RGAE, 1637/1/509/80.
88 Lenin, *PSS*, Vol. XLIV, p. 302.
89 See *Metallopromyshlennost' respubliki i ee nuzhdy*, pp. 5–8.
90 Protocol of OTK meeting, 26 December 1921: RGAE, 1884/68/328/30ob.
91 Protocol of OTK meeting, 9 January 1922: RGAE, 1884/31/1944/107.
92 *Ekonomicheskaia zhizn'*, 18 January 1922, p. 1.
93 Report [by GOMZA, early 1922?]: RGAE, 1637/1/673/31–32ob.
94 Ibid., l.31. The citizen mentioned by GOMZA was probably M. P. Puzanov, an engineer at the NKPS.
95 Ibid., l.32.
96 Protocol of STO meeting, 16 December 1921: RTsKhIDNI, 19/3/277/10.
97 STO resolution, 4 January 1922: RGAE, 4038/1/38/35. See also protocol of STO meeting, 4 January 1922: GARF, r-130/6/1247/3.
98 Protocols of meetings of NKPS Small Collegium, 31 January 1922 and 8 February 1922: RGAE, 1884/28/11/10, 12.
99 See *PPG*, Vol. II, part 1, pp. 58–60, 72.
100 *Biulleten' Tsentral'nogo biuro pechati NKPS*, No. 248/36 (7 March 1922), p. 6; *PPG*, Vol. II, part 1, p. 256 (note 24).
101 Statement to Dzerzhinskii by M. A. Mett and I. Ia. Levin, 6 December 1921: RGAE, 1884/43/600/30–1; meeting about Mozherez, 16 March 1922: 1884/28/600/130–1; meeting about Railway Mission affairs, 30 January 1922: 1884/28/2/247–8. With regard to the sleeping cars, Lomonosov reports that the French government supported the deal which he

negotiated in Paris in late March: 'Vospominaniia', Vol. 8, pp. 973–5, 989, 991, 1001–2. The final outcome is unknown.
102 Minute by Fomin, 21 January 1922, on copy of STO resolution, 4 January 1922: RGAE, 4038/1/38/35; protocol of NKPS Small Collegium meeting, 24 January 1922: RGAE, 1884/28/11/5a; report to STO, No. 38/c [January 1922?]: RTsKhIDNI, 5/1/149/99.
103 Lomonosov, 'Vospominaniia', Vol. 8, p. 897.
104 Ibid., Vol. 8, p. 702.
105 Lomonosov describes his role in these (ultimately fruitless) talks at great length: ibid., Vol. 8, pp. 481–3, 695–6, 726–7, 730–4, 759, 772–88, 860–5, 869–71, 876–80, 910–11, 915, 962–3, 1005. See also protocols of meetings on 11 November 1921 and 18 November 1921, and memorandum by C. Günther, 30 November 1921: SRA UD:1920, HP64 Er, Vol. 2758/I; protocol of meeting of Swedish bankers on 17 January 1922: SRA UD:1920, HP64 Er, Vol. 2758/II; draft contract, [January 1922?]: Nohab papers, F1D, Box 3. See also Carlbäck-Isotalo, 'Pengar eller Politik', pp. 214–17.
106 Protocol of meeting about Railway Mission affairs, 30 January 1922: RGAE, 1884/28/2/246–8.
107 Emshanov–Lomonosov, 10 February 1922: RGAE, 4038/1/6/96; Lomonosov, 'Vospominaniia', Vol. 8, p. 951.
108 Lomonosov, 'Vospominaniia', Vol. 8, p. 1023. See also Postnikov–Dzerzhinskii, 2 October 1922: RGAE, 4038/1/39/93–ob.; Dzerzhinskii–Railway Mission, 7 October 1922: RGAE, 4038/1/39/91; list of credits: RGAE, 4038/1/19/–; Lomonosov, *Predvaritel'nyi otchet*, pp. 105–9.
109 Kerzhentsev–STO, 20 January 1922: RTsKhIDNI, 5/1/149/84 (the one reference to steamships (*parokhody*) is a misprint for steam locomotives (*parovozy*)); TsK secretariat–Bogdanov, 28 January 1922: RTsKhIDNI, 5/1/149/83.
110 Bogdanov–TsK secretariat, 8 February 1922: RTsKhIDNI, 5/1/149/87–ob.; TsK secretariat–Tsiurupa, 13 February 1922: RTsKhIDNI, 5/1/149/82; protocol of Politburo meeting, 22 February 1922: RTsKhIDNI, 17/3/270/2–4.
111 Sokol'nikov–Lenin, 4 February 1922: RTsKhIDNI, 5/1/1372/4; Lenin-Sokol'nikov, 4 February 1922: RTsKhIDNI, 558/22734/8214/1559/1; Sokol'nikov–Lenin, 4 February 1922: RTsKhIDNI, 5/1/1372/3. More detailed information was provided a month later: Sokol'nikov–Lenin, 11 March 1922: RTsKhIDNI, 5/1/1372/5–9.
112 Protocol of Politburo meeting, 22 February 1922: RTsKhIDNI, 17/3/270/2–4.
113 Avanesov–Politburo, 17 March 1922: RTsKhIDNI, 17/84/435/10–18ob.
114 Statement to Politburo, [March 1922]: RGAE, 4038/1/31/31 (first half of text only). A fuller text is in *Odinnadtsatyi s"ezd RKP(b)*, pp. 106–8.
115 Gorbunov–Krzhizhanovskii/Fomin/Krasin, 6 March 1922: RTsKhIDNI, 5/1/149/94; Fomin–Gorbunov, 13 March 1922 (note on copy of report by Emshanov to STO No. 38/c [January 1922]): RTsKhIDNI, 5/1/149/99; report by Gosplan Transport Section, and note from Krzhizhanovskii to

Gorbunov, 10 March 1922: RTsKhIDNI, 5/1/149/97–8; Krasin–Gorbunov, 8 March 1922: RTsKhIDNI, 5/1/149/95.
116 Tsiurupa–Krzhizhanovskii, 14 March 1922: RTsKhIDNI, 5/1/149/100; summary of resolution of STO commission, 16 March 1922: RTsKhIDNI, 76/2/76/34; Firsov (Gosplan)–Gorbunov, 17 March 1922: RTsKhIDNI, 5/1/149/104.
117 Protocol of Politburo meeting, 20 March 1922: RTsKhIDNI, 17/3/283/4; draft STO resolution: RTsKhIDNI, 17/3/283/20; summary of TsK plenum resolution, 25 March 1922: RTsKhIDNI, 76/2/76/35. Stalin outlined his views about Krasin to Lenin in: Stalin–Lenin, 22 March 1922: RTsKhIDNI, 5/2/268/1–2.
118 Shliapnikov's speech is in *Odinnadtsatyi s"ezd RKP(b)*, pp. 101–9. For Trotskii's and Lenin's comments see ibid., pp. 130–1 and pp. 139–49 respectively. (These published speeches have not been compared with the original minutes.)
119 *Pravda*, 30 March 1922, pp. 1, 3; *Ekonomicheskaia zhizn'*, 2 April 1922, p. 5.
120 GOMZA proposal, [8 April 1922?]: RGAE, 4038/1/31/26–9; GOMZA–Bogdanov, 19 April 1922: RGAE, 1637/1/509/345–6; draft report to STO, [April 1922?]: RGAE, 1637/1/509/347–ob.
121 See, for instance, protocols of Collegium meetings, 1 and 26 March 1922: RGAE, 1884/28/11/17ob., 22; theses of reports by NKPS Finance Directorate, 30 May 1922: RGAE, 1884/28/14/50–7; protocol of Collegium meeting, 31 May 1922: RGAE, 1884/28/11/24.
122 See VSNKh report to STO, 2 May 1922: RGAE, 4038/1/31/25; Bogdanov–Lomonosov, 11 May 1922: RGAE, 4038/1/31/24; a copy of Rykov's submission to the Politburo is in: Lomonosov, 'Vospominaniia', Vol. 8, pp. 1171–2. For the NKPS response to the VSNKh report see: RGAE, 4038/1/31/22–23ob.
123 Bogdanov–Lomonosov, 11 May 1922: RGAE, 4038/1/31/24; protocol of STO meeting, 19 May 1922: GARF, r-130/6/1248/266. Ikonnikov has noted the involvement of NKRKI in this affair, though implying that it took place in 1921: *Organizatsiia i deiatel'nost' RKI*, pp. 79–80.
124 Summary of Politburo decision: RTsKhIDNI, 76/2/76/35; Lomonosov, 'Dnevnik', Vol. 9, pp. 94–5, 101.
125 *Pravda*, 9 June 1922, p. 1, and 29 June 1922, p. 1.
126 Protocols of meetings of Gosplan Industry Section commission, 1 and 10 June 1922: RGAE, 4372/9/61/121–2 and 113–14; Lomonosov, 'Vospominaniia', Vol. 8, pp. 1163–5; *PPG*, Vol. II, part 1, pp. 222–4.
127 Protocol of meeting on 10 June 1922: RGAE, 4372/9/61/113–4; Lomonosov, 'Dnevnik', Vol. 9, p. 111; and Lomonosov, 'Vospominaniia', Vol. 8, pp. 1164–5.
128 Lomonosov, 'Vospominaniia', pp. 1163–4. See also protocol of meeting on 1 June 1922: RGAE, 4372/9/61/121–2; *PPG*, Vol. II, part 1, p. 217.
129 *PPG*, Vol. II, part 1, pp. 222–4.
130 Protocol of Politburo meeting, 8 June 1922: RTsKhIDNI, 17/3/296/1; Lomonosov, 'Dnevnik', Vol. 9, pp. 102–4, 108, 112.

131 Protocol of Politburo meeting, 15 June 1922: RTsKhIDNI, 17/3/298/1–2, 5. Lomonosov, who was not present at the Politburo meeting, interpreted his inclusion in the commission as an attempt to discredit him: 'Dnevnik', Vol. 9, pp. 113–14; and 'Vospominaniia', Vol. 8, p. 1177.
132 Litvinov–Kerzhentsev, 16 June 1922: RTsKhIDNI, 76/2/76/12–16.
133 See protocol of NKPS Collegium meeting, 14 June 1922: RGAE, 1884/28/11/29; report to NKPS Collegium, 30 June 1922: RGAE, 1884/28/10/196–200; *PPG*, Vol. II, part 1, pp. 243–5; and also *Ekonomicheskaia zhizn'*, 15 June 1922, p. 4.
134 The NKPS report is discussed by VSNKh in a submission to STO: RGAE, 4372/9/61/93–ob.; the NKPS position was attacked by Glavmetall in a report dated 22 June 1922: RGAE, 4372/9/61/75–ob. See also extract from protocol of meeting of Gosplan Presidium, 29 June 1922: RGAE, 4372/9/61/90; protocols of meetings of Industry Section commission on 1 and 7 July 1922: RGAE, 4372/9/61/88–9 and 83–4; *PPG*, Vol. II, part 1, pp. 243–6 (Gosplan Presidium meetings, 13 and 18 July); report by Neopikhanov, 18 July 1922: RGAE, 4372/9/61/67; and Neopikhanov, *Planirovanie transporta*, pp. 287–92.
135 See protocols of Politburo meetings on 22 June 1922: RTsKhIDNI, 17/3/299/5; 26 June: RTsKhIDNI, 17/3/300/2; and 29 June: RTsKhIDNI, 17/3/301/1; Lomonosov, 'Dnevnik', Vol. 9, pp. 115–16, 118, 121–2, and 'Vospominaniia', Vol. 8, pp. 1192–6, 1205, 1214–16. Khrennikov's candidacy as a member of the commission was not confirmed by the Politburo until 22 June: see RTsKhIDNI, 76/2/76/35.
136 See Extract from speech of com. Krasin, 17 June 1922: RGAE, 4038/1/120/64; see also Lomonosov, 'Dnevnik', Vol. 9, pp. 116–17, and 'Vospominaniia', Vol. 8, pp. 1199, 1201, 1206–11. Krasin's two main speeches were published in *Biulleten' pervogo soveshchaniia upolnomochennykh NKVT*, No. 2 (18 June 1922), pp. 1–2, and No. 3 (19 June 1922), pp. 1–6; neither text contains the above Extract.
137 Report by Krasin, 27 June 1922: GARF, r-5446/55/508/6–19; Lomonosov, 'Dnevnik', Vol. 9, pp. 123–5, and 'Vospominaniia', Vol. 8, pp. 1217–27.
138 Draft resolution of Politburo commission: RTsKhIDNI, 17/3/301/5; Lomonosov, 'Vospominaniia', Vol. 8, pp. 1228–31, 1237.
139 Protocol of Politburo meeting, 29 June 1922: RTsKhIDNI, 17/3/301/1; SNK resolution, 3 July 1922: GARF, r-130/6/1a/284; protocol of Politburo meeting, 6 July 1922: RTsKhIDNI, 17/3/302/5.
140 Lomonosov, 'Dnevnik', Vol. 9, pp. 125–6, and 'Vospominaniia', Vol. 8, pp. 1230–1.
141 Protocols of meetings between Tsentrosoiuz and Nohab, 8, 11 and 12 July 1922: Nohab papers, F1D, box 1; Lomonosov, 'Dnevnik', Vol. 9, pp. 129–34, 137–9, and 'Vospominaniia', Vol. 8, pp. 1249–52, 1255–8, 1280–1.
142 Lomonosov, 'Dnevnik', Vol. 9, pp. 142–3, and 'Vospominaniia', Vol. 8, pp. 1271–3.
143 Protocol of meeting between Tsentrosoiuz and Nohab, 18 July 1922, and provisional agreement, 26 July 1922: Nohab papers, F1D, box 1; cancella-

tion agreement, 28 July 1922, and extract from contract for delivery of 500 locomotives, 28 July 1922: RGAE, 4038/1/19/–; Lomonosov, 'Dnevnik', Vol. 9, pp. 144–59, and 'Vospominaniia', Vol. 8, pp. 1283–9, 1292–1307.
144 Extract from contract for delivery of 500 locomotives, 28 July 1922: RGAE, 4038/1/19/–.
145 Lomonosov, 'Vospominaniia', Vol. 8, pp. 1304–5, 1307. Trebilcock, *Vickers Brothers*, p. 132, notes that locomotive salesmen commonly paid bribes and sub-commissions.
146 Lomonosov, 'Vospominaniia', Vol. 8, pp. 1313–16.
147 Neopikhanov, *Planirovanie transporta*, p. 293; protocol of STO meeting, 4 August 1922: GARF, r-130/6/1249/249; *PPG*, Vol. II, part 2, pp. 16, 227 (note 8); STO resolution, 24 August 1922: GARF, r-130/6/1249/381; and protocol of STO meeting, 25 August 1922: GARF, r-130/6/1249/372. Glavmetall published the locomotive contract in 1923: *General'nyi dogovor mezhdu Narodnym komissariatom putei soobshcheniia i Glavnym upravleniem gosudarstvennoi metallicheskoi promyshlennosti*.

7 Denouement

1 Lomonosov, 'Vospominaniia', Vol. 8, pp. 1230–1, 1372–3. Iaroslavskii was probably E. M. Iaroslavskii of the NKRKI: Davies et al. (eds), *Government Officials*, p. 404; Medvedev's identity is unclear.
2 Lomonosov, 'Vospominaniia', Vol. 8, pp. 1399–1401, 1415–17, 1420–5, 1465, 1592–3.
3 This assessment is based on a file originally entitled 'Reviziia Missii': RGAE, 4038/1/19.
4 Staff lists by location and citizenship, [September 1922]: RGAE, 4038/1/19/–.
5 Lomonosov–Trotskii/Lezhava/Rykov/Krzhizhanovskii, 4 August 1920: RGAE, 4038/1/33/155.
6 Report by Graftio to Lenin/Kalinin/Zinov'ev/Ivanov, 14 January 1922: RGAE, 4038/1/19/–.
7 See Lomonosov–People's Commissar for Justice, 20 January 1922: RGAE, 4038/1/19/–.
8 Report about turbines, n.d.: RGAE, 4038/1/19/–.
9 See Komgosor–Lomonosov, 17 July 1921, RGAE, 4038/1/19/–; protocol of SNK meeting, 23 August 1921: RTsKhIDNI, 19/1/438/4; Lomonosov–People's Commissar for Justice, 20 January 1922: RGAE, 4038/1/19/–; Lomonosov, 'Vospominaniia', Vol. 8, p. 596.
10 Report by Graftio, 14 January 1922: RGAE, 4038/1/19/–.
11 Ibid.; Krasin–[Kerzhentsev?], 11 January 1922: RGAE, 4038/1/5/5.
12 See Lomonosov, *Predvaritel'nyi otchet*, 'Prilozhenie V', p. 5. For a critical comment by a Soviet historian about this purchase, see Isaev, 'Bor'ba partii za ekonomicheskuiu nezavisimost'', p. 25.
13 Protocol of SNK meeting, 14 March 1922: GARF, r-130/6/1a/37; protocol of SNK meeting, 21 March 1922: GARF, r-130/6/1a/48–9; Fotieva–Lomonosov, 28 March 1922: RGAE, 4038/1/6/22.

14 Lomonosov, 'Vospominaniia', Vol. 8, pp. 1592–3. Krestinskii and Litvinov had also expressed concern about allegedly high salaries: Krestinskii–Lomonosov, 23 November 1921: RGAE, 4038/1/5/15; and Litvinov–Lomonosov, 2 February 1922: RGAE, 4038/1/17/64–5.
15 Lomonosov, 'Vospominaniia', Vol. 8, pp. 1594–5, 1616; *Izvestiia*, 28 December 1922, p. 5.
16 See Lomonosov, 'Dnevnik', Vol. 11, pp. 4–5, 7–8, and 'Vospominaniia', Vol. 8, pp. 1836–7, 1839–40, 1845–56 (list of allegations with Lomonosov's response to each one).
17 See, for example, the lists of faults detected on the first locomotives by spring 1922: RGAE, 4038/1/4/83–4, 137–9. An example of similar criticism of Soviet-built Class E locomotives is: Report to GOMZA Technical Department, 26 March 1923: RGAE, 1637/1/509/302.
18 There is a copy of the contract in: RGAE, 4038/1/19/–.
19 Protocol of Politburo troika meeting, 24 March 1923: GARF, r-5446/55/238/44–5.
20 Lomonosov, 'Dnevnik', Vol. 11, pp. 5, 10–11, and 'Vospominaniia', Vol. 8, p. 1856.
21 Report to SNK: RTsKhIDNI, 5/1/149/201–529.
22 Lomonosov, 'Vospominaniia', Vol. 8, pp. 1191–2.
23 Protocol of Politburo meeting, 29 June 1922: RTsKhIDNI, 17/3/301/1; protocol of Politburo meeting, RTsKhIDNI, 17/3/302/5 (confirmed the decision of 29 June); SNK resolution, 3 July 1922: GARF, r-130/6/1a/284; Lomonosov, 'Vospominaniia', Vol. 8, pp. 1228, 1246–7.
24 Lomonosov, 'Vospominaniia', Vol. 8, pp. 1526, 1535.
25 Lomonosov, 'Dnevnik', Vol. 10, pp. 64, 66, 68–9, and 'Vospominaniia', Vol. 8, pp. 1541–3; protocol of SNK meeting, 31 October 1922: RTsKhIDNI, 19/1/529/2–3. On the Central Committee and control of foreign trade see, for example, Deutscher, *Prophet Unarmed*, pp. 66–8; and O'Connor, *Engineer of Revolution*, pp. 166–87.
26 Extract from protocol of SNK meeting, 9 January 1923: RGAE, 4038/1/20/104; Fomin–Lomonosov, 26 February 1923: RGAE, 4038/1/20/26; extract from protocol of SNK meeting, 13 March 1923: RGAE, 4038/1/20/13; SNK resolution, 29 March 1923: RGAE, 4038/1/20/7–8; Lomonosov, 'Dnevnik', Vol. 10, pp. 174–5, and 'Vospominaniia', Vol. 8, pp. 1772, 1821, 1909–11.
27 Statute for NKPS delegation, [March 1923?]: RGAE, 4038/1/20/100–1.
28 Lomonosov, 'Vospominaniia', Vol. 9, p. 326.
29 Contracts still uncompleted as of 15 April 1923 are indicated in Lomonosov, *Predvaritel'nyi otchet*, 'Prilozhenie V'. The last Nohab locomotive was accepted for shipment by the Russian inspector on 15 December 1924: RGAE, 1884/70/3/26, 52.
30 The financial problems are discussed in: report by Rudyi, [March 1924]: GARF, r-5446/55/505/62–5; Rudyi–Rudzutak, 22 March 1924: GARF, r-5446/55/505/68–72; Rudzutak–Politburo, [April 1924]: GARF, r-5446/55/505/73–5; report about implementation of Tsentrosoiuz and Soviet

government orders in Sweden, 1920–5: RGAE, 1884/70/3/36–52. The date of the final shipment is confirmed in RGAE, 1884/70/4/142.
31. NKPS–Gosplan Sub-Commission for Foreign Trade, 6 February 1923: RGAE, 4372/9/130/29ob.–32; Gosplan Industry Section–Gosplan Transport Section, 1 March 1923: RGAE, 4372/9/130/25–ob.; extract from protocol of meeting of Gosplan Transport Section, 3 March 1923: RGAE, 4372/9/130/23.
32. Lomonosov, 'Vospominaniia', Vol. 8, p. 1345; the Vitkovice firm has been identified from Teichova, *Economic Background to Munich*, p. 112.
33. See Rykov–Lomonosov/NKVT/NKPS, 4 October 1922: RGAE, 4038/1/21/103; Dzerzhinskii–Bogdanov, 11 October 1922: RGAE, 4038/1/21/108; Dzerzhinskii–Rykov/Kamenev, 11 October 1922: RGAE, 4038/1/21/107; protocol of SNK meeting, 31 October 1922: RTsKhIDNI, 19/1/529/1–2; Lomonosov, 'Vospominaniia', Vol. 8, pp. 1372, 1384, 1409, 1539–40, 1591. The NKPS protested against Sovnarkom's decision (taken on 16 November 1922), and the issue was referred to the NKRKI and so-called Small Sovnarkom. In meetings on 2 and 5 January 1923 the NKPS maintained that only a small quantity of parts was needed, and wanted a special gold allocation for them. But on 9 February the Small Sovnarkom included the parts in the NKPS quarterly domestic purchasing plan. See report by Chernov (Glavmetall) to VSNKh Presidium, 30 April 1923: RGAE, 4086/1/179/16.
34. Lomonosov, 'Vospominaniia', Vol. 8, p. 1666, and Vol. 9, p. 89. The contract's termination is discussed in Heywood, 'Estonia's Industrial Policy'.
35. Lomonosov, 'Vospominaniia', Vol. 8, pp. 1655, 1763.
36. Ibid., Vol. 8, pp. 1824–6 and Vol. 9, pp. 7, 89, 92, 99, 495.
37. Ibid., Vol. 8, pp. 1371, 1386, 1426, 1432–8, 1471, 1478; minutes of meetings on 29 September 1922 and 4 October 1922, protocol of meeting of special commission, 2 October 1922: in Nohab papers, F1D, box 5.
38. Soviet dieselisation debates in the 1920s and Lomonosov's involvement are discussed in Westwood, *Soviet Locomotive Technology*, pp. 14–22, 34–74.
39. Lomonosov and Shveter, *Proekty teplovozov*, pp. 16–20, 'Prilozheniia I–III'; Lomonosov, *Predvaritel'nyi otchet*, 'Prilozhenie V', pp. 10–11; Lomonosov–Dzerzhinskii, 17 May 1921, and resolution by Emshanov, 19 August 1921: RGAE, 4038/1/46/50.
40. For Lomonosov's view of his quarrel with Shelest see Lomonosov and Shveter, *Proekty teplovozov*, pp. 16–18 and 'Prilozhenie II', pp. 9–22. The Shelest family's version is in Goriacheva and Shelest, *Aleksei Nesterovich Shelest*, pp. 44–74. For criticism of both parties see Westwood, *Soviet Locomotive Technology*, pp. 47–8.
41. Lomonosov, *Teplovoz Iu^E No. 001*; Lomonosov and Shveter, *Proekty teplovozov*, pp. 119–29; Rakov, *Lokomotivy otechestvennykh zheleznykh dorog*, pp. 359–62. Another diesel-electric locomotive was designed by Professor Gakkel' and built concurrently in Petrograd but was not a success: ibid., pp. 356–9.

42 Westwood, *Soviet Locomotive Technology*, pp. 67–71; Rakov, *Lokomotivy otechestvennykh zheleznykh dorog*, pp. 362–4.
43 This publication is *Vneshniaia torgovliia SSSR za 1918–1940gg*.
44 Weissman, *Herbert Hoover and Famine Relief*, pp. 198–9.
45 Dohan, 'Foreign Trade', p. 321. A full account of the reserve's depletion, including non-trade expenditure, has yet to appear.
46 These changes are analysed in Heywood, 'Change in the Russian and Soviet Steam Locomotive Stock'. For present purposes the main statistical sources are: *Statisticheskii sbornik Ministerstva putei soobshcheniia*; and *Materialy po statistike putei soobshcheniia (vypusk 53-i)*. The first main Soviet-era products were redesigns of the E and S classes, known as E^U and S^U; the 'u' denoted 'strengthened' (*usilennyi*).
47 *Statisticheskii sbornik Ministerstva putei soobshcheniia*, Table IIIA, p. 8; *Materialy po statistike putei soobshcheniia (vypusk 53-i)*, pp. 36–9.
48 *Statisticheskii sbornik Ministerstva putei soobshcheniia*, Table IIIA, p. 8, and 'Prilozhenie k tablitse IIIA i V', p. 4; *Materialy po statistike putei soobshcheniia (vypusk 53-i)*, pp. 2, 5–6. See also Heywood, 'Change in the Russian and Soviet Steam Locomotive Stock', pp. 30, 37.
49 See Heywood, 'Change in the Russian and Soviet Steam Locomotive Stock', pp. 32–4.
50 See ibid., pp. 33–4. With regard to the Class Ye, only 744 out of the 881 dispatched from the USA were in stock because (i) eight were lost at sea in 1915, (ii) 124 of those sent in 1918–19 were on the Chinese Eastern Railway, and (iii) losses of parts meant that not all the thirty engines sent to Novorossisk could be assembled. See chapter 1, note 156.
51 *Statisticheskii sbornik Ministerstva putei soobshcheniia*, Table IIIA, pp. 11–13; *Materialy po statistike putei soobshcheniia (vypusk 36-i)*, p. VIII; *Materialy po statistike putei soobshcheniia (vypusk 53-i)*, p. 39; *Materialy po statistike putei soobshcheniia (vypusk 74-i): Chast' II*, p. 14.
52 On Soviet industrialisation discussions in the mid-1920s see Erlich, *Soviet Industrialization Debate*.
53 *General'nyi dogovor mezhdu NKPS i GUMP VSNKh*, pp. 3–6.
54 See Neopikhanov, *Planirovanie transporta*, pp. 501–22; Ianushevskii, *Perspektivy zheleznodorozhnogo khoziaistva*, pp. 8–9, 85–6.
55 Khromov, *Dzerzhinskii na khoziaistvennom fronte*, p. 41.
56 Neopikhanov, *Planirovanie transporta*, pp. 293–9; Khromov, *Dzerzhinskii na khoziaistvennom fronte*, pp. 41–8.
57 Meeting of VSNKh Main Concession Committee, 14 March 1923: RGAE, 1884/43/600/273–6; report about Mozherez, 10 April 1923: RGAE, 1884/43/600/284–6.
58 *XXXIII soveshchatel'nyi s''ezd inzhenerov podvizhnogo sostava*, pp. 257–63.
59 Neopikhanov, *Planirovanie transporta*, p. 298.
60 On the scissors crisis see, for instance, Nove, *Economic History*, pp. 93–6; Khromov, *Dzerzhinskii na khoziaistvennom fronte*, p. 68.
61 See, for example, Dzerzhinskii, *Izbrannye proizvedeniia*, Vol. 1, pp. 356–60; Dzerzhinskii, *V Sovet truda i oborony SSSR: Dokladnaia zapiska po voprosu o*

metallo-promyshlennosti; *Otvet Glavmetalla na dokladnuiu zapisku Narkomputi tov. Dzerzhinskogo v STO ot 20/XI-1923 goda*; Dzerzhinskii, *Doklad Narodnogo komissara putei soobshcheniia tov. Dzerzhinskogo na konferentsii Soiuza zheleznodorozhnikov, 3 dekabria 1923 goda*; and Khromov, *Dzerzhinskii na khoziaistvennom fronte*, pp. 48–50.

62 Khromov, *Dzerzhinskii na khoziaistvennom fronte*, pp. 50–1. The special government commission is discussed separately in ibid., pp. 108–16.
63 Ibid., pp. 51–3. Traffic statistics are given in Westwood et al., 'The Railways', p. 312.
64 The modernisation debate is the focus of Nagatsuna, 'A Utopian Ideologue'. See also Westwood, *History of Russian Railways*, pp. 226–80, for an overview of the period, and Rees, *Stalinism and Soviet Rail Transport*.
65 Westwood, 'Transport', p. 158.
66 Ibid., p. 168.
67 Lewis, 'Foreign Economic Relations' provides a good overview of the main issues and trends.
68 Lomonosov and Shveter, *Proekty teplovozov*, 'Prilozhenie III', p. 110.
69 Lomonosov's later life is described in Aplin, 'Lomonosov', pp. xviii–xx.
70 Krasovskii's fall is considered in Nagatsuna, 'A Utopian Ideologue', pp. 9–10. The 'Shakhty' affair involved the arrest and trial of fifty-five people in the mining industry, mostly non-party technical specialists, on charges of counter-revolutionary sabotage. One allegation was the deliberate purchase of unsuitable or unnecessary machinery, and five of the accused were executed. The information about Borisov was obtained in conversation with N. A. Zenzinov in December 1996.
71 For example: *Soveshchanie Stakhanovtsev–Krivonosovtsev*, pp. 157–8. On the fate of Dobrovol'skii and other NKPS engineers, see Westwood, *Soviet Locomotive Technology*, pp. 66, 221 (note 59).
72 The deaths of Lezhava, Krestinskii, Kerzhentsev and Fomin are recorded in Davies et al. (eds), *Government Officials*, pp. 290, 310, 321, 330. Emshanov's death is dated in Lenin, *PSS*, Vol. LI, p. 495.
73 Report about implementation of Tsentrosoiuz and Soviet government orders in Sweden, 1920–5: RGAE, 1884/70/4/142. The locomotive's service details are from: Technical Passport of Steam Locomotive 4444, Class E^{SH} (courtesy of the Traction Directorate, Ministry of Ways of Communication of the Russian Federation).

Bibliography

Unpublished sources

Archival collections

Arkhiv vneshnei politiki Rossiiskoi Federatsii, Moscow

Fond 04 Sekretariat narkoma inostrannykh del SSSR G. V. Chicherina
Fond 082 Referentura po Germanii
Fond 140 Referentura po Shvetsii

Cambridge University Library, Cambridge

Vickers Archive

Friedrich Krupp GmbH, Historisches Archiv, Essen

Werksarchiv IV 1361 Niederschrift von Hagemann: Russisches Lokomotivgeschäft, 1920–1937

Gosudarstvennyi arkhiv Rossiiskoi Federatsii, Moscow

Fond 1779 Kantseliariia Vremennogo pravitel'stva
Fond 7742 Ministerstvo putei soobshcheniia Vremennogo pravitel'stva
Fond r-130 Sovet narodnykh komissarov RSFSR
Fond r-1235 Vserossiiskii tsentral'nyi ispolnitel'nyi komitet
Fond r-4085 Narodnyi komissariat raboche-krest'ianskoi inspektsii RSFSR
Fond r-5446 Sovet narodnykh komissarov SSSR
Fond r-5674 STO pri SNK SSSR
Fond r-6751 STO pri SNK RSFSR
Fond r-6941 Materialy OTK pri STO RSFSR

Hoover Institution, Stanford, Calif.

M. V. Bernatskii papers
W. L. Darling papers
George H. Emerson papers

Benjamin O. Johnson papers
M. Laserson papers
John F. Stevens papers
Russia: Posol'stvo (U.S.)

House of Lords Record Office, London

Historical Collection 187: Davidson papers
Historical Collection 191: Bonar Law papers
Historical Collection 192: Lloyd George papers

Internationaal Instituut voor Sociale Geschiedenis, Amsterdam

L. B. Krasin papers

Landsarkivet, Gothenburg

Nydqvist & Holm AB papers

Leeds District Archive, Leeds

Acc. 1839 Papers relating to the Leeds Forge Company Ltd

Leeds Russian Archive, University of Leeds, Leeds

MS 716 G. V. Lomonossoff Collection:
   'Vospominaniia' Vol. 5 ('Na Fontanke, 1912–1917'), MS 716.2.1.5
   Vol. 6 ('Komandirovka v Ameriku, 1917–1919'), MS 716.2.1.6
   Vol. 7 ('V Evrope bez Risy, 1919–1920'), MS 716.2.1.7
   Vol. 8 ('Zheleznodorozhnaia Missiia, 1920–1923'), MS 716.2.1.8
   Vol. 9 ('Postroika i ispytanie teplovozov, 1923–1926'), MS 716.2.1.9
   'Dnevnik' Vols. 4–6 MSS 716.3.4, 716.3.5, 716.3.6
   Vols. 8–11 MSS 716.3.7, 716.3.8, 716.3.9, 716.3.10

Library of Congress, Washington, D.C.

Newton D. Baker papers
John F. Stevens papers

National Railway Museum, York

Materials relating to Sir W. G. Armstrong Whitworth & Company Ltd

New York State Archives, State Education Dept, Albany, N.Y.

Lusk Committee papers (photocopies in Leeds Russian Archive, MS 716, Appendix 2)

Bibliography

Public Record Office, London

ADM 233 Admiralty, Wireless News 1918–21
BT 90 Advisory Committee to the Department of Overseas Trade
BT 197 Board of Trade Advisory Council
BT 198 Board of Trade Council
CAB 23 Cabinet Minutes
CAB 24 Cabinet Memoranda
ECG 1 Export Credits Advisory Committee
FO 368 Foreign Office, Trade and Commercial Correspondence
FO 371 Foreign Office, General Political Correspondence
GFM 34 German Foreign Ministry papers

Rossiiskii gosudarstvennyi arkhiv ekonomiki, Moscow

Fond 413 Narodnyi komissariat vneshnei torgovli
Fond 1637 GOMZA
Fond 1884 Narodnyi komissariat putei soobshcheniia
Fond 3429 Vysshii sovet narodnogo khoziaistva
Fond 4038 Rossiiskaia zheleznodorozhnaia missiia zagranitsei
Fond 4086 Glavmetall
Fond 4372 Gosplan

Rossiiskii gosudarstvennyi istoricheskii arkhiv, St Petersburg

Fond 31 Komitet po delam metallurgicheskoi promyshlennosti
Fond 120 Sovet predstavitelei parovozostroitel'nykh zavodov
Fond 247 Otdel zagotovlenii MPS

Rossiiskii tsentr khraneniia i izucheniia dokumentov noveishei istorii, Moscow

Fond 5 Sekretariat V. I. Lenina
Fond 17 Tsentral'nyi komitet KPSS
Fond 19 —
Fond 76 F. E. Dzerzhinskii
Fond 137 L. B. Krasin
Fond 158 A. D. Tsiurupa
Fond 159 G. V. Chicherin
Fond 296 V. P. Miliutin
Fond 323 L. B. Kamenev
Fond 355 G. M. Krzhizhanovskii
Fond 558 I. V. Stalin

Svenska Riksarkivet, Stockholm

Utrikesdepartamentets arkiv

Tyne and Wear Archives Service, Newcastle-upon-Tyne
Papers of Sir W. G. Armstrong Whitworth & Company Ltd

United States National Archives, Washington, D.C.
RG 39 Bureau of Accounts (Treasury)
RG 40 Department of Commerce
RG 43 US Participation in International Conferences, Commissions and Expositions
RG 56 Department of the Treasury
RG 59 Department of State
RG 61 War Industries Board
RG 62 Council of National Defense
RG 107 Office of the Secretary of War
RG 165 War Department General and Special Staff
RG 182 War Trade Board
RG 261 Former Russian Agencies
RG 407 Adjutant General

PhD dissertations

Argenbright, R. T., 'The Russian Railroad System and the Founding of the Communist State, 1917–1922' (University of California at Berkeley, 1990).

Breuning, E. C. M., 'German Foreign Policy Between East and West, 1921–1926' (University of Oxford, 1966).

Buchanan, H. R., 'Soviet Economic Policy for the Transition Period: The Supreme Council of the National Economy, 1917–1920' (Indiana University, 1972).

Dohan, M. R., 'Soviet Foreign Trade in the NEP Economy and Soviet Industrialisation Strategy' (Massachusetts Institute of Technology, 1969).

Fithian, F. J., 'Soviet–American Economic Relations, 1918–1933: American Business in Russia during the Period of Non-Recognition' (University of Nebraska, 1964).

Gaworek, N. H., 'Allied Economic Warfare Against Soviet Russia From November 1917 to March 1921' (University of Wisconsin, 1970).

Gregor, R., 'Lenin's Foreign Policy, 1917–1922: Ideology or National Interest?' (University of London, 1966).

Heywood, A. J., 'Reviving Soviet–Western Trade in the Early 1920s: A Study of Soviet Imports of Railway Equipment and Related Contracts' (University of Leeds, 1991).

Himmer, G. R. jnr, 'German–Soviet Economic Relations, 1918–1922' (Johns Hopkins University, 1972).

Hurt, B. E., 'Russian Economic Development, 1881–1914, With Special Reference to the Railways and the Role of the Government' (University of London, 1963).

Iusupov, A. F., 'Anglo-sovetskie ekonomicheskie otnosheniia v 1921–1924gg.' (University of Leningrad, 1982).
Lovtsov, L. V., 'Kommunisticheskaia partiia v bor'be za vosstanovlenie i razvitie zheleznodorozhnogo transporta nashei strany (1921–1925gg.)' (University of Moscow, 1970).
Magerovsky, E. L., 'The People's Commissariat for Foreign Affairs, 1917–1946' (Columbia University, 1975).
Mauerman, A., 'Deiatel'nost' Kommunisticheskoi partii po obespecheniiu raboty zheleznodorozhnogo transporta v pervye gody Sovetskoi vlasti (okt. 1917–1920gg.)' (University of Moscow, 1968).
Morse, W. P., 'Leonid Borisovich Krasin: Soviet Diplomat, 1918–1926' (University of Wisconsin, 1971).
Mueller, G. H., 'The Road to Rapallo: Germany's Relations with Russia, 1919–1922' (University of North Carolina, 1970).
Nikitin, V. I., 'Razrabotka i osushchestvlenie Kommunisticheskoi partiei vneshneekonomicheskoi politiki Sovetskogo gosudarstva so stranami kapitalisticheskogo zapada (1917–1922gg.)' (University of Moscow, 1969).
Priest, L. W., 'The Cordon Sanitaire, 1918–1922' (Stanford University, 1954).
Reilly, P. V., 'Lev Karakhan and the Development of Early Soviet Foreign Policy' (New York University, 1980).
Reitzer, L. F., 'United States–Russian Economic Relations, 1917–1920' (University of Chicago, 1950).
Roley, P. L., 'In Search of an Accommodation: Anglo-Soviet Relations, 1919–1921' (University of Illinois, 1966).
Rotter, S., 'Soviet and Comintern Policy Toward Germany, 1919–1923: A Case Study of Strategy and Tactics' (Columbia University, 1954).
Rudchenko, A. M., 'Istoriia stanovleniia i razvitiia sovetsko-germanskikh ekonomicheskikh otnoshenii (1917–1925gg.)' (University of Moscow, 1972).
St John, J. D., 'John F. Stevens: American Assistance to Russian and Siberian Railroads, 1917–1922' (University of Oklahoma, 1969).
Struger, M., 'Nikolai Nikolaevich Krestinsky and Soviet–German Relations, 1921–1930' (University of Wisconsin, 1973).
Tuve, J. E., 'The Role of Foreign Trade and Foreign Capital in the Development of the USSR to 1927' (Case Western Reserve University, 1970).
White, C. A., 'Prelude to Trade: A Re-assessment of Anglo-American Trade and Commercial Relations with Soviet Russia, 1918–1924' (University of Cambridge, 1988).
Woodward, D. R., 'The West and the Containment of Russia, 1914–1923' (University of Georgia, 1965).

Research papers

Andreev, A. G., 'Deiatel'nost' Sovetskogo biuro v N'iu-Iorke v 1919–1920gg.: K voprosu o sovetsko-amerikanskikh otnosheniiakh v 1917–1920gg.' (Leningrad, 1983; Academy of Sciences INION Library, MS 14,413).
Heywood, A. J., 'Estonia's Industrial Policy, 1920–1924: A View from the East'

(paper presented at the XII Conference on Baltic Studies in Scandinavia, Stockholm, June 1993).

Nagatsuna, K., 'A Utopian Ideologue in Soviet Industrialisation: S. A. Bessonov and Transport Reconstruction Debates, 1928–1930' (paper presented to the Soviet Industrialisation Project Seminar, University of Birmingham, January 1989).

Miscellaneous

Technical passport of E^{SH} No. 4444 (courtesy of the Ministry of Ways of Communication of the Russian Federation).

Published sources

Contemporary newspapers and periodicals

Biulleten' Narodnogo komissariata putei soobshcheniia
Biulleten' pervogo soveshchaniia upolnomochennykh NKVT
Biulleten' Tsentral'nogo biuro pechati NKPS
Dekapod
Economist
Ekonomicheskaia zhizn'
Ekonomist
Gudok
Izvestiia
Izvestiia Petrogradskogo soveta
Krasnaia gazeta
Krasnyi put'
Krasnyi put' zheleznodorozhnika
Mezhdunarodnaia zhizn'
Narodnoe khoziaistvo
Novyi mir
Petrogradskaia pravda
Pravda
Promyshlennost' i torgovlia
Put'
Puti soobshcheniia severa
Russian Economist
Sotsialisticheskoe khoziaistvo
Tekhnika i ekonomika putei soobshcheniia
Times
Transport
Vestnik glavnogo upravleniia promyshlennosti
Vestnik metallopromyshlennosti
Vestnik Narodnogo komissariata inostrannykh del
Vestnik Narodnogo komissariata torgovli i promyshlennosti

Vestnik promyshlennosti i torgovli
Vestnik promyshlennosti i transporta
Vestnik promyshlennosti, torgovli i transporta
Vestnik putei soobshcheniia
Vneshniaia torgovlia
Zheleznodorozhnaia tekhnika i ekonomika
Zheleznodorozhnik

Documents, reports, statistics, contemporary works and memoirs

Akten zur Deutschen Auswärtigen Politik, 1918–1945: Serie A, 1918–1925 (Göttingen: Vandenhoeck & Ruprecht, 1982–).
Analiz sostoianiia transporta na 1–oe oktiabria 1923–24 goda po sravneniiu s sostoianiem na 1–oe oktiabria 1922–23 goda (Moscow, 1924).
Arskii, R., *Metall i ego znachenie v Sovetskoi Rossii* (Peterburg [sic]: Gosudarstvennoe izdatel'stvo, 1920).
  Kontsessii (Rostov na Donu: Gosudarstvennoe izdatel'stvo, 1921).
  Promyshlennoe polozhenie Sovetskoi Rossii i perspektivy tovaroobmena (Peterburg [sic]: Gosudarstvennoe izdatel'stvo, 1921).
  Sostoianie transporta i ego remont (Moscow: Glavpolitput', 1920).
  Transport i prodovol'stvie (Moscow: NKPS, 1920).
  Vosem' let na khoziaistvennom fronte (Leningrad: Priboi, 1925).
Bakh, M. G., *Politiko-ekonomicheskie vzaimootnosheniia mezhdu SSSR i Pribaltikoi za desiat' let (1917–1927)* (Moscow: Izdatel'stvo Kommunisticheskoi akademii, 1928).
Barou, N., *Russian Co-operation Abroad: Foreign Trade, 1912–1928* (London: King, 1930).
Beable, W. H., *Commercial Russia* (London: Constable, 1918).
Bezrukikh, P. E., *Sovetskii transport za desiat' let (1917–1927)* (Leningrad: Krasnaia gazeta, 1927).
Binovich, L. E., *Dostizheniia sovetskogo transporta* (Moscow: Transpechat', 1924).
Boublikoff, A. A. [Bublikov, A. A.], *The Necessity for Russo-American Co-operation in Russian Railway Construction* (New York: Youroveta Home and Foreign Trade Co., 1918).
Buharin, N. and Preobrazhensky, E. [Bukharin, N. I. and Preobrazhenskii, E. A.], *The ABC of Communism: A Popular Explanation of the Program of the Communist Party of Russia* ([n.p.], 1922).
Cameron Watt, D. (ed.), *British Documents on Foreign Affairs: Reports and Papers from the Confidential Print, Part II, Series A: The Soviet Union, 1917–1939*, 15 vols. ([n.p.], 1984–6).
Chernov, A. S., *Metallopromyshlennost' SSSR* (Moscow: Izdanie avtora, 1925).
Chicherin, G. V., *Stat'i i rechi po voprosam mezhdunarodnoi politiki* (Moscow: Izdatel'stvo sotsial'no-ekonomicheskoi literatury, 1961).
Conditions in Russia: Hearings before the Committee on Foreign Affairs, House of Representatives, Sixty-sixth Congress, Third Session on H. Res. 635 requesting the Secretary of State to furnish the House of Representatives certain information

as to conditions in Russia (Washington, DC: Government Printing Office, 1921).

Deiatel'nost' Russkoi [sic] *zheleznodorozhnoi missii zagranitsei* (Berlin, 1921).

'Deiatel'nost' Tsentral'nogo komiteta partii v dokumentakh (sobytiia i fakhty: 3–31 ianvaria, 1920g.', in *Izvestiia TsK KPSS*, No. 8 (1990) pp. 185–99.

Dekrety Sovetskoi vlasti (Moscow: Gosudarstvennoe izdatel'stvo politicheskoi literatury, 1957–).

Dernberg, S., Zaidevits, Kh., Zemskov, I. N. et al. (eds), *Sovetsko-germanskie otnosheniia ot peregovorov v Brest-Litovske do podpisaniia Rapall'skogo dogovora*, 2 vols (Moscow: Izdatel'stvo politicheskoi literatury, 1968–71).

Desiatyi s"ezd RKP(b), mart 1921 goda: Stenograficheskii otchet (Moscow: Gosudarstvennoe izdatel'stvo politicheskoi literatury, 1963).

Deviatyi s"ezd RKP(b), mart–aprel' 1920 goda: Protokoly (Moscow: Gosudarstvennoe izdatel'stvo politicheskoi literatury, 1960).

Doklad Glavnogo upravleniia gosudarstvennoi metallicheskoi promyshlennosti Sovetu truda i oborony: Otvet na dokladnuiu zapisku Narodnogo komissara putei soobshcheniia tov. Dzerzhinskogo (Moscow, 1923).

Dzerzhinskaia, S., *V gody velikikh boev*, 2nd edn (Moscow: Mysl', 1975).

Dzerzhinskii, F. E., *Doklad Narodnogo komissara putei soobshcheniia tov. Dzerzhinskogo na konferentsii Soiuza zheleznodorozhnikov, 3 dekabria 1923 goda* (Moscow: Transpechat', 1923).

Izbrannye proizvedeniia v dvykh tomakh, 2 vols (Moscow: Izdatel'stvo politicheskoi literatury, 1977).

V Sovet truda i oborony SSSR: Dokladnaia zapiska po voprosu o metallopromyshlennosti F. E. Dzerzhinskogo (Moscow: Transpechat', 1923).

Emshanov, A. I., *Tezisy doklada o rabote transporta za 1920–i god* (Moscow, 1921).

Fomin, V. V., *Lenin i transport*, 2nd edn (Moscow: Politizdat, 1973).

Piatiletie sovetskogo transporta 1917–1922gg. i ego blizhaishie perspektivy (Moscow: Ekonomicheskaia zhizn', 1923).

Francis, D. R., *Russia from the American Embassy, April 1916–November 1918* (New York: Charles Scribner's Sons, 1921).

General'nyi dogovor mezhdu Narodnym komissariatom putei soobshcheniia i Glavnym upravleniem gosudarstvennoi metallicheskoi promyshlennosti Vysshego soveta narodnogo khoziaistva po voprosu o novom i remontnom parovozostroenii na zavodakh GUMP VSNKh (Moscow: Izdanie Glavnogo upravlenii gosudarstvennoi metallicheskoi promyshlennosti, 1923).

Godovoi otchet NKID k IX s"ezdu sovetov (1920–1921) (Moscow: Narkomindel, 1921).

Golikov, G. N., Antoniuk, D. I., Mchedlov, M. P. et al. (eds), *Vladimir Il'ich Lenin: Biograficheskaia khronika*, 12 vols (Moscow: Izdatel'stvo politicheskoi literatury, 1970–82).

Golopolosov, A. I., *Obzor zheleznodorozhnogo transporta (po dannym Chrezvychainoi komissii)* (Moscow: NKRKI, 1920).

Gosudarstvennye mashinostroitel'nye zavody (Moscow, 1921).

Gregory, J. D., *On the Edge of Diplomacy: Rambles and Reflections, 1902–28* (London: Hutchinson, 1928).

Grinevetskii, V. I., *Poslevoennye perspektivy russkoi promyshlennosti* (Moscow, 1922).
Problema teplovoza i ee znachenie dlia Rossii (Moscow: Izdatel'stvo Teplotekhnicheskogo instituta, 1923).
Groman, V. G. (ed.), *Gosudarstvennaia promyshlennost' SSSR v 1921–1923gg. i ee finansovoe polozhenie: Opyt izucheniia dinamiki vazhneishikh otraslei russkoi promyshlennosti* (Moscow: Gosudarstvennoe izdatel'stvo, 1925).
Groman, V. G. and Kaufman, M. Ia., *Vneshniaia torgovlia i narodnoe khoziaistvo Rossii: Sbornik statei* (Moscow: Vsia Rossiia, 1923).
Groman, V. G., Kaufman, M. Ia. and Zamengof, M. (eds), *Vneshniaia torgovlia Rossii v 1922–1923 khoziaistvennom godu: (Sbornik statei)* (Moscow: Ekonomicheskaia zhizn', 1923).
Vneshniaia torgovlia SSSR (za 1923 god) (Moscow: Redaktsionno-izdatel'skii otdel NKVT, 1924).
Gromyko, A. A. and Ponomarev, B. N. (eds), *Dokumenty vneshnei politiki SSSR*, 21 vols (Moscow: Gosudarstvennoe izdatel'stvo politicheskoi literatury, 1957–77).
Harcave, S. (trans. and ed.), *The Memoirs of Count Witte: A Portrait of the Twilight Years of Tsarism by the Man who Built Modern Russia* (Armonk, N.Y.: M. E. Sharpe, 1990).
Hilger, G. and Meyer, A. G., *The Incompatible Allies: A Memoir History of German–Soviet Relations, 1918–1941* (New York: Macmillan, 1953).
Ianushevskii, P. S., *Perspektivy zheleznodorozhnogo khoziaistva RSFSR* (Moscow: Izdanie redaktsionno-izdatel'skogo otdela NKPS, 1923).
Il'inskii, D. P. and Ivanitskii, V. P., *Ocherk istorii russkoi parovozostroitel'noi i vagonstroitel'noi promyshlennosti* (Moscow: Transpechat', 1929).
Ioffe, Ia. A., *Organizatsiia interventsii i blokady Sovetskoi respubliki, 1918–1920: Ocherk* (Moscow and Leningrad: Gosizdat, 1930).
Iurovskii, L. N., *Denezhnaia politika sovetskoi vlasti, 1917–1927* (Moscow: Finansovoe izdatel'stvo, 1928).
Ivanovskii, N. V., *Perspektivy zheleznodorozhnogo khoziaistva v Rossii: Doklad VIII vserossiiskomu elektrotekhnicheskomu s''ezdu v Moskve, zaslushannyi 4-go oktiabria 1921g.* (Petrograd, 1921).
Iz opyta sostavleniia plana material'nogo snabzheniia transporta na 1922–23 god (Moscow: Transpechat', [n.d.]).
Kaufman, M. Ia., *Organizatsiia i regulirovanie vneshnei torgovli Rossii* (Moscow and Leningrad: Ekonomicheskaia zhizn', 1925).
Vneshniaia torgovlia Rossii (1918–1921gg.) (Petrograd: Akademicheskoe izdatel'stvo, 1922).
Khromov, S. S., Vaganov, F. M., Anikeev, V. V. et al. (eds), *Protokoly Prezidiuma Vysshego Soveta Narodnogo Khoziaistva (dekabr' 1917g.–1918g.)* (Moscow: Nauka, 1991).
Klemenchich, V., *Itogi raboty zheleznykh dorog za tri goda 1917–1920gg.* (Moscow: Izdanie Tsektrana i Politupravleniia NKPS, 1920).
Komitet po oborudovaniiu russkogo podvizhnogo sostava amerikanskoi stsepkoi: Organizatsionnoe soveshchanie (Moscow, 1920).

Korotkevich, M., *Problema planomernogo vosstanovleniia transporta* (Moscow, 1922).
Koudrey, V., *Once a Commissar* (New Haven, Conn.: Yale University Press, 1937).
Krasin, L. B., *Sovetskii schet inostrannym kapitalistam* (Leningrad: Priboi, 1925).
Vneshtorg i vneshniaia ekonomicheskaia politika sovetskogo pravitel'stva (Peterburg [sic]: Gosudarstvennoe izdatel'stvo, 1921).
Voprosy vneshnei torgovli, 2nd edn (Moscow: Mezhdunarodnye otnosheniia, 1970).
Zachem nam nuzhny vneshnie zaimy (Moscow: Gosudarstvennoe izdatel'stvo, 1925).
Zadachi zheleznodorozhnikov (Moscow: Glavpolitput', 1920).
Krasin, L. B. (comp.), *Narodnyi komissariat putei soobshcheniia za dva goda Revoliutsii: Otchet VII-mu vserossiiskomu s"ezdu sovetov* (Moscow, 1919).
Krasovskii, P., *Evoliutsiia i razvitie tipa parovozov za poslednie 25 let* (Moscow: Sektsiia inzhenerno-tekhnicheskikh rabotnikov Mosk.-Kurskoi zh.d., 1926).
Krassin, Lubov [Krasina, L. V.], *Leonid Krassin: His Life and Work* (London: Skeffington, 1929).
Kratkii obzor deiatel'nosti NKPS v 1920g.: Materialy k dokladu VIII-mu s"ezdu sovetov (Moscow: NKPS, 1921).
Krylov, A. N., *Moi vospominaniia* (Moscow: AN SSSR, 1945).
Kul'zhinskii, S. and El'kin, L., *Parovoznyi park kazennykh zheleznykh dorog: Mery k ego uluchsheniiu v sviazi s sokrashcheniem raskhodov proekta raspredeleniia moshchnykh parovozov tipa 4/5 po seti kazennykh zheleznykh dorog* (St Petersburg, 1910).
Larsons, M. [Lazerson, M. Ia.], *Na sovetskoi sluzhbe: Zapiski spetsa* (Paris: Rodnik, 1930).
V sovetskom labirinte: Epizody i siluety (Paris: Strela, 1932).
Lenin, V. I., *Polnoe sobranie sochinenii*, 5th edn, 55 vols (Moscow: Izdatel'stvo politicheskoi literatury, 1960–5).
Leninskii sbornik, 40 vols. (Moscow: Gosudarstvennoe izdatel'stvo/Izdatel'stvo politicheskoi literatury, 1925–85).
Levi, L. M., *Rasstroistvo zheleznodorozhnogo transporta, ego nedosredstvennye prichiny i prosteishie mery protivodeistviia* (Kiev, 1916).
Lezhava-Kuibysheva, O. A., 'Na khoziaistvennom fronte', in *Istoriia SSSR*, No. 4 (1974), pp. 133–47.
Liberman, S. I. [Libermann, S. I.], *Building Lenin's Russia* (University of Chicago Press, 1945).
Libermann, S. I., *Dela i liudi: Na sovetskoi stroike* (New York: New Democracy Books, 1944).
Lied, J., *Sidelights on the Economic Situation in Russia* (Moscow, 1922).
Lipets, A. I., *Parovozy tipa 'dekapod' (1–5–0), postroennye v Amerike dlia Russkikh kazennykh zheleznykh dorog* (New York, 1920).
Liubimov, V., *Vzaimozameniaemost' chastei parovozov* E^{SH} *i* E^{G} (Berlin, 1923).
Lomonosov, Iu.V., *Parovozy 0–5–0 E, E^{SH}, E^{G}* (Berlin, 1924).

Predvaritel'nyi otchet Iu.V. Lomonosova o deiatel'nosti Rossiiskoi zheleznodorozhnoi missii zagranitseiu za vse vremia ee sushchestvovaniia (1920–1923) (Berlin, 1923).
Teplovoz Iu^E No. 001 i ego ispytanie v Germanii (Berlin, 1925).
Vospominaniia o Martovskoi revoliutsii 1917 goda (Stockholm and Berlin, 1921).
Lomonosov, Iu.V. (ed.), *Perevozka parovozov E^{SH} i E^G iz za-granitsy* (Berlin, 1923).
Lomonosov, Iu.V. and Shveter, E., *Proekty teplovozov, razrabotannye v 1921–1925gg. v Germanii dlia SSSR* (Berlin, 1926).
Lopukhin, V. B., 'Posle 25 oktiabria' (publikatsiia L. Burtseva), in *Minuvshee: Istoricheskii al'manakh*, Vol. I (Paris: Atheneum, 1986), pp. 9–98.
Maiskii, I. M., *Vneshniaia politika RSFSR, 1917–1922* (Moscow: Krasnaia nov', 1922).
Materialy po statistike putei soobshcheniia, vypusk 36-i: Zheleznodorozhnyi transport v 1923/24 operatsionnom godu (Moscow: Transpechat', 1925).
Materialy po statistike putei soobshcheniia, vypusk 53-i: Zheleznodorozhnyi transport v 1924/25 operatsionnom godu (Moscow: Transpechat', 1926).
Materialy po statistike putei soobshcheniia, vypusk 74-i: Zheleznodorozhnyi transport v 1925/26 operatsionnom godu (Moscow: Transpechat', 1927).
Meijer, J. M. (ed.), *The Trotsky Papers*, 2 vols. (The Hague: Mouton, 1964–71).
Metallopromyshlennost' respubliki i ee nuzhdy (Moscow, 1921).
Metallopromyshlennost' SSSR v 1922–1923 operatsionnom godu: Doklad Glavnogo upravleniia gosudarstvennoi metallicheskoi promyshlennosti na VI vserossiiskom s"ezde metallistov v 1923g. (Moscow, 1923).
Mikhailov, I. D., *Doklad o sovremennom sostoianii nashego zheleznodorozhnogo transporta Vserossiiskomu prodovol'stvennomu s"ezdu v Moskve, 21 maia 1917g.* (Petrograd, 1917).
Evoliutsia russkogo transporta, 1913–1925gg. (Moscow: Ekonomicheskaia zhizn', 1925).
Raschet oborudovaniia magistral'nykh zheleznykh dorog v tiagovom otnoshenii: Oborudovanie uchastkov sluzhby tiagi (Petrograd, 1918).
Transport: Ego sovremennoe sostoianie (Moscow, 1919).
Miliutin, V. P., *Narodnoe khoziaistvo Sovetskoi Rossii: (Kratkii ocherk organizatsii upravleniia i polozheniia promyshlennosti Sovetskoi Rossii)* (Moscow, 1920).
Morris, I. N., *From an American Legation in Sweden, 1914–1922* (New York: Alfred A. Knopf, 1923).
MPS, Inzhenernyi Sovet: Zhurnaly Komissii podvizhnogo sostava i tiagi (St Petersburg, 1913–17).
Naporko, A. (comp.), *Zheleznodorozhnyi transport SSSR v dokumentakh Kommunisticheskoi partii i Sovetskogo pravitel'stva* (Moscow: Gosudarstvennoe transportnoe zheleznodorozhnoe izdatel'stvo, 1957).
Narodnyi komissariat putei soobshcheniia: Sbornik statei k S"ezdu sovetov (Moscow, 1920).
Neopikhanov, A. A., *Russkii transport i ego planirovanie* (Moscow and Petrograd: Gosudarstvennoe izdatel'stvo, 1924).
[Nevskii, V. I.], *Doklad ot Narodnogo komissara putei soobshcheniia predsedateliu Soveta narodnykh komissarov tovarishchu Leninu* (Moscow, 1919).

NKPS v 1920 godu: Materialy po rabote Tsentral'nykh uchrezhdenii i mestnykh organov zheleznodorozhnogo i vodnogo transporta (Moscow, 1921).
Novitsky, V. J. [Novitskii, V.], 'The Fate of the Russian Gold Reserve', in *The Russian Economist*, Vol. 1, No. 2 (1921), pp. 346–57.
Obzor sostoianiia i raboty transporta v 1921 godu: Materialy k dokladu IX-mu s"ezdu sovetov (Moscow, 1921).
Odinnadtsatyi s"ezd RKP(b), mart-aprel' 1922 goda: Stenograficheskii otchet (Moscow: Gosudarstvennoe izdatel'stvo politicheskoi literatury, 1961).
Ostapenko, S. S., *Transport i voina* (Ekaterinoslav, 1916).
Otchet o deiatel'nosti Glavnoi inspektsii putei soobshcheniia Respubliki za 1921 god i plan rabot na 1922 god (Moscow, 1922).
Otchet o deiatel'nosti Narodnogo komissariata vneshnei torgovli (s 15–go maia po 15–e noiabria 1920g.) (Moscow: Gosudarstvennoe izdatel'stvo, 1920).
Otchet OTK v Sovet truda i oborony za dekabr' i 2–iu polovinu 1920g. (Moscow, 1921).
Otvet Glavmetalla na dokladnuiu zapisku Narkomputi tov. Dzerzhinskogo v STO ot 20/XI-1923 goda (Moscow, 1923).
Papers Relating to the Foreign Relations of the United States (Washington, DC: Government Printing Office, 1864–).
Pasvolsky, L. and Moulton, H. G., *Russian Debts and Russian Reconstruction: A Study of the Relation of Russia's Foreign Debts to Her Economic Recovery* (New York: McGraw-Hill, 1924).
Petrusevich, G. I., *Istoriia razvitiia zheleznodorozhnykh gruzovykh potokov s 80–kh godov* (Moscow: Transpechat', 1930).
Rabota zheleznodorozhnogo transporta s oktiabria 1922g. po mart 1924g. (Moscow: Transpechat', 1924).
Rapoport, A. Iu., *Sovetskoe torgpredstvo v Berline: Iz vospominanii bespartiinogo spetsa* (New York, 1981).
Rogovskii, N. I., Akhapkin, Iu. A, Grechishnikov, P. V. et al. (eds), *Protokoly Prezidiuma Gosplana za 1921–1922 gody* (Moscow: Ekonomika, 1979).
Rozvadovskaia, M. F. and Slutskaia, V. M. (eds), *Rytsar' revoliutsii: Vospominaniia sovremennikov o Felikse Edmundoviche Dzerzhinskom* (Moscow: Izdatel'stvo politicheskoi literatury, 1967).
Russian Government's Plan of Future Railroad Construction (New York: Youroveta Home and Foreign Trade Co., [n.d.]).
Russkaia promyshlennost' v 1922 godu: (Materialy k 10–mu s"ezdu sovetov) (Moscow: Redaktsionno-izdatel'skii otdel VSNKh, 1923).
Rykov, A. I., *Stat'i i rechi*, 2 vols. (Leningrad: Gosudarstvennoe izdatel'stvo, 1927–8).
Sarab'ianov, V. N., *Metallopromyshlennost' Rossii* (Moscow: Gosudarstvennoe izdatel'stvo, 1921).
Shatunovskii, Ia., *Obshchie printsipy organizatsii remonta i postroiki parovozov v sviazi s khoziaistvennym i trudovym polozheniem Sovetskoi Rossii* (Moscow: NKPS, 1920).
  Vosstanovlenie transporta: Puti soobshcheniia i puti revoliutsii (Moscow and Petrograd, 1920).

Shcheglovitov, V. N. and Karelin, P. P., *Transport: Doklady V. N. Shcheglovitova i P. P. Karelina obshchemu sobraniiu ispolnitel'nogo komiteta Moskovskogo okruga, 15 aprelia 1917 goda* (Moscow, 1917).
Shchukin, N., *Istoricheskii ocherk deiatel'nosti Komissii podvizhnogo sostava i tiagi pri Inzhenernom sovete* (Petrograd, [n.d.]).
Shmukker, M. M., *Finansy kazennoi seti zheleznykh dorog Rossii v sviazi s biudzhetom (1890–1913gg.)* (Vol'sk, 1913).
Ocherki finansov i ekonomiki zheleznodorozhnogo transporta Rossii za 1913–1922 gody (Moscow: Transpechat', 1923).
Shtein, B. E., *Torgovaia politika i torgovye dogovory Sovetskoi Rossii, 1917–1922gg.* (Moscow and Petrograd: Gosudarstvennoe izdatel'stvo, 1923).
Vneshniaia torgovaia politika SSSR (Moscow and Leningrad: Tsentral'noe upravlenie pechati VSNKh SSSR, 1925).
Sidorov, A. L., Volobuev, P. V., Gaponenko, L. S. et al. (eds), *Ekonomicheskoe polozhenie Rossii nakanune Velikoi oktiabr'skoi sotsialisticheskoi revoliutsii: Dokumenty i materialy, mart–oktiabr' 1917g.*, 3 vols (Moscow: AN SSSR, 1957–67).
Solomon, G. A., *Among the Red Autocrats: My Experience in the Service of the Soviets* (New York: Our Hope, 1935).
Soveshchanie Stakhanovtsev–Krivonosovtsev zheleznodorozhnogo transporta (Moscow: Partizdat TsK VKP(b), 1936).
Stalin, I. V., *Sochineniia*, Vol. V (Moscow: Gosudarstvennoe Izdatel'stvo Politicheskoi Literatury, 1947).
Statisticheskii sbornik Ministerstva putei soobshcheniia (vypusk sto sorok pervyi): Zheleznye dorogi v 1913g., Chast' I (Petrograd, 1916).
Svedeniia i materialy o rabote zheleznykh dorog RSFSR v 1919 i 1920gg.: Sostavlennye na mart 1920 goda (Moscow, 1920).
Sverdlov, V. M., *Doklad V. M. Sverdlova o polozhenii russkikh zheleznykh dorog i o merakh, neobkhodimykh dlia vosstanovleniia transporta* (Moscow, 1920).
Vse na transport! (Moscow, 1920).
Toplivosnabzhenie i transport v 1921g. (Moscow, 1922).
Troianovskii, A. (ed.), *Nasha trestirovannaia promyshlennost'* (Moscow: NKRKI, 1922).
Trotskii, L. D., *Sochineniia*, 12 vols (Moscow and Leningrad: Gosudarstvennoe izdatel'stvo, 1925–7).
Trotsky, L. [Trotskii, L. D.], *My Life* (New York: Grosset and Dunlap, 1960).
Trudy XXXIII soveshchatel'nogo s"ezda inzhenerov sluzhby puti russkikh zheleznykh dorog 1922 goda (Moscow: NKPS Transpechat', [n.d.]).
Trudy XXXII-go soveshchatel'nogo s"ezda inzhenerov sluzhby tiagi (Moscow, 1923).
Trudy XXXIV soveshchatel'nogo s"ezda inzhenerov podvizhnogo sostava i tiagi v Moskve s 1-go po 9-oe aprelia 1925 goda (Moscow, 1924).
XXXIII soveshchatel'nyi s"ezd inzhenerov podvizhnogo sostava i tiagi v Moskve, 18 iiunia 1923 goda (Moscow, 1924).
Vauclain, S. M., *Steaming Up!* (San Marino, Calif.: Golden West Books, 1973).
'Vedomost' ob importe metallicheskikh izdelii v RSFSR (1920–1924gg.)', in *Istoricheskii arkhiv*, No. 5 (1960), pp. 117–21.

Vinogradov, L. K. and Kut'ev, V. F. (comps), 'Dokumenty F. E. Dzerzhinskogo po khoziaistvennym voprosam (1922–1926gg.): Dokumenty Instituta marksizma-leninizma pri TsK KPSS', in *Istoricheskii arkhiv*, No. 2 (1960), pp. 44–91.

Vneshniaia torgovlia Rossii za pervuiu tret' 1922g. (Moscow: Izdanie NKVT, 1922).

Vneshniaia torgovlia RSFSR (s dekabria 1920 po dekabr' 1921g.): Otchet k IX-mu vserossiiskomu s"ezdu sovetov (Moscow, 1921).

Vneshniaia torgovlia SSSR: Statisticheskii sbornik, 1918–1966 (Moscow: Mezhdunarodnye otnosheniia, 1967).

Vneshniaia torgovlia SSSR za 1918–1940gg.: Statisticheskii obzor (Moscow: Vneshtorgizdat, 1960).

Vserossiiskii s"ezd rabotnikov zheleznodorozhnogo i vodnogo transporta: Materialy k predstoiashchemu s"ezdu (Moscow, 1921).

Woodward, E. L. and Butler, R. (eds), *Documents on British Foreign Policy, 1919–1939: First Series*, 27 vols (London: HMSO, 1946–86).

Zakliuchenie Prezidiuma VSNKh po dokladu Glavmetalla i NKPS (Moscow, 1923).

Zheleznodorozhnyi i vodnyi transport v 1921–1922gg.: Otchet NKPS ko 2–mu vserossiiskomu s"ezdu ob"edinennogo soiuza rabotnikov zheleznodorozhnogo i vodnogo transporta (Moscow: Izdanie Tsentral'nogo biuro pechati NKPS, 1922).

Zvezdin, Z. K., Pavlovskii, I. G., Gundobin, N. A. et al. (eds), *Zheleznodorozhnyi transport v vosstanovitel'nyi period* (Moscow: Transport, 1979).

Selected secondary works

Afonina, G. M., *Kratkie svedeniia o razvitii otechestvennykh zheleznykh dorog s 1838 po 1990gg.* (Moscow: MPS RF, 1995).

Åhlander, O., 'Staat, Wirtschaft und Handelspolitik: Schweden und Deutschland, 1918–1921' (published PhD, University of Lund, 1983).

Akhtamzian, A. A., 'Osnovnye etapy sovetskoi vneshnei politiki (1917–1967gg.)', in *Voprosy istorii*, No. 10 (1967), pp. 113–34.

— *Rapall'skaia politika: Sovetsko-germanskie diplomaticheskie otnosheniia v 1922–1932 godakh* (Moscow: Mezhdunarodnye otnosheniia, 1974).

Alekseeva, I. V., *Agoniia serdechnogo soglasiia: Tsarizm, burzhuaziia i ikh soiuzniki po Antante, 1914–1917gg.* (Leningrad: Lenizdat, 1990).

Andrew, C., *Secret Service: The Making of the British Intelligence Community* (London: Heinemann, 1985).

Aplin, H. A., 'Iurii Vladimirovich Lomonosov (1876–1952)', in his *Catalogue of the Lomonossoff Collections* (Leeds University Press, 1988), pp. vii–xx.

Baevskii, D. A., *Ocherki po istorii khoziaistvennogo stroitel'stva perioda grazhdanskoi voiny* (Moscow: AN SSSR, 1957).

Bailes, K. E., *Technology and Society under Lenin and Stalin: Origins of the Soviet Technical Intelligentsia, 1917–1941* (Princeton University Press, 1978).

Bakhov, A. S., *Na zare sovetskoi diplomatii: Organy sovetskoi diplomatii v 1917–1922gg.* (Moscow: Mezhdunarodnye otnosheniia, 1966).

Balawyder, A., *Canadian–Soviet Relations between the World Wars* (University of Toronto Press, 1972).
Batty, P., *The House of Krupp* (London: Secker and Warburg, 1966).
Baykov, A., *The Development of the Soviet Economic System* (Cambridge University Press, 1946).
  Soviet Foreign Trade (Princeton University Press, 1946).
Berdrow, W., *The Krupps: 150 Years' Krupp History, 1787–1937, Based on Documents and Work Archives* (Berlin: Schmidt, 1937).
Blackwell, W. L., *The Beginnings of Russian Industrialisation, 1800–1860* (Princeton University Press, 1968).
Bogdanovich, A. O., Burnosov, N. N., Zenzinov, N. A. et al. (eds), *Ministry i Narkomy Putei Soobshcheniia* (Moscow: Transport, 1995).
Bradley, D. L., *The Locomotive History of the South Eastern and Chatham Railway* (London: RCTS, 1980).
Brotherstone, T. and Dukes, P. (eds.), *The Trotsky Reappraisal* (Edinburgh University Press, 1992).
Carlbäck-Isotalo, H., 'Ekonomicheskie sviazi Sovetskoi Rossii i Shvetsii v 1917–1924gg.', in O. V. Chernysheva (ed.), *Severnaia Evropa: Problemy noveishei istorii: Sbornik nauchnykh trudov* (Moscow: Nauka, 1988), pp. 33–48.
  'Pengar eller Politik: Ekonomiska förbindelser mellan Sverige och Sovjet, 1917–1924', in *Historisk Tidskrift*, 1985, pp. 187–233.
  'Sweden and Russia in Dissolution, 1918–1919: Some Political and Economical Aspects of the Swedish Government Policies towards the Baltic Countries, the Ukraine and other new states', in Hiden, J. and Loit, A. (eds), *The Baltic in International Relations between the Two World Wars* (University of Stockholm, 1988), pp. 209–33.
Carr, E. H., *German–Soviet Relations between the Two World Wars* (Baltimore: Johns Hopkins Press, 1951).
  The Bolshevik Revolution, 1917–1923, 3 vols (London: Macmillan, 1950–3).
Carroll, E. M., *Soviet Communism and Western Opinion, 1919–1921* (Chapel Hill, N.C.: University of North Carolina Press, 1965).
Carsten, F. L., *Britain and the Weimar Republic: The British Documents* (London: Batsford Academic, 1984).
Chernysheva, O. V. (ed.), *Severnaia Evropa: Problemy noveishei istorii: Sbornik nauchnykh trudov* (Moscow: Nauka, 1988).
Chubar'ian, A. O., *V. I. Lenin i formirovanie sovetskoi vneshnei politiki* (Moscow: Nauka, 1972).
Chubar'ian, A. O., Farbman, N. V., Nikonova, S. V. et al. (eds.), *Evropa v mezhdunarodnykh otnosheniiakh, 1917–1939* (Moscow: Nauka, 1979).
Coates, W. P. and Coates, Z. K., *A History of Anglo-Soviet Relations* (London: Lawrence and Wishart, 1943).
Coopersmith, J., *The Electrification of Russia, 1880–1926* (Ithaca: Cornell University Press, 1992).
Craig, G. A. and Gilbert, F. (eds.), *The Diplomats, 1919–1939* (Princeton University Press, 1953).

Davenport-Hines, R. P. T., *Dudley Docker: The Life and Times of a Trade Warrior* (Cambridge University Press, 1984).
Davies, N., 'The Missing Revolutionary War: The Polish Campaigns and the Retreat from Revolution in Soviet Russia', in *Soviet Studies*, Vol. 27, No. 2 (1975), pp. 178–95.
Davies, R. W. (ed.), *From Tsarism to the New Economic Policy: Continuity and Change in the Economy of the USSR* (Basingstoke: Macmillan, 1990).
Davies, R. W., Harrison, M. and Wheatcroft, S. G. (eds), *The Economic Transformation of the Soviet Union, 1913–1945* (Cambridge University Press, 1994).
Davies, R. W., Ilic, M. J., Jenkins, H. P. et al. (eds), *Soviet Government Officials, 1922–41: A Handlist* (University of Birmingham, 1989).
Day, R. B., *Leon Trotsky and the Politics of Economic Isolation* (London: Cambridge University Press, 1973).
Debo, R. K., *Revolution and Survival: The Foreign Policy of Soviet Russia, 1917–1918* (Liverpool University Press, 1979).
  Survival and Consolidation: The Foreign Policy of Soviet Russia, 1918–1921 (Montreal & Kingston: McGill–Queen's University Press, 1992).
Deutscher, I., *The Great Contest: Russia and the West* (London: Oxford University Press, 1960).
  The Prophet Armed: Trotsky, 1879–1921 (London: Oxford University Press, 1954).
  The Prophet Unarmed: Trotsky, 1921–1929 (London: Oxford University Press, 1959).
Dobb, M., *Soviet Economic Development since 1917*, 6th edn (London: Routledge and Kegan Paul, 1966).
Dohan, M. R., 'Foreign Trade', in Davies, R. W. (ed.), *From Tsarism to the New Economic Policy: Continuity and Change in the Economy of the USSR* (Basingstoke: Macmillan, 1990), pp. 212–34, 321–31.
Dongarov, A. G., *Inostrannyi kapital v Rossii i SSSR* (Moscow: Mezhdunarodnye otnosheniia, 1990).
Drobizhev, V. Z., *Glavnyi shtab sotsialisticheskoi promyshlennosti: (Ocherk istorii VSNKh, 1917–1932gg.)* (Moscow: Mysl', 1966).
Edson, W. D., 'The Russian Decapods', in *Railway and Locomotive Historical Society Bulletin*, No. 124 (1971), pp. 64–75.
Efimkin, A. P., ' "My zaplatili nemetskim imperialistam zoloto ... " ', in *Istoriia SSSR*, No. 5 (1990), pp. 147–51.
Efremtsev, G. P., *Istoriia Kolomenskogo zavoda: Ocherk istorii Kolomenskogo teplovozostroitel'nogo zavoda imeni V. V. Kuibysheva za 110 let (1863–1973)* (Moscow: Mysl', 1973).
Elwood, R. C. (ed.), *Russian and East European History: Selected Papers from the Second World Congress for Soviet and East European Studies (Garmisch-Partenkirchen Sept. 30–Oct. 4 1980)* (Berkeley: Berkeley Slavic Specialties, 1984).
Emets, V. A., *Ocherki vneshnei politiki Rossii v period pervoi mirovoi voiny: Vzaimootnosheniia Rossii s soiuznikami po voprosam vedeniia voiny* (Moscow: Nauka, 1977).

Erlich, A., *The Soviet Industrialization Debate, 1924–1928* (Cambridge, Mass.: Harvard University Press, 1960).
Erokhin, A., '"Spetsial'no sledit' za etim delom ... ": Rasskaz o knigakh iz lichnoi biblioteki V. I. Lenina', in *Pravda*, 4 February 1984, p. 3.
Fadeev, G. M., Kraskovskii, E. Ia., Uzdin, M. M. et al. (eds), *Istoriia zheleznodorozhnogo transporta Rossii, tom 1: 1836–1917* (St Petersburg: Ivan Fedorov, 1994).
Falkus, M. E., *The Industrialisation of Russia, 1700–1914* (London: Macmillan, 1972).
Fiddick, T. C., *Russia's Retreat from Poland, 1920: From Permanent Revolution to Peaceful Coexistence* (Basingstoke: Macmillan, 1990).
Fink, C., *The Genoa Conference: European Diplomacy, 1921–1922* (Chapel Hill, N.C.: University of North Carolina Press, 1984).
Fink, C., Frohn, A. and Heideking, J. (eds), *Genoa, Rapallo and European Reconstruction in 1922* (Cambridge University Press, 1991).
Fischer, L., *Russia's Road from Peace to War: Soviet Foreign Relations, 1917–1941* (New York: Harper and Row, 1969).
The Soviets in World Affairs: A History of the Relations between the Soviet Union and the Rest of the World, 1917–1929, 2 vols (London: Cape, 1930).
Freund, G., *Unholy Alliance: Russian–German Relations from the Treaty of Brest-Litovsk to the Treaty of Berlin* (London: Chatto and Windus, 1957).
Ganelin, R. Sh., *Rossiia i SShA, 1914–1917gg.: Ocherki istorii russko-amerikanskikh otnoshenii* (Leningrad: Nauka, 1969).
Sovetsko-amerikanskie otnosheniia v kontse 1917–nachale 1918g. (Leningrad: Nauka, 1975).
Gatrell, P., *The Tsarist Economy, 1850–1917* (London: Batsford, 1986).
Gatzke, H. W., 'Russo-German Military Collaboration during the Weimar Republic', in *American Historical Review*, Vol. 53, No. 3 (1958), pp. 565–97.
Genkina, E. B., *Gosudarstvennaia deiatel'nost' V. I. Lenina, 1921–1923* (Moscow: Nauka, 1969).
Protokoly Sovnarkoma RSFSR kak istoricheskii istochnik (Moscow: Nauka, 1982).
Gerschenkron, A., *Economic Backwardness in Historical Perspective: A Book of Essays* (Cambridge, Mass.: Harvard University Press, 1962).
Gerson, L. D., 'Felix Dzerzhinsky as People's Commissar of Transport, 1921–1924', in Elwood, R. C. (ed.), *Russian and East European History: Selected Papers from the Second World Congress for Soviet and East European Studies (Garmisch-Partenkirchen Sept. 30–Oct. 4 1980)* (Berkeley: Berkeley Slavic Specialties, 1984), pp. 220–57.
Geyer, D., *Russian Imperialism: The Interaction of Domestic and Foreign Policy, 1860–1914* (Leamington Spa: Berg, 1987).
Gimpel'son, E. G., *Velikii oktiabr' i stanovlenie sovetskoi sistemy upravleniia narodnym khoziaistvom (noiabr' 1917–1920gg.)* (Moscow: Nauka, 1977).
Gladkov, I. A., *Ocherki sovetskoi ekonomiki, 1917–1920gg.* (Moscow: Gosudarstvennoe izdatel'stvo politicheskoi literatury, 1956).
Glenny, M. V., 'The Anglo-Soviet Trade Agreement, March 1921', in *The Journal of Contemporary History*, Vol. 5, No. 2 (1970), pp. 63–82.

'Leonid Krasin: The Years before 1917: An Outline', in *Soviet Studies*, Vol. 22, No. 2 (1971), pp. 192–221.
Goriacheva, V. P. and Shelest, P. A., *Aleksei Nesterovich Shelest – pioner teplovozostroeniia, 1878–1954* (Moscow: Nauka, 1989).
Gorokhov, I. M., Zamiatin, L. and Zemskov, I., *G. V. Chicherin – diplomat leninskoi shkoly* (Moscow: Izdatel'stvo politicheskoi literatury, 1966).
Gromyko, A. A. and Ponomarev, V. P. (eds), *Istoriia vneshnei politiki SSSR, 1917–1985, Vol. 1 ('1917–1945')* (Moscow: Nauka, 1986).
Gvishiani, L. A., *Sovetskaia Rossiia i SShA (1917–1920)* (Moscow: Mezhdunarodnye otnosheniia, 1970).
Haigh, R. H., Morris, D. S. and Peters, A. R., *German–Soviet Relations in the Weimar Era: Friendship from Necessity* (Aldershot: Gower Press, 1985).
Soviet Foreign Policy: The League of Nations and Europe, 1917–1939 (Aldershot: Gower Press, 1986).
Haywood, R. M., *The Beginnings of Railway Development in Russia in the Reign of Nicholas I, 1835–1842* (Durham, N.C.: Duke University Press, 1969).
Heywood, A. J., 'The Armstrong Affair and the Making of the Anglo-Soviet Trade Agreement, 1920–1921', in *Revolutionary Russia*, Vol. 5, No. 1 (June 1992), pp. 53–91.
'The Baltic Commercial "Bridge" in the 1920s: Some Early Soviet Perspectives', in Loit, A., Johansson, A., Kangeris, K. et al. (eds), *Emancipation and Interdependence: The Baltic States as New Entities in the International Economy, 1918–1940* (University of Stockholm, 1994).
Change in the Russian and Soviet Steam Locomotive Stock, 1913–1928 (University of Birmingham, 1991; Centre for Russian and East European Studies, SIPS Discussion Paper No. 31).
'Trade or Isolation? Soviet Imports of Railway Equipment, 1920–1922', in Hiden, J. and Loit, A. (eds), *Contact or Isolation? Soviet–Western Relations in the Inter-War Period, 1917–1940* (University of Stockholm, 1991), pp. 137–60.
Hiden, J. and Loit, A. (eds), *The Baltic in International Relations between the Two World Wars* (University of Stockholm, 1988).
Contact or Isolation? Soviet–Western Relations in the Inter-War Period, 1917–1940 (University of Stockholm, 1991).
Himmer, R., 'Soviet Policy Toward Germany During the Russo-Polish War, 1920', in *Slavic Review*, Vol. 35, No. 4 (1976), pp. 665–82.
Hinkkanen-Lievonen, M.-L., *British Trade and Enterprise in the Baltic States, 1919–1925* (Helsinki: Suomen Historiallinen Seura, 1984).
Hogenhuis-Seliverstoff, A., *Les relations Franco-Soviétiques, 1917–1924* (Paris: Publications de la Sorbonne, 1981).
Hunter, H., *Soviet Transportation Policy* (Cambridge, Mass.: Harvard University Press, 1957).
Iakhontov, Iu., 'Tysiacha parovozov dlia Lenina', in *Pravda*, 27 January 1969, p. 5.
Iakobson, P. V., *Istoriia teplovoza v SSSR* (Moscow: Transzheldorizdat, 1960).

Ianush, L. B., *Russkie parovozy za 50 let* (Moscow-Leningrad: Gosudarstvennoe nauchno-tekhnicheskoe izdatel'stvo mashinostroitel'noi literatury, 1950).
Ikonnikov, S. N., *Organizatsiia i deiatel'nost' RKI v 1920–1925gg.* (Moscow: AN SSSR, 1960).
Ioffe, A. E., *Mezhdunarodnye sviazi sovetskoi nauki, tekhniki i kul'tury, 1917–1932* (Moscow: Nauka, 1975).
Iordanov, L., *Krasnyi ekselents: Povest' o B. Stomoniakove* (Moscow: Progress, 1985).
Isaev, V. A., 'Bor'ba partii za ekonomicheskuiu nezavisimost' Sovetskogo gosudarstva v oblasti turbostroeniia', in *Vestnik Leningradskogo gosudarstvennogo universiteta*, No. 14 (1969), pp. 23–32.
Jackson, A. A., 'The Great Government Locomotive Sales of 1919–1927', in *Railway World* (July 1986), pp. 408–11.
Johnsson, W., *Nydqvist & Holm: 100 År, 1847–1947* (Trollhättan, 1947) (reprinted by Trollhättan Kommun, 1985).
Karpova, R. F., *L. B. Krasin – sovetskii diplomat* (Moscow: Izdatel'stvo sotsial'no-ekonomicheskoi literatury Mysl', 1962).
  'Priznanie SSSR de-iure Norvegiei, Shvetsiei i Daniei', in *Skandinavskii sbornik*, Vol. XII (Tallinn: Eesti Raamat, 1967), pp. 92–104.
  'Sovetskie otnosheniia so skandinavskimi stranami, 1920–1923gg.', in *Skandinavskii sbornik*, Vol. X (Tallinn: Eesti Raamat, 1965), pp. 135–69.
  'Zakliuchitel'nyi etap anglo-sovetskikh peregovorov 1920–1921gg.', in *Vestnik Leningradskogo gosudarstvennogo universiteta*, No. 14 (1962), pp. 34–46.
Kennan, G. F., *Russia and the West under Lenin and Stalin* (Boston, Mass.: Little, Brown and Co., 1961).
  Soviet–American Relations, 1917–1920, 2 vols (Princeton University Press, 1956–58).
  Soviet Foreign Policy, 1917–1941 (Princeton, NJ: Van Nostrand, 1960).
Kharlamov, M. A., Ioffe, A. E., Kan, A. S. et al. (eds.), *Leninskaia vneshniaia politika sovetskoi strany, 1917–1924* (Leningrad: Nauka, 1969).
Khromov, P. A., *Ekonomicheskoe razvitie Rossii v XIX–XX vekakh, 1800–1917* (Moscow: Gosudarstvennoe izdatel'stvo politicheskoi literatury, 1950).
Khromov, S. S., *F. E. Dzerzhinskii na khoziaistvennom fronte, 1921–1926* (Moscow: Mysl', 1977).
  F. E. Dzerzhinskii vo glave metallopromyshlennosti (Moscow: Izdatel'stvo Moskovskogo universiteta, 1966).
Kim, M. P., *Ekonomicheskaia politika sovetskogo gosudarstva v perekhodnyi period ot kapitalizma k sotsializmu* (Moscow: Nauka, 1986).
Klass, G. von, *Krupps: The Story of an Industrial Empire* (London: Sidgwick and Jackson, 1954).
Knei-Paz, B., *The Social and Political Thought of Leon Trotsky* (Oxford: Clarendon Press, 1978).
Kobliakov, I. K., *Ot Bresta do Rapallo: Ocherki istorii sovetsko-germanskikh otnoshenii s 1918g. po 1922g.* (Moscow, 1954).

Kochan, L., *Russia and the Weimar Republic* (Cambridge: Bowes and Bowes, 1954).
'The Russian Road to Rapallo', in *Soviet Studies*, Vol. 2, No. 2 (1950–1), pp. 109–22.
Kostiuchenko, S., Khrenov, I. and Fedorov, Iu., *Istoriia Kirovskogo zavoda, 1917–1945* (Moscow: Mysl', 1966).
Kovalenko, D. A., *Oboronnaia promyshlennost' Sovetskoi Rossii v 1918–1920gg.* (Moscow: Nauka, 1970).
Kremnev, V., *Krasin* (Moscow: Molodaia gvardiia 1968).
Kubitskaia, O. A., 'Stanovlenie parovozostroitel'noi monopolii v Rossii (1900–1907gg.)', in *Samoderzhavie i krupnyi kapital v Rossii v kontse XIX– nachale XXv.: Sbornik statei* (Moscow: AN SSSR, 1982), pp. 134–58.
Kuuse, J., 'The Development of the Swedish Engineering Industry: a rejoinder', in *Scandinavian Economic History Review*, Vol. 26, No. 1 (1978), pp. 164–7.
'Foreign Trade and the Breakthrough of the Engineering Industry in Sweden, 1890–1920', in *Scandinavian Economic History Review*, Vol. 25, No. 1 (1977), pp. 1–36.
Kuz'mich, V., 'Pervye sovetskie', in *Gudok*, 6 October 1987, p. 4.
'Tovarishchu Lomonosovu ...', in *Gudok*, 31 October 1987, p. 4.
Lebedev, N. I., *Velikii oktiabr' i perestroika mezhdunarodnykh otnoshenii* (Moscow: Nauka, 1978).
Lebedev, V. V., *Russko-amerikanskie ekonomicheskie otnosheniia (1900–1917gg.)* (Moscow: Mezhdunarodnye otnosheniia, 1964).
Le Fleming, H. M. and Price, J. H., *Russian Steam Locomotives*, 2nd edn (Newton Abbot: David and Charles, 1972).
Lerner, W., *Karl Radek: The Last Internationalist* (Stanford University Press, 1970).
Lewin, M., *Lenin's Last Struggle* (London: Faber and Faber, 1969).
Political Undercurrents in Soviet Economic Debates (London: Pluto Press, 1975).
Lewis, R. A., 'Foreign Economic Relations', in Davies, R. W., Harrison, M. and Wheatcroft, S. G. (eds.), *The Economic Transformation of the Soviet Union, 1913–1945* (Cambridge University Press, 1994), pp. 198–215.
Science and Industrialisation in the USSR: Industrial Research and Development, 1917–1940 (London: Macmillan, 1979).
Lincoln, W. B., *Passage through Armageddon: The Russians in War and Revolution, 1914–1918* (Oxford University Press, 1994).
Linke, H. G., *Deutsch–Sowjetische Beziehungen bis Rapallo* (Cologne: Verlag Wissenschaft und Politik, 1970).
Loit, A., Johansson, A., Kangeris, K. et al. (eds.), *Emancipation and Interdependence: The Baltic States as New Entities in the International Economy, 1918–1940* (University of Stockholm, 1994).
Lorenson, E., 'Istoriia tysiachi parovozov (o postavke v SSSR tovarnykh lokomotivov iz Shvetsii v 1920g.)', in *Novoe vremia*, No. 24 (1964), pp. 24–6.
Lovtsov, L. V., 'Iz istorii bor'by Kommunisticheskoi partii za sozdanie

otechestvennogo teplovozostroeniia', in *Stranitsy velikogo puti: Iz istorii bor'by KPSS za pobedu kommunizma: Sbornik statei aspirantov, Chast' III* (Moscow: Izdatel'stvo Moskovskogo universiteta, 1970), pp. 100–33.

KPSS v bor'be za vosstanovlenie i razvitie zheleznodorozhnogo transporta (1921–1925gg.) (Moscow: Izdatel'stvo Moskovskogo universiteta, 1980).

'Leninskii printsip edinstva resheniia khoziaistvennykh i politicheskikh zadach v rukovodstve partii vosstanovleniem zheleznodorozhnogo transporta (1921–1925gg.)', in *Iz istorii bor'by KPSS za pobedu sotsializma i kommunizma: Sbornik statei* (Moscow: Izdatel'stvo Moskovskogo universiteta, 1971).

Lowe, J. W., *British Steam Locomotive Builders* (Cambridge: Goose, 1975).

Makeenko, M. M., *Ocherk razvitiia mashinostroeniia SSSR v 1921–1928gg.* (Kishinev: Kartia moldoveniaske, 1962).

Malakhinova, R. P., 'F. E. Dzerzhinskii na sotsialisticheskoi stroike', in *Voprosy istorii*, No. 11 (1967), pp. 157–68.

Malle, S., *The Economic Organisation of War Communism, 1918–1921* (Cambridge University Press, 1985).

Marks, S. G., *Road to Power: The Trans-Siberian Railroad and the Colonisation of Asian Russia, 1850–1917* (London: I. B. Tauris, 1991).

Mawdsley, E., *The Russian Civil War* (Boston, Mass.: Allen and Unwin, 1987).

Mints, I. I. (ed.), *Sovetskaia Rossiia i kapitalisticheskii mir v 1917–1923gg.* (Moscow: Gospolitizdat, 1957).

Mitchell, D. W., *A History of Russian and Soviet Sea Power* (London: André Deutsch, 1974).

Mokrshitskii, E. I., *Istoriia parovozostroeniia SSSR, 1846–1940gg.* (Moscow: Gosudarstvennoe transportnoe zheleznodorozhnoe izdatel'stvo, 1941).

Neilson, K., *Strategy and Supply: The Anglo-Russian Alliance, 1914–17* (London: George Allen and Unwin, 1984).

Nikol'skii, A. S., 'Sozdanie i ekspluatatsiia parka parovozov serii S', in *Voprosy istorii estestvoznaniia i tekhniki*, No. 2 (1992), pp. 38–49.

Nilsson, C. -A., 'Foreign Trade and the Breakthrough of the Engineering Industry in Sweden: A Comment', in *Scandinavian Economic History Review*, Vol. 26, No. 1 (1978), pp. 156–63.

Norman, E. A., 'Teplovoz professora Lomonosova – pervenets sovetskogo i mirovogo teplovozostroeniia', in *Voprosy istorii estestvoznaniia i tekhniki*, No. 4 (1985), pp. 116–25.

Northedge, F. S. and Wells, A., *Britain and Soviet Communism: The Impact of a Revolution* (London: Macmillan, 1982).

Nove, A., *An Economic History of the USSR* (Harmondsworth: Penguin Books, 1976).

'Soviet Planning and Grinevetskii – A Comment', in *Survey*, No. 70/71 (1969), pp. 169–72.

O'Connor, T. E., *Diplomacy and Revolution: G. V. Chicherin and Soviet Foreign Affairs, 1918–1930* (Ames, Iowa: Iowa State University Press, 1988).

The Engineer of Revolution: L. B. Krasin and the Bolsheviks, 1870–1926 (Boulder, Colo.: Westview Press, 1992).

Orlov, B. P., *Razvitie transporta SSSR, 1917–1962* (Moscow: AN SSSR, 1963).
Oznobishin, D. V., *Ot Bresta do Iureva: Iz istorii vneshnei politiki sovetskoi vlasti, 1917–1920gg.* (Moscow: Nauka, 1966).
P. P–w, 'Gunnar W. Anderson död', in *Tidningen Trollhättan*, [30?] May 1960.
Page, F. M. and de Pater, A. D., *Russian Locomotives, Vol. 1 ('1836–1904')* (Sutton Coldfield: Retrieval Press, 1987).
Page, F. M. and Nurminen, J., *Russian Locomotives, Vol. 2 ('1905–1924')* (Sutton Coldfield: Retrieval Press, 1992).
Pakhman, T. A., *Leninskii plan tekhnicheskogo perevooruzheniia zheleznodorozhnogo transporta i ego pretvorenie v zhizn'* (Moscow: Obshchestvo 'Znanie' RSFSR, 1971).
Pavliuchenkov, S. A., *Krest'ianskii Brest, ili predistoriia bol'shevitskogo NEPa* (Moscow: Russkoe knigoizdatel'skoe tovarishchestvo, 1996).
Pethybridge, R. W., 'Railways and Press Communications in Soviet Russia in the Early NEP Period', in *Soviet Studies*, Vol. 38, No. 2 (1986), pp. 194–206.
'The Significance of Communications in 1917', in *Soviet Studies*, Vol. 19, No. 1 (1967–8), pp. 109–14.
The Spread of the Russian Revolution: Essays on 1917 (London: Macmillan, 1972).
Phillips, H. D., *Between the Revolution and the West: A Political Biography of Maxim M. Litvinov* (Boulder, Colo.: Westview Press, 1992).
Pogge von Strandmann, H., 'Grossindustrie und Rapallopolitik: Deutsch–Sowjetische Handelsbeziehungen in der Weimarer Republik', in *Historische Zeitschrift*, Vol. 222 (Munich: Oldenburg, 1976), pp. 265–341.
Pogrebinskii, A. P., 'Komitet po zheleznodorozhnym zakazam i ego likvidatsiia v 1914g.', in *Istoricheskie zapiski*, Vol. LXXXIII (Moscow: AN SSSR, 1969), pp. 233–43.
'Popytki regulirovaniia zheleznodorozhnogo transporta tsarskoi Rossii v gody pervoi mirovoi voiny: (k voprosu o kharaktere gosudarstvenno-monopolisticheskogo kapitalizma v Rossii)', in *Voprosy politicheskoi ekonomiki* (Moscow, 1958), pp. 242–71.
Popov, V. I. (comp.), *Dipkur'ery: Ocherki o pervykh sovetskikh diplomaticheskikh kur'erakh* (Moscow: Izdatel'stvo politicheskoi literatury, 1970).
Popova, E. I., 'Missiia Stevensa i proval zheleznodorozhnoi politiki SShA v Rossii i Kitae v 1917–1922gg.', in *Istoricheskie zapiski*, Vol. LX (Moscow: AN SSSR, 1957), pp. 31–85.
Rakov, V. A., *Lokomotivy otechestvennykh zheleznykh dorog, 1845–1955* (Moscow: Transport, 1995).
Lokomotivy zheleznykh dorog Sovetskogo Soiuza: Ot pervykh parovozov do sovremennykh lokomotivov (Moscow: Gosudarstvennoe transportnoe zheleznodorozhnoe izdatel'stvo, 1955).
Rakow, W. A. [Rakov, V. A.], *Russische und sowjetische Dampflokomotiven* (Berlin: Transpress, 1986).
Rassweiler, A. D., *The Generation of Power: The History of Dneprostroi* (Oxford University Press, 1988).

Reed, B., 'Lomonossoff: A Diesel Traction Pioneer', in *Railroad History*, Bulletin 128 (1973), pp. 35–49.
Rees, E. A., *Stalinism and Soviet Rail Transport, 1928–41* (Basingstoke: Macmillan, 1995).
 State Control in Soviet Russia: The Rise and Fall of the Workers' and Peasants' Inspectorate, 1920–1934 (Basingstoke: Macmillan, 1987).
Remington, T. F., *Building Socialism in Bolshevik Russia: Ideology and Industrial Organization, 1917–1921* (University of Pittsburgh Press, 1984).
Rigby, T. H., *Lenin's Government: Sovnarkom, 1917–1922* (Cambridge University Press, 1979).
Rosenbaum, K., *Community of Fate: German–Soviet Diplomatic Relations, 1922–1928* (Syracuse University Press, 1965).
Rosenfeld, G., *Sowjet-Russland und Deutschland, 1917–1922* (Cologne: Pahl-Rugenstein Verlag, 1984).
Rozenfel'd, Ia. S. and Klimenko, K. I., *Istoriia mashinostroeniia SSSR (s pervoi poloviny XIX veka do nashikh dnei)* (Moscow: AN SSSR, 1961).
Ryzhikov, V. A., *Sovetsko-angliiskie otnosheniia: Osnovnye etapy istorii* (Moscow: Mezhdunarodnye otnosheniia, 1987).
Scott, J. D., *Vickers: A History* (London: Weidenfeld and Nicolson, 1962).
Senin, A. S., 'Aleksei Ivanovich Rykov', in *Voprosy istorii*, No. 9 (1988), pp. 85–115.
Service, R., *The Bolshevik Party in Revolution: A Study in Organisational Change, 1917–1923* (London: Macmillan, 1979).
 Lenin: A Political Life, Volume 3: The Iron Ring (Basingstoke: Macmillan, 1995).
Shabunin, A., 'Vrio narkomputi Lev Trotskii', in *Gudok*, 24 June 1989, p. 4.
Shadur, L. A., *Razvitie otechestvennogo vagonnogo parka* (Moscow: Transport, 1988).
Shishkin, V. A., *Sovetskoe gosudarstvo i strany zapada v 1917–1923gg.: Ocherki istorii stanovleniia ekonomicheskikh otnoshenii* (Leningrad: Nauka, 1969).
 'Stanovlenie sovetsko-skandinavskikh ekonomicheskikh otnoshenii (1917–1923)', in *Istoricheskie sviazi skandinavii i Rossii IX–XXvv.: Sbornik statei* (Leningrad: Nauka, 1970), pp. 164–203.
 V bor'be s blokadoi: O stanovlenii sovetskoi vneshnei torgovli (Moscow: Politizdat, 1979).
 V. I. Lenin i vneshneekonomicheskaia politika sovetskogo gosudarstva (1917–1923gg.) (Leningrad: Nauka, 1977).
Sidorov, A. L., *Ekonomicheskoe polozhenie Rossii v gody pervoi mirovoi voiny* (Moscow: AN SSSR, 1973).
 Istoricheskie predposylki Velikoi oktiabr'skoi sotsialisticheskoi revoliutsii (Moscow: Nauka, 1970).
 'Zheleznodorozhnyi transport Rossii v pervoi mirovoi voine i obostrenie ekonomicheskogo krizisa v strane', in *Istoricheskie zapiski*, Vol. XXVI (Moscow: AN SSSR, 1948), pp. 3–64.
Siegel, K. A. S., *Loans and Legitimacy: The Evolution of Soviet–American Relations, 1919–1933* (Lexington, Ky.: University Press of Kentucky, 1996).

Siegelbaum, L. H., *The Politics of Industrial Mobilisation in Russia, 1914–1917: A Study of the War Industries Committees* (London: Macmillan, 1983).
Simonov, N. S., 'Sovetskaia finansovaia politika v usloviiakh nepa (1921–1927gg)', in *Istoriia SSSR*, No. 5 (1990), pp. 42–59.
Smele, J. D., 'White Gold: The Imperial Russian Gold Reserve in the Anti-Bolshevik East, 1918–? (An Unconcluded Chapter in the History of the Russian Civil War)', in *Europe–Asia Studies*, Vol. 46, No. 8 (1994), pp. 1317–47.
Smith, C. J., *Finland and the Russian Revolution, 1917–1922* (Athens, Ga.: University of Georgia Press, 1958).
Smith, G. A., *Soviet Foreign Trade: Organization, Operations and Policy, 1918–1971* (New York: Praeger, 1973).
Smolinski, L., 'A Rejoinder', in *Survey*, No. 70/71 (1969), pp. 172–77.
'Grinevetskii and Soviet Industrialisation', in *Survey*, No. 67 (1968), pp. 100–15.
Söderlund, E. F., 'The Swedish Iron Industry during the First World War and the Post-War Depression', in *Scandinavian Economic History Review*, Vol. 6, No. 1 (1958), pp. 53–94.
Sokolov, V. V., 'Stanovlenie sovetsko-avstriiskikh otnoshenii (1917–1924gg.)', in *Novaia i noveishaia istoriia*, No. 3 (1979), pp. 22–38.
Solov'eva, A. M., *Zheleznodorozhnyi transport Rossii vo vtoroi polovine XIX veka* (Moscow: Nauka, 1975).
Sonkin, M. E., *Okno vo vneshnii mir: Ekonomicheskie sviazi Sovetskogo gosudarstva v 1917–1921gg.* (Moscow: Mysl', 1964).
Sosnovskii, L. A. and Zenzinov, N. A., *Otechestvennye uchenye-zheleznodorozhniki: kratkii biograficheskii slovar'-spravochnik* (Gomel': BelIIZhT, 1993).
Steklov, V. Iu., *V. I. Lenin i Elektrifikatsiia*, 3rd edn (Moscow: Nauka, 1982).
Stites, R., *Revolutionary Dreams: Utopian Vision and Experimental Life in the Russian Revolution* (Oxford University Press, 1989).
Stone, N., *The Eastern Front, 1914–1917* (Abingdon: Purnell, 1976).
Strumilin, S. G., *Statistiko-ekonomicheskie ocherki* (Moscow: Gosudarstvennoe statisticheskoe izdatel'stvo, 1958).
Suboch, N. I., 'Gorenie', in *Elektricheskaia i teplovoznaia tiaga*, No. 9 (1987), pp. 40–2.
Sundström, E., *Ånglok tillverkade i Sverige* (Stockholm: Högbergs Tryckeri AB, 1974).
Sutton, A. C., *Western Technology and Soviet Economic Development*, Vol. 1 ('1917–1930') (Stanford, Calif.: Hoover Institution Publications, 1968).
Suvorova, L. N., 'Za "fasadom" "Voennogo kommunizma": Politicheskaia vlast' i rynochnaia ekonomika', in *Otechestvennaia istoria*, No. 4 (1993), pp. 48–59.
Symons, L. and White, C., *Russian Transport: An Historical and Geographical Survey* (London: Bell, 1975).
Teichova, A., *An Economic Background to Munich: International Business and Czechoslovakia, 1918–1939* (London: Cambridge University Press, 1974).

Trebilcock, C., *The Vickers Brothers: Armaments and Enterprises, 1854–1914* (London: Europa, 1977).
Trukhnov, G. M., *Iz istorii sovetsko-germanskikh otnoshenii (1920–1922gg.)* (Minsk: Izdatel'stvo BGU, 1974).
Trush, M. I., *Mezhdunarodnaia deiatel'nost' V. I. Lenina: Zashchita zavoevanii sotsialisticheskoi revoliutsii, 1919–1920*, 2nd edn (Moscow: Izdatel'stvo politicheskoi literatury, 1988).
Tsuji, Y., 'The Debate on the Trade Unions, 1920–1921', in *Revolutionary Russia*, Vol. 2, No. 1 (1989), pp. 31–100.
Uldricks, T. J., *Diplomacy and Ideology: The Origins of Soviet Foreign Relations, 1917–1930* (London: Sage, 1979).
  'Russia and Europe: Diplomacy, Revolution and Economic Development in the 1920s', in *International History Review*, Vol. 1, No. 1 (1979), pp. 55–83.
Ullman, R. H., *Anglo-Soviet Relations, 1917–1921*, 3 vols (Princeton University Press, 1961–72).
Vasil'ev, N., *Transport Rossii v voine 1914–1918* (Moscow: Voenizdat, 1939).
Velidov, A. S., Kozichev, M. A., Solov'ev, A. A. et al. (eds), *Feliks Edmundovich Dzerzhinskii: Biografiia*, 3rd edn (Moscow: Izdatel'stvo politicheskoi literatury, 1986).
Volkogonov, D. A., *Trotskii: politicheskii portret*, 2 vols (Moscow: Novosti, 1992).
Volobuev, P. V., *Ekonomicheskaia politika Vremennogo pravitel'stva* (Moscow: AN SSSR, 1962).
  'Vremennoe pravitel'stvo i vopros o preodolenii razrukhi na zheleznodorozhnom transporte', in *Istoricheskie zapiski*, Vol. LXIX (Moscow: AN SSSR, 1961), pp. 253–67.
Von Laue, T. H., *Sergei Witte and the Industrialization of Russia* (New York: Columbia University Press, 1963).
'Vykort – lok – världsaffärer', in *Göteborgs Handels- och Sjöfarts Tidning*, 8 April 1972, p. 1.
Warren, K., *Armstrongs of Elswick: Growth in Engineering and Armaments to the Merger with Vickers* (Basingstoke: Macmillan, 1989).
Weissman, B. M., *Herbert Hoover and Famine Relief to Soviet Russia, 1921–23* (Stanford, Calif.: Hoover Institution Press, 1974).
Westwood, J. N., *A History of Russian Railways* (London: George Allen and Unwin Ltd, 1964).
  Soviet Locomotive Technology during Industrialisation, 1928–1952 (London: Macmillan, 1982).
  'Transport', in Davies, R. W., Harrison, M. and Wheatcroft, S. G. (eds), *The Economic Transformation of the Soviet Union, 1913–1945* (Cambridge University Press, 1994), pp. 158–81.
Westwood, J. N., Hunter, H., Ambler, P. J. et al., 'The Railways', in Davies, R. W. (ed.), *From Tsarism to the New Economic Policy: Continuity and Change in the Economy of the USSR* (Basingstoke: Macmillan, 1990), pp. 169–88, 307–14.
White, C. A., *British and American Commercial Relations with Soviet Russia, 1918–1924* (Chapel Hill, N.C.: University of North Carolina Press, 1992).

White, S., *Britain and the Bolshevik Revolution: A Study in the Politics of Diplomacy, 1920–1924* (London: Macmillan, 1979).

The Origins of Detente: The Genoa Conference and Soviet–Western Relations, 1921–1922 (Cambridge University Press, 1985).

The Soviet Leadership: Politburo, Orgburo and Secretariat of the CPSU, 1919–1990 (Lorton House paper, No. 3, 1991).

Williams, A. J., *Trading with the Bolsheviks: The Politics of East–West trade, 1920–39* (Manchester University Press, 1992).

Wistrich, R., *Trotsky: Fate of a Revolutionary* (London: Robson Books, 1979).

Zaleski, E., *Planning for Economic Growth in the Soviet Union, 1918–1932* (Chapel Hill, N.C.: University of North Carolina Press, 1971).

Zarkhii, S. N., *Narkomput' F. Dzerzhinskii* (Moscow: Transport, 1977).

Zarnitskii, S. V. and Sergeev, A. N., *Chicherin* (Moscow: Molodaia gvardiia, 1966).

Zarnitskii, S. V. and Trofimova, L. I., *Sovetskoi strany diplomat* (Moscow: Izdatel'stvo politicheskoi literatury, 1968).

Zenzinov, N. A., 'Vydaiushchiisia rossiiskii zheleznodorozhnyi inzhener', in *Zheleznodorozhnyi transport*, No. 4 (1993), pp. 57–63.

Zubov, N. I., *F. E. Dzerzhinskii: Biografiia*, 3rd edn (Moscow: Izdatel'stvo politicheskoi literatury, 1971).

Index

Åkerström 70
Alco – *see* American Locomotive Company
Aleksandrov workshops 19, 68
Allgemeine Deutsche Gewerkschaftsbunde 121
Allied Purchasing Commission 42
Allied Supreme Economic Council 77, 93, 102, 111
Allis Chalmers Company 129
All-Russian Central Executive Committee (VTsIK) 73, 76, 78–79, 166, 175, 177, 206
   transport policy 78
   vetoes railway contracts 175, 177
All-Russian Congress of Soviets, Eighth 3, 136, 139–140
All-Russian Congress of Soviets, Ninth 166, 184
All-Russian Congress of Soviets, Seventh 49, 69, 86
All-Russian Congress of Trades Unions, Third 79–80
All-Russian Cooperative Society Ltd (Arcos) 112, 212
Al'perovich, E. 80, 180
American Car and Foundry Company 39
American Expeditionary Force in France 40, 42–43
American Foreign Trade Corporation 107
American Locomotive Company (Alco) 30, 35, 39, 44, 123
American Relief Administration 165
American Steel Car Company 90
American Steel, Engineering and Automobile Products AG (Amstea) 268

Anchits, engineer 91, 107
Anderson, Bibi 7
Anderson, Gunnar W. 69, 96–97, 99–102, 125, 130–131, 154–155, 177, 188, 195, 197–199, 204, 208, 211, 231, 233
   acquisition of Nohab 100–101
   career 96
   locomotive contract 99–102, 131, 195, 197–199, 204, 211, 231, 233
   subcontracting to Germany 101–102, 125, 130–131, 154–155
   Swedish Concern 96, 99, 101, 125
   visit to Soviet Russia, 1919 69, 96
Anglo–Soviet Trade Agreement, 1921 110, 116, 120, 152, 159, 163, 165, 197
Archangel 21, 24–27, 41, 47, 57
Arcos Ltd – *see* All-Russian Cooperative Society Ltd
Armstrong Whitworth – *see* Sir W. G. Armstrong Whitworth and Company
Arskii, R. 67, 73, 75, 79, 86
Aschberg, Olof 33, 70, 121, 125, 128, 132
Atlas Diesel AB 95
Austria 110, 151, 154–155, 201
automatic brakes 31–32, 61–62
automatic couplings 31, 58, 61–62, 222
Avanesov, V. A. 175, 187, 190, 200–204, 206

Baker, Newton D. 40, 43
Bakhmet'ev, B. A. 37–40, 43–45, 61, 88, 104
Baldwin Locomotive Works 27, 30–31, 35, 39, 44, 46, 88–90, 113, 125, 174
   see also Vauclain, Samuel
Bamberger, Ludwig 109, 123, 154

311

Index

Barclay, Colville Adrian de Rune 93, 102
Baring Brothers Bank Ltd 32
Bark, P. L. 33–35
Bartels, Walter 71
Basic Transport Commission (OTK) 137–138, 157–158, 171, 173, 175–178, 183–184, 187
   NKPS imports 137, 171, 173, 175–178
   NKPS Order No. 1042 138
   oil-tanker orders 175
   overhaul of locomotives abroad 157–158, 176–177
   recommends repatriation of NKPS foreign orders 184, 187
Behrendt, Gustav 127
Bel'gard, S. K. 128, 153
Belgium, State Railways 35
Belonozhkin, A. I. 68
Beneš, Eduard 119
Berg, Harald 121–123, 154
Berg, Victor – *see* Victor Berg company
blockade, Allied naval 1, 3, 48, 63, 67–69, 75–77, 79, 93, 101–102, 111, 116, 121
Blunt, Lt. Col. F. R. 253
Bofors AB 95
Bogdanov, P. A. 180, 189, 191–192, 208
boilers 115, 125, 130, 157, 177–178, 182, 190, 203, 205, 208, 210–213, 216, 229
   see also Sir W. G. Armstrong Whitworth and Company
boiler tubes 54, 70, 72, 125, 133, 143, 153–154, 171, 174, 181, 185, 190, 211–212, 216–218, 229
Bolshevik Revolution – *see* October Revolution
Bonar Law, A. 117
Bonnier, Tor 121–123, 193, 231
Borisov, I. N. 147–150, 158, 165, 169, 223
Borsig 123
Brändström, Elsa 107
Branting, Hjalmar 94–95, 102, 125, 132
Brest-Litovsk, Treaty of 65–67
brick, fire-resistant 69, 172, 174–176, 181, 219
Briansk Machine-Building Works 53, 55, 185, 192
Briske & Prohl 70–72, 122, 124
British Baltic Commercial Corporation 174

Brockdorff-Rantzau, Ulrich Graf von 71
Brown Boveri & Co. 209
Buchanan, Sir George 33–34
Bücher, Hermann 127–128, 154
Bukharin, N. I. 63, 65, 167
Bullitt, William C. 71

Canada 129–130, 151, 156, 175
Canadian Car and Foundry Company 175, 211
Canadian Locomotive Company 30
Central Committee – *see* Russian Communist Party
Central Cooperative Society (Tsentrosoiuz) 75, 78, 81, 85–86, 91–93, 96, 98–101, 103–104, 121, 125, 131, 133, 145–146, 151, 155, 182, 207, 231
   assessment of foreign contracts 131, 145–146
   Lomonosov's mandates 104
   representatives appointed to Nohab 103
   trade delegation to Europe 81, 85, 93–94, 99, 111–112, 116–118, 122
Central War Industries Committee 66
Cheka – *see* Extraordinary Commission
Chekhovskii, K. N. 150
Chernov, A. S. 184
Chicherin, G. V. 69, 85–86, 93, 97, 104–105, 107, 109, 112, 125, 135, 143, 145–146, 151–153, 168
   calls for resumption of Soviet–Western trade 69, 86
   Lomonosov's mandates 104–105, 125
   opposition to Swedish contracts, 1920 145–146, 151–153
   policy firmness towards Britain 112
Chubar', V. Ia. 68
Churchill, Winston S. 112, 116–117
claims – *see* debts
Colby, Bainbridge 88
Comintern – *see* Communist International
Commission for Rolling-stock and Traction 22–23, 28, 30
Commission of Ways of Communication in America 30, 39, 45–47, 61, 150
Committee for Railway Orders 20, 27

Index   313

Communist International (Comintern) 75, 156, 232
Compagnie Internationale des Wagons-Lits 187
concessions 3–4, 68–69, 74, 119, 141, 164, 166, 187
Conference of Russian Communist Party, Eleventh 166
Congress of Economic Councils, Third 76, 103
Congress of Representatives of Trade and Industry 28
Congress of Russian Communist Party, Eleventh 191
Congress of Russian Communist Party, Ninth 74, 77–78, 80–81, 137
Congress of Russian Communist Party, Tenth 163–164, 194, 232
Congress of Traction Engineers, Thirty-Third 221
Coombes, W. H. 90
cooperative societies 77–78, 99, 111, 166
   see also Central Cooperative Society
Council of Foreign Trade 106, 141, 143–146, 152–153
Council of Labour and Defence (STO) 137, 142, 169, 171–173, 175–176, 178–179, 183–184, 187, 189, 191–193, 196, 199, 202, 207–208, 220, 222
   Armstrong contract 178
   Basic Transport Commission 137, 171, 173, 183
   cancellation of foreign contracts 187, 189, 191–193, 208
   Estonian locomotive overhaul contract 176, 208
   Gosplan review of NKPS supplies and foreign contracts 169, 172, 179, 187, 193, 198, 199
   locomotive-building and overhaul plans 137, 183–184, 192, 196, 199, 220, 222
   moratorium on new foreign contracts 169, 172–173
   oil-tanker contract 175
   imports plans 142, 169, 172–173
   water turbines contract 202
Council of Ministers 27–29
Council of People's Commissars (Sovnarkom) 5, 6, 8, 59, 65, 74, 78–80, 98, 104–105, 108, 135, 137, 137, 141–146, 150, 153, 155, 158, 165, 168, 170, 173, 175, 177–179, 181, 187–189, 191, 197, 200, 202–203, 205–2306, 208–209, 231
   abolition of Railway Mission 205–206
   arbitration role 141, 181
   Armstrong contract 177
   Avanesov's audit commission 200, 203
   Commission for Gold Affairs 173, 175, 179, 187, 189, 202–203
   Dzerzhinskii commission 197, 205
   foreign trade monopoly 65, 231
   gold expenditure for NKPS imports 5, 78–80, 98, 141–144, 146, 155, 158, 173, 175, 177–179, 188–189, 203, 208, 225
   Lomonosov reprimanded 203
   Lomonosov's mandates 104–105, 150, 153, 168, 197, 231
   moratorium on new foreign contracts 143, 158
   oil-tanker contract 173
   reviews imports plans 135, 141–142, 146, 158, 178
   shipment of railway imports 178
   water turbines contract 202
Crosby, Oscar T. 43–44
Curzon, Lord 102, 112, 116–117
Cuthell, White, Bayles and Appel, Inc. 92
Czechoslovakia 110, 119, 151, 154–155, 166, 201, 207

D'Abernon, Lord 269
Daily Herald 79
debts, Russia's foreign 1, 5, 15, 64, 67, 166
   abrogation of 1, 5, 64, 67
   claims against Soviet government 5, 94, 96, 99, 116
decapods – *see* locomotive classes
Denikin, General A. I. 49
Derutra 189
Deutsche Bank 128–129, 154
Deutsche Ökonomie GmbH 121–123, 125
dieselisation 38, 57–58, 62, 189, 208–210, 229

Disconto-Gesellschaft 128–129
Dobrovol'skii, N. I. 223
Dortmund Union 211
Dzerzhinskii, F. E. 164–165, 169, 172, 191, 193, 195–197, 200, 204–205, 220–223
  abolition of Railway Mission 197, 205
  appointed to NKPS 164–165, 172
  appointed to VSNKh 221
  commission to review NKPS foreign orders and Railway Mission 193, 195–197, 204
  defends Lomonosov 195, 200
  distrust of Krasin 169
  locomotive construction plans 220–222
  positive attitude to imports 172

Economist 164
economy, national 1–9, 13–23, 48–52, 56–57, 59–60, 62–63, 67, 72–82, 114, 135–136, 138–140, 157, 159, 163–166, 181, 200, 219–223, 225–228, 233–234
  crisis 2, 69, 23, 28, 30, 48–52, 135–136, 165, 181, 223, 225–228
  investment in 6, 14–19, 58–59, 80, 225–228, 233–234
  modernisation of 1, 5–6, 9, 13–23, 56–57, 62, 67, 72–76, 80–82, 135–136, 139–140, 157, 159, 164, 219, 221–223, 225–228, 233–234
  reconstruction of 1, 9, 56–57, 59–60, 62, 67, 72–82, 135–136, 139–140, 157, 159, 164–165, 173, 200, 219–223, 225–228, 233–234
Eesti Pank – *see* Estonia, Bank of
Ekonomicheskaia zhizn' 59, 67, 80, 86, 138, 181, 183, 192
electrification 1–3, 6, 48, 57, 61–62, 72–73, 81–82, 125–136, 139–140, 223, 225–226
  see also GOELRO; Lenin; All-Russian Congress of Soviets, Eighth
Elizarov, M. T. 53
Emshanov, A. I. 157, 165, 167, 171–172, 188–189, 191, 204, 206–208, 214, 223
  appointed as NKPS plenipotentiary 204
  cancellation of NKPS foreign locomotive contracts 188–189, 191, 204, 208, 214
  desire for imports 171–172, 188–189
Enskilda Bank 130
Erofeev, N. 57–58
Eskilstuna III 69, 93, 96
Esslingen machine-building works – *see* Maschinenfabrik Esslingen
Estonia 76–77, 88–92, 107, 110, 113, 115, 125, 157, 159, 170, 196, 194, 201, 207–208, 211–212, 214–215, 217
  Bank of 92
  government of 90–91, 107
  locomotive overhaul contract 107, 110, 113, 115, 157, 159, 176, 194, 201, 207–208, 210–212, 214–215, 217
  proposed NKPS Information and Technical Bureau 148
  Soviet peace talks and treaty with, 1919–20 76–77
Estonian Trading Company 107
Extraordinary Commission (Cheka) 58, 175, 200
Eyres, Lincoln 79

Falu Works 94–95
famine relief 165, 172, 179, 212–214, 230, 234
February Revolution 24, 32–33, 36, 38, 66
Filippov, L. V. 148–149, 151
Finland 70, 154, 170, 176
  shipment of locomotives via 170
First World War 3, 13, 20–21, 23–47, 51, 59, 65–66, 68–70, 105–106, 150, 154, 222, 225
  armaments crisis 23–24, 29, 47
  financial agreements 32–35, 37, 70
  foreign trade problems 3, 24–26, 31–32
  locomotive production 28–30
  military imports 26–27
  railway construction 25–26, 35
  railway equipment contracts 24, 26–30, 35, 39, 44–45, 69
  railway imports 13, 24, 26–47, 105–106
  railway investment 25–26, 28–29, 35–36, 222
  railway performance 24–26, 35–36, 40–42

supply committees 26, 30–31, 39
wagon production 30
see also Central War Industries Committee; Commission of Ways of Communication in America; Russian Government Committee in London; Russian Supply Committee in America; Special Council for Defence; Special Council for Shipments
Five-Year Plan, First 219, 222
Fomin, V. V. 81, 139, 148, 158, 165, 178, 188, 191, 206, 220, 223
  appointment of Trotskii to NKPS 81
  cancellation of NKPS foreign locomotive contracts 188, 191
  defends Lomonosov 178
  defends Trotskii 139
  desire for imports 188, 191
foreign trade – *see* trade, foreign
France 14, 26–27, 32, 34, 37, 40, 42, 64, 130–131, 187
  government of 102
  pressure on Swedish government 97, 130–131
  support for gold embargo 130
Francis, David R. 37
Fren, V. N. 107, 127, 150
Friedrich Krupp AG 109, 121–122, 133, 154, 211
  first contract for locomotive tyres 133, 211
  Krasin negotiations 109, 121–122
  see also Bamberger, Ludwig; Berg, Harald; Hagemann, Otto; Verband of German Locomotive-Building Companies
Frumkin, M. I. 205–206
fuel crisis 25, 35, 49–51, 135–136, 138–139, 157, 182, 184

Gakkel', Ia. M. 282
Gartvan, R. Ia. 194
Genoa conference on European reconstruction, 1922 166, 187, 190, 193
Germany 9, 14–15, 20, 26–27, 36, 63–68, 70–72, 75, 77, 93, 103, 108, 110, 114, 117–134, 142–146, 148–149, 151–158, 165–167, 169, 171, 184, 194, 201, 205, 207, 209, 228, 231, 233

  assistance to Kopp and Lomonosov 70–72, 131, 231
  attitudes to Allied policy 71–72, 121, 129
  banks' refusal to handle Soviet gold 130
  financial negotiations 128–133, 154–156
  Kopp recognised 71
  Lomonosov's negotiations, 1919 70–72
  'March Action' 156, 233
  Ministry of Foreign Affairs 9, 70–71, 126–129
  Ministry of Trade and Industry 126–127
  requests British support for Soviet contracts 117–119, 129–130
  Soviet economic relations with 63, 65–67, 117–121, 134, 145, 194
  Soviet–German Trade Agreement, 1921 165
Gerstner, Franz Anton von 18
Glass, J. R. 115
Glavmetall 180–181, 184, 190
Glover Locomotive Works 92
GOELRO 2–3, 73, 75, 135–136, 138–140, 157, 223, 225, 227–228, 233
  see also electrification; Basic Transport Commission; planning
gold reserve 4–6, 15, 80–82, 98, 135, 140–146, 151–159, 164, 172, 176, 181–184, 187, 189, 205, 212, 214–216, 222, 225, 227–231, 233–234
  Allied embargo of 72, 77, 101, 118, 130, 228, 231
  allocations from 5–6, 80–82, 98, 141–145, 144–145, 155, 158, 165, 177–179, 187, 189, 202, 225, 228–230, 233
  decision to spend on railway imports, 1920 5–7, 80–82, 142, 203, 222, 225, 228, 234
  German banks' refusal to handle 130
  obstacles to expenditure in Germany 121, 128–130
  reviews of expenditure priorities 135, 140–141, 143–146, 158–159, 172, 176, 178–179, 187, 190, 228–230

gold reserve (cont.)
  size of 5, 140, 164, 172, 179, 189–190, 212, 216, 225, 227–230, 234
  Swedish readiness to handle 98, 118–119, 128, 130–133, 151, 228
  Tsentrosoiuz control of sales 99, 131, 146, 153, 155
GOMZA 53, 55, 185–186, 190, 192–194
  campaign against NKPS foreign contracts 185–186, 190, 192–194
  locomotive production 55
  rolling-stock overhaul 193
Gordin 125
Gosplan – *see* State Planning Commission
Graftio, G. O. 202
Great Britain 9, 15–16, 18, 20, 24, 26, 32–36, 37, 40–41, 45, 72, 86, 90–94, 102–103, 108, 110–121, 124–125, 129–132, 142, 152, 156–157, 159, 163, 165, 176–177, 183, 197, 201, 207, 209, 223, 231, 233
  Admiralty 116
  Anglo–Soviet Trade Agreement, 1921 110, 116, 120, 152, 159, 163, 165, 197
  Cabinet 111, 116–119
  claims against Soviet government 116
  Department for Overseas Trade 163
  disposal of wartime supplies 45, 111
  financial support for German contract 117–119, 120–130
  Foreign Office 9, 34–35, 102, 177
  influence of Soviet railway contracts on British policy 116–120, 231
  Ministry of Food 94
  Ministry of Munitions 34, 111
  negotiations with Krasin, 1920–21 103, 108, 110–120, 124, 152
  pressure on Swedish government 97, 131–132
  property ownership test cases 116, 176
  Trade Mission in Moscow 163
  Treasury 32, 34–35
  War Office 34
  wartime loans to Russia 32–35, 43, 45
  see also Lloyd George, David; Sir W. G. Armstrong Whitworth and Company
Grinevetskii, V. I. 56–57, 63, 73

Grinshtein, A. I. 171, 178
Guaranty Trust Company 125
Gudok 137, 171, 183
Gukovskii, I. E. 77, 90–91, 103, 107, 148, 159, 174, 212

Hagemann, Otto 121, 123, 127–128
Hague international conference, 1922 195
Hamrin, Emil 94–97, 101–102
Haniel von Haimhausen, Edgar K. A. 127
Hannoversche Maschinenbau AG 71
Harbin workshops 31, 33, 36
Hartmann AG – *see* Sächsische Maschinenfabrik Richard Hartmann AG
Hellberg, Wilhelm 69, 99, 132
Henschel & Sohn 123, 133, 211
Hilger, Gustav 262
Hinger, A. W. 88–89
Hodgson, R. M. 177
Hohenzollern AG für Lokomotivbau 209
Holmquist 211
Hoover, Herbert H. 165
Horne, Sir Robert 119

Ianushevskii, P. S. 179, 220–221
Iaroslavskii, [E. M.] 200
imports policy 5–7, 14, 19, 24, 26–30, 36–37, 47, 67–69, 73–82, 85, 134–135, 140–142, 145–146, 151, 158–159, 164–167, 169, 172, 178–182, 184–186, 190, 200, 203–204, 207, 210, 212, 214–216, 222–223, 225–234
  duties (tariffs) 15, 19
  food products 158, 165, 179, 181–182, 192, 212, 215, 228
  NEP's impact on 140, 164, 166–167, 173, 180–181, 227–230
  priorities, 1920 5–6, 74–76, 78–79, 81–82, 134–135, 140–142, 145–146, 158–159, 225–228, 233–234
  substitution 15, 19–20
industrialisation 1, 6, 13–23, 64, 73, 76, 82, 222–223, 225–226, 228, 234
  Soviet 1, 64, 73, 76, 82, 222–223, 225–226, 228, 234
  tsarist 1, 6, 13–23, 82, 222–223, 226

industry, heavy engineering 15, 19–21,
    27–30, 36, 47, 53–56, 67, 76, 80, 82,
    102, 140, 142, 157, 164–165, 171,
    180–187, 190, 192–196, 199,
    207–208, 219–222, 226–229,
    233–234
  capacity 20–22, 27–30, 54–55, 80,
    102, 181–186, 219, 222
  cartels 20, 27
  locomotive-building plans 29, 36,
    80–81, 192–193, 196, 199, 220–222
  opposition to imports 20, 29, 76, 80,
    180–187, 189–194, 207–208, 219,
    229, 233
  overhauls of rolling-stock 55–56, 67,
    138–139, 143, 157, 220–222
  protectionism 19–20, 23–24, 47, 82,
    180–182, 229, 233
  tension with railways 19–20, 23,
    28–30, 47, 138–139, 180–196,
    220–222
  wartime performance 28–30, 36
  see also Glavmetall; GOMZA;
    Supreme Council of the National
    Economy
Inter-Allied Railway Committee 253
Inter-Allied Technical Board 253
intervention, Allied military 1, 52, 63,
    65, 68, 129
investment, foreign 1, 3, 5–6, 14–19, 23,
    57, 63–64, 73–74, 140, 163–164, 187,
    226–227
Ioffe, A. A. 66, 77
Ion, E. F. 125, 201–202
Irving, B. 113, 115
Italy 21, 34, 110, 142, 154–155, 166
Iugostal' Machine-Building Trust 192
Ivanov, General N. I. 38
Ivitskii, V. P. 94–95, 106, 112–113, 115,
    141–142
  liaison with British industry 112
  report about Armstrong Whitworth
    112–113
  revision of imports plans 106,
    141–142
  Swedish locomotive contract, 1920
    94–95, 106
Izvestiia 75

Johnson, Colonel Benjamin O. 87
Jorgen Hals AS 268

Kamenev, L. B. 140, 158, 167, 169, 223
  distrust of Krasin 169
  patron of Lomonosov 169, 223
  review of imports plan 158
Karakhan, L. M. 150
Kerzhentsev, P. M. 152, 166–169, 171,
    188–189, 191, 195, 198–199, 207,
    223, 231–232
  ambassador to Sweden 152
  negotiations with Swedish
    government, 1921–22 166, 188, 198
  part-cancellation of Swedish
    locomotive contract 188–189, 191,
    195, 198–199
  relations with Lomonosov 167–169,
    171, 189, 195, 207, 231–232
Khar'kov Transport Machine-Building
    Works 55, 192
Khrennikov, S. A. 194, 196, 199
Khinchuk, L. M. 104, 145–146
Kilmarnock, Lord 121
Kirsanov, P. N. 223
Knox, General Alfred 41
Kobozev, P. A. 53
Kogan, A. G. 194
Kolchak, Admiral A. V. 49
Kolegaev, A. L. 143, 147–150
Kolomna Machine-Building Works 36,
    53, 55, 185
Komgosor 202
Könemann, Dr 127
Konovalov, A. I. 137
Kopp, V. L. 71, 77, 108–109, 121–123,
    126–129, 131–132
  calls for resumption of trade 77
  locomotive negotiations in Germany
    108–109, 121–123, 126–129
  negotiations with Markevich
    128–129, 132
  recognition by German government
    71, 121
  relations with Lomonosov 126–127
  value of his German contracts, 1920
    134
Krasin, L. B. 38, 49, 53, 59–63, 66–69,
    71–82, 85, 90–106, 108–117,
    119–135, 141, 143, 145, 147,
    151–153, 155–156, 158, 166–171,
    173–177, 179–180, 182–183, 191,
    193, 196–197, 201–206, 210, 223,
    226, 228, 230–234

Krasin, L. B. (*cont.*)
  American locomotive discussions 90–92, 125, 173–174
  Anglo–Soviet negotiations, 1920–21 74, 103, 108, 110–117, 119–120, 124, 152, 177, 197
  appointment to NKPS, 1919 53, 59, 69
  appointment to NKTiP, 1918 67
  appointment to Tsentrosoiuz delegation 78
  Armstrong locomotive overhaul contract 113–116, 120, 169, 176–179, 231
  Canadian locomotive discussions 129–130
  fears about gold exports 152–153
  German locomotive negotiations, 1920–21 120–134, 156, 197
  German trade negotiations, 1918 66–67
  Lomonosov's mandates 105, 108, 153, 197
  oil-tanker contracts 175, 179
  railway reconstruction 59–62, 78, 80–82, 143, 173, 203
  relations with Lomonosov and Railway Mission 105–106, 108–109, 122–124, 134, 152–153, 156, 167–171, 183, 193, 196–197, 204, 206, 231–232
  Revalis locomotive contract 91–92, 154, 174
  Stalin's criticisms of 168–169, 191
  Swedish Concern credit contract 96, 99
  Swedish locomotive negotiations, contracts, 1920–22 92–103, 106, 141, 145, 151, 191, 197, 201, 203–204, 210, 231, 233
  Swedish trade negotiations, 1918–19 68–69, 96
  theses about foreign trade, 1920 74, 204, 226
  Tsentrosoiuz delegation 78, 81, 85, 93–94, 99
  Tsentrosoiuz mandate 98, 104
  use of intermediaries 93, 121–122, 193, 230–231
  water turbines contract 201–202
  see also People's Commissariat of Foreign Trade

Krasina, L. 66
Krasovskii, P. I. 176, 194–195, 221, 223
Krestinskii, N. N. 78, 128, 166–167, 203–204, 207, 209, 223
Kronshtadt rebellion 158–159
Krumin, G. 138
Krupp – *see* Friedrich Krupp AG
Krylov, A. N. 170
Krzhizhanovskii, G. M. 191, 202

Lansbury, George 79
Lansing, Robert 42–43
Lapirov-Skoblo, M. Ia. 68
Lazerson, M. Ia. 115, 128–129, 132, 150, 155
Leeds Forge Company 175, 211
Legien, Karl 121–122, 128
Lend-Lease locomotive deliveries 174
Lenin, V. I. 1, 3, 5–8, 49, 61, 63–65, 72–73, 75–76, 79, 93, 103–105, 119, 126, 133, 135, 140–141, 145, 150, 153, 156, 163–164, 166–168, 170–171, 177, 184, 189, 191, 194, 201–204, 206, 221, 225, 232–233
  assessment of first German railway contracts 145
  attitude to Railway Mission 150, 168, 170
  concessions policy 141, 163–164
  economic strategy 1, 72–73, 76, 163–164, 167, 194, 203–204, 225
  electrification 1, 3, 73, 135, 140
  foreign trade 1, 5–7, 65, 76, 79, 104–105, 156, 163–164, 166–168, 170, 184, 194, 203–204, 206, 225, 233
  international revolution 1, 6, 63–64
  labour conscription 75
  peaceful coexistence 5–6, 64, 164
  postwar reconstruction 1, 3, 5–6, 72–73, 76, 135, 140, 164, 167, 194, 203–204, 225
  relations with Lomonosov 8, 61, 103, 150, 168, 170–171, 206, 232
  water turbines contract 201–202
Levi, L. M. 35, 47
Lezhava, A. I. 75, 109, 143, 145–146, 150–151, 158, 167–168, 171, 201, 223
  creation of Railway Mission 150
  resignation refused by Politburo 171

Linke-Hofmann Werke AG 175, 211
Lion 121–122
Litvinov, M. M. 69, 72, 77–78, 85, 93, 97–98, 129, 145, 150–151, 155, 167, 191, 193, 195–196, 198–199
  creation of Railway Mission 150
Lloyd George, David 72, 110–112, 114, 116–120, 129, 152, 163
  aide-mémoire from Simons 117–120, 129
Ljungman, Andreas 97
loans, foreign 14–15, 18–19, 26, 32–37, 42–44, 70, 74, 89, 96, 99, 140, 143, 146, 155, 158–159, 164, 166, 178–179, 182, 185, 187–188, 190, 198, 222, 226–229
  NKVT optimism 166
  proposed Swedish, 1921–22 188, 198
  relative lack of 140, 158, 166, 179, 222, 227–228
  see also Genoa conference; investment; Swedish Concern
locomotive-building (in Russia) 19–23, 28–30, 54–56, 68–69, 80–81, 86, 180–187, 192–196, 219–222, 232, 234
  cartelisation of industry 20
  commencement 19–20
  new contracts opposed by NKPS, 1922 192–196
  new policy, 1919 54–56
  new plan, summer 1922 195–196, 199
  state support for 19–20, 80, 181–187, 192–196
  see also Glavmetall; GOMZA
locomotive classes
  A 0-6-0+0-6-0 Mallet 27–28, 35, 46
  E 0-10-0 22–23, 27–28, 30, 36, 61–62, 70, 82, 85, 105–106, 123–124, 127, 154, 156, 158, 184–186, 198, 210–211, 219, 224, 233–234
  Flamme 2-10-0 35, 106
  G-10 0-10-0 (German) 127
  O 0-8-0 107, 139, 176–177
  G-12 2-10-0 (German) 122
  R 0-10-0 (Swedish) 99, 105
  S 2-6-2 22, 28, 219
  Shch 2-8-0 22, 28, 177
  Ye 2-10-0 'decapod' 28–31, 33–35, 37, 39–40, 42–47, 61–62, 70–71, 82,
    85–92, 105, 107, 110, 123, 125, 127, 154, 173–174, 219, 233
locomotives
  cancellation of contracts for 45–46, 105–106, 151–152, 174, 179, 184, 187–199, 200–201, 205, 209–211, 219, 229–230
  diesel 38, 58, 189, 208–210, 212–213, 223, 229
  faults 31, 203, 205, 209
  increasing availability, 1920 136
  Lend-Lease deliveries 174
  modernisation of stock 62, 82, 139, 173, 184, 208–210, 217, 219, 221–222, 224, 226–229, 233–234
  'powerful' types 22–23, 219
  proposed expansion of stock (1914) 22–23, 219
  proposed new designs (1914, 1919, 1923) 22–23, 58, 62, 221
  repair strategy 25, 55–57, 67–68, 136–139, 157, 172, 193
  second-hand purchases 35, 105–106
  shipments to Russia 7, 31, 46, 167, 169–170, 175, 178–179, 188–190, 207–208, 229
  'sickness' 36, 51–52, 193, 217, 234
  technical standardisation 58, 61, 106
  see also industry, heavy engineering; Nydqvist & Holm AB; Verband of German Locomotive-Building Companies
Lomonosov, Iu. V. 6, 8, 23, 38–39, 44–45, 47, 61–62, 69–72, 76, 89, 91, 101, 103–109, 114–118, 120, 122–135, 143, 145–156, 158–159, 167–171, 173–178, 182–183, 188–190, 193–199, 200–210, 212, 223, 231–234
  abolition of Railway Mission 170–171, 197, 200, 204–206, 232
  acting Head of Tsentrosoiuz Delegation in Sweden 125
  alleged negligence and dishonesty 203–205
  American locomotive negotiations, 1920–21 91, 107, 125, 154, 173–174
  appointment as Sovnarkom plenipotentiary 103–105, 150, 153, 168, 231
  Armstrong contract 114–116, 169,

Lomonosov, Iu. V. (*cont.*)
  176–178, 201, 203, 205, 208, 210–211
 Branting meetings 125
 Canadian locomotive discussions 129–130, 156
 cancellation of NKPS foreign locomotive contracts 151–152, 187–190, 193–199, 201, 205, 209–211
 career 38
 creates Railway Mission 150–151, 231Ó
 diesel locomotives 38, 189, 208–210, 212–213, 223
 Estonian locomotive overhaul contract 107, 115, 176, 194, 201, 208
 financial negotiations and operations 126, 128–133, 154–156, 171, 178, 182, 188–190, 196–199, 201–205, 208
 German locomotive negotiations, 1920–21 109, 118, 120–135, 154–157
 Kamenev's patronage 169, 223
 loans to Nohab 131, 182, 198
 mandates (Sovnarkom, Tsentrosoiuz) 103–105, 150, 168, 197
 negotiations in Europe, 1919 70–72, 122
 Nohab locomotive negotiations 101, 123, 125, 130–133, 182, 197–199, 208
 oil-tanker contracts 175
 opposes Chicherin over Nordiska agreement 151–152
 Palmstierna meetings 125, 132
 proposed order for 100 locomotives, 1922 188
 relations with colleagues 38, 105, 108–109, 126, 146–147, 149–150, 152–153, 155–156, 167–171, 189, 193, 195–197, 199–200, 202–206, 209, 231–232
 report (final) to Sovnarkom 204–205
 reprimanded by Sovnarkom 203
 shipment of railway imports 167, 169–170, 178, 188–189, 206, 208
 'shock programme' of NKPS orders 153–154, 169
 speech to Third Congress of Economic Councils, 1920 76, 103
 Stalin's support for 168–169
 subordinated directly to Sovnarkom 104–105, 150, 168, 231
 technical quality control 103, 108, 123–124, 146–147, 151, 202–203, 233
 Central Committee commission, 1921 167–168
 wartime work in United States 38–39, 44–45, 47, 89, 104
 water turbines contract 125, 201–202
Lomonosova, R. N. 155, 199
Lomov, M. A. 56, 76
London Joint City and Midland Bank 198
Lugansk Machine-Building Works 55, 192
Lutovinov, Iu. Kh. 165–166, 170

Main Artillery Directorate 26–27
Mallet locomotives 27–28, 35, 46
Maltzan, Adolf 126–127
Mannesmann company 133, 211
Markevich, Otto 128–129, 132
Martens, L. K. 61, 69, 85, 88–89, 91–92, 108–109, 154, 180, 184
Maschinenfabrik Esslingen 209
McAdoo, William G. 37, 39–40, 43–44
McCall, R. B. 115
Medved'ev 200
Mendelssohn & Co. 128–129, 154
Metallgesellschaft (Frankfurt) 122
metal industry – *see* industry
Mikhailov, I. D. 86, 144
Mikhailov, V. M. 167
military imports 214–215, 230
Miliukov, P. N. 37
Miliutin, V. P. 78, 139
Ministry of Finances 26, 32
Ministry of Trade and Industry 27
Ministry of Ways of Communication (MPS) 17, 19–20, 22–24, 26–39, 41, 45–47, 49, 147, 219
 Committee for Railway Orders 20, 27
 control of railway system 19
 interest in postwar modernisation 25–26, 29, 35–36, 47
 wartime orders 24–37, 39–47
Mirbach, Wilhelm Graf von 120
Mission of Ways of Communication in

America – see Commission of Ways of Communication in America
modernisation 1–3, 5–7, 9, 13–23, 25–26, 29, 35–36, 47–49, 56–63, 73, 76, 78, 80–82, 106, 135–140, 143, 157, 159, 173, 187, 208, 210, 219, 222–228, 233–234
Moll, Victor 132
Molotov, V. M. 167, 189
Motala Works 94–95
Mozherez (Moscow Railway Repair Factory) 59, 68, 187–188, 221
Müller, Hermann 72
Murmansk 21, 24, 26, 41
Murmansk Railway 24, 30, 33, 41, 57

Naglovskii, A. 166
Nekrasov, N. V. 42
Neopikhanov, A. A. 196
Nevskii Ship- and Machine-Building Works 55, 68, 192
Nevskii, V. I. 53
New Economic Policy 2, 5, 7, 9, 140, 159, 163–166, 171, 180–181, 227–230
  financial discipline 140, 180–181, 228
  financial retrenchment 164, 169, 171–173, 179, 228–229
  impact on foreign trade 5, 7, 164–166, 173, 180, 228–230
New Statesman 163
Nicholas I, tsar of Russia 16, 18
Nicholas II, tsar of Russia 32–34
Nikolaevsk 26
Nohab – see Nydqvist & Holm AB
Nol'tein, E. E. 58
Nordiska Handelsbanken 99–100, 130–133, 146, 151–152, 155–156
  Anderson–Nohab locomotive contract 99–100
  Chicherin seeks cancellation of agreement 151–152
  finance for German locomotive contract via Nohab 130–133, 146, 155
  gold sales 99, 131–133, 146, 155–156
  Swedish Concern credit contract 99
North British Locomotive Company 269
Norway 66, 166

Novorossiisk 175
Nydqvist family 100–101
Nydqvist & Holm AB (Nohab) 8, 94–97, 99–103, 105, 110, 116, 122, 125, 130–133, 141–144, 149, 182–183, 185, 188, 194–198, 200–202, 205, 207–212, 214–215, 219, 230
  acquired by Anderson 100–101
  amendments to locomotive contract 100, 182, 196–199
  financial difficulties 197, 207
  initial contacts with Krasin 94–95, 97
  locomotive contract's terms 99–101
  part-cancellation of locomotive contract 142, 188, 194–198, 200–201, 205, 209–211, 214–215, 219, 230
  possible transfer of contract to Germany 101–102, 130, 143
  Soviet loans 131, 182, 198
  Soviet technical inspection personnel 103, 149, 233
  subcontracting production 101–102, 130
  water turbines contract 125, 201–202, 207, 210–211, 213, 215–216

Observer 77
October Revolution 1, 13, 26, 38, 44–45, 61, 66, 68, 137, 147, 223
  impact on wartime foreign contracts 44–45
oil-tanker contracts 151, 174–177, 179, 185, 190, 207, 210–212, 217, 229
O'Malley, Owen 102
Orgburo – see Russian Communist Party
Osinskii, N. (V. V. Obolenskii) 64–65, 158
Ostapenko, S. S. 35

Palmstierna, Baron Erik 93–94, 98–99, 102, 107, 112, 125, 131–132, 151
  assists Soviet locomotive order in Germany 131–132
  attitude to Allied policy 93, 99, 102
  authorisation of Soviet contracts 98–99, 102
  demands return of Swedish state property 98–99, 125, 151

Palmstierna, Baron Erik (*cont.*)
  expectations of Soviet trade 93–94
  recognises Lomonosov as Tsentrosoiuz representative 125
peaceful coexistence 5, 6, 64
People's Commissariat of Agriculture 141, 179, 215
People's Commissariat of Finances 8, 189, 195, 216
People's Commissariat of Food Procurement 145, 179, 215
People's Commissariat of Foreign Affairs 145, 150, 152, 171
People's Commissariat of Foreign Trade (NKVT) 7–8, 74, 79–80, 114, 141, 146, 148, 150, 153, 165–171, 178, 180–183, 188, 190–191, 193–194, 196–197, 201–207, 231–232
  audit of trade delegations, 1922 201–202
  coordination with Railway Mission 150–151, 153, 167–171, 193, 196–197, 203–207, 231–232
  creation of 74, 141
  monopoly of foreign trade 7, 153, 166–168, 180, 183, 197, 231
  relations with VSNKh 180–183
People's Commissariat of Trade and Industry (NKTiP) 65, 67, 69, 74, 141
People's Commissariat of Ways of Communication (NKPS) 7, 49–50, 52–54, 56, 58–60, 62, 65–69, 76, 78–79, 81–82, 85, 87, 91, 95, 98, 103–108, 113–114, 125, 135–150, 153–154, 157–159, 164–173, 175–176, 178–196, 199–200, 203–209, 212, 214–225, 227–233
  Armstrong locomotive overhaul contract 114, 157–158, 176–179
  Bureau for Foreign Orders 66–67
  Collegium 8, 108, 136–137, 157, 169, 171, 195, 206, 223
  Commission for the Improvement of Transport 59
  Communications Directorate 147, 150
  critique of GOMZA campaign, 1922 187–188, 192–193, 195–196
  desire for imports 7, 65–66, 69, 79, 106, 138, 141–144, 154, 157, 169, 171–173, 175–176, 181, 187–189, 207, 228
  Directorate of Economics and Materials 53–54, 66, 106, 143, 147–149, 172, 218
  Estonian locomotive overhaul contract 107, 176, 194
  financial policy 165, 181, 184
  imports plans 7, 69, 79, 106, 141–146, 153–154, 158, 169, 172–173, 178–179, 182, 189, 207, 216–217, 225–226, 228, 234
  Inspectorate of Ways of Communication 176
  labour militarisation 136–137
  locomotive-building plans 55–56, 80–81, 183–184, 192–193, 195–196, 199, 200, 219–222, 232
  Main Directorate 147–148
  Main Directorate for Waterways 147
  oil-tanker contracts 175–176, 179, 185
  Operations Directorate 81
  Order No. 1042 138–139, 142, 157, 172
  Order No. 1157 138, 142, 157, 172
  political support lost, 1920 135, 140, 145, 157, 159, 222–223, 227–228
  postwar priorities 56–63, 225–226
  priority for imports, 1920 74, 78–79, 135, 145, 159, 222, 225–226, 228, 233–234
  propaganda 137
  reconstruction strategy 9, 48–49, 56–63, 78–82, 105–106, 135, 137–140, 144, 157, 159, 165, 173, 187, 203, 219–228, 233–234
  relations with NKVT 148, 169, 205–207
  relations with Railway Mission 150, 169, 178, 205–206
  relations with VSNKh 137–139, 141–144, 171, 175, 178, 181, 184, 188–189, 192, 200, 207, 219–222, 232
  rolling-stock reconstruction and modernisation 56–63, 82, 105–106, 137–139, 141–144, 157–159, 172–173, 208–210, 217, 219, 221–222, 224, 226–229, 233–234
  Secretariat for Foreign Orders 148, 172

Special Technical Conference for
  Foreign Orders 147–148
storage of serviceable locomotives
  136, 182, 185
Technical Committee 60–62, 82,
  105–106, 204, 209
Technical Directorate 76, 137–138,
  147, 149, 157
Traction Department 176, 194
trades unions 137, 139
Trotskii's appointment, 1920 81, 85
unacceptability of new foreign
  locomotive types 105–106
workshops 53, 68, 74, 138, 157, 170,
  183
People's Commissariat of Workers' and
  Peasants' Inspection (NKRKI) 139,
  175–177, 190, 193, 200, 204
  assesses NKPS imports 176, 204–205
  attacks NKPS 139
  investigation of Railway Mission
    204–205
  opposes overhauling locomotives
    abroad 176–177
Perno, F. F. 214
Peters, William 163–164, 166
Petrograd 33, 37–41, 55, 58, 67–69, 94,
  170, 192
Phoenix Wagon Works 30
Poland 24–25, 89–90, 108, 112, 116, 118,
  120, 122, 134, 136, 142, 180, 190,
  209
Politburo – *see* Russian Communist
  Party
Polovtseva, V. N. 77
Porter Company, H. K. 30
Pravda 49, 75, 139, 192, 194
Pravosudovich, M. E. 137
Preobrazhenskii, E. A. 63
Pressed Steel Car Company 90
Preston, Sir Walter 178
Prodvagon 28–30
protectionism 13, 18–20, 23–24, 47, 82,
  180–187, 226–227, 229–230
Provisional government 24, 36, 44, 46
  attitude towards USA 36–37
  railway crisis 36
Putilov Machine-Building Company 55,
  58, 62, 68, 192
Putilov, A. I. 33
Puzanov, M. P. 185

Rabinov, Maks 91–92
Radek, K. B. 75
Raevskii, A. S. 62
rails 19–20, 22, 24–25, 28, 30–31, 33–34,
  42, 45–46, 54, 58, 60, 67, 90, 142,
  144, 174, 185, 190, 211–213,
  216–217, 223, 229
  disposal of wartime supplies 45–46
  domestic production 19, 28, 30, 54
  imports of 19, 24–25, 28, 30, 33–34,
    142, 144, 174, 185, 190, 211–213,
    216–217, 223, 229
railway construction 6, 13, 15–19,
  21–23, 25–26, 35, 57–58, 61, 74, 187,
  222
railway imports policy, 1920–23 5–9,
  13, 24, 47, 78–82, 134–135, 151,
  158–159, 164, 200, 203–205,
  210–220, 225–230, 233–234
  origins 5–7, 13, 24, 47, 82, 203–205,
    225–227
  overall results 210–220, 228–229
Railway Mission – *see* Russian Railway
  Mission Abroad
railways
  Archangel–Vologda 24, 27, 41, 47, 57
  Chinese Eastern 31, 41, 46, 87
  Dneiper 224
  Murmansk 24, 30, 33, 41, 47
  Nicholas 68, 115, 224
  North Western 224
  October 224
  Perm' 157
  St Petersburg–Moscow 19
  St Petersburg–Tsarskoe Selo 16, 18
  Tashkent 208
  trans-Siberian (route) 16–17, 20, 24,
    40–41, 47, 57
  Turkestan-Siberian (Turksib) 222
  Western 224
railway transport
  civil war crisis of 8–9, 48–56,
    136–137, 139, 165, 171–172,
    225–226
  civil war damage 53
  common-carrier system 17
  condition in 1914 21–23, 56–57
  finances 19, 21–22, 57, 165, 181, 184,
    192
  investment 13, 16–19, 21–23, 25–26,
    36, 47, 58, 63, 73–74, 135, 139–140,

railway transport (*cont.*)
    159, 184, 187, 217, 219–222, 225, 227–228, 234
  modernisation 7, 22, 25–26, 29, 35–36, 47–49, 56–63, 73, 76, 78, 80–82, 106, 135, 137–140, 143–144, 157, 159, 173, 184, 187, 208–210, 219, 221–222, 224, 226–229, 233–234
  nationalisation 19
  political support lost, 1920 135, 140, 145, 157, 159, 222–223, 227–228
  procurement policy 5–7, 18–19, 23–24, 29–30, 76, 82, 171–173, 181–84, 203–205, 226
  proposed 'railway ruble' 187
  traffic 17, 21–25, 36, 40–41, 50–51, 53, 57, 60–62, 78, 136, 165, 172, 186, 188–189, 195–196, 220–222
Rapallo, Treaty of 166, 194
reconstruction strategy 1–3, 5–9, 48–49, 56–57, 60–65, 72–76, 85, 135–136, 139–140, 157, 159, 164–165, 173, 219, 222–228, 233–234
  role of railways 5–9, 48–49, 56–57, 60, 62, 72–73, 78–82, 135–136, 139–140, 157, 159, 165, 173, 222–223, 225–228, 233–234
  roles for foreign resources 1, 3, 5, 60–61, 63–65, 73–76, 78–82, 164, 222–223, 226–227, 231, 233
  sector-by-sector approach 49, 81–82, 140, 159, 225–227
Red Army 53, 67, 81, 86, 124
Reichsbetrieb 123
Remington Arms Company 27
Revalis Company 91–92, 96, 107, 154, 174, 211
Review of Reviews 163
Rheinmetall (Rheinische Metallwaren- und Maschinenfabrik) 211
Riga 30, 170
Riga, Mayor of 90
Riga, Treaty of 190
Rogov, A. G. 53
Romanov, V. V. 149
Rotshtein, F. A. 151
Rudyi, Iu.V. 87, 206–207, 209, 214
Rudzutak, Ia. E. 221
Rukhlov, S. V. 27–32

Russia Company 36
Russian Communist Party (Bolshevik)
  Central Committee 8, 38, 49, 65, 72, 77, 81, 140, 145, 151, 158, 163, 165, 167–169, 181, 187–189, 191, 204, 206, 221–222
  arbitration role 167, 181
  commission about Railway Mission, 1921 167–169
  commission reviews imports plan 158, 165
  foreign trade monopoly 167, 206
  Orgburo 8, 140–141, 167
  Politburo 8, 77–78, 98, 101, 104, 109, 122, 140, 152, 163, 165, 171, 177, 181, 189–193, 195–197, 203, 205
  abolition of Railway Mission 197, 205
  appoints Dzerzhinskii commission 193
  arbitration role 181
  confirms Swedish agreements 152
  expenditure on imports 98, 190
  Lomonosov's mandate 104
  rejects German locomotive offer 109, 122
Russian Government Committee in London 26
Russian Railway Mission Abroad 6, 8, 110, 150–151, 153, 155, 159, 167–171, 174, 179, 183, 187–189, 191, 193, 196–197, 199–210, 213–216, 223, 231–233
  abolition 170–171, 197, 200, 204–206, 232
  audit of its commercial activity, 1922 200–204
  bonus payments 201–203
  communist contingent 201, 233
  complaints against 153, 155, 167–171, 189, 191, 193, 196–197, 199–205, 231–232
  coordination with NKVT 153, 167–171, 183, 197, 203–207, 231–232
  creation and legal status of 6, 150, 168, 197, 231
  final contracts 207–210
  Lenin's support for 150, 168, 206
  NKPS support for 169, 188, 205–206
  opposed by Kerzhentsev 167–169, 171, 189, 232

Index

opposed by Krasin 153, 155, 167–171, 196–197, 206, 232
payroll 201
raison d'être 150, 167–169
salaries 201–203
Shipping Department 170
structure 150–151, 168
technical quality control 151, 207, 233
value of orders 210–216
Russian Railway Service Corps 41, 87
Russian Supply Committee in America 26, 30–31, 39
Russo-Baltic Wagon Works 30
Rykov, A. I. 75–76, 145, 180, 192, 204, 208

Sandström 255
Sächsische Maschinenfabrik Richard Hartmann AG 123
Savel'ev, M. 67, 73
Sazherez (Samara Railway Repair Factory) 59, 68, 188
'scissors crisis' 221
scrap metal, sales of 188–189, 207–208
Serebriakov, L. P. 145, 206
Sereda, S. P. 145
'Shakhty' affair 223
Shatunovskii, Ia. 79, 86
Shchukin, N. L. 23, 28–30, 33, 59, 149
Shchukin Commission – *see* Commission for Rolling Stock and Traction
Sheinman, A. L. 104
Shelest, A. N. 58, 107, 208–209
Shelest, N. P. 107
Shliapnikov, A. G. 139, 191
Shtein, B. E. 3
Shulenburg, S. I. 30, 37, 39
Siemens-Schückert Electrical Company 66, 103
Simons, Dr Walter 117–120, 129
aide-mémoire to Lloyd George 117–119, 129
Sir W. G. Armstrong Whitworth and Company 111–116, 120, 157–158, 169, 176–179, 183, 190, 201, 203, 205, 208–211, 229, 231–232
boilers 177–178, 190, 203, 205, 208, 210–212, 229
locomotive overhaul contract 113–116, 120, 157–159, 176–177, 183, 231
Skandinaviska Bank 130
SKF 100
Skidelski 34
Skoda works 207
'Socialism in One Country' 222, 227
Sokol'nikov, G. Ia. 167, 190
Solomon, G. A. 107, 110, 153, 155, 157, 176
Sormovo Machine-Building Works 53, 55, 94, 149, 185
Sovnarkom – *see* Council of People's Commissars
spare parts 24–25, 33, 45–46, 51, 53, 72, 74, 78–81, 93, 111, 121, 137–138, 141–145, 149, 153–154, 157, 159, 170–173, 175–177, 181–182, 188–189, 192–193, 195, 207–208, 211–213, 216–217, 228–229, 233–234
imports in WWI 24–25, 33, 45–46
needed for seed campaign, 1922 188–189
shortages 51, 53, 138, 142–143, 157, 171–172, 181, 188–189, 192–193, 216–217, 228, 234
Special Council for Defence 25, 35, 38
Special Council for Shipments 30
Stalin, I. V. 2, 139–140, 167–169, 191–192, 196, 222, 228
attacks Krasin 168–169, 191
industrialisation 2, 9, 222, 228
praises GOELRO plan 140
supports Lomonosov 168, 169
Stamfordham, Lord 117
Standard Steel Car Company 39
Stark 70
State Commission for the Electrification of Russia – *see* GOELRO
State Duma 26, 59
State Planning Commission (Gosplan) 8, 158, 164, 166, 169, 172–173, 175–176, 178–179, 181, 183, 187, 190–196, 199–200, 202, 207, 214, 220–222, 230, 232
arbitration role 181, 195–196, 221, 232
Energy Section 202
Estonian locomotive overhaul contract 176, 194
Industry Section 194, 196, 199
oil-tanker contracts 175

Index

State Planning Commission (*cont.*)
  Presidium 179, 194, 196, 199
  review of NKPS supplies and foreign contracts 169, 172–173, 175, 191, 193–195
  reviews of imports plans 158, 169, 172–173, 175, 189, 190, 207, 230
  shipment of railway imports 178–179
  Sub-Commission for Foreign Trade and Concessions 172, 178–179
  Transport Section 179, 196, 220
Steinbach 154
Stepanova-Skvortsova, I. I. 265
Stevens, John F. 40–44, 47, 87
Stiunkel', B. 181–184
Stockhammern, Karl Edler von 71–72
Stol 103
Stomoniakov, B. S. 96, 165, 167–170, 197, 204, 231
subversion 116–117, 119, 233
Sudakov, P. I. 184, 190–191
supermainlines 57, 62, 187
Supreme Council of the National Economy (VSNKh) 56, 64, 67, 75, 78, 80, 106, 137–144, 148, 171, 175, 178–184, 188–196, 199–202, 207, 219–222, 232–233
  campaign against railway imports 180–184, 188–196, 207–208
  Committee for Foreign Trade 140–141, 144, 180, 201
  Council of Foreign Trade 106, 141, 143–146, 152–153
  Department of Metal 56, 80, 138, 141, 180
  Elektrostroi 201
  foreign trade monopoly 180–183
  Glavmetall 180–181, 184, 190
  imports plans 106, 141–142, 144, 179–182
  Komgosor 202
  locomotive-building plans 56, 80–81, 183–184, 192–193, 195–196, 199–200, 220–222, 232
  protectionism 180–187
  relations with NKPS 137–139, 141–144, 171, 175, 178, 181, 184, 188–189, 192, 200, 219–222, 232
  'shock' factories 138
Svenska Järnvägsverkstad AB 95
Svenska Riksbank – *see* Sweden, Bank of

Sverdlov, V. M. 137, 144
Svirstroi 125, 201
Sweden 9, 66, 68–70, 91–107, 118–119, 125, 128, 130–133, 145–146, 148–149, 151–156, 166, 171, 185–186, 188, 191, 194–198, 200–202, 204, 208, 224, 228, 231
  assistance for Soviet locomotive contract in Germany 130–133
  attitude to Allied policy 68, 93, 99, 102, 130–132, 228
  Bank of 95, 99, 130–132, 152
  claims against Soviet government 94, 96, 99
  engineering industry 70, 93, 97, 102, 131
  expectations of Soviet trade 93–94
  General Association of Exporters 96
  government's approval for Tsentrosoiuz contracts 98–99, 102, 133
  Lomonosov's visit, 1919 70
  Minister of Finances 93, 133
  Minister of Justice 204
  Ministry of Foreign Affairs 9, 93–95
  part-cancellation of locomotive contract 188, 191, 194–198
  Red Cross personnel 94, 107
  rejection of draft Trade Agreement, 1922 166, 188, 194
  Soviet boycott of 93
  Trade Agreement, 1924 166
  trade agreement negotiations, 1921–22 166, 188, 198
  Tsentrosoiuz delegation 93–94, 98–99, 125, 151, 171
  trade representative in Russia 98
  see also gold reserve; Palmstierna; Anderson, Gunnar; Nydqvist & Holm AB
Swedish Concern 96, 99, 101, 125, 158–159, 201
  credit contract's terms 99
  water turbines contract 125, 201
  see also Anderson, Gunnar; Krasin, L. B.
Switzerland 116, 119, 154, 209

Tallinn 77, 90–93, 103, 107–108, 123, 125, 148, 151–153, 155–156, 170
Tereshchenko, M. I. 37

Index

trade agreements 3, 78, 103, 108, 110–111, 115–116, 120, 129, 163, 165–166, 188, 194, 197
   Anglo–Soviet, 1921 110, 116, 120, 152, 159, 163, 165, 197
   Soviet–German, 1921 165
trade delegations 3, 98–99, 104, 125, 148, 150, 152, 165–166, 169–171, 177, 201–202, 205–206
   Berlin 3, 148, 165, 169–171
   London 3, 177, 212
   see also All-Russian Cooperative Society Ltd
trade, foreign (external) 1–9, 15, 24, 26, 48, 53, 63–69, 72–82, 85, 112, 121, 133–134, 140–141, 145, 151–152, 159, 163–166, 180, 182, 184, 206, 212–216, 223, 225–234
   collapse of 3–4, 26, 48, 53
   desirability of 1, 4–5, 64, 66–68, 73–76, 85, 112, 140–141, 151, 226–227
   interwar patterns 223, 230
   legal framework for 3
   pre-1914 patterns 15–16, 226, 230
   priorities 74, 78–82, 141, 145, 225, 227, 234
   revival of 2–4, 65, 112, 121, 133–134, 159, 184, 223, 225, 228–230, 233–234
   see also People's Commissariat of Foreign Trade
trades unions controversy 139
Trepov, A. F. 26, 32–35
Trotskii, L. D. 49, 63–67, 73–81, 85–86, 103–106, 109, 133, 135–141, 143, 145, 150, 157, 173, 191, 195, 206, 226
   appointment to NKPS 81, 85
   attitude to imports 73–77, 79–80, 86, 105–106, 138, 141, 143, 145
   Basic Transport Commission 137–138
   controversy about his NKPS work 135, 139
   economic strategy 73–81, 136–140, 173, 226
   foreign trade monopoly 206
   international revolution 63–65
   Lomonosov's mandate 104–105, 150
   relations with Stalin 139–140
   resignation from NKPS 140, 157

trades unions 137, 139
transport crisis 49, 136–139
transport reconstruction policy 78, 81, 85, 136–140, 173
tsarist government 13–26, 28–29, 32–34, 36, 46, 64, 66, 181, 226
Tsentrosoiuz – *see* Central Cooperative Society
Tsiurupa, A. D. 158, 163, 190–191
turbines – *see* water turbines contract
tyres 30, 36, 70, 72, 121, 125, 133, 143, 153, 171, 181, 185, 190, 211–213, 216–218, 229

Uggla, Erland 95, 97, 101–102
Ugol' Trust 179
Union of Metalworkers 80, 190–191
United Mechanical Factories of Estonia 211
United Railway Equipment Company 122
United States 9, 20–21, 27–28, 30, 35–37, 39–46, 61, 66–67, 70, 79, 85–92, 108, 117–119, 125, 130, 142, 150, 154–155, 165, 173–174, 180, 187
   analysis of Russian railway crisis 40–43, 47
   Council of National Defense 39, 42–43
   deliveries to White forces, 1918–19 46–47
   Director General of Military Railroads 46
   disposal of wartime supplies 45–47, 86, 88, 92
   industrial capacity 43, 70, 85–86, 118, 142
   inter-Allied supply policy 39–40, 42–43
   minor Soviet railway contracts 92, 174
   restrictions on trade with Soviet Russia 45, 88, 90, 92, 154, 173–174
   Revalis contract 91–92, 154, 174
   Shipping Board 92
   State Department 39, 88, 90, 92, 174
   Treasury Department 37, 39–40, 42–43, 45, 88
   War Department 39–40, 42–43, 45–46, 88, 91–92, 173–174

United States (*cont.*)
   wartime loans to Russia 36–37, 42–44

Vauclain, Samuel 27–28, 39, 44–45, 89
Velikie Luki 170
Ventspils 170
Verband of German Locomotive-
   Building Companies 71, 121–124,
   126–128, 130–132, 154, 156, 211,
   231, 233
   financial discussions 128–133, 154, 156
   initial contacts with Krasin 121–124
   locomotive negotiations 121–124,
   126–133, 154, 156
   subcontracted locomotive order from
   Nohab 130–133
Versailles, Treaty of 71, 118
Vickers Ltd 269
Victor Berg company 121, 133, 154–156,
   211
Vikzhedor 52–53
Vikzhel 52–53
Vitkovice Mining and Foundry works
   207
Vitte, S. Iu. 14, 17, 82, 222, 226
Vladivostok 20–21, 24–26, 31, 33, 36,
   40, 43
Volkhovstroi 125, 201–202, 207,
   210–213, 215
Vorovskii, V. V. 68, 151, 166
Voskresenskii, B. D. 95, 106, 112,
   141–142
   liaison with British industry 112
   report to NKPS 142
   revision of imports plans 106, 141
Votkinsk Machine-Building Works 55
Vrangel, General P. N. 136, 180

wagons 21, 24–40, 42–47, 52–53, 57–62,
   67, 70, 79, 82, 85–86, 106, 111,
   137–138, 151, 153–154, 157, 165,
   170, 174–177, 179–180, 183, 185,
   190, 193, 210–213, 216–217, 225,
   227, 229
   contracts in WWI 24–25, 28–30, 36,
   39, 44–45
   deliveries in WWI 30–32, 46–47
   high-capacity designs 29, 31–32, 62
   oil-tanker contracts 151, 174–177,
   179, 185, 190, 207, 210–212, 217, 229
   shortages 21, 25, 28–29, 36, 40, 47, 52,
   57
War Communism 2, 5, 7, 48–49, 136,
   222–223, 225, 227
   postwar reconstruction 5, 48–49,
   56–57, 72–82, 136, 222–223, 225
water turbines contract 125, 201–202,
   207–208, 210–213, 215
waterways, inland 14, 138, 147
West, Sir Glynn Hamilton 115
Wheeling Mold 92
Willard, Daniel F. 39, 43–45
Wilson, President Woodrow 45
Windrower, Captain 90–91
Wise, E. F. 94, 111
Wolf, Otto 211
Woolwich Arsenal 111
Workers' Opposition 139, 165, 191
workshop equipment 24, 33, 36, 39, 74,
   78, 111, 143, 158, 169
World, The 79

Zernov, V. S. 149
Zinov'ev, G. E. 78, 167

Cambridge Russian, Soviet and Post-Soviet Studies

105 ANTHONY HEYWOOD
   Modernising Lenin's Russia
   Economic reconstruction, foreign trade and the railways

104 HIRAOKI KUROMIYA
   Freedom and terror in the Donbas
   A Ukrainian–Russian Borderland, 1870s–1990s

103 ILYA PRIZEL
   National identity and foreign policy
   Nationalism and leadership in Poland, Russia and Ukraine

102 ALENA LEDENEVA
   Russia's economy of favours
   Blat, networking and informal exchanges

101 RUDOLF L. TŐKÉS
   Hungary's negotiated revolution
   Economic reform, social change and political succession

100 PETER SOLOMON
   Soviet criminal justice under Stalin

99 MARK HARRISON
   Accounting for war
   Soviet production, employment, and the defence burden, 1940–1945

98 KAZIMIERZ Z. POZNANSKI
   Poland's protracted transition
   Institutional change and economic growth, 1971–1993

97 ANITA J. PRAZMOWSKA
   Britain and Poland, 1939–1943
   The betrayed ally

96 JOHN DOYLE KLIER
   Imperial Russia's Jewish question 1855–1881

95 DON C. RAWSON
   Russian rightists and the revolution of 1905

94 GRAEME GILL
   The collapse of a single party system
   The disintegration of the Communist Party of the Soviet Union

93 DONALD FILTZER
   Soviet workers and the collapse of *perestroika*
   The Soviet labour process and Gorbachev's reforms, 1985–1991

92 PETER GATRELL
   Government, industry and rearmament in Russia, 1900–1914
   The last argument of tsarism

91 LINDA RACIOPPI
   Soviet policy towards South Asia since 1970

90 WENDY GOLDMAN
Women, the State and the family
Soviet family policy and social life, 1917–1936

89 JONATHAN C. VALDEZ
Internationalism and the ideology of Soviet influence in Eastern Europe

88 PETER RUTLAND
The politics of economic stagnation in the Soviet Union
The role of local party organs in economic management

87 DONALD FILTZER
Soviet workers and de-Stalinization
The consolidation of the modern system of Soviet production relations 1953–1964

86 MILICA UVALIC
Investment and property rights in Yugoslavia
The long transition to a market economy

85 AVRIL PITTMAN
From Ostpolitik to reunification: West German–Soviet political relations since 1974

84 GEORGE O. LIBER
The Soviet nationality policy and social change in the Ukrainian SSR 1923–1934
The urban harvest

83 CHRISTOPH BLUTH
Soviet strategic arms policy before SALT

82 JOHN P. WILLERTON
Patronage and politics in the USSR

81 JAMES HUGHES
Stalin, Siberia and the crisis of the New Economic Policy

80 ILIANA ZLOCH-CHRISTY
East–West financial relations
Current problems and future prospects

79 MICHAEL D. KENNEDY
Professionals, power and Solidarity in Poland
A critical sociology of Soviet-type society

78 GARETH M. WINROW
The foreign policy of the GDR in Africa

77 JOZEF M. VAN BRABANT
The planned economies and international economic organizations

76 WILLIAM MOSKOFF
The bread of affliction: the food supply in the USSR during World War II

75 YAACOV RO'I
The struggle for Soviet Jewish emigration 1948–1967

74 GRAEME GILL
The origins of the Stalinist political system

73 SANTOSH K. MEHROTRA
India and the Soviet Union: trade and technology transfer

72 ILYA PRIZEL
Latin America through Soviet eyes
The evolution of Soviet perceptions during the Brezhnev era 1964–1982

71 ROBERT G. PATMAN
The Soviet Union in the Horn of Africa
The diplomacy of intervention and disengagement

70 IVAN T. BEREND
The Hungarian economic reforms 1953–1988

69 CHRIS WARD
Russia's cotton workers and the New Economic Policy
Shop-floor culture and state policy 1921–1929

68 LASZLO CSABA
Eastern Europe in the world economy

67 MICHAEL E. URBAN
An algebra of Soviet power
Elite circulation in the Belorussian Republic 1966–1986

66 JANE L. CURRY
Poland's journalists: professionalism and politics

65 MARTIN MYANT
The Czechoslovak economy 1948–1988
The battle for economic reform

64 XAVIER RICHET
The Hungarian model: markets and planning in a socialist economy

63 PAUL G. LEWIS
Political authority and party secretaries in Poland 1975–1986

62 BENJAMIN PINKUS
The Jews of the Soviet Union
The history of a national minority

61 FRANCESCO BENVENUTI
The Bolsheviks and the Red Army, 1918–1922

60 HIROAKI KUROMIYA
Stalin's industrial revolution
Politics and workers, 1928–1932

59 LEWIS SIEGELBAUM
Stakhanovism and the politics of productivity in the USSR, 1935–1941

58 JOZEF M. VAN BRABANT
Adjustment, structural change and economic efficiency
Aspects of monetary cooperation in Eastern Europe

57 ILIANA ZLOCH-CHRISTY
Debt problems of Eastern Europe

56 SUSAN BRIDGER
Women in the Soviet countryside
Women's roles in rural development in the Soviet Union

55 ALLEN LYNCH
The Soviet study of international relations

54 DAVID GRANICK
Job rights in the Soviet Union: their consequences

53 ANITA PRAZMOWSKA
Britain, Poland and the Eastern Front, 1939

52 ELLEN JONES AND FRED GRUPP
Modernization, value change and fertility in the Soviet Union

51 CATHERINE ANDREYEV
Valasov and the Russian liberation movement
Soviet reality and émigré theories

50 STEPHEN WHITE
The origins of détente
The Genoa Conference and Soviet–Western relations 1921–1922

49 JAMES MCADAMS
East Germany and détente
Building authority after the Wall

48 S. G. WHEATCROFT AND R. W. DAVIES (EDS.)
Materials for a balance of the Soviet national economy 1928–1930

47 SYLVANA MALLE
The economic organization of war communism, 1918–1921

46 DAVID S. MASON
Public opinion and political change in Poland, 1980–1982

45 MARK HARRISON
Soviet planning in peace and war 1938–1945

44 NIGEL SWAIN
Collective farms which work

43 J. ARCH GETTY
Origins of the great purges
The Soviet Communist Party reconsidered, 1933–1938

42 TADEUSZ SWIETOCHOWSKI
Russian Azerbaijan 1905–1920
The shaping of national identity in a muslim community

41 RAY TARAS
Ideology in a socialist state
Poland 1956–1983

38 DAVID A. DYKER
The process of investment in the Soviet Union

35 WILLIAM J. CONYNGHAM
The modernization of Soviet industrial management

34 ANGELA STENT
From embargo to Ostpolitik
The political economy of West German–Soviet relations 1955–1980

32 BLAIR A. RUBLE
Soviet trade unions
Their development in the 1970s

30 JOZEF M. VAN BRABANT
Socialist economic integration
Aspects of contemporary economic problems in Eastern Europe

22 JAMES RIORDAN
Sport in Soviet society
Development of sport and physical education in Russia and the USSR